# A·N·N·U·A·L EDITIONS

# Sociology

*Thirty-Second Edition*

## 03/04

D1372918

**EDITOR**

**Kurt Finsterbusch**

*University of Maryland, College Park*

Kurt Finsterbusch received a bachelor's degree in history from Princeton University in 1957 and a bachelor of divinity degree from Grace Theological Seminary in 1960. His Ph.D. in sociology, from Columbia University, was conferred in 1969. Dr. Finsterbusch is the author of several books, including *Understanding Social Impacts* (Sage Publications, 1980), *Social Research for Policy Decisions* (Wadsworth Publishing, 1980, with Annabelle Bender Motz), and *Organizational Change as a Development Strategy* (Lynne Rienner Publishers, 1987, with Jerald Hage). He is currently teaching at the University of Maryland, College Park, and, in addition to serving as editor for *Annual Editions: Sociology*, he is also editor of *Annual Editions: Social Problems,* and McGraw-Hill/Dushkin's *Taking Sides: Clashing Views on Controversial Social Issues.*

*McGraw-Hill/Dushkin*

530 Old Whitfield Street, Guilford, Connecticut 06437

Visit us on the Internet
*http://www.dushkin.com*

# Credits

1. **Culture**
   Unit photo—© 2003 by PhotoDisc, Inc.
2. **Socialization and Social Control**
   Unit photo—© 2003 by PhotoDisc, Inc.
3. **Groups and Roles in Transition**
   Unit photo—© 2003 by Cleo Freelance Photography.
4. **Stratification and Social Inequalities**
   Unit photo—© 2003 by Sweet By & By/Cindy Brown.
5. **Social Institutions: Issues, Crises, and Changes**
   Unit photo—© 2003 by Sweet By & By/Cindy Brown.
6. **Social Change and the Future**
   Unit photo—© 2003 by Sweet By & By/Cindy Brown.

# Copyright

Cataloging in Publication Data
Main entry under title: Annual Editions: Sociology. 2003/2004.
1. Sociology—Periodicals. 2. United States—Social conditions—2002—Periodicals.
I. Finsterbusch, Kurt, *comp.* II. Title: Sociology.
ISBN 0–07–283867–1          658'.05          ISSN 0277–9315

Thirty-Second Edition

Cover image © 2003 PhotoDisc, Inc.
Printed in the United States of America    1234567890BAHBAH543    Printed on Recycled Paper

# To the Reader

In publishing ANNUAL EDITIONS we recognize the enormous role played by the magazines, newspapers, and journals of the public press in providing current, first-rate educational information in a broad spectrum of interest areas. Many of these articles are appropriate for students, researchers, and professionals seeking accurate, current material to help bridge the gap between principles and theories and the real world. These articles, however, become more useful for study when those of lasting value are carefully collected, organized, indexed, and reproduced in a low-cost format, which provides easy and permanent access when the material is needed. That is the role played by ANNUAL EDITIONS.

The new millennium has arrived with difficult new issues such as how to deal with new levels of terrorism, while many of the old issues remain unresolved. There is much uncertainty. Almost all institutions are under stress. The political system is held in low regard because it seems to accomplish so little, to cost so much, and to focus on special interests more than the public good. The economy is in a recession in the short term and in the long term it suffers from foreign competition, trade deficits, economic uncertainties, and a worrisome concentration of economic power in the hands of relatively few multinational corporations. Complaints about the education system continue, because grades K–12 do not teach basic skills well and college costs are too high. Health care is too expensive, many Americans lack health care coverage, and some diseases are becoming resistant to our medicines. The entertainment industry is booming, but many people worry about its impact on values and behavior. News media standards seem to be set by the tabloids. Furthermore, the dynamics of technology, globalization, and identity groups are creating crises, changes, and challenges. Crime rates have declined somewhat, but they are still at high levels. The public is demanding more police, more jails, and tougher sentences, but less government spending. Government social policies seem to create almost as many problems as they solve. Laborers, women, blacks, and many other groups complain of injustices and victimization. The use of toxic chemicals has been blamed for increases in cancer, sterility, and other diseases. Marriage and the family have been transformed, in part by the women's movement and in part by the stress that current conditions create for women who try to combine family and careers. Schools, television, and corporations are commonly vilified. Many claim that morality has declined to shameful levels. Add to all this the problems of population growth, ozone depletion, and global warming, and it is easy to be pessimistic. Nevertheless, crises and problems also create opportunities.

The present generation may determine the course of history for the next 200 years. Great changes are taking place, and new solutions are being sought where old answers no longer work. The issues that the current generation faces are complex and must be interpreted within a sophisticated framework. The sociological perspective provides such a framework. It expects people to act in terms of their positions in the social structure, the political, economic, and social forces operating on them, and the norms that govern the situation.

*Annual Editions: Sociology 03/04* should help you to develop the sociological perspective that will enable you to determine how the issues of the day relate to the way that society is structured. The articles provide not only information but also models of interpretation and analysis that will guide you as you form your own views. In addition, both the *topic guide* and the *World Wide Web* pages can be used to further explore the book's topics.

This thirty-second edition of *Annual Editions: Sociology* emphasizes social change, institutional crises, and prospects for the future. It provides intellectual preparation for acting for the betterment of humanity in times of crucial change. The sociological perspective is needed more than ever as humankind tries to find a way to peace, prosperity, health, and well-being that can be maintained for generations in an improving environment. The numerous obstacles that lie in the path of these important goals require sophisticated responses. The goals of this edition are to communicate to students the excitement and importance of the study of the social world and to provoke interest in and enthusiasm for the study of sociology.

*Annual Editions: Sociology* depends upon reader response in order to develop and change. You are encouraged to return the postage-paid *article rating form* at the back of the book with your opinions about existing articles, recommendations of articles you think have sociological merit for subsequent editions, and advice on how the anthology can be made more useful as a teaching and learning tool.

*Kurt Finsterbusch*

Kurt Finsterbusch
*Editor*

*Dedicated to Meredith Ramsay for all that she has taught me about issues of great human concern.*

# Contents

## UNIT 1
## Culture

Five selections consider what our culture can learn from primitive peoples, what forces are shaping today's cultures and lifestyles, and the impact of crises on culture.

*Part A.  Modern, Traditional, and Unusual Cultures*

*Part B.  American Culture and Cultural Change*

The concepts in bold italics are developed in the article. For further expansion, please refer to the Topic Guide and the Index.

# UNIT 2
# Socialization and Social Control

Four articles examine the effects of social influences on childhood, personality, and human behavior with regard to the socialization of the individual.

# UNIT 3
# Groups and Roles in Transition

Seven articles discuss some of the social roles and group relationships that are in transition in today's society. Topics include primary and secondary groups and the reevaluation of social choices.

The concepts in bold italics are developed in the article. For further expansion, please refer to the Topic Guide and the Index.

# UNIT 4
# Stratification and Social Inequalities

Nine selections discuss the social stratification and inequalities that exist in today's society with regard to the rich, the poor, blacks, and gender issues.

The concepts in bold italics are developed in the article. For further expansion, please refer to the Topic Guide and the Index.

The concepts in bold italics are developed in the article. For further expansion, please refer to the Topic Guide and the Index.

# UNIT 5
# Social Institutions: Issues, Crises, and Changes

Eight articles examine several social institutions that are currently in crisis. Selections focus on the political, economic, and social spheres, as well as the overall state of the nation.

The concepts in bold italics are developed in the article. For further expansion, please refer to the Topic Guide and the Index.

# UNIT 6
## Social Change and the Future

Eight selections discuss the impact that population, technology, environmental stress, and social values will have on society's future.

The concepts in bold italics are developed in the article. For further expansion, please refer to the Topic Guide and the Index.

## Part D.    The Reshaping of the World

The concepts in bold italics are developed in the article. For further expansion, please refer to the Topic Guide and the Index.

# Topic Guide

This topic guide suggests how the selections in this book relate to the subjects covered in your course. You may want to use the topics listed on these pages to search the Web more easily.

On the following pages a number of Web sites have been gathered specifically for this book. They are arranged to reflect the units of this *Annual Edition*. You can link to these sites by going to the DUSHKIN ONLINE support site at *http://www.dushkin.com/online/*.

## ALL THE ARTICLES THAT RELATE TO EACH TOPIC ARE LISTED BELOW THE BOLD-FACED TERM.

**Abortion**
32. Seeking Abortion's Middle Ground

**Abuse**
9. Pedophilia

**African Americans**
21. Racism Isn't What It Used to Be

**Aggression**
6. Boys Will Be Boys
25. Violence Against Women

**Agriculture**
37. Grains of Hope

**Atmosphere**
35. Feeling the Heat: Life in the Greenhouse

**Business**
16. Where Everyone's a Minority
29. Work, Work, Work, Work!

**Capitalism**
19. Corporate Welfare
28. In Corporate America, It's Cleanup Time
29. Work, Work, Work, Work!

**Children and childhood**
2. The Mountain People
6. Boys Will Be Boys
9. Pedophilia
10. The American Family
11. Divorce and Cohabitation: Why We Don't Marry
12. Should You Stay Together for the Kids?
30. Schools That Develop Children

**Cities**
16. Where Everyone's a Minority

**Civil rights**
21. Racism Isn't What It Used to Be

**Climate**
35. Feeling the Heat: Life in the Greenhouse

**Community**
2. The Mountain People
23. The Melting Pot, Part I: Are We There Yet?
27. Where the Public Good Prevailed
30. Schools That Develop Children
35. Feeling the Heat: Life in the Greenhouse
41. Community Building: Steps Toward a Good Society

**Compensation, income**
18. The Great CEO Pay Heist

**Conservation**
37. Grains of Hope

**Corporate strategy and human resources**
18. The Great CEO Pay Heist

**Corporate welfare**
19. Corporate Welfare

**Crime**
3. More Moral
8. Preventing Crime: The Promising Road Ahead
9. Pedophilia
28. In Corporate America, It's Cleanup Time

**Cultural customs**
1. Modernization's Challenge to Traditional Values: Who's Afraid of Ronald McDonald?

**Culture**
1. Modernization's Challenge to Traditional Values: Who's Afraid of Ronald McDonald?
2. The Mountain People
3. More Moral
4. American Culture Goes Global, or Does It?
5. What's so Great About America?
6. Boys Will Be Boys
7. Born to Be Good?
10. The American Family
11. Divorce and Cohabitation: Why We Don't Marry
13. Now for the Truth About Americans and Sex
14. Shades of Gay
15. When Careers Collide
23. The Melting Pot, Part I: Are We There Yet?
24. The Past and Prologue
27. Where the Public Good Prevailed
29. Work, Work, Work, Work!
30. Schools That Develop Children
32. Seeking Abortion's Middle Ground
39. Why Don't They Like Us?
41. Community Building: Steps Toward a Good Society

**Demography**
23. The Melting Pot, Part I: Are We There Yet?
34. Sixteen Impacts of Population Growth

**Desegregation**
21. Racism Isn't What It Used to Be

**Developing countries**
1. Modernization's Challenge to Traditional Values: Who's Afraid of Ronald McDonald?
37. Grains of Hope

# World Wide Web Sites

The following World Wide Web sites have been carefully researched and selected to support the articles found in this reader. The easiest way to access these selected sites is to go to our DUSHKIN ONLINE support site at *http://www.dushkin.com/online/*.

# AE: Sociology 03/04

The following sites were available at the time of publication. Visit our Web site—we update DUSHKIN ONLINE regularly to reflect any changes.

## General Sources

### Library of Congress
*http://www.loc.gov*

Examine this extensive Web site to learn about resource tools, library services/resources, exhibitions, and databases in many different subfields of sociology.

### Social Science Information Gateway (SOSIG)
*http://sosig.esrc.bris.ac.uk*

SOSIG is an online catalog of Internet resources relevant to social science education and research. Resources are selected by librarians or subject specialists.

### Sociological Tour Through Cyberspace
*http://www.trinity.edu/~mkearl/index.html*

Prepared by Michael Kearl at Trinity University, this extensive site provides essays, commentaries, data analyses, and links on death and dying, family, the sociology of time, social gerontology, social psychology, and more.

## UNIT 1: Culture

### American Studies Web
*http://www.georgetown.edu/crossroads/asw/*

This eclectic site provides links to a wealth of resources on the Web related to American studies: gender studies, environment, race, and more. It is of great help when doing research in demography, genealogy, and population studies.

### Anthropology Resources Page
*http://www.usd.edu/anth/*

Many cultural topics can be accessed at this site from the University of South Dakota. Click on the links to find information about differences and similarities in values and lifestyles among the world's peoples.

### Human Rights and Humanitarian Assistance
*http://www.etown.edu/vl/humrts.html*

Through this part of the World Wide Web Virtual Library, you can conduct research into a number of human-rights topics in order to gain a greater understanding of issues affecting indigenous peoples in the modern era. The site also provides links to many other subjects related to sociology.

### Sociology Library
*http://www.library.upenn.edu/resources/subject/social/sociology/sociology.html*

A number of indexes of cultural and ethnic studies, criminology, population, and demographics are provided on this Web site.

## UNIT 2: Socialization and Social Control

### Center for Leadership Studies
*http://www.situational.com*

The Center for Leadership Studies (CLS) is organized for the research and development of the full range of leadership in individuals, teams, organizations, and communities.

### Crime Times
*http://www.crime-times.org*

This interesting site lists research reviews and other information regarding causes of criminal, violent, and psychopathic behavior. It is provided by the Wacker Foundation, publishers of *Crime Times*.

### Ethics Updates/Lawrence Hinman
*http://ethics.acusd.edu*

This site provides both simple concept definition and complex analysis of ethics, original treatises, and sophisticated search-engine capability. Subject matter covers the gamut, from ethical theory to applied ethical venues. There are many opportunities for user input.

### National Institute on Drug Abuse (NIDA)
*http://165.112.78.61/*

Use this site index of the National Institute on Drug Abuse for access to NIDA publications and communications, information on drugs of abuse, and links to other related Web sites.

### Sexual Assault Information Page
*http://web.archive.org/web/*/http://www.cs.utk.edu/~bartley/saInfoPage.html*

This invaluable site provides dozens of links to information and resources on a variety of sexual assault–related topics, including child sexual abuse, date rape, incest, secondary victims, and offenders. It also provides some material of interest in the pornography debate.

### Social Influence Website
*http://www.influenceatwork.com/*

This Web site is devoted to social influence—the modern scientific study of persuasion, compliance, and propaganda.

## UNIT 3: Groups and Roles in Transition

### American Men's Studies Association
*http://www.vix.com/pub/men/orgs/writeups/amsa.html*

The American Men's Studies Association is an organization of scholars, therapists, and others interested in the exploration of masculinity in modern society. Click on Men's Issues.

### The Gallup Organization
*http://www.gallup.com*

Links to an extensive archive of public opinion poll results and special reports on a huge variety of topics related to American society are available on this Gallup Organization home page.

### Grass-Roots.org
*http://www.iglou.com/why/ria.htm*

Grass-roots.org offers this site as part of its program called Reinvesting in America (its effort to help people fight hunger and

# www.dushkin.com/online/

poverty in their communities). Various resources and models for grassroots action are included here.

## Marriage and Family Therapy
*http://www.aamft.org/index_nm.asp*

This site has links to numerous marriage and family therapy topics. Online directories, books and articles are also available.

## The North-South Institute
*http://www.nsi-ins.ca/ensi/index.html*

Searching this site of the North-South Institute—which works to strengthen international development cooperation and enhance gender and social equity—will help you find information on a variety of issues related to social transitions.

## PsychNet/American Psychological Association
*http://www.apa.org/psychnet/*

By exploring this site, you will be able to find links to an abundance of articles and other resources related to interpersonal relationships throughout the life span.

## SocioSite: Feminism and Woman Issues
*http://www.pscw.uva.nl/sociosite/TOPICS/Women.html*

Open this enormous sociology site of the University of Amsterdam's Sociological Institute to gain insights into a number of issues that affect both men and women. It provides biographies of women through history, an international network for women in the workplace, links to gay studies, affirmative action, family and children's issues, and much more. Return to the site's home page for many other sociological links.

# UNIT 4: Stratification and Social Inequalities

## Americans With Disabilities Act Document Center
*http://www.jan.wvu.edu/links/adalinks.htm*

This Web site contains copies of the Americans With Disabilities Act of 1990 (ADA) and ADA regulations. This Web site also provides you with links to other Internet sources of information concerning disability issues.

## American Scientist
*http://www.amsci.org/amsci/amsci.html*

Investigating this Web site of the *American Scientist* will help students of sociology to access a variety of articles and to explore issues and concepts related to race and gender.

## Give Five
*http://www.independentsector.org/give5/givefive.html*

The Give Five Web site is a project of Independent Sector, a national coalition of foundations, voluntary organizations, and corporate giving programs working to encourage giving, volunteering, not-for-profit initiatives, and citizen action.

## Joint Center for Poverty Research
*http://www.jcpr.org*

Finding research information related to poverty is possible at this site. It provides working papers, answers to FAQs, and facts about who is poor in America. Welfare reform is also addressed.

## NAACP Online: National Association for the Advancement of Colored People
*http://www.naacp.org*

The principal objective of the NAACP is to ensure the political, educational, social, and economic equality of minority group citizens in the United States.

## Patterns of Variability: The Concept of Race
*http://www.as.ua.edu/ant/bindon/ant270/lectures/race/race1.htm*

This site provides a handy, at-a-glance reference to the prevailing concepts of race and the causes of human variability since ancient times. It can serve as a valuable starting point for research and understanding into the concept of race.

## The Urban Institute
*http://www.urban.org/welfare/overview.htm*

The Urban Institute offers lengthy discussions of issues related to welfare and its reform. This page starts with the assertion that "No one likes the current welfare system."

# UNIT 5: Social Institutions: Issues, Crises, and Changes

## Center for the Study of Group Processes
*http://www.uiowa.edu/~grpproc/*

The mission of the Center for the Study of Group Processes includes promoting basic research in the field of group processes and enhancing the professional development of faculty and students in the field of group processes.

## International Labour Organization (ILO)
*http://www.ilo.org*

ILO's home page leads to links that describe the goals of the organization and summarizes international labor standards and human rights. Its official UN Web site locator can point to many other useful resources.

## IRIS Center
*http://www.iris.umd.edu*

The project on Institutional Reform and the Informal Sector (IRIS) aims to understand transitional and developing economies. Examine this site to learn about research into government institutions and policies that helps to promote successful economic change in the global age.

## Marketplace of Political Ideas/University of Houston Library
*http://info.lib.uh.edu/politics/markind.htm*

Here is a collection of links to campaign, conservative/liberal perspectives, and political-party sites, including General Political, Democratic, Republican, and Third-Party sites.

## National Center for Policy Analysis
*http://www.ncpa.org*

Through this site, you can reach links that provide discussions of an array of topics that are of major interest in the study of American politics and government from a sociological perspective, including regulatory policy, affirmative action, and income.

## National Institutes of Health (NIH)
*http://www.nih.gov*

Consult this site for links to extensive health information and scientific resources of interest to sociologists from the NIH, one of eight health agencies of the Public Health Service.

# UNIT 6: Social Change and the Future

## Communications for a Sustainable Future
*http://csf.colorado.edu*

This site will lead you to information on topics in international environmental sustainability. It pays particular attention to the political economics of protecting the environment.

## Gil Gordon Associates
*http://www.gilgordon.com*

This site consolidates a wide variety of information from around the world on the subject of telecommuting, teleworking, the virtual office, alternative officing, and related topics.

# www.dushkin.com/online/

### Human Rights and Humanitarian Assistance
*http://www.etown.edu/vl/humrts.html*

Through this part of the World Wide Web Virtual Library, you can conduct research into a number of human-rights concerns around the world. The site also provides links to many other subjects related to important social issues.

### The Hunger Project
*http://www.thp.org*

Browse through this nonprofit organization's site to explore how it tries to achieve its goal: the end to global hunger through leadership at all levels of society. The Hunger Project contends that the persistence of hunger is at the heart of the major security issues threatening our planet.

### National Immigrant Forum
*http://www.immigrationforum.org/index.htm*

This pro-immigrant organization offers this site to examine the effects of immigration on the U.S. economy and society. Click on the links for discussion of underground economies, immigrant economies, and other topics.

### Terrorism Research Center
*http://www.terrorism.com/index.shtml*

The Terrorism Research Center features definitions and original research on terrorism, counterterrorism documents, a comprehensive list of Web links, and monthly profiles of terrorist and counterterrorist groups.

### United Nations Environment Program (UNEP)
*http://www.unep.ch*

Consult this home page of UNEP for links to environmental topics of critical concern to sociologists. The site will direct you to useful databases and global resource information.

### William Davidson Institute
*http://www.wdi.bus.umich.edu*

The William Davidson Institute at the University of Michigan Business School is dedicated to the understanding and promotion of economic transition. Consult this site for discussion of topics related to the changing global economy and the effects of globalization in general.

We highly recommend that you review our Web site for expanded information and our other product lines. We are continually updating and adding links to our Web site in order to offer you the most usable and useful information that will support and expand the value of your Annual Editions. You can reach us at: *http://www.dushkin.com/annualeditions/*.

# UNIT 1
# Culture

## Unit Selections

1. **Modernization's Challenge to Traditional Values: Who's Afraid of Ronald McDonald?** Ronald Inglehart and Wayne E. Baker
2. **The Mountain People**, Colin M. Turnbull
3. **More Moral**, David Whitman
4. **American Culture Goes Global, or Does It?** Richard Pells
5. **What's so Great About America?** Dinesh D'Souza

## Key Points to Consider

- What do you think are the core values in American society?

- What are the strengths and weaknesses of cultures that emphasize either cooperation or individualism?

- What is the relationship between culture and identity?

- What might a visitor from a primitive tribe describe as shocking and barbaric about American society?

 **Links: www.dushkin.com/online/**
These sites are annotated in the World Wide Web pages.

**American Studies Web**
*http://www.georgetown.edu/crossroads/asw/*

**Anthropology Resources Page**
*http://www.usd.edu/anth/*

**Human Rights and Humanitarian Assistance**
*http://www.etown.edu/vl/humrts.html*

**Sociology Library**
*http://www.library.upenn.edu/resources/subject/social/sociology/sociology.html*

The ordinary, everyday objects of living and the daily routines of life provide a structure to social life that is regularly punctuated by festivals, celebrations, and other special events (both happy and sad). These routine and special times are the stuff of culture, for culture is the sum total of all the elements of one's social inheritance. Culture includes language, tools, values, habits, science, religion, literature, and art.

It is easy to take one's own culture for granted, so it is useful to pause and reflect on the shared beliefs and practices that form the foundations for our social life. Students share beliefs and practices and thus have a student culture. Obviously the faculty has one also. Students, faculty, and administrators share a university culture. At the national level, Americans share an American culture. These cultures change over time and especially between generations. As a result, there is much variety among cultures across time and across nations, tribes, and groups. It is fascinating to study these differences and to compare the dominant values and signature patterns of different groups.

The two articles in the first subsection deal with traditional cultures that are under considerable stress today. In the first the authors study the differences between the cultures of rich and poor countries using an ambitious cross-national survey. The peoples of poor countries are more anchored in traditions and less imbued with secular/rational values or involved in self-expression. The study also clearly shows some of the important effects that economic development has on culture. The second article, by Colin Turnbull, reports how the Ik tribe suffered the loss of its tribal lands and was forced to live in a harsh environment. When a society's technology is very primitive, its environment has a profound impact on its social structure and culture. We would expect, therefore, that such a momentous change in the tribe's environment would require some interesting adaptations. The change that occurred, however, was shocking. Literally all aspects of life changed for the tribe's members in a disturbingly sinister way. Moreover, the experience of this tribe leads Turnbull to question some of the individualistic tendencies of America.

In the next subsection, David Whitman attacks the moral decline thesis. He shows that most moral indicators have improved in the last 25 years. Drug and alcohol use, heavy drinking and drunk driving, cheating on taxes, political corruption, and crime have declined noticeably. Controlling for inflation, charitable giving has increased 50 percent. Church attendance and religion-based behavior have not declined. Though a few trends in moral indicators are negative, most are positive and the vast improvement on some social issues, such as discrimination, leads Whitman to conclude that America is more moral today than it was 25 years ago.

The culture of America continues to have an impact on the world. In fact, many people throughout the world are critical of

American culture and thus are angered by its worldwide influence. Osama bin Laden is the most famous of such critics. In the next article, Richard Pells acknowledges that American culture has a considerable impact around the world, but challenges the thesis that the culture of America is Americanizing the world as many critics argue. He points out that much of American culture is imported and has spread throughout the world because it has incorporated foreign styles and ideas. The final article of this section argues that America has much to be proud about. Its author, Dinesh D'Souza, is an immigrant himself so he can see America both as an outsider and as an insider. He is able to identify many wonderful aspects of America that amaze and attract foreigners. He emphasizes the whole population's sense of equality and freedom of choice, in addition to the wealth that even the poor have here, when compared to the poor other countries.

# Modernization's Challenge to Traditional Values: Who's Afraid of Ronald McDonald?

"Modernization" means "Americanization" to many who fear a coming McWorld. But a study by two social researchers indicates that traditional values will keep most countries from becoming clones of the United States.

*By Ronald Inglehart and Wayne E. Baker*

The World Values Survey—a two-decade-long examination of the values of 65 societies coordinated by the University of Michigan's Institute for Social Research—is the largest investigation ever conducted of attitudes, values, and beliefs around the world. This study has carried out three waves of representative national surveys: the first in 1981–1982, the second in 1990–1991, and the third in 1995–1998. The fourth wave is being completed in 1999–2001. The study now represents some 80% of the world's population. These societies have per capita GNPs ranging from $300 to more than $30,000. Their political systems range from long-established stable democracies to authoritarian states.

The World Values Survey data have been used by researchers around the world for hundreds of publications in more than a dozen languages. Studies that have been based on the data cover a wide range of topics, including volunteerism in Europe, political partisanship and social class in Ireland, democratization in Korea, liberalization in Mexico, future values in Japan, and the religious vote in Western Europe.

This article examines the relationship between cultural values and economic globalization and modernization: What impact does economic development have on the values of a culture, and vice versa? Is a future "McWorld" inevitable?

## Rich Values, Poor Values

The World Values Survey data show us that the world views of the people of rich societies differ systematically from those of low-income societies across a wide range of political, social, and religious norms and beliefs. The two most significant dimensions that emerged reflected, first, a polarization between *traditional* and *secular-rational* orientations toward authority and, second, a polarization between *survival* and *self-expres-*

*sion* values. By *traditional* we mean those societies that are relatively authoritarian, place strong emphasis on religion, and exhibit a mainstream version of preindustrial values such as an emphasis on male dominance in economic and political life, respect for authority, and relatively low levels of tolerance for abortion and divorce. Advanced societies, or *secular-rational*, tend to have the opposite characteristics.

A central component of the survival vs. self-expression dimension involves the polarization between materialist and postmaterialist values. Massive evidence indicates that a cultural shift throughout advanced industrial society is emerging among generations who have grown up taking survival for granted. Values among this group emphasize environmental protection, the women's movement, and rising demand for participation in decision making in economic and political life. During the past 25 years, these values have become increasingly widespread in almost all advanced industrial societies for which extensive time-series evidence is available.

Economic development brings with it sweeping cultural change, some modernization theorists tell us. Others argue that cultural values are enduring and exert more influence on society than does economic change. Who's right?

One goal of the World Values Survey is to study links between economic development and changes in values. A key question that we ask is whether the globalization of the economy will necessarily produce a homogenization (or, more specifically, an Americanization) of culture—a so-called "McWorld."

In the nineteenth century, modernization theorists such as Karl Marx and Friedrich Nietzsche made bold predictions about the future of industrial society, such as the rise of labor and the decline of religion. In the twentieth century, non-Western societies were expected to abandon their traditional cultures and assimilate the technologically and morally "superior" ways of the West.

Clearly now, at the start of the twenty-first century, we need to rethink "modernization." Few people today anticipate a proletarian revolution, and non-western societies such as East Asia have surpassed their Western role models in key aspects of modernization, such as rates of economic growth. And few observers today attribute moral superiority to the West.

## Two Dimensions of Cross-Cultural Variation

1. Traditional vs. Secular-Rational Values
   **Traditional** values emphasize the following:
   - God is very important in respondent's life.
   - Respondent believes it is more important for a child to learn obedience and religious faith than independence and determination.
   - Respondent believes abortion is never justifiable.
   - Respondent has strong sense of national pride.
   - Respondent favors more respect for authority.
   **Secular-Rational** values emphasize the opposite.
2. Survival vs. Self-Expression Values
   **Survival** values emphasize the following:
   - Respondent gives priority to economic and physical security over self-expression and quality of life.
   - Respondent describes self as not very happy.
   - Respondent has not signed and would not sign a petition.
   - Respondent believes homosexuality is never justifiable.
   - Respondent believes you have to be very careful about trusting people.
   **Self-Expression** values emphasize the opposite.

Source: World Values Survey (http://wvs.isr.umich.edu)

On the other hand, one core concept of modernization theory still seems valid: Industrialization produces pervasive social and cultural consequences, such as rising educational levels, shifting attitudes toward authority, broader political participation, declining fertility rates, and changing gender roles. On the basis of the World Values Surveys, we believe that economic development has systematic and, to some extent, predictable cultural and political consequences. Once a society has embarked on industrialization—the central element of the modernization process—certain changes are highly likely to occur. But economic development is not the *only* force at work.

In the past few decades, modernization has become associated with *post*-industrialization: the rise of the knowledge and service-oriented economy. These changes in the nature of work had major political and cultural consequences, too. Rather than growing more materialistic with increased prosperity, postindustrial societies are experiencing an increasing emphasis on quality-of-life issues, environmental protection, and self-expression.

While industrialization increased human dominance over the environment—and consequently created a dwindling role for religious belief—the emergence of postindustrial society is stimulating further evolution of prevailing world views in a different direction. Life in postindustrial societies centers on services rather than material objects, and more effort is focused on communicating and processing information. Most people spend their productive hours dealing with other people and symbols.

Thus, the rise of postindustrial society leads to a growing emphasis on self-expression. Today's unprecedented wealth in advanced societies means an increasing share of the population grows up taking survival for granted. Their value priorities shift from an overwhelming emphasis on economic and physical security toward an increasing emphasis on subjective well-being and quality of life. "Modernization," thus, is not linear—it moves in new directions.

## How Values Shape Culture

Different societies follow different trajectories even when they are subjected to the same forces of economic development, in part because situation-specific factors, such as a society's cultural heritage, also shape how a particular society develops. Recently, Samuel Huntington, author of *The Clash of Civilizations* (Simon & Schuster, 1996), has focused on the role of religion in shaping the world's eight major civilizations or "cultural zones": Western Christianity, Orthodox, Islam, Confucian, Japanese, Hindu, African, and Latin American. These zones were shaped by religious traditions that are still powerful today, despite the forces of modernization.

## Distinctive cultural zones persist two centuries after the industrial revolution began.

Other scholars observe other distinctive cultural traits that endure over long periods of time and continue to shape a society's political and economic performance. For example, the regions of Italy in which democratic institutions function most successfully today are those in which civil society was relatively well developed in the nineteenth century and even earlier, as Robert Putnam notes in *Making Democracy Work* (Princeton University Press, 1993). And a cultural heritage of "low trust" puts a society at a competitive disadvantage in global markets because it is less able to develop large and complex social institutions, Francis Fukuyama argues in *Trust: The Social Virtues and the Creation of Prosperity* (Free Press, 1995).

The impression that we are moving toward a uniform "McWorld" is partly an illusion. The seemingly identical McDonald's restaurants that have spread throughout the world actually have different social meanings and fulfill dif-

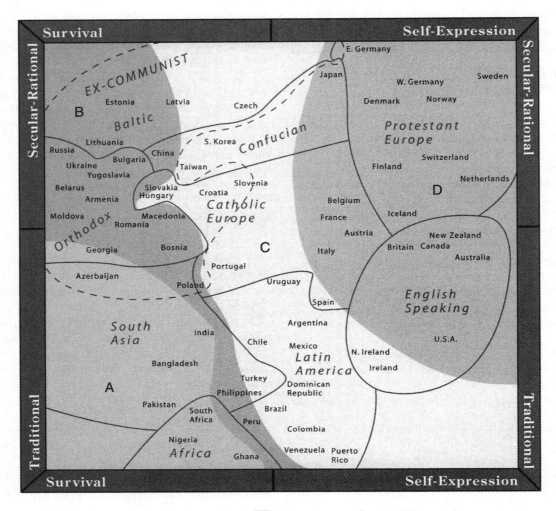

Less than $2,000 GNP per capita  A    C  $5,000 to $15,000 GNP per capita

$2,000 to $5,000 GNP per capita  B    D  More than $15,000 GNP per capita

ferent social functions in different cultural zones. Eating in a McDonald's restaurant in Japan is a different social experience from eating in one in the United States, Europe, or China.

Likewise, the globalization of communication is unmistakable, but its effects may be overestimated. It is certainly apparent that young people around the world are wearing jeans and listening to U.S. pop music; what is less apparent is the persistence of underlying value differences.

## Mapping and Predicting Values

Using the 1995–1998 wave of the World Values Survey, we produced a map of the world's values, showing the locations of 65 societies on the two cross-cultural dimensions—traditional vs. secular-rational values and survival vs. self-expression values.

What the map shows us is that cross-cultural variation is highly constrained. That is, if the people of a given society place a strong emphasis on religion, that society's relative position on many other variables can be predicted—such as attitudes toward abortion, national pride, respect for authority, and child-drearing. Similarly, survival vs. self-expression values reflect wide-ranging but tightly correlated clusters of values: Materialistic (survival-oriented) societies can be predicted to value maintaining order and fighting inflation, while postmaterialistic (self-expression-oriented) societies can be predicted to value freedom, interpersonal trust, and tolerance of outgroups.

Economic development seems to have a powerful impact on cultural values: The value systems of rich countries differ systematically from those of poor countries. If we superimpose an income "map" over the values map, we see that all 19 societies with an annual per capita GNP of over $15,000 rank relatively high on both dimensions, placing them in the upper right-hand corner. This economic zone cuts across the boundaries of the Protestant, ex-Communist, Confucian, Catholic, and English-speaking cultural zones.

On the other hand, all societies with per capita GNPs below $2,000 fall into a cluster at the lower left of the map, in an economic zone that cuts across the African, South Asian, ex-Communist, and Orthodox cultural zones. The remaining societies fall into two intermediate cultural-economic zones. Economic development seems to move societies in a common direction, regardless of their cultural heritage. Nevertheless, distinctive cultural zones persist two centuries after the industrial revolution began.

Of course, per capita GNP is only one indicator of a society's level of economic development. Another might be the percentage of the labor force engaged in the agricultural sector, the industrial sector, or the service sector. The shift from an agrarian mode of production to industrial production seems to bring with it a shift from traditional values toward increasing rationalization and secularization.

But a society's cultural heritage also plays a role: All four of the Confucian-influenced societies (China, Taiwan, South Korea, and Japan) have relatively secular values, regardless of the proportion of their labor forces in the industrial sector. Conversely, the historically Roman Catholic societies (e.g., Italy, Portugal, and Spain) display relatively traditional values when compared with Confucian or ex-Communist societies with the same proportion of industrial workers. And virtually all of the historically Protestant societies (e.g., West Germany, Denmark, Norway, and Sweden) rank higher on the survival/self-expression dimension than do all of the historically Roman Catholic societies, regardless of the extent to which their labor forces are engaged in the service sector.

We can conclude from this that changes in GNP and occupational structure have important influences on prevailing world views, but traditional cultural influences persist.

Religious traditions appear to have had an enduring impact on the contemporary value systems of the 65 societies. But a society's culture reflects its entire historical heritage. A central historical event of the twentieth century was the rise and fall of a Communist empire that once ruled one-third of the world's population. Communism left a clear imprint on the value systems of those who lived under it. East Germany remains culturally close to West Germany despite four decades of Communist

rule, but its value system has been drawn toward the Communist zone. And although China is a member of the Confucian zone, it also falls within a broad Communist-influenced zone. Similarly, Azerbaijan, though part of the Islamic cluster, also falls within the Communist superzone that dominated it for decades.

## The Deviant U.S.

The World Value Map clearly shows that the United States is a deviant case. We do not believe it is a prototype of cultural modernization for other societies to follow, as some postwar modernization theorists have naively assumed. The United States has a much more traditional value system than any other advanced industrial society.

On the traditional/secular-rational dimension, the United States ranks far below other rich societies, with levels of religiosity and national pride comparable to those found in developing societies. The United States does rank among the most advanced societies along the survival/self-expression dimension, but even here it does not lead the world. The Swedes and the Dutch seem closer to the cutting edge of cultural change than do the Americans.

Modernization theory implies that as societies develop economically their cultures tend to shift in a predictable direction. Our data supports this prediction. Economic differences are linked with large and pervasive cultural differences. But we find clear evidence of the influence of long-established cultural zones.

Do these cultural clusters simply reflect economic differences? For example, do the societies of Protestant Europe have similar values simply because they are rich? No. The impact of a society's historical-cultural heritage persists when we control for GDP per capita and the structure of the labor force. On a value such as *interpersonal trust* (a variable on the surival / self-expression dimension), even rich Catholic societies rank lower than rich Protestant ones.

Within a given society, however, Catholics rank about as high on *interpersonal trust* as do Protestants. The shared historical experience of given nations, not individual personality, is crucial. Once established, the cross-cultural differences linked with religion have become part of a national culture that is transmitted by the educational institutions and mass media of given societies to the people of that nation. Despite globalization, the nation remains a key unit of shared experience, and its educational and cultural institutions shape the values of almost everyone in that society.

## The Persistence of Religious and Spiritual Beliefs

As a society shifts from an agrarian to an industrial economy and survival comes to be taken for granted, traditional religious beliefs tend to decline. Nevertheless, as the twenty-first century opens, cleavages along religious lines remain strong. Why has religion been so slow to disappear?

History has taken an ironic turn: Communist-style industrialization was especially favorable to secularization, but the collapse of Communism has given rise to pervasive insecurity—

and a return to religious beliefs. Five of the seven ex-Communist societies for which we have time-series data show rising church attendance.

Throughout advanced industrial societies we see two contrasting trends: the decline of attendance at religious services on the one hand, and on the other the persistence of religious beliefs and the rise of spirituality. The need for answers to spiritual questions such as why we are here and where we are going does not die out in postindustrial society. Spiritual concerns will probably always be part of the human outlook. In fact, in the three successive waves of the World Values Survey, concern for the meaning and purpose of life became *stronger* in most advanced industrial societies.

## Conclusion: Whither Modernization?

Economic development is associated with pervasive, and to an extent predictable, cultural changes. Industrialization promotes a shift from traditional to secular-rational values; postindustrialization promotes a shift toward more trust, tolerance, and emphasis on well-being. Economic collapse propels societies in the opposite direction.

Economic development tends to push societies in a common direction, but rather than converging they seem to move along paths shaped by their cultural heritages. Therefore, we doubt that the forces of modernization will produce a homogenized world culture in the foreseeable future.

Certainly it is misleading to view cultural change as "Americanization." Industrializing societies in general are not becoming like the United States. In fact, the United States seems to be a deviant case: Its people hold much more traditional values and beliefs than do those in any other equally prosperous society. If any societies exemplify the cutting edge of cultural change, it would be the Nordic countries.

Finally, modernization is probabilistic, not deterministic. Economic development tends to transform a given society in a predictable direction, but the process and path are not inevitable. Many factors are involved, so any prediction must be contingent on the historical and cultural context of the society in question.

## Modernization and McDonald's

McDonald's restaurants have become a dominant symbol of the globalization of the economy and target of the wrath of globalization's many opponents. But local values still wield great influence on culture, so don't look for McWorld to emerge anytime soon, say social researchers Ronald Inglehart and Wayne E. Baker.

Nevertheless, the central prediction of modernization theory finds broad support: Economic development is associated with major changes in prevailing values and beliefs. The world views of rich societies differ markedly from those of poor societies. This does not necessarily imply cultural convergence, but it does predict the general direction of cultural change and (insofar as the process is based on intergenerational population replacement) even gives some idea of the rate at which such change is likely to occur.

In short, economic development will cause shifts in the values of people in developing nations, but it will not produce a uniform global culture. The future may *look* like McWorld, but it won't feel like one.

**About the Authors**

Ronald Inglehart is professor of political science and program director at the Institute for Social Research, University of Michigan, Ann Arbor, Michigan 48106. E-mail RFI@umich.edu. The World Values Survey Web site is http://wvs.isr.umich.edu/.

Wayne E. Baker is professor of organizational behavior and director of the Center for Society and Economy, University of Michigan Business School, and faculty associate at the Institute for Social Research. He may be reached by e-mail at wayneb@umich.edu; his Web site is www.bus.umich.edu/cse.

This article draws on their paper "Modernization, Cultural Change, and the Persistence of Traditional Values" in the American Sociological Review (February 2000).

Originally published in the March/April 2001 issue of *The Futurist,* pp. 16-21. Used with permission from the World Future Society, 7910 Woodmont Avenue, Suite 450, Bethesda, Maryland 20814. Telephone: 310/656-8274; Fax: 301/951-0394; (http://www.wfs.org).

# The Mountain People

**Colin M. Turnbull**

In what follows, there will be much to shock, and the reader will be tempted to say, "how primitive, how savage, how disgusting," and, above all, "how inhuman." The first judgments are typical of the kind of ethno- and egocentricism from which we can never quite escape. But "how inhuman" is of a different order and supposes that there are certain values inherent in humanity itself, from which the people described here seem to depart in a most drastic manner. In living the experience, however, and perhaps in reading it, one finds that it is oneself one is looking at and questioning; it is a voyage in quest of the basic human and a discovery of his potential for inhumanity, a potential that lies within us all.

Just before World War II the Ik tribe had been encouraged to settle in northern Uganda, in the mountainous northeast corner bordering on Kenya to the east and Sudan to the north. Until then they had roamed in nomadic bands, as hunters and gatherers, through a vast region in all three countries. The Kidepo Valley below Mount Morungole was their major hunting territory. After they were confined to a part of their former area, Kidepo was made a national park and they were forbidden to hunt or gather there.

The concept of family in a nomadic society is a broad one; what really counts most in everyday life is community of residence, and those who live close to each other are likely to see each other as effectively related, whether there is any kinship bond or not. Full brothers, on the other hand, who live in different parts of the camp may have little concern for each other.

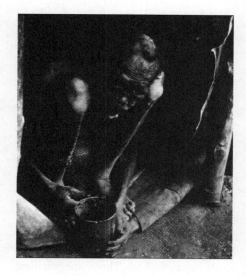

It is not possible, then, to think of the family as a simple, basic unit. A child is brought up to regard any adult living in the same camp as a parent, and age-mate as a brother or sister. The Ik had this essentially social attitude toward kinship, and it readily lent itself to the rapid and disastrous changes that took place following the restriction of their movement and hunting activities. The family simply ceased to exist.

It is a mistake to think of small-scale societies as "primitive" or "simple." Hunters and gatherers, most of all, appear simple and straightforward in terms of their social organization, yet that is far from true. If we can learn about the nature of society from a study of small-scale societies, we can also learn about human relationships. The smaller the society, the less emphasis there is on the formal system and the more there is on interpersonal and intergroup relations. Security is seen in terms of these rela-

tionships, and so is survival. The result, which appears so deceptively simple, is that hunters frequently display those characteristics that we find so admirable in man: kindness, generosity, consideration, affection, honesty, hospitality, compassion, charity. For them, in their tiny, close-knit society, these are necessities for survival. In our society anyone possessing even half these qualities would find it hard to survive, yet we think these virtues are inherent in man. I took it for granted that the Ik would possess these same qualities. But they were as unfriendly, uncharitable, inhospitable and generally mean as any people can be. For those positive qualities we value so highly are no longer functional for them; even more than in our own society they spell ruin and disaster. It seems that, far from being basic human qualities, they are luxuries we can afford in times of plenty or are mere mechanisms for survival and security. Given the situation in which the Ik found themselves, man has no time for such luxuries, and a much more basic man appears, using more basic survival tactics.

*Turnbull had to wait in Kaabong, a remote administration outpost, for permission from the Uganda government to continue to Pirre, the Ik water hole and police post. While there he began to learn the Ik language and became used to their constant demands for food and tobacco. An official in Kaabong gave him, as a "gift," 20 Ik workers to build a house and a road up to it. When they arrived at Pirre, however, wages for the workers were negotiated by wily Atum, "the senior of all the Ik on Morungole."*

The police seemed as glad to see me as I was to see them. They hungrily

asked for news of Kaabong, as though it were the hub of the universe. They had a borehole and pump for water, to which they said I was welcome, since the water holes used by the Ik were not fit for drinking or even for washing. The police were not able to tell me much about the Ik, because every time they went to visit an Ik village, there was nobody there. Only in times of real hunger did they see much of the Ik, and then only enough to know that they were hungry.

The next morning I rose early, but even though it was barely daylight, by the time I had washed and dressed, the Ik were already outside. They were sitting silently, staring at the Land Rover. As impassive as they seemed, there was an air of expectancy, and I was reminded that these were, after all, hunters, and the likelihood was that I was their morning's prey. So I left the Land Rover curtains closed and as silently as possible prepared a frugal breakfast.

Atum was waiting for me. He said that he had told all the Ik that Iciebam [friend of the Ik] had arrived to live with them and that I had given the workers a "holiday" so they could greet me. They were waiting in the villages. They were very hungry, he added, and many were dying. That was probably one of the few true statements he ever made, and I never even considered believing it.

There were seven villages in all. Village Number One was built on a steep slope, and even the houses tilted at a crazy angle. Atum rapped on the outer stockade with his cane and shouted a greeting, but there was no response. This was Giriko's village, he said, and he was one of my workers.

"But I thought you told them to go back to their villages," I said.

"Yes, but you gave them a holiday, so they are probably in their fields," answered Atum, looking me straight in the eye.

At Village Number Two there was indisputably someone inside, for I could hear loud singing. The singing stopped, a pair of hands gripped the stockade and a craggy head rose into view, giving me an undeniably welcoming smile. This was Lokelea. When I asked him what he had been singing about, he answered, "Because I'm hungry."

Village Number Three, the smallest of all, was empty. Village Number Four had only 8 huts, as against the 12 or so in Lokelea's village and the 18 in Giriko's. The outer stockade was broken in one section, and we walked right in. We ducked through a low opening and entered a compound in which a woman was making pottery. She kept on at her work but gave us a cheery welcome and laughed her head off when I tried to speak in Icietot. She willingly showed me details of her work and did not seem unduly surprised at my interest. She said that everyone else had left for the fields except old Nangoli, who, on hearing her name mentioned, appeared at a hole in the stockade shutting off the next compound. Nangoli mumbled toothlessly at Losike, who told Atum to pour her some water.

As we climbed up to his own village, Number Five, Atum said that Losike never gave anything away. Later I remembered that gift of water to Nangoli. At the time I did not stop to think that in

this country a gift of water could be a gift of life.

Atum's village had nearly 50 houses, each within its compound within the stout outer stockade. Atum did not invite me in.

A hundred yards away stood Village Number Six. Kauar, one of the workers, was sitting on a rocky slab just outside the village. He had a smile like Losike's, open and warm, and he said he had been waiting for me all morning. He offered us water and showed me his own small compound and that of his mother.

Coming up from Village Number Seven, at quite a respectable speed, was a blind man. This was Logwara, emaciated but alive and remarkably active. He had heard us and had come to greet me, he said, but he added the inevitable demand for tobacco in the same breath. We sat down in the open sunlight. For a brief moment I felt at peace.

After a short time Atum said we should start back and called over his shoulder to his village. A muffled sound came from within, and he said, "That's my wife, she is very sick—and hungry." I offered to go and see her, but he shook his head. Back at the Land Rover I gave Atum some food and some aspirin, not knowing what else to give him to help his wife.

I was awakened well before dawn by the lowing of cattle. I made an extra pot of tea and let Atum distribute it, and then we divided the workers into two teams. Kauar was to head the team building the house, and Lokelatom, Losike's husband, was to take charge of the road workers.

While the Ik were working, their heads kept turning as though they were expecting something to happen. Every now and again one would stand up and peer into the distance and then take off into the bush for an hour or so. On one such occasion, after the person had been gone two hours, the others started drifting off. By then I knew them better; I looked for a wisp of smoke and followed it to where the road team was cooking a goat. Smoke was a giveaway, though, so they economized on cooking and ate most food nearly raw. It is a curious hangover from what must once have been a moral code that Ik will offer food if surprised in the act of eating, though they now go to enormous pains not to be so surprised.

I was always up before dawn, but by the time I got up to the villages they were always deserted. One morning I followed the little *oror* [gulley] up from *oror a pirre'i* [Ravine of Pirre] while it was still quite dark, and I met Lomeja on his way down. He took me on my first illicit hunt in Kidepo. He told me that if he got anything he would share it with me and with anyone else who managed to join us but that he certainly would not take anything back to his family. "Each one of them is out seeing what he can get

for himself, and do you think they will bring any back for me?"

Lomeja was one of the very few Ik who seemed glad to volunteer information. Unlike many of the others, he did not get up and leave as I approached. Apart from him, I spent most of my time, those days, with Losike, the potter. She told me that Nangoli, the old lady in the adjoining compound, and her husband, Amuarkuar, were rather peculiar. They helped each other get food and water, and they brought it back to their compound to eat together.

I still do not know how much real hunger there was at that time, for most of the younger people seemed fairly well fed, and the few skinny old people seemed healthy and active. But my laboriously extracted genealogies showed that there were quite a number of old people still alive and allegedly in these villages, though they were never to be seen. Then Atum's wife died.

Atum told me nothing about it but kept up his demands for food and medicine. After a while the beady-eyed Lomongin told me that Atum was selling the medicine I was giving him for his wife. I was not unduly surprised and merely remarked that that was too bad for his wife. "Oh no," said Lomongin, "she has been dead for weeks."

It must have been then that I began to notice other things that I suppose I had chosen to ignore before. Only a very few of the Ik helped me with the language. Others would understand when it suited them and would pretend they did not understand when they did not want to listen. I began to be forced into a similar isolationist attitude myself, and although I cannot say I enjoyed it, it did make life much easier. I even began to enjoy, in a peculiar way, the company of the silent Ik. And the more I accepted it, the less often people got up and left as I approached. On one occasion I sat on the *di* [sitting place] by Atum's rain tree for three days with a group of Ik, and for three days not one word was exchanged.

The work teams were more lively, but only while working. Kauar always played and joked with the children when they came back from foraging. He used to volunteer to make the two-day walk into Kaabong and the even more tiring

two-day climb back to get mail for me or to buy a few things for others. He always asked if he had made the trip more quickly than the last time.

Then one day Kauar went to Kaabong and did not come back. He was found on the last peak of the trail, cold and dead. Those who found him took the things he had been carrying and pushed his body into the bush. I still see his open, laughing face, see him giving precious tidbits to the children, comforting some child who was crying, and watching me read the letters he carried so lovingly for me. And I still think of him probably running up that viciously steep mountainside so he could break his time record and falling dead in his pathetic prime because he was starving.

Once I settled down into my new home, I was able to work more effectively. Having recovered at least some of my anthropological detachment, when I heard the telltale rustling of someone at my stockade, I merely threw a stone. If when out walking I stumbled during a difficult descent and the Ik shrieked with laughter, I no longer even noticed it.

Anyone falling down was good for a laugh, but I never saw anyone actually trip anyone else. The adults were content to let things happen and then enjoy them; it was probably conservation of energy. The children, however, sought their pleasures with vigor. The best game of all, at this time, was teasing poor little Adupa. She was not so little—in fact she should have been an adult, for she was nearly 13 years old—but Adupa was a little mad. Or you might say she was the only sane one, depending on your point of view. Adupa did not jump on other people's play houses, and she lavished enormous care on hers and would curl up inside it. That made it all the more jump-on-able. The other children beat her viciously.

Children are not allowed to sleep in the house after they are "put out," which is at about three years old, four at the latest. From then on they sleep in the open courtyard, taking what shelter they can against the stockade. They may ask for permission to sit in the doorway of their parents' house but may not lie down or sleep there. "The same thing applies to old people," said Atum, "if they can't build a house of their own and, of course, *if* their children let them stay in their compounds."

I saw a few old people, most of whom had taken over abandoned huts. For the first time I realized that there really was starvation and saw why I had never known it before: it was confined to the aged. Down in Giriko's village the old ritual priest, Lolim, confidentially told me that he was sheltering an old man who had been refused shelter by his son. But Lolim did not have enough food for himself, let alone his guest; could I… I liked old Lolim, so, not believing that Lolim had a visitor at all, I brought him a double ration that evening. There was rustling in the back of the hut, and Lolim helped ancient Lomeraniang to the entrance. They shook with delight at the sight of the food.

When the two old men had finished eating, I left; I found a hungry-looking and disapproving little crowd clustered outside. They muttered to each other about wasting food. From then on I brought food daily, but in a very short time Lomeraniang was dead, and his son refused to come down from the village above to bury him. Lolim scratched a hole and covered the body with a pile of stones he carried himself, one by one.

Hunger was indeed more severe than I knew, and, after the old people, the children were the next to go. It was all quite impersonal—even to me, in most cases, since I had been immunized by the Ik themselves against sorrow on their behalf. But Adupa was an exception. Her madness was such that she did not know just how vicious humans could be. Even worse, she thought that parents were for loving, for giving as well as receiving. Her parents were not given to fantasies. When she came for shelter, they drove her out; and when she came because she was hungry, they laughed that Icien laugh, as if she had made them happy.

Adupa's reactions became slower and slower. When she managed to find food—fruit peels, skins, bits of bone, half-eaten berries—she held it in her hand and looked at it with wonder and delight. Her playmates caught on quickly; they put tidbits in her way and watched her simple drawn little face wrinkle in a smile. Then as she raised her

hand to her mouth, they set on her with cries of excitement, fun and laughter, beating her savagely over the head. But that is not how she died. I took to feeding her, which is probably the cruelest thing I could have done, a gross selfishness on my part to try to salve my own rapidly disappearing conscience. I had to protect her, physically, as I fed her. But the others would beat her anyway, and Adupa cried, not because of the pain in her body but because of the pain she felt at the great, vast, empty wasteland where love should have been.

It was *that* that killed her. She demanded that her parents love her. Finally they took her in, and Adupa was happy and stopped crying. She stopped crying forever because her parents went away and closed the door tight behind them, so tight that weak little Adupa could never have moved it.

The Ik seem to tell us that the family is not such a fundamental unit as we usually suppose, that it is not essential to social life. In the crisis of survival facing the Ik, the family was one of the first institutions to go, and the Ik as a society have survived.

The other quality of life that we hold to be necessary for survival—love—the Ik dismiss as idiotic and highly dangerous. But we need to see more of the Ik before their absolute lovelessness becomes truly apparent.

In this curious society there is one common value to which all Ik hold tenaciously. It is *ngag*, "food." That is the one standard by which they measure right and wrong, goodness and badness. The very word for "good" is defined in terms of food. "Goodness" is "the possession of food," or the "*individual* possession of food." If you try to discover their concept of a "good man," you get the truly Icien answer: one who has a full stomach.

We should not be surprised, then, when the mother throws her child out at three years old. At that age a series of *rites de passage* begins. In this environment a child has no chance of survival on his own until he is about 13, so children from age bands. The junior band consists of children between three and seven, the senior of eight- to twelve-year-olds. Within the band each child seeks another close to him in age for defense against the older children. There friendships are temporary, however, and inevitably there comes a time when each turns on the one that up to then had been the closest to him; that is the *rite de passage*, the destruction of that fragile bond called friendship. When this has happened three or four times, the child is ready for the world.

The weakest are soon thinned out, and the strongest survive to achieve leadership of the band. Such a leader is eventually driven out, turned against by his fellow band members. Then the process starts all over again; he joins the senior age band as its most junior member.

The final *rite de passage* is into adulthood, at the age of 12 or 13. By then the candidate has learned the wisdom of acting on his own, for his own good, while acknowledging that on occasion it is profitable to associate temporarily with others.

One year in four the Ik can count on a complete drought. About this time it began to be apparent that there were going to be two consecutive years of drought and famine. Men as well as women took to gathering what wild fruits and berries they could find, digging up roots, cutting grass that was going to seed, threshing and eating the seed.

Old Nangoli went to the other side of Kidepo, where food and water were more plentiful. But she had to leave her husband, Amuarkuar, behind. One day he appeared at my *odok* and asked for water. I gave him some and was going to get him food when Atum came storming over and argued with me about wasting water. In the midst of the dispute Amuarkuar quietly left. He wandered over to a rocky outcrop and lay down there to rest. Nearby was a small bundle of grass that evidently he had cut and had been dragging painfully to the ruins of his village to make a rough shelter. The grass was his supreme effort to keep a home going until Nangoli returned. When I went over to him, he looked up and smiled and said that my water tasted good. He lay back and went to sleep with a smile on his face. That is how Amuarkuar died, happily.

There are measures that can be taken for survival involving the classical institutions of gift and sacrifice. These are weapons, sharp and aggressive. The object is to build up a series of obligations so that in times of crisis you have a number of debts you can recall; with luck one of them may be repaid. To this end, in the circumstances of Ik life, considerable sacrifice would be justified, so you have the odd phenomenon of these otherwise singularly self-interested people going out of their way to "help" each other. Their help may very well be resented in the extreme, but is done in such a way that it cannot be refused, for it has already been given. Someone may hoe another's field in his absence or rebuild his stockade or join in the building of a house.

The danger in this system was that the debtor might not be around when collection was called for and, by the same token, neither might the creditor. The future was too uncertain for this to be anything but one additional survival measure, though some developed it to a fine technique.

There seemed to be increasingly little among the Ik that could by any stretch of the imagination be called social life, let alone social organization. The family does not hold itself together; economic interest is centered on as many stomachs as there are people; and cooperation is merely a device for furthering an interest that is consciously selfish. We often do

the same thing in our so-called "altruistic" practices, but we tell ourselves it is for the good of others. The Ik have dispensed with the myth of altruism. Though they have no centralized leadership or means of physical coercion, they do hold together with remarkable tenacity.

In our world, where the family has also lost much of its value as a social unit and where religious belief no longer binds us into communities, we maintain order only through coercive power that is ready to uphold a rigid law and through an equally rigid penal system. The Ik, however, have learned to do without coercion, either spiritual or physical. It seems that they have come to a recognition of what they accept as man's basic selfishness, of his natural determination to survive as an individual before all else. This they consider to be man's basic right, and they allow others to pursue that right without recrimination.

In large-scale societies such as our own, where members are individual beings rather than social beings, we rely on law for order. The absence of both a common law and a common belief would surely result in lack of any community of behavior; yet Ik society is not anarchical. One might well expect religion, then, to play a powerful role in Icien life, providing a source of unity.

The Ik, as may be expected, do not run true to form. When I arrived, there were still three ritual priests alive. From them and from the few other old people, I learned something of the Ik's belief and practice as they had been before their world was so terribly changed. There had been a powerful unity of belief in Didigwari—a sky god—and a body of ritual practice reinforcing secular behavior that was truly social.

Didigwari himself is too remote to be of much practical significance to the Ik. He created them and abandoned them and retreated into his domain somewhere in the sky. He never came down to earth, but the *abang* [ancestors] have all known life on earth; it is only against them that one can sin and only to them that one can turn for help, through the ritual priest.

While Morungole has no legends attached to it by the Ik, it nonetheless figures in their ideology and is in some ways regarded by them as sacred. I had

noticed this by the almost reverential way in which they looked at it—none of the shrewd cunning and cold appraisal with which they regarded the rest of the world. When they talked about it, there was a different quality to their voices. They seemed incapable of talking about Morungole in any other way, which is probably why they talked about it so very seldom. Even that weasel Lomongin became gentle the only time he talked about it to me. He said, "If Atum and I were there, we would not argue. It is a good place." I asked if he meant that it was full of food. He said yes. "Then why do Ik never go there?" "They do go there." "But if hunting is good there, why not live there?" "We don't hunt there, we just go there." "Why?" "I told you, it is a good place." If I did not understand him, that was my fault; for once he was doing his best to communicate something to me. With others it was the same. All agreed that it was "a good place." One added, "That is the Place of God."

Lolim, the oldest and greatest of the ritual priests, was also the last. He was not much in demand any longer, but he was still held in awe, which means kept at a distance. Whenever he approached a *di*, people cleared a space for him, as far away from themselves as possible. The Ik rarely called on his services, for they had little to pay him with, and he had equally little to offer them. The main things they did try to get out of him were certain forms of medicine, both herbal and magical.

Lolim said that he had inherited his power from his father. His father had taught him well but could not give him the power to hear the *abang*—that had to come from the *abang* themselves. He had wanted his oldest son to inherit and had taught him everything he could. But his son, Longoli, was bad, and the *abang* refused to talk to him. They talked instead to his oldest daughter, bald Nangoli. But there soon came the time when all the Ik needed was food in their stomachs, and Lolim could not supply that. The time came when Lolim was too weak to go out and collect the medicines he needed. His children all refused to go except Nangoli, and then she was jailed for gathering in Kidepo Park.

Lolim became ill and had to be protected while eating the food I gave him. Then the children began openly ridiculing him and teasing him, dancing in front of him and kneeling down so that he would trip over them. His grandson used to creep up behind him and with a pair of hard sticks drum a lively tattoo on the old man's bald head.

I fed him whenever I could, but often he did not want more than a bite. Once I found him rolled up in his protective ball, crying. He had had nothing to eat for four days and no water for two. He had asked his children, who all told him not to come near them.

The next day I saw him leaving Atum's village, where his son Longoli lived. Longoli swore that he had been giving his father food and was looking after him. Lolim was not shuffling away; it was almost a run, the run of a drunken man, staggering from side to side. I called to him, but he made no reply, just a kind of long, continuous and horrible moan. He had been to Longoli to beg him to let him into his compound because he knew he was going to die in a few hours, Longoli calmly told me afterward. Obviously Longoli could not do a thing like that: a man of Lolim's importance would have called for an enormous funeral feast. So he refused. Lolim begged Longoli then to open up Nangoli's *asak* for him so that he could die in *her* compound. But Longoli drove him out, and he died alone.

Atum pulled some stones over the body where it had fallen into a kind of hollow. I saw that the body must have lain parallel with the *oror*. Atum answered without waiting for the question: "He was lying looking up at Mount Meraniang."

Insofar as ritual survived at all, it could hardly be said to be religious, for it did little or nothing to bind Icien society together. But the question still remained: Did this lack of social behavior and communal ritual or religious expression mean that there was no community of belief?

Belief may manifest itself, at either the individual or the communal level, in what we call morality, when we behave according to certain principles supported by our belief even when it seems against

our personal interest. When we call ourselves moral, however, we tend to ignore that ultimately our morality benefits us even as individuals, insofar as we are social individuals and live in a society. In the absence of belief, law takes over and morality has little role. If there was such a thing as an Icien morality, I had not yet perceived it, though traces of a moral past remained. But it still remained a possibility, as did the existence of an unspoken, unmanifest belief that might yet reveal itself and provide a basis for the reintegration of society. I was somewhat encouraged in this hope by the unexpected flight of old Nangoli, widow of Amuarkuar.

When Nangoli returned and found her husband dead, she did an odd thing: she grieved. She tore down what was left of their home, uprooted the stockade, tore up whatever was growing in her little field. Then she fled with a few belongings.

Some weeks later I heard that she and her children had gone over to the Sudan and built a village there. This migration was so unusual that I decided to see whether this runaway village was different.

Lojieri led the way, and Atum came along. One long day's trek got us there. Lojieri pulled part of the brush fence aside, and we went in and wandered around. He and Atum looked inside all the huts, and Lojieri helped himself to tobacco from one and water from another. Surprises were coming thick and fast. That households should be left open and untended with such wealth inside… That there should have been such wealth, for as well as tobacco and jars of water there were baskets of food, and meat was drying on racks. There were half a dozen or so compounds, but they were separated from each other only by a short line of sticks and brush. It was a village, and these were homes, the first and last I was to see.

The dusk had already fallen, and Nangoli came in with her children and grandchildren. They had heard us and came in with warm welcomes. There was no hunger here, and in a very short time each kitchen hearth had a pot of food cooking. Then we sat around the central fire and talked until late, and it was another universe.

There was no talk of "how much better it is here than there"; talk revolved around what had happened on the hunt that day. Loron was lying on the ground in front of the fire as his mother made gentle fun of him. His wife, Kinimei, whom I had never seen even speak to him at Pirre, put a bowl of fresh-cooked berries and fruit in front of him. It was all like a nightmare rather than a fantasy, for it made the reality of Pirre seem all the more frightening.

The unpleasantness of returning was somewhat alleviated by Atum's suffering on the way up the stony trail. Several times he slipped, which made Lojieri and me laugh. It was a pleasure to move rapidly ahead and leave Atum gasping behind so that we could be sitting up on the *di* when he finally appeared and could laugh at his discomfort.

The days of drought wore on into weeks and months and, like everyone else, I became rather bored with sickness and death. I survived rather as did the young adults, by diligent attention to my own needs while ignoring those of others.

More and more it was only the young who could go far from the village as hunger became starvation. Famine relief had been initiated down at Kasile, and those fit enough to make the trip set off. When they came back, the contrast between them and the others was that between life and death. Villages were villages of the dead and dying, and there was little difference between the two. People crawled rather than walked. After a few feet some would lie down to rest, but they could not be sure of ever being able to sit up again, so they mostly stayed upright until they reached their destination. They were going nowhere, these semianimate bags of skin and bone; they just wanted to be with others, and they stopped whenever they met. Perhaps it was the most important demonstration of sociality I ever saw among the Ik. Once they met, they neither spoke nor did anything together.

Early one morning, before dawn, the village moved. In the midst of a hive of activity were the aged and crippled, soon to be abandoned, in danger of being trampled but seemingly unaware of it. Lolim's widow, Lo'ono, whom I had never seen before, also had been abandoned and had tried to make her way down the mountainside. But she was totally blind and had tripped and rolled to the bottom of the *oror a pirre'i;* there she lay on her back, her legs and arms thrashing feebly, while a little crowd laughed.

At this time a colleague was with me. He kept the others away while I ran to get medicine and food and water, for Lo'ono was obviously near dead from hunger and thirst as well as from the fall. We treated her and fed her and asked her to come back with us. But she asked us to point her in the direction of her son's new village. I said I did not think she would get much of a welcome there, and she replied that she knew it but wanted to be near him when she died. So we gave her more food, put her stick in her hand and pointed her the right way. She suddenly cried. She was crying, she said, because we had reminded her that there had been a time when people had helped each other, when people had been kind and good. Still crying, she set off.

The Ik up to this point had been tolerant of my activities, but all this was too much. They said that what we were doing was wrong. Food and medicine were for the living, not the dead. I thought of Lo'ono. And I thought of other old people who had joined in the merriment when they had been teased or had a precious morsel of food taken from their mouths. They knew that it was silly of them to expect to go on living, and, having watched others, they knew that the spectacle really was quite funny. So they joined in the laughter. Perhaps if we had left Lo'ono, she would have died laughing. But we prolonged her misery for no more than a few brief days. Even worse, we reminded her of when things had been different, of days when children had cared for parents and parents for children. She was already dead, and we made her unhappy as well. At the time I was sure we were right, doing the only "human" thing. In a way we *were*—we were making life more comfortable for ourselves. But now I wonder if the Ik way was not right, if I too should not have laughed as Lo'ono flapped about, then left her to die.

Ngorok was a man at 12. Lomer, his older brother, at 15 was showing signs of strain; when he was carrying a load, his face took on a curious expression of pain

that was not physical pain. Giriko, at 25 was 40, Atum at 40 was 65, and the very oldest, perhaps a bare 50, were centenarians. And I, at 40, was younger than any of them, for I still enjoyed life, which they had learned was not "adult" when they were 3. But they retained their will to survive and so offered grudging respect to those who had survived for long.

Even in the teasing of the old there was a glimmer of hope. It denoted a certain intimacy that did not exist between adjacent generations. This is quite common in small-scale societies. The very old and the very young look at each other as representing the future and the past. To the child, the aged represent a world that existed before their own birth and the unknown world to come.

And now that all the old are dead, what is left? Every Ik who is old today was thrown out at three and has survived, and in consequence has thrown his own children out and knows that they will not help him in his old age any more than he helped his parents. The system has turned one full cycle and is now self-perpetuating; it has eradicated what we know as "humanity" and has turned the world into a chilly void where man does not seem to care even for himself, but survives. Yet into this hideous world Nangoli and her family quietly returned because they could not bear to be alone.

For the moment abandoning the very old and the very young, the Ik as a whole must be searched for one last lingering trace of humanity. They appear to have disposed of virtually all the qualities that we normally think of as differentiating us from other primates, yet they survive without seeming to be greatly different from ourselves in terms of behavior. Their behavior is more extreme, for we do not start throwing our children out until kindergarten. We have shifted responsibility from family to state, the Ik have shifted it to the individual.

It has been claimed that human beings are capable of love and, indeed, are dependent upon it for survival and sanity. The Ik offer us an opportunity for testing this cherished notion that love is essential to survival. If it is, the Ik should have it.

Love in human relationships implies mutuality, a willingness to sacrifice the

self that springs from a consciousness of identity. This seems to bring us back to the Ik, for it implies that love is self-oriented, that even the supreme sacrifice of one's life is no more than selfishness, for the victim feels amply rewarded by the pleasure he feels in making the sacrifice. The Ik, however, do not value emotion above survival, and they are without love.

But I kept looking, for it was the one thing that could fill the void their survival tactics had created; and if love was not there in some form, it meant that for humanity love is not a necessity at all, but a luxury or an illusion. And if it was not among the Ik, it meant that mankind can lose it.

The only possibility for any discovery of love lay in the realm of interpersonal relationships. But they were, each one, simply alone, and seemingly content to be alone. It was this acceptance of individual isolation that made love almost impossible. Contact, when made, was usually for a specific practical purpose having to do with food and the filling of a stomach, a single stomach. Such contacts did not have anything like the permanence or duration required to develop a situation in which love was possible.

The isolation that made love impossible, however, was not completely proof against loneliness, I no longer noticed normal behavior, such as the way people ate, running as they gobbled, so as to have it all for themselves. But I did notice that when someone was making twine or straightening a spear shaft, the focus of attention for the spectators was not the person but the action. If they were caught watching by the one being watched and their eyes met, the reaction was a sharp retreat on both sides.

When the rains failed for the second year running, I knew that the Ik as a society were almost certainly finished and that the monster they had created in its place, that passionless, feelingless association of individuals, would spread like a fungus, contaminating all it touched. When I left, I too had been contaminated. I was not upset when I said good-bye to old Loiangorok. I told him I had left a sack of *posho* [ground corn meal] with the police for him, and I said I would send money for more when that ran out.

He dragged himself slowly toward the *di* every day, and he always clutched a knife. When he got there, or as far as he could, he squatted down and whittled at some wood, thus proving that he was still alive and able to do things. The *posho* was enough to last him for months, but I felt no emotion when I estimated that he would last one month, even with the *posho* in the hands of the police. I underestimated his son, who within two days had persuaded the police that it would save a lot of bother if he looked after the *posho*. I heard later that Loiangorok died of starvation within two weeks.

So, I departed with a kind of forced gaiety, feeling that I should be glad to be gone but having forgotten how to be glad. I certainly was not thinking of returning within a year, but I did. The following spring I heard that rain had come at last and that the fields of the Ik had never looked so prosperous, nor the country so green and fertile. A few months away had refreshed me, and I wondered if my conclusions had not been excessively pessimistic. So, early that summer, I set off to be present for the first harvests in three years.

I was not surprised too much when two days after my arrival and installation at the police post I found Logwara, the blind man, lying on the roadside bleeding, while a hundred yards up other Ik were squabbling over the body of a hyena. Logwara had tried to get there ahead of the others to grab the meat and had been trampled on.

First I looked at the villages. The lush outer covering concealed an inner decay. All the villages were like this to some extent, except for Lokelea's. There the tomatoes and pumpkins were carefully pruned and cleaned, so that the fruits were larger and healthier. In what had been my own compound the shade trees had been cut down for firewood, and the lovely hanging nests of the weaver birds were gone.

The fields were even more desolate. Every field without exception had yielded in abundance, and it was a new sensation to have vision cut off by thick crops. But every crop was rotting from sheer neglect.

The Ik said that they had no need to bother guarding the fields. There was so much food they could never eat it all, so why not let the birds and baboons take some? The Ik had full bellies; they were good. The *di* at Atum's village was much the same as usual, people sitting or lying about. People were still stealing from each other's fields, and nobody thought of saving for the future.

It was obvious that nothing had really changed due to the sudden glut of food except that interpersonal relationships had deteriorated still further and that Icien individualism had heightened beyond what I thought even Ik to be capable of.

The Ik had faced a conscious choice between being humans and being parasites and had chosen the latter. When they saw their fields come alive, they were confronted with a problem. If they reaped the harvest, they would have to store grain for eating and planting, and every Ik knew that trying to store anything was a waste of time. Further, if they made their fields look too promising, the government would stop famine relief. So the Ik let their fields rot and continued to draw famine relief.

The Ik were not starving any longer; the old and infirm had all died the previous year, and the younger survivors were doing quite well. But the famine relief was administered in a way that was little short of criminal. As before, only the young and well were able to get down from Pirre to collect the relief; they were given relief for those who could not come and told to take it back. But they never did—they ate it themselves.

The facts are there, though those that can be read here form but a fraction of what one person was able to gather in under two years. There can be no mistaking the direction in which those facts point, and that is the most important thing of all, for it may affect the rest of mankind as it has affected the Ik. The Ik have "progressed," one might say, since the change that has come to them came with the advent of civilization to Africa. They have made of a world that was alive a world that is dead—a cold, dispassionate world that is without ugliness because it is without beauty, without hate because it is without love, and without any realization of truth even, because it simply is. And the symptoms of change in our own

society indicate that we are heading in the same direction.

Those values we cherish so highly may indeed be basic to human society but not to humanity, and that means that the Ik show that society itself is not indispensable for man's survival and that man is capable of associating for purposes of survival without being social. The Ik have replaced human society with a mere survival system that does not take human emotion into account. As yet the system i[s] imperfect, for although survival is assured, it is at a minimal level and there is still competition between individuals. With our intellectual sophistication and advanced technology we should be able to perfect the system and eliminate competition, guaranteeing survival for a given number of years for all, reducing the demands made upon us by a social system, abolishing desire and consequently that ever-present and vital gap between desire and achievement, treating us, in a word, as individuals with one basic individual right—the right to survive.

Such interaction as there is within this system is one of mutual exploitation. That is how it already is with the Ik. In our own world the mainstays of a society based on a truly social sense of mutuality are breaking down, indicating that perhaps society as we know it has outworn its usefulness and that by clinging to an outworn system we are bringing about our own destruction. Family, economy, government and religion, the basic categories of social activity and behavior, no longer create any sense of social unity involving a shared and mutual responsibility among all members of our society. At best they enable the individual to survive as an individual. It is the world of the individual, as is the world of the Ik.

The sorry state of society in the civilized world today is in large measure due to the fact that social change has not kept up with technological change. This mad, senseless, unthinking commitment to technological change that we call progress may be sufficient to exterminate the human race in a very short time even without the assistance of nuclear warfare. But since we have already become individualized and desocialized, we say that extermination will not come in our time, which shows about as much sense of family devotion as one might expect from the Ik.

Even supposing that we can avert nuclear holocaust or the almost universal famine that may be expected if population keeps expanding and pollution remains unchecked, what will be the cost if not the same already paid by the Ik? They too were driven by the need to survive, and they succeeded at the cost of their humanity. We are already beginning to pay the same price, but we not only still have the choice (though we may not have the will or courage to make it), we also have the intellectual and technological ability to avert an Icien end. Any change as radical as will be necessary is not likely to bring material benefits to the present generation, but only then will there be a future.

The Ik teach us that our much vaunted human values are not inherent in humanity at all but are associated only with a particular form of survival called society and that all, even society itself, are luxuries that can be dispensed with. That does not make them any less wonderful, and if man has any greatness, it is surely in his ability to maintain these values, even shortening an already pitifully short life rather than sacrifice his humanity. But that too involves choice, and the Ik teach us that man can lose the will to make it. That is the point at which there is an end to truth, to goodness and to beauty, an end to the struggle for their achievement, which gives life to the individual and strength and meaning to society. The Ik have relinquished all luxury in the name of individual survival, and they live on as a people without life,

without passion, beyond humanity. We pursue those trivial, idiotic technological encumbrances, and all the time we are losing our potential for social rather than individual survival, for hating as well as loving, losing perhaps our last chance to enjoy life with all the passion that is our nature.

---

*Anthropologist Colin M. Turnbull, author of* The Forest People *and* The Lonely Africans, *went to study the Ik of Uganda, who he believed were still primarily hunters, in order to compare them with other hunting-and-gathering societies he had studied in totally different environments. He was surprised to discover that they were no longer hunters but primarily farmers, well on their way to starvation and something worse in a drought-stricken land.*

From *Intellectual Digest,* April 1973. © 1972 by Colin M. Turnbull. Reprinted by permission of Simon & Schuster.

America's moral non-decline.

# MORE MORAL

*By David Whitman*

By the time the Lewinsky scandal erupted, three out of four Americans already believed that moral values had weakened in the past quarter-century. Now, thanks to Bill Clinton's Oval Office high jinks, the case that moral standards are eroding seems stronger than ever. In his new bestseller *The Death of Outrage*, William Bennett argues that the lack of public outcry over the president's adultery and prevarication is but one more sign that people's "commitment to long-standing American ideals has been enervated." Al Gore would disagree with Bennett's analysis of Clinton, but he, too, believes that "there is indeed a spiritual crisis in modern civilization."

Yet, for all the bipartisan hand-wringing about moral decline, there is surprisingly little evidence that Americans *act* more immorally today than they did a quarter-century ago. In fact, just the opposite seems to be true—as even a few conservatives are beginning to concede. In the current issue of the right-leaning magazine *The American Enterprise*, editor-in-chief Karl Zinsmeister urges fellow conservatives not "to accuse the American people of becoming morally rotten. Especially when there exist abundant data suggesting that the residents of our land are actually becoming *less* morally rotten." It is still true, of course, that millions of citizens continue to err and sin, and that the culture now has a surfeit of coarseness, from noxious rap lyrics to the "Jerry Springer Show." But, if one looks beyond the anecdotes, the picture of how people behave is unexpectedly encouraging.

Compared with their predecessors of a quarter-century ago, Americans today are less likely to drink to excess, take drugs, rely on the dole, drive drunk, or knowingly evade paying taxes. They give more money to charity and spend as much or more time in church. And they are more likely than their predecessors to do good Samaritan work among the poor, sick, and elderly. Despite fears of random violence, FBI reports suggest that fewer people were murdered by strangers in 1997 (2,067) than in 1977 (about 2,500), even though the U.S. population grew by 47 million during that time. The dramatic drop in the number of Americans victimized by murder, burglary, and theft represents another well-known illustration of moral progress, but there are many more.

For example, Americans now donate significantly more money to charity than they did a generation ago, as Everett Carll Ladd, director of the Roper Center for Public Opinion Research, documents in a forthcoming book. Adjusted for inflation, Americans gave about $525 per adult to charity in 1996. That is 50 percent more than Americans on average donated in 1970 ($349) and roughly triple what people gave in 1950 ($179). Starting in 1977, pollsters also began regularly asking adults whether they were involved in charity or social services, such as helping the poor, the sick, or the elderly. The ranks of those participating roughly doubled from 26 percent in 1977 to 54 percent in 1995. Volunteer work by college students is up, too. In 1998, 74 percent of college freshmen had done volunteer work the preceding year, the highest such figure since researchers started tracking it in 1984.

Charity has often gone hand in hand with religion, so perhaps it is not surprising to learn that religious faith, too, is not in decline. On the contrary, America remains a deeply religious nation, with a reinvigorated evangelical movement. In 1997, the Gallup Poll replicated one of its earliest surveys on Americans' religious practices from 1947. The 50-year update found that the same percentage of Americans pray (90 percent), believe in God (96 percent), and attend church once a week. One of the few differences between the two eras was that Americans were actually more likely to give grace or give thanks aloud in 1997 than in 1947 (63 percent compared with 43 percent).

Both adults and teens are now as likely to belong to a church or synagogue as their counterparts were 25 years ago, and they attend religious services a bit more often. Two months ago, at the start of December, 42 percent of adults reported attending a service at a church or synagogue the previous week—a tad higher than the 40 percent or so who said they had attended services in 1972, 1950, and 1940. As the political scientist Seymour Martin Lipset writes in his book *American Exceptionalism,* "Religious affiliation and belief in America are much higher in the twentieth century than in the nineteenth, and have not decreased in the post–World War II era."

While everyone "knows" that cheating on tests has exploded in recent decades, the few studies that have looked at trends over time suggest a different picture. A 1996 analysis by Donald McCabe and Linda Klebe Trevino of Rutgers University at nine state universities did find that cheating on tests and exams increased significantly from 1963 to 1993. But serious cheating on written work, such as plagiarism and turning in work done by others, had declined slightly, leading the researchers to conclude that "the dramatic upsurge in cheating heralded by the media was not found."

Cheating on taxes also appears to be no worse than in the recent past. Since 1973, the Internal Revenue Service has tracked the "voluntary compliance rate," a figure used to describe the percentage of total tax liability that individuals and corporations pay voluntarily. In 1992, the voluntary compliance rate for the individual income tax was roughly 83 percent, a hair higher than in 1973.

As for another vice—drug use—Americans seem to be doing better, not worse. Use of illicit drugs peaked in 1979, when 14.1 percent of the population reported having used an illicit drug the previous month, more than double the 1997 figure of 6.4 percent. Cocaine use peaked in 1985; Americans were four times as likely to use cocaine then as they are today. The trends are similar among high school seniors (though marijuana use has risen since 1992).

At the same time, heavy alcohol consumption, binge drinking, and drunken driving have all declined. Heavy alcohol use—defined as having five or more drinks on the same occasion on each of five or more days in the previous months—at its lowest point since 1985, when the federal government first started tracking the figure. In 1985, 8.3 percent of the population were heavy drinkers compared with 5.4 percent in 1997, a drop of about a third. The decline in drunken driving has been equally marked. In 1997, the number of people killed in alcohol-related crashes dropped to less than 40 percent of all traffic fatalities for the first time since the government started tracking this statistic in 1975. Americans consumed about as much alcohol per person in 1995 as in 1945—and drank substantially less than in 1970.

For all the talk of scandal, and despite the official statistics, political corruption seems to be waning, too. In 1996, 952 individuals were indicted in federal prosecutions for public corruption, more than triple the number in 1975. Yet most historians believe the apparent rise in corruption stems from the proliferation of special prosecutors and inspector generals, not from a real upsurge in unethical conduct. New disclosure rules, government intercessions in allegedly corrupt unions, a law enforcement crackdown on the mob, the disappearance of Tammany Hall–style urban political machines and "good-time Charlie" governors, and a more watchful press all seem to have reduced bribes, hush money, and other blatant types of political corruption. Even William Bennett concedes in *The Death of Outrage* that "in general, politics today is less corrupt than perhaps at any point in American history."

Granted, not all the news on the moral front is good. One institution that undeniably weakened in the past quarter-century is the family. Since the early '70s, out-of-wedlock childbearing has skyrocketed. Child abuse and neglect have risen, too—thanks mainly to the advent of crack—and most noncustodial parents still don't pay their child support.

Yet other much-lamented changes in family life do not really demonstrate a rise (or fall) in collective virtue. The surge in divorce suggests that Americans now lack a sense of commitment, but most divorced couples do not think they are acting immorally—more often, they think they have done the right thing by ending a troubled marriage. Many couples similarly defend cohabitation, once deemed to be "living in sin," as a sensible trial run at marriage.

Some moral behavior that has improved in the past quarter-century, particularly the reduction in criminality and drug-taking, is still worse today than it was in the 1950s. But, even when stacked up against the "good ol' days," there are plenty of signs of moral progress. In the 1950s, well over half of the nation's black population lived under almost apartheid-like conditions through much of the South. Millions of women faced sexual discrimination and were denied the right to pursue a calling of their own. Society treated the elderly shabbily, with more than one in three living in poverty (compared with one in ten today). The disabled faced blatant, ugly bigotry, as did homosexuals.

Why hasn't the news about moral progress reached the public? In part, the reason is that it is often thought that people were more moral in earlier eras. Back in 1939, a Gallup Poll showed that 62 percent of the population believed that Americans were happier and more contented in the horse-and-buggy days; a survey taken by Elmo Roper two years earlier found that half of the population felt religion was then losing its influence on American life as well.

But part of the explanation for the public disbelief is that Americans experience an "optimism gap." When members of the public voice distress about family breakdown they are almost always referring to other people's families. Yet the vast majority of citizens do not have serious moral qualms about themselves or their families. Surveys show that most people think they are more moral than the average American, and members of the public repeatedly describe their own families as happy ones with strong ties.

In 1997, *U.S. News & World Report* conducted a revealing survey of 1,000 adults who were asked to rate the chances that various celebrities would one day get into heaven. Topping the list of famous people bound for heaven was Mother Teresa, who had not yet died. Nearly 80 percent of those polled thought it likely that the Nobel Peace Prize winner would one day get her wings. But the survey's most startling finding was that the individuals voted most likely to get into heaven were, well, those being polled. Eighty-seven percent felt that they were heaven-bound, compared with 79 percent who thought the same of Mother Teresa.

Most Americans, in short, hold a generous opinion of their own morals, even while they remain acutely aware of others' failings. But, if Americans can convince themselves that they are bound for heaven, it may also be time to acknowledge that the rest of the nation is not making a beeline for purgatory.

---

DAVID WHITMAN is a senior writer at *U.S. News & World Report* and the author of *The Optimism Gap: The I'm OK—They're Not Syndrome and the Myth of American Decline* (Walker and Company).

# American Culture Goes Global, or Does It?

*By RICHARD PELLS*

Since september 11, newspaper and magazine columnists and television pundits have told us that it is not only the economic power of the United States or the Bush administration's "unilateralist" foreign policy that breeds global anti-Americanism. Dislike for the United States stems also, they say, from its "cultural imperialism." We have been hearing a good deal about how American mass culture inspires resentment and sometimes violent reactions, not just in the Middle East but all over the world.

Yet the discomfort with American cultural dominance is not new. In 1901, the British writer William Stead published a book called, ominously, *The Americanization of the World*. The title captured a set of apprehensions—about the disappearance of national languages and traditions, and the obliteration of the unique identities of countries under the weight of American habits and states of mind—that persists today.

More recently, globalization has become the main enemy for academics, journalists, and political activists who loathe what they see as a trend toward cultural uniformity. Still, they usually regard global culture and American culture as synonymous. And they continue to insist that Hollywood, McDonald's, and Disneyland are eradicating regional and local eccentricities—disseminating images and subliminal messages so beguiling as to drown out competing voices in other lands.

Despite those allegations, the cultural relationship between the United States and the rest of the world over the past 100 years has never been one-sided. On the contrary, the United States was, and continues to be, as much a consumer of foreign intellectual and artistic influences as it has been a shaper of the world's entertainment and tastes.

That is not an argument with which many foreigners (or even many Americans) would readily agree. The clichés about America's cultural "hegemony" make it difficult for most people to recognize that modern global culture is hardly a monolithic entity foisted on the world by the American media.

Neither is it easy for critics of Microsoft or AOL Time Warner to acknowledge that the conception of a harmonious and distinctively American culture—encircling the globe, implanting its values in foreign minds—is a myth.

In fact, as a nation of immigrants from the 19th to the 21st centuries, and as a haven in the 1930s and '40s for refugee scholars and artists, the United States has been a recipient as much as an exporter of global culture. Indeed, the influence of immigrants and African-Americans on the United States explains why its culture has been so popular for so long in so many places. American culture has spread throughout the world because it has incorporated foreign styles and ideas. What Americans have done more brilliantly than their competitors overseas is repackage the cultural products we receive from abroad and then retransmit them to the rest of the planet. In effect, Americans have specialized in selling the dreams, fears, and folklore of other people back to them. That is why a global mass culture has come to be identified, however simplistically, with the United States.

Americans, after all, did not invent fast food, amusement parks, or the movies. Before the Big Mac, there were fish and chips. Before Disneyland, there was Copenhagen's Tivoli Gardens (which Walt Disney used as a prototype for his first theme park, in Anaheim, a model later re-exported to Tokyo and Paris).

Nor can the origins of today's international entertainment be traced only to P.T. Barnum or Buffalo Bill. The roots of the new global culture lie as well in the European modernist assault, in the early 20th century, on 19th-century literature, music, painting, and architecture—particularly in the modernist refusal to honor the traditional boundaries between high and low culture. Modernism in the arts was improvisational, eclectic, and irreverent. Those traits have also been characteristic of, but not peculiar to, mass culture.

The hallmark of 19th-century culture, in Europe and also in Asia, was its insistence on defending the purity of literature, classical music, and representational painting against the intrusions of folklore and popular amusements. No one confused Tolstoy with dime novels, opera with Wild West shows, the Louvre with Coney Island. High culture was supposed to be educational, contemplative, and uplifting—a way of preserving the best in human civilization.

Such beliefs didn't mean that a Dickens never indulged in melodrama, or that a Brahms disdained the use of popular songs. Nor did Chinese or Japanese authors and painters refuse to draw on oral or folkloric traditions. But the 19th-century barriers between high and low culture were resolutely, if imperfectly, maintained.

The artists of the early 20th century shattered what seemed to them the artificial demarcations between different cultural forms. They also challenged the notion that culture was a means of intellectual or moral improvement. They did so by emphasizing style and craftsmanship at the expense of philosophy, religion, or ideology. They deliberately called attention to language in their novels, to optics in their paintings, to the materials in and function of their architecture, to the structure of music instead of its melodies.

And they wanted to shock their audiences. Which they succeeded in doing. Modern painting and literature—with its emphasis on visually distorted nudes, overt sexuality, and meditations on violence—was attacked for being degrading and obscene, and for appealing to the baser instincts of humanity. In much the same way, critics would later denounce the vulgarity of popular culture.

Although modernism assaulted the conventions of 19th-century high culture in Europe and Asia, it inadvertently accelerated the growth of mass culture in the United States. Indeed, Americans were already receptive to the blurring of cultural boundaries. In the 19th century, symphony orchestras in the United States often included band music in their programs, and opera singers were asked to perform both Mozart and Stephen Foster.

So, for Americans in the 20th century, Surrealism, with its dreamlike associations, easily lent itself to the wordplay and psychological symbolism of advertising, cartoons, and theme parks. Dadaism ridiculed the snobbery of elite cultural institutions and reinforced, instead, an existing appetite (especially among the immigrant audiences in the United States) for low-class, anti-bourgeois nickelodeons and vaudeville shows. Stravinsky's experiments with atonal (and thus unconventional and unmelodic) music validated the rhythmic innovations of American jazz. Writers like Hemingway, detesting the rhetorical embellishments of 19th-century prose, invented a terse, hard-boiled language, devoted to reproducing as authentically as possible the elemental qualities of personal experience. That laconic style became a model for modern journalism, detective fiction, and movie dialogue.

All of those trends provided the foundations for a genuinely new culture. But the new culture turned out to be neither modernist nor European. Instead, the United States transformed what was still a parochial culture, appealing largely to the young and the rebellious in Western society, into a global phenomenon.

The propensity of Americans to borrow modernist ideas, and to transform them into a global culture, is clearly visible in the commercial uses of modern architecture. The European Bauhaus movement—intended in the 1920s as a socialist experiment in working-class housing—eventually provided the theories and techniques for the construction of skyscrapers and vacation homes in the United States. But the same architectural ideas were then sent back to Europe after World War II as a model for the reconstruction of bombed-out cities like Rotterdam, Cologne, and Frankfurt. Thus, the United States converted what had once been a distinctive, if localized, rebellion by Dutch and German architects into a generic "international style."

But it is in popular culture that the reciprocal relationship between America and the rest of the world can best be seen. There are many reasons for the ascendancy of American mass culture. Certainly, the ability of American-based media conglomerates to control the production and distribution of their products has been a major stimulus to the worldwide spread of American entertainment. But the power of American capitalism is not the only, or even the most important, explanation for the global popularity of America's movies and television shows.

The effectiveness of English as a language of mass communications has been essential to the acceptance of American culture. Unlike, for example, German, Russian, or Chinese, the simple structure and grammar of English, along with its tendency to use shorter, less-abstract words and more-concise sentences, are all advantageous for the composers of song lyrics, ad slogans, cartoon captions, newspaper headlines, and movie and TV dialogue. English is thus a language exceptionally well-suited to the demands and spread of American mass culture.

## American musicians and entertainers have followed modernist artists like Picasso and Braque in drawing on elements from high and low culture.

Another factor is the size of the American audience. A huge domestic market has made it possible for many American filmmakers and TV executives to retrieve most of their production costs and make a profit within the borders of the United States. That economic cushion has enabled them to spend more money on stars, sets, special effects, location shooting, and merchandising—the very ingredients that attract international audiences as well.

Yet even with such advantages, America's mass culture may not be all that American. The American audience is not only large; because of the influx of immigrants and refugees, it is also international in its complexion. The heterogeneity of America's population—its regional, ethnic, religious, and racial diversity—has forced the media, since the early years of the 20th century, to experiment with messages, images, and story lines that have a broad multicultural appeal. The Hollywood studios, mass-circulation magazines, and television networks have had to learn how to speak to a variety of groups and classes at home. That has given them the techniques to appeal to an equally diverse audience abroad. The American domestic market has, in essence, been a laboratory, a place to develop cultural products that can then be adapted to the world market.

An important way that the American media have succeeded in transcending internal social divisions, national borders, and language barriers is by mixing up cultural styles. American musicians and entertainers have followed the example of modernist artists like Picasso and Braque in drawing on elements from high and low culture, combining the sacred and the profane. Advertisers have adapted the techniques of Surrealism and Abstract Expressionism to make their products more intriguing. Composers like Aaron Copland, George Gershwin, and Leonard Bernstein incorporated folk melodies, religious hymns, blues, gospel songs, and jazz into their symphonies, concertos, operas, and ballets. Indeed, an art form as quintessentially American as jazz evolved during the 20th century into an amalgam of African, Caribbean, Latin American, and modernist European music. That blending of forms in America's mass culture has enhanced its appeal to multiethnic domestic and international audiences by capturing their varied experiences and tastes.

NOWHERE ARE FOREIGN INFLUENCES more evident than in the American movie industry. For better or worse, Hollywood became, in the 20th century, the cultural capital of the modern world. But it was never an exclusively American capital. Like past cultural centers—Florence, Paris, Vienna—Hollywood has functioned as an international community, built by immigrant entrepreneurs and drawing on the talents of actors, directors, writers, cinematographers, editors, and costume and set designers from all over the world. The first American movie star, after all, was Charlie Chaplin, whose comic skills were honed in British music halls.

Moreover, during much of the 20th century, American moviemakers thought of themselves as acolytes, entranced by the superior works of foreign directors. In the 1920s, few American directors could gain admittance to a European pantheon that included Sergei Eisenstein, F.W. Murnau, G.W. Pabst, Fritz Lang, and Carl Dreyer. The postwar years, from the 1940s to the mid-'60s, were once again a golden age of filmmaking in Britain, Sweden, France, Italy, Japan, and India. An extraordinary generation of foreign directors—Ingmar Bergman, Federico Fellini, Michelangelo Antonioni, François Truffaut, Jean-Luc Godard, Akira Kurosawa, Satyajit Ray—were the world's most celebrated auteurs.

Nevertheless, it is one of the paradoxes of the European and Asian cinemas that their greatest success was in spawning American imitations. After the release, in 1967, of *Bonnie and Clyde* (originally to have been directed by Truffaut or Godard), the newest geniuses—Francis Ford Coppola, Martin Scorsese, Robert Altman, Steven Spielberg, Woody Allen—were American. They may have owed their improvisational methods and autobiographical preoccupations to Italian neo-Realism and the French New Wave. But who, in any country, needed to see another *La Dolce Vita* when you could enjoy *Nashville*? Why try to decipher *Jules and Jim* or *L'Avventura* when you could see *Annie Hall* or *The Godfather*? Wasn't it conceivable that *The Seven Samurai* might not be as powerful or as disturbing a movie as *The Wild Bunch*?

It turned out that foreign filmmakers had been too influential for their own good. They helped revolutionize the American cinema, so that, after the 1960s and '70s, it became hard for any other continent's film industry to match the worldwide popularity of American movies.

Once again, however, we need to remember that Hollywood movies have never been just American. To take another example, American directors, in all eras, have emulated foreign artists and filmmakers by paying close attention to the style and formal qualities of a movie, and to the need to tell a story visually. Early-20th-century European painters wanted viewers to recognize that they were looking at lines and color on a canvas rather than at a reproduction of the natural world. Similarly, many American films—from the multiple narrators in *Citizen Kane*, to the split-screen portrait of how two lovers imagine their relationship in *Annie Hall*, to the flashbacks and flash-forwards in *Pulp Fiction*, to the roses blooming from the navel of Kevin Spacey's fantasy dream girl in *American Beauty*—deliberately remind the audience that it is watching a movie instead of a play or a photographed version of reality. American filmmakers (not only in the movies but also on MTV) have been willing to use the most sophisticated techniques of editing and camera work, much of it inspired by European directors, to create a modernist collage of images that captures the speed and seductiveness of life in the contemporary world.

Hollywood's addiction to modernist visual pyrotechnics is especially evident in the largely nonverbal style of many of its contemporary performers. The tendency to mumble was not always in vogue. In the 1930s and '40s, the sound and meaning of words were important not only in movies but also on records and the radio. Even though some homegrown stars, like John Wayne and Gary Cooper, were famously terse, audiences could at least hear and understand what they were saying. But the centrality of language in the films of the 1930s led, more often, to a dependence in Hollywood on British actors (like Cary Grant), or on Americans who sounded vaguely British (like Katharine Hepburn and Bette Davis). It is illustrative of how important foreign (especially British) talent was to Hollywood in an earlier era that the two most famous Southern belles in American fiction and drama—Scarlett O'Hara and Blanche DuBois— were played in the movies by Vivien Leigh.

The verbal eloquence of pre-World War II acting, in both movies and the theater, disappeared after 1945. After Marlon Brando's revolutionary performance in *A Streetcar Named Desire*, in the 1947 stage version and the 1951 screen version, the model of American acting became inarticulateness—a brooding and halting introspection that one doesn't find in the glib and clever heroes or heroines of the screwball comedies and gangster films of the '30s. Brando was trained in the Method, an acting technique originally developed in Stanislavsky's Moscow Art Theater in prerevolutionary Russia, then imported to New York by members of the Group Theater during the 1930s. Where British actors, trained in Shakespeare, were taught to subordinate their personalities to the role as written, the Method encouraged actors to improvise, to summon up childhood memories, and to explore their inner feelings, often at the expense of what the playwright or screenwriter intended. Norman Mailer once said that Brando, in his pauses and his gazes into the middle distance, always seemed to be searching for a better line than the one the writer had composed. In effect, what Brando did (along with his successors and imitators, from James Dean to Warren Beatty to Robert De Niro) was to lead a revolt against the British school of acting, with its reverence for the script and the written (and spoken) word.

Thus, after World War II, the emotional power of American acting lay more in what was not said, in what could not even be communicated in words. The Method actor's reliance on physical mannerisms and even silence in interpreting a role has been especially appropriate for a cinema that puts a premium on the inexpressible. Indeed, the influence of the Method, not only in the United States but also abroad (where it was reflected in the acting styles of Jean-Paul Belmondo and Marcello Mastroianni), is a classic example of how a foreign idea, originally meant for the stage, was adapted in postwar America to the movies, and then conveyed to the rest of the world as a paradigm for both cinematic and social behavior. More important, the Method's disregard for language permitted global audiences—even those not well-versed in English—to understand and appreciate what they were watching in American films.

FINALLY, American culture has imitated not only the modernists' visual flamboyance, but also their emphasis on personal expression and their tendency to be apolitical and anti-ideological. The refusal to browbeat an audience with a social message has accounted, more than any other factor, for the worldwide popularity of American entertainment. American movies, in particular, have customarily focused on human relationships and private feelings, not on the problems of a particular time and place. They tell tales about romance, intrigue, success, failure, moral conflicts, and survival. The most memorable movies of the 1930s (with the exception of *The Grapes of Wrath*) were comedies and musicals about mismatched people falling in love, not socially conscious films dealing with issues of poverty and unemployment. Similarly, the finest movies about World War II (like *Casablanca*) or the Vietnam War (like *The Deer Hunter*) linger in the mind long after those conflicts have ended because they explore their characters' intimate emotions rather than dwelling on headline events.

Such intensely personal dilemmas are what people everywhere wrestle with. So Europeans, Asians, and Latin Americans flocked to *Titanic* (as they once did to *Gone With the Wind*) not because it celebrated American values, but because people all over the world could see some part of their own lives reflected in the story of love and loss.

America's mass culture has often been crude and intrusive, as its critics—from American academics like Benjamin Barber to German directors like Wim Wenders—have always complained. In their eyes, American culture is "colonizing" everyone else's subconscious, reducing us all to passive residents of "McWorld."

But American culture has never felt all that foreign to foreigners. And, at its best, it has transformed what it received from others into a culture that everyone, everywhere, can embrace, a culture that is both emotionally and, on occasion, artistically compelling for millions of people throughout the world.

So, despite the current hostility to America's policies and values—in Europe and Latin America as well as in the Middle East and Asia—it is important to recognize how familiar much of American culture seems to people abroad. If anything, our movies, television shows, and theme parks have been less "imperialistic" than cosmopolitan. In the end, American mass culture has not transformed the world into a replica of the United States. Instead, America's dependence on foreign cultures has made the United States a replica of the world.

*Richard Pells is a professor of history at the University of Texas at Austin. His books include* Not Like Us: How Europeans Have Loved, Hated, and Transformed American Culture Since World War II (*Basic Books, 1997*).

Originally published in *The Chronicle of Higher Education*, April 12, 2002, pp. B7, B9. © 2002 by Richard Pells. Reprinted by permission.

# What's So Great About America?

## By Dinesh D'Souza

The newcomer who sees America for the first time typically experiences emotions that alternate between wonder and delight. Here is a country where *everything works*: The roads are paper-smooth, the highway signs are clear and accurate, the public toilets function properly, when you pick up the telephone you get a dial tone. You can even buy things from the store and then take them *back* if you change your mind. For the Third World visitor, the American supermarket is a marvel to behold: endless aisles of every imaginable product, 50 different types of cereal, multiple flavors of ice cream, countless unappreciated inventions like quilted toilet paper, fabric softener, roll-on deodorant, disposable diapers.

The immigrant cannot help noticing that America is a country where the poor live comparatively well. This fact was dramatized in the 1980s, when CBS television broadcast an anti-Reagan documentary, "People Like Us," which was intended to show the miseries of the poor during an American recession. The Soviet Union also broadcast the documentary, with the intention of embarrassing the Reagan administration. But it had the opposite effect. Ordinary people across the Soviet Union saw that the poorest Americans had television sets and cars. They arrived at the same conclusion that I witnessed in a friend of mine from Bombay who has been trying unsuccessfully to move to the United States for nearly a decade. I asked him, "Why are you so eager to come to America?" He replied, "Because I really want to live in a country where the poor people are fat."

The point is that the United States is a country where the ordinary guy has a good life. This is what distinguishes America from so many other countries. Everywhere in the world, the rich person lives well. Indeed, a good case can be made that if you are rich, you live better in countries other than America, because you enjoy the pleasures of aristocracy. In India, where I grew up, the wealthy have innumerable servants and toadies groveling before them and attending to their every need.

In the United States, on the other hand, the social ethic is egalitarian, regardless of wealth. For all his riches, Bill Gates could not approach a homeless person and say, "Here's a $100 bill. I'll give it to you if you kiss my feet."

Most likely the homeless guy would tell Gates to go to hell. The American view is that the rich guy may have more money, but he isn't in any fundamental sense better than you are. The American janitor or waiter sees himself as performing a service, but he doesn't see himself as inferior to those he serves. And neither do the customers see him that way: They are generally happy to show him respect and appreciation on a plane of equality. America is the only country in the world where we call the waiter "Sir," as if he were a knight.

The moral triumph of America is that it has extended the benefits of comfort and affluence, traditionally enjoyed by very few, to a large segment of society. Very few people in America have to wonder where their next meal is coming from. Even sick people who don't have money or insurance will receive medical care at hospital emergency rooms. The poorest American girls are not humiliated by having to wear torn clothes. Every child is given an education, and most have the chance to go on to college. The common man can expect to live long enough and have enough free time to play with his grandchildren.

Ordinary Americans not only enjoy security and dignity, but also comforts that other societies reserve for the elite. We now live in a country where construction workers regularly pay $4 for a cappuccino, where maids drive nice cars, where plumbers take their families on vacation to Europe. As Irving Kristol once observed, there is virtually no restaurant in America to which a CEO can go to lunch with the absolute assurance that he will not find his secretary also dining there. Given the standard of living of the ordinary American, it is no wonder that socialist or revolutionary schemes have never found a wide constituency in the United States. As Werner Sombart observed, all socialist utopias in America have come to grief on roast beef and apple pie.

Thus it is entirely understandable that people would associate the idea of America with a better life. For them, money is not an end in itself; money is the means to a longer, healthier, and fuller life. Money allows them to purchase a level of security, dignity, and comfort not available in other countries. Money also frees up time for family life, community involvement, and spiritual pursuits, and so provides moral as well as material gains.

**Y**et even this offers an incomplete picture of why America is so appealing to so many outsiders. Let me illustrate with the example of my own life. Not long ago, I asked myself: What would my existence have been like had I never come to the United States, if I had stayed in India? Materially, my life has improved, but not in a fundamental sense. I grew up in a middle-class family in Bombay. My father was a chemical engineer; my mother, an office secretary. I was raised without great luxury, but neither did I lack for anything. My standard of living in America is higher, but it is not a radical difference. My life has changed far more dramatically in other ways.

Had I remained in India, I would probably have lived my entire existence within a one-mile radius of where I was born. I would undoubtedly have married a woman of my identical religious, socioeconomic, and cultural background. I would almost certainly have become a medical doctor, an engineer, or a software programmer. I would have socialized within my ethnic community and had few real friends outside that group. I would have a whole set of opinions that could be predicted in advance; indeed, they would not be very different from what my father believed, or his father before him. In sum, my destiny would to a large degree have been given to me.

Instead, I came to Arizona in 1978 as a high-school exchange student, then a year later enrolled at Dartmouth College. There I fell in with a group of students who were actively involved in politics; soon I had switched my major from economics to English literature. My reading included books like Plutarch's *Moralia*; Hamilton, Madison, and Jay's *Federalist Papers*; and Evelyn Waugh's *Brideshead Revisited*. They transported me to places a long way from home and implanted in my mind ideas that I had never previously considered. By the time I graduated, I decided that I should become a writer. America permits many strange careers: This is a place where you can become, say, a comedian. That is very different from most places.

If there is a single phrase that encapsulates life in the Third World, it is that "birth is destiny." A great deal of importance is attached to what tribe you come from, whether you are male or female, and whether you are the eldest son or not. Once your tribe, caste, sex and family position have been established at birth, your life takes a course that is largely determined for you.

In America, by contrast, you get to write the script of your own life. When your parents say to you, "What do you want to be when you grow up?" the question is open ended, it is you who supply the answer. Your parents can advise you: "Have you considered law school?" "Why not become the first doctor in the family?" It is considered very improper, however, for them to try to force your decision. Indeed, American parents typically send their teenage children away to college where they live on their own and learn independence. This is part of the process of forming your mind, choosing a field of interest for yourself, and developing your identity.

It is not uncommon in the United States for two brothers who come from the same gene pool and were raised in similar circumstances to do quite different things: The eldest becomes a gas station attendant, the younger moves up to be vice president at Oracle; the eldest marries his high-school sweetheart and raises four kids; the youngest refuses to settle down; one is the Methodist that he was raised to be, the other becomes a Christian Scientist. What to be, where to live, whom to marry, what to believe, what religion to practice—these are all decisions that Americans make for themselves.

In America your destiny is not prescribed; it is constructed. Your life is like a blank sheet of paper and you are the artist. This notion of being the architect of your own destiny is the incredibly powerful idea that is behind the worldwide appeal of America. Young people especially find the prospect of authoring their own lives irresistible. The immigrant discovers that America permits him to break free of the constraints that have held him captive, so that the future becomes a landscape of his own choosing.

If there is a single phrase that captures this, it is "the pursuit of happiness." As writer V. S. Naipaul notes, "much is contained" in that simple phrase: "the idea of the individual, responsibility, choice, the life of the intellect, the idea of vocation, perfectibility, and achievement. It is an immense human idea. It cannot be reduced to a fixed system. It cannot generate fanaticism. But it is known [around the world] to exist; and because of that, other more rigid systems in the end blow away."

**B**ut where did the "pursuit of happiness" come from? And why has it come in America to mean something much more than simple selfishness? America's founders were religious men. They believed that political legitimacy derives from God. Yet they were determined not to permit theological differences to become the basis for political conflict.

The American system refused to establish a national church, instead recognizing all citizens as free to practice their own religion. From the beginning the United States was made up of numerous sects. The Puritans dominated in Massachusetts, the Anglicans in Virginia, the Catholics were concentrated in Maryland, so it was in every group's interest to "live and let live." The ingenuity of the American solution is evident in Voltaire's remark that where there is one religion, you have tyranny; where there are two, you have religious war; but where they are many, you have freedom.

One reason the American founders were able to avoid religious oppression and conflict is that they found a way to channel people's energies away from theological quarrels and into commercial activity. The American system is founded on property rights and trade, and *The Federalist* tells us that protection of the obtaining of property is "the first object of government." The founders reasoned that people who are working assiduously to better their condition are not likely to go around spearing their neighbors.

Capitalism gives America a this-worldly focus that allows death and the afterlife to recede from everyday view. Along with their heavenly aspirations, the gaze of the people is shifted to earthly progress. This "lowering of the sights" convinces many critics that American capitalism is a base, degraded system and that the energies that drive it are crass and immoral.

These modern critiques draw on some very old prejudices. In the ancient world, labor was generally despised. The Greeks looked down on merchants and traders as low-lifes. "The gentleman understands what is noble," Confucius writes in his *Analects*, "the small man understands what is profitable." In the Indian caste system the *vaisya* or trader occupies nearly the lowest rung of the ladder—one step up from the despised "untouchable." The Muslim historian Ibn Khaldun suggests that even gain by conquest is preferable to gain by trade, because conquest embodies the virtues of courage and manliness. In these traditions, the honorable life is devoted to philosophy or the priesthood or military valor. "Making a living" was considered a necessary, but undignified, pursuit. Far better to rout your adversary, kill the men, enslave the women and children, and make off with a bunch of loot than to improve your lot by buying and selling stuff.

Drawing on the inspiration of philosophers like John Locke and Adam Smith, the American founders altered this moral hierarchy. They argued that trade based on consent and mutual gain was preferable to plunder. The founders established a regime in which the self-interest of entrepreneurs and workers would be directed toward serving the wants and needs of others. In this view, the ordinary life, devoted to production, serving the customer, and supporting a family, is a noble and dignified endeavor. Hard work, once considered a curse, now becomes socially acceptable, even honorable. Commerce, formerly a degraded thing, now becomes a virtue.

Of course the founders recognized that in both the private and the public sphere, greedy and ambitious people can pose a danger to the well-being of others. Instead of trying to outlaw these passions, the founders attempted a different approach. As the fifty-first book of *The Federalist* puts it, "Ambition must be made to counteract ambition." In a free society, "the security for civil rights [consists] in the multiplicity of interests." The framers of the Constitution reasoned that by setting interests against each other, by making them compete, no single one could become strong enough to imperil the welfare of the whole.

In the public sphere the founders took special care to devise a system that would minimize the abuse of power. They established limited government, in order that the power of the state would remain confined. They divided authority between the national and state governments. Within the national framework, they provided for separation of powers, so that the legislature, executive, and judiciary would each have its own domain of authority. They insisted upon checks and balances, to enhance accountability.

The founders didn't ignore the importance of virtue, but they knew that virtue is not always in abundant supply. According to Christianity, the problem of the bad person is that his will is corrupted, a fault endemic to human nature. America's founders knew they could not transform human nature, so they devised a system that would thwart the schemes of the wicked and channel the energies of flawed persons toward the public good.

The experiment that the founders embarked upon more than two centuries ago has largely succeeded in achieving its goals. Tribal and religious battles such as we see in Lebanon, Mogadishu, Kashmir, and Belfast don't happen here. Whites and African Americans have lunch together. Americans of Jewish and Palestinian descent collaborate on software problems and play racquetball after work. Hindus and Muslims, Serbs and Croats, Turks and Armenians, Irish Catholics and British Protestants, all seem to have forgotten their ancestral differences and joined the vast and varied American parade. Everybody wants to "make it," to "get ahead," to "hit it big." And even as they compete, people recognize that somehow they are all in this together, in pursuit of some great, elusive American dream. In this respect America is a glittering symbol to the world.

America's founders solved two great problems which are a source of perennial misery and conflict in many other societies—the problem of scarcity, and the problem of religious and tribal conflict. They invented a new regime in which citizens would enjoy a wide range of freedoms—economic freedom, political freedom, and freedom of speech and religion—in order to shape their own lives and pursue happiness. By protecting religion and government from each other, and by directing the energies of the citizens toward trade and commerce, the American founders created a rich, dynamic, and peaceful society. It is now the hope of countless millions all across the world.

*Dinesh D'Souza, Rishwain Fellow at the Hoover Institution, is author of* What's So Great About America, *from which this is adapted.*

From *The American Enterprise*, April/May 2002, pp. 22-25. © 2002 by The American Enterprise. Reprinted by permission.

# UNIT 2

# Socialization and Social Control

## Unit Selections

6. **Boys Will Be Boys**, Barbara Kantrowitz and Claudia Kalb
7. **Born to Be Good?** Celia Kitzinger
8. **Preventing Crime: The Promising Road Ahead**, Gene Stephens
9. **Pedophilia**, John Cloud

## Key Points to Consider

- What are the major differences between the ways that boys and girls are socialized?

- How can the ways in which children are socialized in America be improved?

- Why is socialization a lifelong process?

- What are the principal factors that make people what they are?

- What are the major ways to reduce crime in the United States, and how effective are they?

- How can the recently revealed problem of pedophilia in the Roman Catholic Church be explained?

 **Links: www.dushkin.com/online/**
These sites are annotated in the World Wide Web pages.

**Center for Leadership Studies**
   *http://www.situational.com*
**Crime Times**
   *http://www.crime-times.org*
**Ethics Updates/Lawrence Hinman**
   *http://ethics.acusd.edu*
**National Institute on Drug Abuse (NIDA)**
   *http://165.112.78.61/*
**Sexual Assault Information Page**
   *http://web.archive.org/web/*/http://www.cs.utk.edu/~bartley/saInfoPage.html*
**Social Influence Website**
   *http://www.influenceatwork.com/*

Why do we behave the way we do? Three forces are at work: biology, socialization, and the human will or internal decision maker. The focus in sociology is on socialization, which is the conscious and unconscious process whereby we learn the norms and behavior patterns that enable us to function appropriately in our social environment. Socialization is based on the need to belong, because the desire for acceptance is the major motivation for internalizing the socially approved attitudes and behaviors. Fear of punishment is another motivation. It is utilized by parents and institutionalized in the law enforcement system. The language we use, the concepts we apply in thinking, the images we have of ourselves, our gender roles, and our masculine and feminine ideals are all learned through socialization. Socialization may take place in many contexts. The most basic socialization takes place in the family, but churches, schools, communities, the media, and workplaces also play major roles in the process.

The first subsection deals with issues concerning the basic influences on the development of our character and behavior patterns. Barbara Kantrowitz and Claudia Kalb review the latest research on child development and compare the development of boys and girls, but with an emphasis on boys because boys have been slighted in the research of previous decades. The authors conclude that "boys and girls really are from two different planets," and that boys are commonly misunderstood. It is normal for them to have "an abundance of energy and the urge to conquer," but they usually are penalized by adults for these traits. Nevertheless, they hold each other to norms of masculinity and toughness. In the second article of this section, Celia Kitzinger seeks to explain why people are so good. Is it because they are rewarded for being good? Is it because people have a natural feeling of empathy that allows them to enjoy the pleasure and suffer the pain of others? Or does the answer lie in the human capacity for moral reasoning of which we are so proud? Kitzinger's answer to each question is "yes, in part." The more basic answer, however, is social pressure, which urges us to be good. At times it also urges us to be bad.

The next subsection deals with crime, law enforcement, and social control—major concerns today because crime and violence seem to be out of control. The first article in this subsection, "Preventing Crime: The Promising Road Ahead," tries to find out what works and what does not work in preventing crime. Gene Stephens looks at over 500 studies of crime prevention programs and finds that many popular programs have little or no effect.

The next article covers a recent newsmaker, pedophilia. In it, John Cloud tries to find out why people sexually molest children. According to the psychological community, pedophilia, which is the sexual desire of adults for children, is a psychiatric illness that is estimated to afflict 4 percent of the population. Fortunately not all pedophiles act on their urges. Unfortunately, many children are sexually abused by nonpedophiles. It is also important to note that pedophilia is treatable.

# Boys will be Boys

**Developmental research has been focused on girls; now it's their brothers' turn. Boys need help, too, but first they need to be understood.**

BY BARBARA KANTROWITZ AND CLAUDIA KALB

IT WAS A CLASSIC MARS-VENUS ENCOUNTER. Only in this case, the woman was from Harvard and the man—well, boy—was a 4-year-old at a suburban Boston nursery school. Graduate student Judy Chu was in his classroom last fall to gather observations for her doctoral dissertation on human development. His greeting was startling: he held up his finger as if it were a gun and pretended to shoot her. "I felt bad," Chu recalls. "I felt as if he didn't like me." Months later and much more boy-savvy, Chu has a different interpretation: the gunplay wasn't hostile—it was just a way for him to say hello. "They don't mean it to have harsh consequences. It's a way for them to connect."

## The Wonder (and Worry) Years

There may be no such thing as *child* development anymore. Instead, researchers are now studying each gender's development separately and discovering that boys and girls face very different sorts of challenges. Here is a rough guide to the major phases in their development.

**Boys**

**0-3 years** At birth, boys have brains that are 5% larger than girls' (size doesn't affect intelligence) and proportionately larger bodies—disparities that increase with age.

**4-6 years** The start of school is a tough time as boys must curb aggressive impulses. They lag behind girls in reading skills, and hyperactivity may be a problem.

| Age 1 | 2 | 3 | 4 | 5 | 6 | 7 |
|-------|---|---|---|---|---|---|

**Girls**

**0-3 years** Girls are born with a higher proportion of nerve cells to process information. More brain regions are involved in language production and recognition.

**4-6 years** Girls are well suited to school. They are calm, get along with others, pick up on social cues, and reading and writing come easily to them.

**7-10 years** While good at gross motor skills, boys trail girls in finer control. Many of the best students but also nearly all of the poorest ones are boys.

**11-13 years** A mixed bag. Dropout rates begin to climb, but good students start pulling ahead of girls in math skills and catching up some in verbal ones.

**14-16 years** Entering adolescence, boys hit another rough patch. Indulging in drugs, alcohol and aggressive behavior are common forms of rebellion.

| 8 | 9 | 10 | 11 | 12 | 13 | 14 | 15 | 16 |
|---|---|----|----|----|----|----|----|----|

**7-10 years** Very good years for girls. On average, they outperform boys at school, excelling in verbal skills while holding their own in math.

**11-13 years** The start of puberty and girls' most vulnerable time. Many experience depression; as many as 15% may try to kill themselves.

**14-16 years** Eating disorders are a major concern. Although anorexia can manifest itself as early as 8, it typically afflicts girls starting at 11 or 12; bulimia at 15.

SOURCES: DR. MICHAEL THOMPSON, BARNEY BRAWER. RESEARCH BY BILL VOURVOULIAS—NEWSWEEK

# Trouble Spots: Where Boys Run Into Problems

Not all boys are the same, of course, but most rebel in predictable patterns and with predictable weapons: underachievement, aggression and drug and alcohol use. While taking chances is an important aspect of the growth process, it can lead to real trouble.

### When Johnny Can't Read

Girls have reading disorders nearly as often as boys, but are able to overcome them. Disability rates, as identified by:

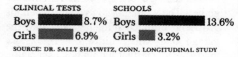

| CLINICAL TESTS | | SCHOOLS | |
|---|---|---|---|
| Boys | 8.7% | Boys | 13.6% |
| Girls | 6.9% | Girls | 3.2% |

SOURCE: DR. SALLY SHAYWITZ, CONN. LONGITUDINAL STUDY

### Suicidal Impulses

While girls are much more likely to try to kill themselves, boys are likelier to die from their attempts.

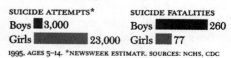

| SUICIDE ATTEMPTS* | | SUICIDE FATALITIES | |
|---|---|---|---|
| Boys | 3,000 | Boys | 260 |
| Girls | 23,000 | Girls | 77 |

1995, AGES 5–14. *NEWSWEEK ESTIMATE. SOURCES: NCHS, CDC

### Binge Drinking

Boys binge more on alcohol. Those who had five or more drinks in a row in the last two weeks:

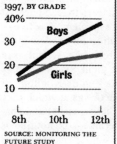

1997, BY GRADE

Boys

Girls

8th 10th 12th

SOURCE: MONITORING THE FUTURE STUDY

### Aggression That Turns to Violence

Boys get arrested three times as often as girls, but for some nonviolent crimes the numbers are surprisingly even.

Arrests of 10- to 17-year-olds: ■ Boys ■ Girls

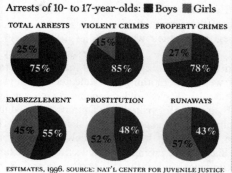

| TOTAL ARRESTS | VIOLENT CRIMES | PROPERTY CRIMES |
|---|---|---|
| 25% / 75% | 15% / 85% | 27% / 78% |
| EMBEZZLEMENT | PROSTITUTION | RUNAWAYS |
| 45% / 55% | 52% / 48% | 43% / 57% |

ESTIMATES, 1996. SOURCE: NAT'L CENTER FOR JUVENILE JUSTICE

### Eating Disorders

Boys can also have eating disorders. Kids who used laxatives or vomited to lose weight:

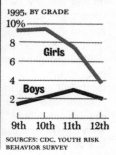

1995, BY GRADE

Girls

Boys

9th 10th 11th 12th

SOURCES: CDC, YOUTH RISK BEHAVIOR SURVEY

Researchers like Chu are discovering new meaning in lots of things boys have done for ages. In fact, they're dissecting just about every aspect of the developing male psyche and creating a hot new field of inquiry: the study of boys. They're also producing a slew of books with titles like "Real Boys: Rescuing Our Sons From the Myths of Boyhood" and "Raising Cain: Protecting the Emotional Life of Boys" that will hit the stores in the next few months.

What some researchers are finding is that boys and girls really are from two different planets. But since the two sexes have to live together here on Earth, they should be raised with special consideration for their distinct needs. Boys and girls have different "crisis points," experts say, stages in their emotional and social development where things can go very wrong. Until recently, girls got all the attention. But boys need help, too. They're much more likely than girls to have discipline problems at school and to be diagnosed with attention deficit disorder (ADD). Boys far outnumber girls in special-education classes. They're also more likely to commit violent crimes and end up in jail. Consider the headlines: Jonesboro, Ark.; Paducah, Ky.; Pearl, Miss. In all these school shootings, the perpetrators were young adolescent boys.

Even normal boy behavior has come to be considered pathological in the wake of the feminist movement. An abundance of physical energy and the urge to conquer—these are normal male characteristics, and in an earlier age they were good things,

even essential to survival. "If Huck Finn or Tom Sawyer were alive today," says Michael Gurian, author of "The Wonder of Boys," "we'd say they had ADD or a conduct disorder." He says one of the new insights we're gaining about boys is a very old one: boys will be boys. "They are who they are," says Gurian, "and we need to love them for who they are. Let's not try to rewire them."

Indirectly, boys are benefiting from all the research done on girls, especially the landmark work by Harvard University's Carol Gilligan. Her 1982 book, "In a Different Voice: Psychological Theory and Women's Development," inspired Take Our Daughters to Work Day, along with best-selling spinoffs like Mary Pipher's "Reviving Ophelia." The traditional, unisex way of looking at child development was profoundly flawed, Gilligan says: "It was like having a one-dimensional perspective on a two-dimensional scene." At Harvard, where she chairs the gender-studies department, Gilligan is now supervising work on males, including Chu's project. Other researchers are studying mental illness and violence in boys.

While girls' horizons have been expanding, boys' have narrowed, confined to rigid ideas of acceptable male behavior no matter how hard their parents tried to avoid stereotypes. The macho ideal still rules. "We gave boys dolls and they used them as guns," says Gurian. "For 15 years, all we heard was that [gender differences] were all about socialization. Parents who raised their kids through that period said in the end, 'That's not true. Boys and girls can be

awfully different.' I think we're awakening to the biological realities and the sociological realities."

But what exactly is the essential nature of boys? Even as infants, boys and girls behave differently. A recent study at Children's Hospital in Boston found that boy babies are more emotionally expressive; girls are more reflective. (That means boy babies tend to cry when they're unhappy; girl babies suck their thumbs.) This could indicate that girls are innately more able to control their emotions. Boys have higher levels of testosterone and lower levels of the neurotransmitter serotonin, which inhibits aggression and impulsivity. That may help explain why more males than females carry through with suicide, become alcoholics and are diagnosed with ADD.

The developmental research on the impact of these physiological differences is still in the embryonic stage, but psychologists are drawing some interesting comparisons between girls and boys (chart). For girls, the first crisis point often comes in early adolescence. Until then, Gilligan and others found, girls have an enormous capacity for establishing relationships and interpreting emotions. But in their early teens, girls clamp down, squash their emotions, blunt their insight. Their self-esteem plummets. The first crisis point for boys comes much earlier, researchers now say. "There's an outbreak of symptoms at age 5, 6, 7, just like you see in girls at 11, 12, 13," says Gilligan. Problems at this age include bed-wetting and separation anxiety. "They don't have the language or experience" to articulate it fully, she says, "but the feelings are no less intense." That's why Gilligan's student Chu is studying preschoolers. For girls at this age, Chu says, hugging a parent goodbye "is almost a nonissue." But little boys, who display a great deal of tenderness, soon begin to bury it with "big boy" behavior to avoid being called sissies. "When their parents drop them off, they want to be close and want to be held, but not in front of other people," says Chu. "Even as early as 4, they're already aware of those masculine stereotypes and are negotiating their way around them."

It's a phenomenon that parents, especially mothers, know well. One morning last month, Lori Dube, a 37-year-old mother of three from Evanston, Ill., visited her oldest son, Abe, almost 5, at his nursery school, where he was having lunch with his friends. She kissed him, prompting another boy to comment scornfully: "Do you know what your mom just did? She kissed you!" Dube acknowledges, with some sadness, that she'll have to be more sensitive to Abe's new reactions to future public displays of affection. "Even if he loves it, he's getting these messages that it's not good."

There's a struggle—a desire and need for warmth on the one hand and a pull toward independence on the other. Boys like Abe are going through what psychologists long ago declared an integral part of growing up: individualization and disconnection from parents, especially mothers. But now some researchers think that process is too abrupt. When boys repress normal feelings like love because of social pressure, says William Pollack, head of the Center for Men at Boston's McLean Hospital and author of the forthcoming "Real Boys," "they've lost contact with the genuine nature of who they are and what they feel. Boys are in a silent crisis. The only time we notice it is when they pull the trigger."

No one is saying that acting like Rambo in nursery school leads directly to tragedies like Jonesboro. But researchers do think that boys who are forced to shut down positive emotions are left with only one socially acceptable outlet: anger. The cultural ideals boys are exposed to in movies and on TV still emphasize traditional masculine roles—warrior, rogue, adventurer—with heavy doses of violence. For every Mr. Mom, there are a dozen Terminators. "The feminist movement has done a great job of convincing people that a woman can be nurturing and a mother and a tough trial lawyer at the same time," says Dan Kindlon, an assistant professor of psy-

chiatry at Harvard Medical School. "But we haven't done that as much with men. We're afraid that if they're too soft, that's all they can be."

And the demands placed on boys in the early years of elementary school can increase their overall stress levels. Scientists have known for years that boys and girls develop physically and intellectually at very different rates (time-line). Boys' fine motor skills—the ability to hold a pencil, for example—are usually considerably behind girls. They often learn to read later. At the same time, they're much more active— not the best combination for academic advancement. "Boys feel like school is a game rigged against them," says Michael Thompson, coauthor with Kindlon of "Raising Cain." "The things at which they excel—gross motor skills, visual and spatial skills, their exuberance—do not find as good a reception in school" as the things girls excel at. Boys (and girls) are also in academic programs at much younger ages than they used to be, increasing the chances that males will be forced to sit still before they are ready. The result, for many boys, is frustration, says Thompson: "By fourth grade, they're saying the teachers like girls better."

A second crisis point for boys occurs around the same time their sisters are stumbling, in early adolescence. By then, say Thompson and Kindlon, boys go one step further in their drive to be "real guys." They partake in a "culture of cruelty," enforcing male stereotypes on one another. "Anything tender, anything compassionate or too artistic is labeled gay," says Thompson. "The homophobia of boys in the 11, 12, 13 range is a stronger force than gravity."

Boys who refuse to fit the mold suffer. Glo Wellman of the California Parenting Institute in Santa Rosa has three sons, 22, 19 and 12. One of her boys, she says, is a "nontypical boy: he's very sensitive and caring and creative and artistic." Not surprisingly, he had the most difficulty growing up, she says. "We've got a long way to go to help boys... to have a sense that they can be anything they want to be."

In later adolescence, the once affectionate toddler has been replaced by a sulky stranger who often acts as though torture would be preferable to a brief exchange of words with Mom or Dad. Parents have to try even harder to keep in touch. Boys want and need the attention, but often just don't know how to ask for it. In a recent national poll, teenagers named their parents as their No. 1 heroes. Researchers say a strong parental bond is the most important protec-

tion against everything from smoking to suicide.

For San Francisco Chronicle columnist Adnir Lara, that message sank in when she was traveling to New York a few years ago with her son, then 15. She sat next to a woman who told her that until recently she would have had to change seats because she would not have been able to bear the pain of seeing a teenage son and mother together. The woman's son was 17 when his girlfriend dumped him; he went into the garage and killed himself. "This story made me aware that with a boy especially, you have to keep talking because they don't come and talk to you," she says. Lara's son is now 17; she also has a 19-year-old daughter. "My daughter stalked me. She followed me from room to room. She was yelling, but she was in touch. Boys don't do that. They leave the room and you don't know what they're feeling." Her son is now 6 feet 3. "He's a man. There are barriers. You have to reach through that and remember to ruffle his hair."

With the high rate of divorce, many boys are growing up without any adult men in their lives at all. Don Elium, coauthor of the best-selling 1992 book "Raising a Son," says that with troubled boys, there's often a common theme: distant, uninvolved fathers, and mothers who have taken on more responsibility to fill the gap. That was the case with Raymundo Infante Jr., a 16-year-old high-school junior, who lives with his mother, Mildred, 38, a hospital administrative assistant in Chicago, and his sister, Vanessa, 19. His parents divorced when he was a baby and he had little contact with his father until a year ago. The hurt built up—in sixth grade, Raymundo was so depressed that he told a classmate he wanted to kill himself. The classmate told the teacher, who told a counselor, and Raymundo saw a psychiatrist for a year. "I felt that I just wasn't good enough, or he just didn't want me," Raymundo says. Last year Raymundo finally confronted his dad, who works two jobs—in an office and on a construction crew—and accused him of caring more about work than about his son. Now the two spend time together on weekends and sometimes go shopping, but there is still a huge gap of lost years.

Black boys are especially vulnerable, since they are more likely than whites to grow up in homes without fathers. They're often on their own much sooner than whites. Black leaders are looking for alternatives. In Atlanta, the Rev. Tim McDonald's First Iconium Baptist Church just chartered a Boy Scout troop. "Gangs are so prevalent because guys want to belong to something," says McDonald. "We've got to give them something positive to belong to." Black educators like Chicagoan Jawanza Kunjufu think mentoring programs will overcome the bias against academic success as "too white." Some cities are also experimenting with all-boy classrooms in predominantly black schools.

Researchers hope that in the next few years, they'll come up with strategies that will help boys the way the work of Gilligan and others helped girls. In the meantime, experts say, there are some guidelines. Parents can channel their sons' energy into constructive activities, like team sports. They should also look for "teachable moments" to encourage qualities such as empathy. When Diane Fisher, a Cincin-

nati-area psychologist, hears her 8- and 10-year-old boys talking about "finishing somebody," she knows she has mistakenly rented a violent videogame. She pulls the plug and tells them: "In our house, killing people is not entertainment, even if it's just pretend."

Parents can also teach by example. New Yorkers Dana and Frank Minaya say they've never disciplined their 16-year-old son Walter in anger. They insist on resolving all disputes calmly and reasonably, without yelling. If there is a problem, they call an official family meeting "and we never leave without a big hug," says Frank. Walter tries to be open with his parents. "I don't want to miss out on any advice," he says.

Most of all, wise parents of boys should go with the flow. Cindy Lang, 36, a full-time mother in Woodside, Calif., is contin-

ually amazed by the relentless energy of her sons, Roger Lloyd, 12, and Chris, 9. "You accept the fact that they're going to involve themselves in risky behavior, like skateboarding down a flight of stairs. As a girl, I certainly wasn't skateboarding down a flight of stairs." Just last week, she got a phone call from school telling her that Roger Lloyd was in the emergency room because he had fallen backward while playing basketball and school officials thought he might have a concussion. He's fine now, but she's prepared for the next emergency: "I have a cell phone so I can be on alert." Boys will be boys. And we have to let them.

*With* KAREN SPRINGEN *in Chicago,* PATRICIA KING *in San Francisco,* PAT WINGERT *in Washington,* VERN E. SMITH *in Atlanta and* ELIZABETH ANGELL *in New York*

# Born <sup>to</sup> be good?

What motivates us to be good, bad or indifferent towards others?
**Celia Kitzinger** examines the psychology of morality.

MANY of us, much of the time, act to benefit others. There are small kindnesses of everyday life—like holding open a door, sharing food or expressing compassion for someone in distress. Things so ordinary that we simply take them for granted.

We are pleased, but not particularly surprised that people commonly care for sick relatives, give money to help famine victims, donate blood to hospitals, or volunteer to assist at hospices. At times what people do for others is truly spectacular. In the US, Lenny Skutnik risked his life diving into the icy waters of the Potomac River to save an airline crash victim; in Nazi Europe many people risked their lives in offering protection to Jews. In both mundane and exceptional ways people often act to help others—which is why psychologists describe human beings not just as 'social' but also as 'pro-social' animals.

But why do people spend so much time and money and effort on others, when we could keep it all for ourselves? One argument is that self-interest lies at the root of all superficially 'moral' behaviour. According to sociobiologists, we are biologically driven towards those forms of altruism—caring for our families, for example—which improve the survival of our genes.[1] Moral actions are simply automatic and instinctive, of no greater or lesser significance than the behaviour of a

mother bird putting her own life at risk leading a predator away from her chicks. Helping people who are not genetically related to us can also be in the best interest of our genes if it sets up the expectation that we—or those who share our genes—will be helped in turn.

There are many subtle ways in which helping others can offer rewards which serve our self-interest. These include the praise of onlookers; gratitude from the person being helped; the warm glow of knowing we have done a good deed; and the benefit of avoiding guilt, shame or punishment. Most people agree that some good behaviour can be attributed to self-interest. But is that all there is?

In an ingenious set of experiments, a group of psychologists set out to test the idea that empathy—the ability to imagine ourselves in the place of another and to feel their emotions—can result in genuine altruism.[2] Subjects were encouraged to be empathetic while watching a 'worker' who they believed was reacting badly to a series of uncomfortable electric shocks. They were then given a chance to help the worker by receiving the shocks themselves. If helping were only self-serving egoism, then people who felt empathy for the victim would simply want to escape from the upsetting experience. But researchers found that those with strong em-

pathetic feelings volunteered to take the worker's place, even when told they they could leave immediately if they refused. The researchers also found that high-empathy people, who were deprived of the opportunity to help, felt just as good when someone else helped instead. This suggests that the offer to help reflected a genuine wish to relieve the victim's suffering, rather than a desire for praise from other people. So it looks as if the cynical view that even good actions have selfish motives may well be wrong. Empathy is common in very small children who often respond to another's distress with crying and sadness, and may attempt to comfort them with a hug or a cuddly toy. Some psychologists believe that behaviour like this signals the start of moral development.[3]

Although empathy may be an important component of moral behaviour, morality cannot rely on empathy alone because this emotion is too circumscribed and partial. It can also lead us to make unfair decisions—taking sides in a dispute, for example. Another explanation for why people behave well is that they are motivated not by emotions but by reasoned moral principles. This is what Lawrence Kohlberg proposes in his 'cognitive-development model' theory.[4] Children, he says, begin at a 'preconventional' level in which they see morality in relation to obedience and punishments from adults. At the second, 'conventional' level, reached in late childhood or early adolescence, they are oriented first to pleasing and helping others and later to maintaining the existing social order. At the third and highest stage of moral development—reached by only a small proportion of adults—people begin to define moral values and principles such as human dignity, justice, universal human rights. According to this theory, morality is a matter of cognitive (not emotional) development: it matters not one whit whether we care about or empathize with other people so long as we respect their rights as human beings.

## These people were not sadists or psychopaths. They were ordinary people

Some critics, notably feminist psychologist Carol Gilligan, have challenged the theory as sexist: men may favour abstract theoretical notions of rights and justice, but women, she says, are more likely to construct morality rooted in their sense of connection with other people, a morality of care and empathy.[5] Others criticize the ethnocentrism of the model, pointing out that Kohlberg has elevated to the highest stage of moral development precisely those views most likely to be held by white, middle-class, educated North Americans.[6]

It's more likely that moral behaviour comes about in a variety of ways: sometimes we may act well in the hope of rewards; other times good behaviour may be motivated by empathy; sometimes it is the outcome of reasoned moral arguments. Crucially, though, neither strong feelings of empathy nor high moral principles guarantee that people will behave well. There is often a gap between moral beliefs and moral action—between how people think and hope they would behave in a situation and how they actually do behave. Some of the classic studies of psychology were prompted by situations in which people failed to act in accordance with their moral values.

In the 1960s a young woman named Kitty Genovese was murdered by a man who raped and stabbed her repeatedly for half an hour in front of 38 residents of a respectable New York City neighbourhood. Nobody went to help her. Only one person finally called the police, after she was dead. This incident prompted a flood of research into what became known as the 'bystander effect' which examined why people don't intervene when others are in pain or in danger.[7] Sometimes people fail to intervene out of callousness or indifference. But more often they fail to act in spite of what they feel they should do, and then feel ashamed afterwards. Why is this?

A common finding is that people are uncertain how to behave because, unsure about what they are seeing, they conform with the behaviour of others, who are equally unsure. Emergencies are rare events which happen suddenly and unexpectedly. How can we know that an emergency is real and is not a prank, a game, or a film being produced? The safest thing is to sit tight and wait to see how others react. If nobody else does anything, then people worry about making fools of themselves. A large group can stand by and do nothing, each lulled into thinking that there is no need to act, each waiting for someone else to make the first move. What looks like callous indifference is actually fear of what other people will think if they make an inappropriate response in an ambiguous situation.

Someone in Kitty Genovese's situation is less likely to be helped if many people are watching than if only one person witnesses the attack. For example, subjects asked to wait in a room before being interviewed heard a woman in the next room apparently fall, hurt herself, and cry out in distress. Of those waiting alone, 70 per cent went to help her, compared with only 7 per cent of those waiting with a stranger who did nothing. Today's altruist may be tomorrow's passive bystander; it all depends on the social situation because people tend to behave in accordance with socially prescribed roles rather than as individuals.

In a well-known study by Stanley Milgram, subjects were recruited through newspaper advertisements for what was described as 'an experiment in learning'. They were seated in front of a shock machine that could administer up 450 volts to the 'learner', a man strapped into a chair.[8] Each time the 'learner' made a mistake the subject had to pull a lever to give him an electric shock, increasing the voltage each time. (In fact, the lever was a dummy, and the 'learner' was acting out his response). At 150 volts the learner started shouting. At 180 volts, he cried out in pain and pleaded to be released. At 300 volts he screamed with pain and yelled about his heart condition. Later still there was only deathly silence. If subjects wanted to stop giving shocks, the experimenter said only 'the experiment requires that you continue'. No threats, no incentives to go on, just the order. Under these conditions—and contrary to the predictions of psychiatrists who had guessed that virtually no-one would obey to the end—nearly two-thirds of subjects delivered the full range of shocks, proceeding beyond the levers marked 'Danger: Severe Shock' to the ones marked 'XXX'.

These people were not sadists or psychopaths. They were ordinary people who believed that you shouldn't hurt others, who often showed empathy for the learner, and who disliked what they were ordered to do. Virtually all of them complained to the experimenter and asked for permission to stop giving shocks. But when ordered to continue the majority did as they were told. As Milgram says: 'With numbing regularity, good people were seen to knuckle under the demands of authority and perform actions that were callous and severe.' Women were as likely as men to deliver shocks up to maximum intensity.

What all these studies illustrate is the extent to which moral behaviour is a social, not an individual issue. In thinking about why people fail to offer help, why they behave punitively, or why they inflict pain on others, we often resort to explanations which depend on individual characteristics—their personal religious beliefs, their capacity for empathy, their understanding of moral principles, or the kind of upbringing they had. But these explanations overlook the key role of social context. The frightening truth uncovered by these classic psychological studies is that it is not too difficult to set up situations in which most of us behave worse than we could have thought possible, out of conformity, fear of what others might think, loss of individual identity or obedience to authority.

The traditional view of moral behaviour is that people are intrinsically selfish beings whose natural anti-social impulses have been curbed by social structures designed to promote obedience to authority, law and order. An alternative possibility is that people are fundamentally pro-social beings, whose ability to act on altruistic impulses and moral principles is sometimes inhibited by precisely these social pressures. At the very least it is obvious that this is sometimes true, and that we need to develop ways of recognizing and challenging those social pressures which result in apathetic or cruel behaviour in our everyday lives.

## Notes

1. Richard Dawkins, *The Selfish Gene,* OUP 1976.

2. CD Batson, *The Altruism Question,* Erlbaum Associates 1991.

3. C Zahn-Waxler & M Radke-Yarrow, 'The Development of Altruism' in N Eisenberg-Berg (ed.) *The Development of Prosocial Behaviour,* Academic Press 1986.
4. L Kohlberg, *The Philosophy of Moral Development,* Harper and Row 1981.
5. C Gilligan, *In a Different Voice,* Harvard University Press 1982.
6. EEL Simpson, 'Moral Development Research: A Case Study of Scientific Cultural Bias', *Human Development 17,* 1974.

7. B Latané & JM Draley, *The Unresponsive Bystander. Why doesn't he help?* Appleton-Century-Croft 1970.

8. S Milgram, 'Some Conditions of Obedience and Disobedience to Authority', *Human Relations 18,* 1965.

***Celia Kitzinger*** teaches psychology at the University of Loughborough, England.

From *New Internationalist,* April 1997, pp. 15-17. © 1997 by New Internationalist Publications, Ltd. Reprinted by permission.

# Preventing Crime: The Promising Road Ahead

**Careful assessments of crime-prevention programs are revealing what really works. Crime problems could be drastically reduced in the years ahead.**

## By Gene Stephens

Street crime in America dropped to historically low levels by the end of the 1990s, according to the Department of Justice. The debate over the cause of this decrease has spurred an empirical search for answers. Some say the decrease is due to more police on the streets and tougher laws, but others believe that community initiatives and crime-prevention programs are behind it. Finding the answers will be critical to the public's safety in the twenty-first century.

Probably the best explanation for the decrease in crime lies in the budding success of the long-dormant "weed and seed" movement envisioned in the 1960s by now-famous criminologist James Q. Wilson. In his *Public Interest* article "Broken Windows," Wilson said neighborhoods in decline were places where the residents had lost hope and pride, where police rarely came except to make arrests, and where offenders could commit crimes almost with impunity.

Wilson suggested that the formula for change was to "weed" out the immediate problem—drug deal-

ers and addicts, public drunks, thieves, street hustlers, and thugs—by crackdowns and arrests, using even minor offenses (loitering, vagrancy, spitting on the sidewalk, jaywalking) to "sweep" the streets clean. After "weeding," the government must then "seed" the community with programs that assist residents in keeping their communities crime free. Such programs might include enterprise zones to bring in jobs, day care, and health clinics. Depending on the character and needs of the neighborhood, drug rehabilitation, after-school centers, tutors, mentors, and many other activities might be required.

Wilson's ideas were embraced by federal officials in the late 1970s and 1980s. He even prepared a series of videos and publications for the National Institute of Justice (NIJ). Weed and seed money flowed from the U.S. Department of Justice to state and local officials, but congressional strings required more weeding than seeding. The "get tough" legislators at federal and state levels supported longer, mandatory sentences for law violators and built more prisons and

jails to hold them. They also encouraged courts to give adult sentences to juveniles as a "deterrent."

Drug addicts were singled out in particular for harsh treatment; by 1999, more than two-thirds of federal prison inmates and 25% of all state prisoners were serving time for drug charges. Drug-prevention efforts were little more than the well-known "Just Say No" motto.

"Get tough" policies also led to "justice" issues, as research indicates most arrests and convictions come from information and/or testimony from "snitches"—usually offenders seeking money or dropped charges or lessened penalties in exchange for their "helping" police and prosecutors.

Finally, after an alarming increase in street violence in the late 1980s and early 1990s, the "seed" idea received increased attention, primarily through the Problem-Oriented Policing and Community-Oriented Policing movement. As the Justice Department began loosening strings on funding, success stories abounded in communities that developed programs to prevent crime rather than just suppress it. Soon, the

Justice Department was praising government-community partnerships, circulating model programs, and funding crime-prevention efforts.

## What Works

In a July 1998 research briefing, NIJ reviewed major findings of a two-year, congressionally mandated, scientific examination of over 500 crime-prevention programs. Completed by a University of Maryland-led team of researchers, the study provides guidance for communities struggling with crime, with the caveat that, since this is the first study of its kind, the evaluations are based on "minimally adequate evidence." (The complete study can be found online at www.preventingcrime.org.)

The shortest list in the report, unfortunately, was of what works: For families, frequent home visits to infants by trained nurses and other helpers reduced child abuse and other injuries. For children under age five, attending preschool or being visited at home weekly by a teacher decreased their chances of being arrested later in life, at least through their teen years. Family therapy and parent training to deal with delinquent and at-risk pre-adolescents lessened risk factors for delinquency, such as aggression and hyperactivity.

In schools, clearly communicated rules, reinforcement of positive behavior, and school-wide initiatives (such as anti-bullying campaigns) reduced crime and delinquency. Lifeskills training such as problem solving, self-control, and stress management were also successful. Behavior-modification programs to train or coach thinking skills diminished substance abuse in high-risk youth.

Ex-offender job training for older males cut down on repeat offenses, while nuisance abatement suits or threats against landlords for failing to address drug problems on their premises reduced drug dealing and crime in privately owned rental housing.

Extra police patrols in high-crime "hot spots" such as nightclubs, bars, and "hangouts" curtailed crime in these areas. Monitoring high-risk repeat offenders with special units lessened their time on the street and their opportunities to commit more crimes by returning them to prison earlier. Arresting employed domestic abusers reduced repeat abuse (probably because of the threat of losing employment).

Incarcerating hard-core serious offenders prevented crimes they would have committed if on the streets, but researchers warn of diminishing returns for incarcerating less active or less serious offenders. Rehabilitation efforts worked if they were "appropriate to their risk factors"; both adults and juveniles receiving such treatment were less likely to re-offend. Even in-prison drug treatment in "therapeutic community programs" minimized repeat offending after release.

## What Doesn't Work

The "doesn't work" list was longer:

Gun-buyback programs and inner-city community mobilization against crime were found ineffective. Guns could be easily obtained in other communities, and inner-city residents feared getting involved because the criminals might retaliate.

In schools, counseling not only failed to abate substance abuse and delinquency, but even increased it in some instances. Experimental psychologists could explain this seemingly illogical phenomenon: Attention-starved children often turn to drugs and delinquency, and counseling (attention) simply reinforces the behavior.

A surprise to many was that the original DARE curriculum—17 lessons taught in fifth and sixth grades by a uniformed police officer—failed to cut down on drug abuse. Since this finding, many DARE programs have been experimenting with follow-up programs at higher grade levels and have employed full-time

School Resource Officers to monitor and help students daily.

Summer jobs and short-term job training programs for at-risk youth failed to decrease crime, as did job training in place of prosecution for adult offenders. This agrees with earlier research (partially by this author) which found that job training and jobs alone could not overcome the multitude of problems facing at-risk youth and offenders.

Possibly most surprising to police was that the highly touted centerpiece of crime-prevention programs, Neighborhood Watch, failed to diminish burglary or other targeted crimes. However, the data was primarily from high-crime areas "where voluntary participation often fails." In other evaluations, Neighborhood Watch was found to be successful, but only when initiated and sustained by citizen groups. Police-initiated efforts were not sustained by residents.

One cause for alarm at a time when more youths are being arrested and treated harshly was the finding that "arrests of juveniles for minor offenses cause them to become more delinquent in the future than if police exercise discretion and merely warn them or use other alternatives to formal charging." The finding that "scared straight" programs (which bring minor juvenile offenders to visit maximum security prisons to see the severity of conditions there) can actually increase crime by these children should also raise a warning flag. Other research agrees, causing experts to conclude that keeping juveniles far away from the criminal-justice system is the best strategy for preventing crime. The system should be reserved for incorrigible or dangerous juvenile offenders.

Increased arrests of drug dealers were unsuccessful in deterring crime. Drug dealing was so fluid that police enforcement could not curtail it for more than a few days.

Correctional boot camps using a traditional military basic-training approach failed to lessen repeat offending, and "shock probation"—short periods of incarceration followed by probation/parole—did not prove any more effective than direct placement under community supervision. In fact, community supervision alone was usually more effective, as it avoids contact with the stigmatizing effects of imprisonment.

Neither home detention with electronic monitoring nor intensive supervision on probation was found to be any more effective in decreasing repeat offending than standard community supervision. If these results hold up under further study, then these expensive programs can be scrapped. The new electronic monitoring by global positioning satellite (which allows the client to go to school, work, therapy, as well as home) may prove more effective.

## What's Promising

The "promising" list was the longest and most useful portion of the research findings:

Gang monitoring has proven tricky: Community workers, probation officers, and police have been able to reduce gang violence so long as they don't increase gang cohesion; if they do, gang crime increases, the study found.

Community-based mentoring and after-school recreation programs have shown promise of diminishing crime and substance abuse. Community-initiated programs appear more likely than government-created programs to be sustained. Big Brothers/Big Sisters, for example, has the expertise and experience that government efforts lack.

Shelters for battered women were likely to lessen repeat victimization, but only if the women took steps beyond staying in the shelter, such as seeking counseling, education, or job training.

"Schools within schools" programs that group students into smaller units for increased supportive interaction and flexibility in instruction abated drug abuse and delinquency in some locations. Improved classroom management and

innovative instructional techniques have also helped.

Both Job Corps, an intensive residential program for at-risk youth, and prison-based vocational programs for adult offenders have shown promise, probably because they provide not only long-term training but also preparation for entering the workplace.

Enterprise zones, which give tax-break incentives to employers and thereby provide jobs in high unemployment neighborhoods, reduced high crime risk factors such as high-school dropout and parental unemployment. So did dispersing public-housing residents out of the inner city and into suburban areas.

A potpourri of solutions have been deemed promising in places of business, neighborhoods, and schools. For example, street closures, barricades, and rerouting can reduce numerous street crimes in neighborhoods. Probably most promising here is a staple of Community-Oriented Policing programs, in which officers use "problem-solving analysis, addressed to the specific crime situation" such as drug dealing in a public housing project or burglary in a neighborhood.

Finally, combining monetary fines with other penalties might curtail repeat offenses. This finding supplements earlier studies in European countries where fines are attached to almost all offenses. Europeans have discovered that material losses will deter crime more effectively than will short sentences or community supervision.

The researchers were careful to avoid any sweeping conclusions from this first review of crime-prevention programs. However, to sum up, it appears that early intervention and proactive prevention programs show the most promise, along with close monitoring and arrests of hard-core offenders and at "hot spot" locations. Long-term, individual training and treatment are effective for those already at risk or in trouble. Beyond this, community-initiated programs fare better than government-created efforts, and government partner-

ships with existing, established programs are more effective than new government programs.

## Other Assessments

At least two other assessments of crime-prevention efforts support the findings reviewed above.

The first crime-prevention textbook based entirely on scientific research, *The Prevention of Crime: Social and Situational Strategies* by Dennis P. Rosenbaum, Arthur J. Lurigio, and Robert C. Davis (Wadsworth Publishing, 1996) reviewed the plethora of prevention approaches and assessed their usefulness. In some cases, researchers found individual safety and community safety at odds. For example, a person carrying a gun in a high-crime neighborhood was slightly safer, but the added gun on the street placed the neighborhood at greater risk.

Another Justice Department agency—the Office of Juvenile Justice and Delinquency Prevention—offers a taxonomy of strategies to cope with gun violence. Its report, "Promising Strategies to Reduce Gun Violence," recommends programs similar to those mentioned already. These include rallies to highlight awareness of the problem, in-school mentoring and conflict resolution programs, gang and drug prevention initiatives, parenting skills programs, and job training for at-risk youth. (Visit http://ojjdp.ncjrs.org for more information.)

## A New Model for Crime Prevention

Programs that can significantly reduce crime are emerging, but citizens must accept these new strategies, and communities must take control of the process from start to finish.

Community-oriented policing requires partnerships between all public and private agencies in the jurisdiction as well as active participation by community residents. Under ideal conditions, citizens lead the effort to analyze neighborhood needs and set priorities for dealing with crime-breeding situations. Thus, community policing is a philosophy rather than a set of specific tactics; each community must determine its own agenda and create its own plan and programs. However, successful efforts have several common principles:

- The community is involved in planning and supervision of police operations.
- Decision making shifts from standard operating procedures to creative, responsible action determined by the street officer.
- Crime-control methods—imposed authority, intimidation, demand for compliance, reaction to crime—are replaced by (or at least secondary to) prevention methods: establishing trust, sharing power, seeking out and alleviating problems that cause crime.

Several problems must be overcome for this approach to become the model for the twenty-first century. First, *creating* community is often necessary. Neighbors are often strangers; they are either transient or so busy that they don't socialize. Police must first identify and develop community leadership and then arrange social activities to begin the cohesion process.

Second, police recruitment and training must be improved. The high-school diploma remains the only educational requirement in a majority of departments, and training is centered on how to make an arrest, fire a gun, drive a car in pursuit, etc. Clearly the needs of community-oriented policing demand a better educated officer who desires to serve the public. Such officers must be trained in organization, communication, mediation, cooperation skills, and creative problem solving.

In addition, the professional pride of the police will have to be kept in check if community-policing efforts are to be successful. Clearly, police need to learn to share power. Police traditionally have been "the law" at the street level and are not used to having outsiders determine the way they do their job. Known for clannishness, police are now being asked to accept direction from others.

A final issue is that police are charged with protecting constitutional rights while doing their job. Thus, if there is a consensus in a community to trample on the rights of a minority group to protect the majority, community-oriented police officers must use their mediation skills to redirect the decision-making process toward legal solutions.

## Restorative Justice

Even the best proactive efforts of a community and police will not be enough to prevent crime in all situations. When crime does occur, restorative justice offers a proactive alternative to the current reactive and retributive courts and corrections systems, especially those in the juvenile justice process.

Restorative justice is not yet a well-developed alternative system; it has emerged piecemeal over the past three decades—from a few community mediation-arbitration programs starting in the 1970s, to growing use of community service and restitution as alternatives to incarceration, to greater attention to rehabilitation of offenders. Through the National Institute of Justice and many private and public agency efforts nationwide, the connections are being made to provide a coordinated system.

The philosophical principles underlying restorative justice hold that crime is an offense against human relationships, not governments. The first priority is to assist victims, and the second priority is to restore community to the degree possible. The offender has responsibilities to the victim and the community, and the community has responsibility to reclaim and reconcile with the offender as the debt is paid.

## Weeding and Seeding in New York City

For much of the last decades of the twentieth century, Americans saw New York City as the epitome of urban decay—dirty, unsafe, and crime ridden. Many New Yorkers agreed: they huddled behind locked doors, afraid to walk the streets or ride the subways.

But in the latter half of the 1990s, the city made a dramatic turnabout—leading an urban renaissance with a huge decrease in street crime, revival of street life, and provision of safe, clean public transportation.

Crime decreased in New York because of a well-orchestrated "weed and seed" operation.

Weeding included shutting down criminal activity by using informants and task forces to "weed" communities of predators, addicts, and petty offenders, and keeping criminals out by temporarily monitoring communities 24-hours-a-day via barricading streets, stopping vehicles, checking pedestrians, and padlocking dwellings where illegal activity was found.

Seeding, carried out simultaneously, included improving quality of life by fixing potholes, removing graffiti and garbage, installing better street lights, and encouraging residents to organize tenant associations and block groups. To keep the gains from eroding, officers stayed involved with citizens on their beats and played an active role in assisting residents.

NYPD officer Garry McCarthy, initiator of the Model Block Programs, summed it up: "All this changed the neighborhood—and the cops. We stand on a corner and interact with people. No more hostile stares from either side."

While police confrontations and shootings actually decreased during this period, a few cases led to large demonstrations against the most flagrant of the weeding tactics. "Get tough" tactics alone cannot provide safety among freedom-loving people. "Weed" and "seed" tactics must be balanced.

—Gene Stephens

When fully developed, the restorative-justice process will begin with arbitration and mediation to determine the details of the incident. Often there is some blame on both sides, such as in an argument that escalates into an assault. The parties involved agree on an acceptable solution, or the arbiter makes the decision for them. The offender must make restitution to the victims and to the community and must apologize face-to-face. Offenders may be given drug treatment, tutoring, or vocational training in order to help them live lawfully in the community. Ideally, the victim, offender, and community are satisfied that justice has been done; peace is restored.

## The Promise of Success

There are, of course, several obstacles that must be overcome to achieve acceptance of this model of community-oriented policing and restorative justice. The criminal justice establishment is a huge, multibillion-dollar complex. Many involved in it are comfortable and secure. They use fear to keep taxpayers' money flowing in.

Being asked to alleviate fear, identify and assist potential offenders, alleviate community ills, and share power with many other groups has led to high levels of resistance among police officers. For example, after the disastrous shoot-out following a Hollywood, California, bank robbery in 1997, police departments across the country cited the higher firepower of the robbers over police as undeniable evidence that police must have better weaponry. A new federal law allowed police to acquire automatic weapons, tanks, aircraft, and other high-tech gadgetry. SWAT teams were revitalized and expanded. (Even some university police established SWAT units.)

While it may be heresy to say this, the Hollywood incident should have redoubled efforts to ferret out and address the problems that led to the robbery and shootout in the first place. No one wins when "good" guys and "bad" guys accelerate their firepower in the community.

It seems, however, that the Community-Oriented Policing—Restorative Justice movement is strong enough to withstand resistance. Even those most opposed are often converted after seeing the successes—reduced crime, reduced fear, and revitalized communities. Consider the story of a Texas police officer:

> You know, years ago I came off a farm in South Texas and took a job as a city police officer. In my mind, I knew who the bad guys were, and I found a lot of fellow officers who felt the same way. We were out to rid society of these parasites. I policed this way for 15 years, and then a new chief came in and started this new-fangled community policing. He put me in a store-front precinct in a downtown district and had me walking a beat. I was so mad, I just sulked the first year. Well that got old, so I began to talk to people on my beat. After a while I learned they were much like me—concerned about their children, worried about drugs, upset about daily problems. As a police officer I had learned how to deal with many of these problems, and pretty soon I found myself referring these people to agencies that could help. For the first time in my career I feel like something other than a human garbage collector. Before, I rode around in my car all day and jumped out to grab what I considered human garbage. Now, I see people as just that—people. And the fact I can help them makes me feel good about myself and my job.

Gene Stephens is a professor in the College of Criminal Justice, University of South Carolina, and editor of *The Police Futurists*. He is contributing editor on criminal justice for THE FUTURIST. His address is University of South Carolina, Columbia, South Carolina 29208. E-mail stephens-gene@sc.edu.

Originally published in the November 1999 issue of *The Futurist*. Used with permission from the World Future Society, 7910 Woodmont Avenue, Suite 450, Bethesda, MD 20814. Telephone: 301/656-8274; Fax: 301/951-0394; http://www.wfs.org. © 1999.

# pe•do•phil•ia

*n.* recurrent, intense, sexually arousing fantasies,
sexual urges or behaviors involving sexual activity with a prepubescent child

—American Psychiatric Association's *Diagnostic and Statistical Manual*

**Why do some people want to touch kids? What can we do about it?
What happens to the victims? Everything you always wanted to know
about one of society's worst taboos—but were too angry to ask**

**BY JOHN CLOUD** BALTIMORE

IT'S EASIER NOT TO ASK TOO MANY QUESTIONS ABOUT PE-
dophilia. The questions make you blush; some of the answers make your skin crawl. But it seems that almost
daily we see another grown man tell his story and weep,
suddenly becoming the terrified kid he once was. All the
revelations, all spilling out at once, have created a fog:
Why are there so many people who want to molest children? How can we stop them? Are we overreacting?

The flood of reports could almost make you think that
everyone who sexually abuses a child is a Roman Catholic priest. In fact, the perpetrators are a disturbingly diverse lot. There's the Chicago-area nurse who molested
up to 18 patients, including a 9-year-old girl who had suffered a brain aneurysm and later died. There's the 33-
year-old Nevada day-care worker who committed hundreds of sexual acts on at least nine children, mostly ages
2 and 3—and videotaped them. Some of the most heart-
breaking allegations involve the American Boychoir
School, a top choral program in Princeton, N.J. More than
a dozen alumni from the 1960s to the '80s now say they
were sexually abused by at least 11 former staff members.
Says John Hardwicke Jr., 44, who claims he was raped repeatedly at the boarding school: "What we all seemed to
share was this sense of darkness."

But it is possible to cast light on this difficult subject.
Though researchers have many unanswered questions

about child sexual abusers, a serious, if small, academic
field is devoted to understanding and preventing their
behavior—and to comprehending its effects on their victims. Such work can require cold-eyed questions that
poke around the edges of our darkest taboos. At the outset, it's important to note that news accounts often con-
flate two phenomena: pedophilia and child sexual abuse.
According to Dr. Fred Berlin, a Johns Hopkins University
professor who founded the National Institute for the
Study, Prevention and Treatment of Sexual Trauma in
Baltimore, Md., pedophilia is a distinct sexual orientation
marked by persistent, sometimes exclusive, attraction to
prepubescent children. Dr. John Bradford, a University of
Ottawa psychiatrist who has spent 23 years studying pedophilia—which is listed as an illness in the manual psychiatrists use to make diagnoses—estimates its
prevalence at maybe 4% of the population. (Those attracted to teenagers are sometimes said to suffer "epheba-
philia," but perhaps because so many youth-obsessed
Americans would qualify, psychiatrists don't classify
ephebophilia as an illness.)

A psychiatric diagnosis of pedophilia merely indicates
one's desires; not all pedophiles act on their urges and actually commit child sexual abuse. Plenty of sexual abuse
of kids is committed by ordinary people not generally attracted to children. That's one reason the incidence of

# The Cases: A Sad Variety of Abuse

Recent allegation show that sex abuse defies any kind of easy stereotype

## THE SCOUTMASTER

### JERROLD SCHWARTZ

The former head of Manhattan's Troop 666 will face trial in May after pleading not guilty to 36 counts of sodomy. His accuser, now 21, claims abuse started at 14. Boy Scouts internally investigated a 1993 complaint against Schwartz, now 42, but says it was unsubstantiated.

## THE EX-COP

### MICHAEL MCDONALD

Charges in the early 1980s that he molested four girls got him fired from the Long Beach, Calif., force but ended in hung juries. In February, McDonald, now 52, was back in court—and sentenced to eight years for abusing a boy, 14.

## THE TEACHER

### MOHSIN BAGHAZAL

The math and religious-studies instructor at an Islamic day school in St. Louis, Mo., was found guilty on three of five counts of child molestation last month. His lawyer argued there was no physical evidence that his client had penetrated his two male students, who were 10 and 11 at the time. Baghazal, 30, plans to appeal.

## THE UNCLE

### HOWARD NEVISON

A 12-year-old boy claims his uncle assaulted him four times between 1993 and 1998. Nevison, 61, denies the charges. Two other male relatives, a cousin and another uncle, have already been convicted of assaulting the boy.

## THE COACH

### THEODORE DUDASH

Police say the 55-year-old fondled the breasts of a player on his 12-and-under girls' softball team while showing her how to bat. Dudash, of Hollywood, Fla., pleaded not guilty last month to three charges of committing a lewd and lascivious act. His lawyer confirmed that Dudash served probation on a similar charge in 1990.

## THE YOUTH WORKER

### CHRISTOPHER REARDON

Officials investigating allegations of abuse say they found hundreds of photos of naked children and handwritten chats that chronicled Reardon's assaults on 29 boys he encountered in his work at a Massachusetts church and YMCA. In August, Reardon, 30, pleaded guilty to 75 charges and was sentenced to 40 years.

## THE CHOIRMASTER

### DONALD HANSON

He is one of several former staff members accused of abusing pupils at New Jersey's American Boychoir School in the 1970s and '80s. Hanson, who ran the choir for 12 years, ending in 1982, is accused in a civil lawsuit of molesting one alumnus several times a day over six months. Hanson's lawyer has declined to comment.

## THE NURSE

### KENNETH PEBENITO

The now 30-year-old father of a 2-year-old daughter pleaded guilty last June to federal charges of ordering child porn through the mail. As part of his plea agreement, he admitted to molesting as many as 18 of his female patients in several Chicago-area hospitals, including a 9-year-old comatose girl who later died.

## THE DAY-CARE OPERATOR

### LADONNA TUCKER

Indiana prosecutors played a tape of Tucker, now 42, apparently describing sex acts she performed with children in her care—ages 4 months to 2 years—as "wonderful." She was convicted of conspiracy to commit child molesting and promoting prostitution, and sentenced this January to 40 years. She is appealing.

child sexual abuse is so maddeningly high. A Department of Health and Human Services study estimates that victimizers sexually abused 93,000 U.S. children in 1999 (the latest year for which data are available). But there is some good news. Last year the Department of Justice reported that the number of substantiated cases of child sexual abuse has been decreasing, from a peak of nearly 150,000 in 1992 to about 104,000 in 1998—a drop of almost one-third. The authors say vigorous incarceration of offenders over the past few years may be partly responsible.

But if we have punished our way out of the problem somewhat, we still don't have a long-term solution. Many people assume that not only priests but also teachers, Boy Scout leaders and other adults who work with kids are responsible for most child sexual abuse, but that's a misconception. Half of child sexual abusers are the parents of the victims; other relatives commit 18% of the offenses. And the sad truth is that preventing incest is nearly impossible. Less than one-third of perpetrators know their victims from outside the home. But non-family abusers may

# The Vatican Finally Speaks Up

Few institutions prize symbolism as much as the Roman Catholic Church does. And over the past few months, as news surfaced about the sexual abuse of children and teens by priests from Boston to Los Angeles and evidence of official cover-ups grew, American Catholics looked to the Vatican for some kind of sign. The silence out of Rome was deafening until last Monday, when the Pope finally issued a call. America's embattled Cardinals—all 13 of them—were summoned to an unprecedented meeting to be solely devoted to the spreading uproar.

The convocation, which is scheduled to take place this week, means the Vatican has finally accepted that the American church's pedophilia problem is Rome's as well. "When there's a problem in the family, you call the members of the family together to discuss it," says a Vatican insider.

That may be so, but many observers believe the dramatic summons, which followed a secret visit to Rome by Boston's Bernard Cardinal Law, who has been under pressure to resign because of his handling of abuse cases in his archdiocese, was the result of a reluctant acknowledgment that the problem was beginning to hurt the church in tangible ways. Some parishioners in the U.S. have threatened to withhold funds until the controversy is addressed. "The profound and potentially long-lasting alienation of the laity is a very significant factor," says Scott Appleby, director of the Cushwa Center for the Study of American Catholicism at the University of Notre Dame. "It means the financial well-being of the church is at risk."

What can the meeting accomplish? That may depend on who leads it. Many feel that the man to watch will be not the frail Pope but Darío Cardinal Castrillón Hoyos, who heads the church's powerful Congregation for the Clergy. But the conservative Pontiff made headlines Saturday, ordering Bishops to "diligently investigate accusations" against priests for breaking their vows of celibacy. "It's a mistake to underestimate him," says George Weigel, the Pope's biographer.

Neither should the symbolism of ecclesiastic spectacle be underestimated. In a departure from Vatican tradition, the Cardinals' meeting is expected to provide daily briefings to the press. Few expect full disclosure of the discussions. The talks may range from debates on a formal policy to prevent and handle further abuse cases to deeper doctrinal conversations about celibacy and female priests. They will certainly set the agenda for the U.S. Conference of Catholic Bishops' meeting, scheduled for June in Dallas. Meanwhile, the appearance of high-level openness may help calm troubled waters.

Weigel expects little material progress from the Vatican sessions. "It's two days," he says. "Two days! And these are extremely complex issues." But at least they are finally being confronted to resolve them.

*—By Walter Kirn, with reporting by Jeff Israely/Rome and Maggie Sieger/Chicago*

be easier to pick out—many are adults who shower uncommon attention on children—and thus easier to stop.

Although news reports focus on horrific serial offenders, experts say it's possible, with treatment, to prevent pedophiles from abusing kids. States have incarcerated many child sexual abusers, but most eventually get out (average sentence: 11 years). Active pedophiles who find their way into the few treatment programs around the country turn out to be less of a risk than those who are locked up for a while and released.

Berlin runs one of the largest such programs in the nation. Since 1991 hundreds of pedophiles have gone to the creaky Victorian building that houses his clinic. Berlin sees their condition as similar to alcoholism—incurable but treatable—and some of his methods sound similar to those of Alcoholics Anonymous. The pedophiles must admit their urges and confront them in group therapy. Counselors help them restructure their lives so that they don't come into contact with children. Berlin prescribes

medication to reduce sex drives for the 30% of his patients who don't respond to nondrug therapy.

There is nothing new or scientifically subtle about these drugs: they squash testosterone levels and therefore suppress sexual hunger. (High, long-term doses of the drugs are known as "chemical castration," a misnomer because sex drive returns if the injections stop.) But together, drugs and counseling can be effective. Contrary to popular perception, a raft of studies has shown that once in treatment, few pedophiles relapse. In 1991 the *American Journal of Forensic Psychiatry* published a study of 400 of Berlin's patients; only 1.2% of those who had complied with his 2 ½-year treatment were known to have molested kids again three years after finishing the course. Surprisingly, only 5.6% of those who were discharged for noncompliance offended in that period. Similarly, a 2002 study by St. Luke Institute, a psychiatric hospital outside Washington, followed 121 priests for one to five years and found that after treatment only three had relapsed, according to the Rev. Stephen Rossetti, who runs St. Luke. "People don't grow up and say, 'I want to be a pedophile,'" says Rossetti. "All the people I've ever talked to hate it."

Other studies that look back over longer periods—five to 10 years—find higher percentages of pedophiles who strike again, as high as 58% for those who refuse treatment. Such disparities highlight how uncertain the study of pedophilia is, but even the higher figure belies the popular notion that if a pedophile is allowed to go free, he will almost always molest again. "It's very easy to say, 'Throw away the key,'" says Berlin. "But many of these people are tortured by these temptations, and they are relieved that we can do something for them."

FEW PEDOPHILES GET THIS HELP, AS BERLIN IS ONE OF ONLY a dozen or so doctors who run such clinics in North America. "We don't have Betty Ford centers for people with sexual disorders," he says. Instead, a 1996 federal law requires sex offenders to register with state authorities. When an offender is released from prison, the state can (and often does) notify neighbors. It's unclear whether the legislation is preventing abuse.

One difficulty in treating pedophiles is that we know little about their condition. Could people become pedophiles because they were sexually victimized as kids? That theory makes common sense, but only one-third of pedophiles say they were abused. Could pedophilia be a brain disease? Bradford of the University of Ottawa says studies of pedophiles' brains have shown differences in the way they react to changes in hormone levels, but he says the research is in its earliest stages. Other scientists have posited several risk factors that can lead to pedophilia, including chromosomal abnormalities, psychological problems during puberty and even being brothers: The *Journal of Psychology* in 2000 reported that "a gap of several years between brothers might deprive the pedophile of companionship in formative years of sexual behavior development."

But such ideas are still guesswork. "If we really want to understand these people and develop good ways to prevent pedophilia, we need a national demographic survey," says Berlin. "The funding is minuscule, so the research is incomplete." And politically fraught. Everyone who works in the field constantly negotiates America's discomfort with children and sex. Yet understanding child sexual abuse means not only exploring its prevalence, causes and treatments—issues that focus on the abuser—but finding the best way to help victims cope as well. And that research is positively radioactive.

Consider the most basic question of such inquiry: What constitutes a victim of child sexual abuse? By definition, pedophiles prey on the prepubescent. No one would seriously argue that a 6- or even 10-year-old can meaningfully consent to sex. But what about those 12 and older, who make up nearly half of all juvenile sex-abuse

victims? The states define the age of consent for sex differently. Most say it is 16, but some say 18. In Hawaii, it's 14. So are teenagers from the onset of puberty (usually about 13) to the age of sexual majority (usually 16) always victims when they have sex with someone older?

Legally speaking, as the differences in legal adulthood indicate, the younger partners are not always treated as victims. Even in states where the age of consent is 18, prosecutors rarely go after, say, a 23-year-old for sleeping with a 17-year-old. Given that up to half of teens say they have had sex while a minor, "millions of statutory-rape cases occur every day," says Michelle Oberman, a DePaul University rape-law specialist.

Different cultures have different views on whether adult-adolescent sex is always wrong. In the Netherlands, the law allows children ages 12 to 16 to make their own decision about sex, though if Mom and Dad feel a relationship is exploitative, they can ask the authorities to investigate. Most Americans would find such a law abhorrent. Recently, the University of Minnesota initiated an unusual review of its university press after it published a book that calls the Dutch law "a good model." Judith Levine's *Harmful to Minors: The Perils of Protecting Children from Sex*, scheduled to arrive in bookstores this month, asserts that "teens often seek out sex with older people... For some teens, a romance with an older person can feel more like salvation than victimization."

SOME HAVE ATTACKED LEVINE'S BOOK AS TRIVIALIZING THE pain that sexual-abuse victims can feel. The idea that a 12-year-old could consent to sex is "just dangerous in every way," child psychologist Joy Silberg said last week on *Good Morning America*. Silberg pointed out that many children who have sex with an adult are "severely sexually traumatized." Some kids tried to bury their trauma, and as we have seen recently with priests' victims, the agony from sexual abuse can emerge much later.

Levine wrote her book to promote teens' sexual health—not abuse—but she could have predicted the storm that is greeting her. In July 1998, *Psychological Bulletin*, a journal of the American Psychological Association, published a dense, jargony paper by three academics led by Bruce Rind of Temple University. The Rind paper examined 59 studies of 35,000 college students who had been sexually abused as minors. The 59 studies had looked at how the victims were faring in terms of anxiety, depression and 16 other mental-health measures. The authors drew an important distinction between a 15-year-old who has sex willingly and a 5-year-old whose father rapes her. But the authors concluded that for most victims the effects of the abuse "were neither pervasive nor typically intense" and that "men reacted much less negatively than women." In fact, 42% of the men who were asked (vs. 16% of the women) looked back on their sexual experience with an adult as positive.

# What to Say to Your Kids

Parents of children who have been victimized by sexual predators tend to describe their family's experience as "unthinkable." But experts in childhood sexual abuse say parents should think about it and talk to their kids about it, because children who know what to look out for are less likely to be victimized. It is important to educate young children about "good touch and bad touch" and "stranger danger," even though the majority of sexual offenses against children are perpetrated by someone the child knows and trusts.

Dr. Leigh Baker, a psychologist in Denver and the author of *Protecting Your Children from Sexual Predators* (St. Martin's Press), has treated hundreds of abused children and interviewed dozens of sexual offenders. Baker and others say the first line of defense against sexual abuse is a child's sense of self. parents should help their children develop confidence in themselves and their bodies, starting when they are in the toddler stage, and answer kids' questions about their private parts with anatomically correct answers.

## TRUST: Parents should talk openly to kids about their bodies

Experts note that focusing on the sexual act is confusing and scary for kids. But when children are at around age 3, parents can talk freely and openly with them about their bodies, explaining, "Your body belongs only to you. It is the one thing you don't have to share with others." Also: "If anyone ever wants to see or touch your private parts, you should tell me right away." Children should also be told that it's fine to say no to anything that makes them uncomfortable, and that includes sitting on Uncle Bob's lap if they don't like it. "If these things are discussed openly at home, then it is much more probable that a child will know when something unusual has happened and report back to parents," Baker says.

Parents should make it clear to their children that "there are no secrets in our family," Baker says, "Pedophiles use secrecy and shame to keep children quiet. Predators are less likely to choose a child for a victim if they know that the child will tell someone." If families establish an open environment of communication in which any questions can be asked and answered without shame or judgment, children will come to parents when things aren't right.

Pedophiles groom their victims by starting benignly, then making them feel special and exclusive, sometimes even using a mother or father's trust to get to a child. Parents should tell their children it's not right for an older person to want to be their special friend with no other grownups around. Parents should also say, "Older people—even teenagers—should not give you special gifts without asking your parents first and should never ask you to keep secrets." Children should be told that if a relationship with an older person they already know changes and that person wants to be alone with them, this is a danger sign.

Finally, children should be told over and over again to follow that feeling they get in their tummy when things just don't seem right. Even if they don't know exactly what is wrong, children, lie the rest of us, can sense a dangerous or threatening situation. "Always follow your gut" is a simple and important piece of safety advice that even young children can understand.

Baker says parents should view sexual abuse as an issue that the whole family is concerned about—not just the kids. "If children have knowledge and they think their parents know what's going on and what to do, that's not frightening—that's empowering," she says. Children who are empowered will be surefooted and confident in life; they will also be less vulnerable to predators who want to do the unthinkable.

*—By Amy Dickinson*

Radio host Laura Schlessinger discovered the Rind review and called it "junk science." House majority whip Tom DeLay of Texas expressed "outrage and disgust" at the psychological association for printing "a study that advocates normalizing pedophilia," and the House voted unanimously to condemn the paper. Critics whispered that one of the review's co-authors, psychologist Robert Bauserman, had written for a Dutch publication that spoke admiringly of "man-boy" relationships. Now an

AIDS official with the state of Maryland, Bauserman said in an e-mail that "it would have been better to find a different outlet" for his writing than the Dutch journal. But he also pointed out that the Rind study had withstood fierce academic scrutiny without being refuted.

Within the field of child psychology, the Rind study was controversial but not dismissed. Other authors had reached similar conclusions. Critics failed to note that Rind and his colleagues stipulated that "lack of harmfulness does not imply lack of wrongfulness" and said their findings warranted no changes in U.S. laws.

MOST AMERICANS ARE SAVVY WHEN IT COMES TO MAKING distinctions between a kid being abused and one coming of age in a healthy way. Lots of viewers laughed five years ago when *Friends* explored the relationship between Phoebe's high-school-age brother and his teacher. ("If that doesn't keep kids in school, what will?" Chandler wondered.) *On Six Feet Under* last season, Claire, a sexually active character in high school, made out with an older photographer, and viewers hardly seemed to notice the age difference. Americans buy plenty of garments from Calvin Klein and Abercrombie & Fitch, which showcase all-but-hairless flesh—often that of teen models—in their arty ads.

Ultimately, *Friends* and *Six Feet Under* stay on the air because the teen-sex story lines find the right side of a standard that makes sense to most people: if an individual is harmed, then it's abuse. Last week the U.S. Supreme Court adopted that standard in a 6-to-3 decision on child pornography. The court rejected a 1996 congressional ban on "virtual" child porn—pictures that use young-looking adults or computer-generated images to simulate children. "These images do not involve, let alone harm, any children in the production process," wrote Justice Anthony Kennedy.

With the church scandal still roiling, it wasn't a propitious moment to strike a blow in favor of kiddie porn, and many lashed out at the court. But those who have studied pedophilia say society never seems quite ready to explore the delicate issues surrounding sex and kids. "People want to see a monster when they say 'pedophile,'" says Berlin. "But the best public-safety approach on pedophilia is to provide these people with treatment. That will prevent future victimization." In other words, asking questions about pedophilia may make us squirm, but it may also be the first step toward ending it.

*—With reporting by Amanda Bower, Sora Song and Dierdre van Dyk/New York*

# UNIT 3
# Groups and Roles in Transition

## Unit Selections

## Key Points to Consider

- Is the family in America in crisis? What indicators of family health have worsened and what indicators have improved?

- What factors are influencing women's roles today? How are they changing women's lives?

- When marriages are working badly, should the couple stay together for the kids?

- Is the American male in crisis? If so, why?

- What factors create community? How can they be brought into being under today's conditions? What are the impediments to community? What are the consequences of weak communities? Does the Internet strengthen community?

 **Links: www.dushkin.com/online/**
These sites are annotated in the World Wide Web pages.

**American Men's Studies Association**
*http://www.vix.com/pub/men/orgs/writeups/amsa.html*

**The Gallup Organization**
*http://www.gallup.com*

**Grass-Roots.org**
*http://www.iglou.com/why/ria.htm*

**Marriage and Family Therapy**
*http://www.aamft.org/index_nm.asp*

**The North-South Institute**
*http://www.nsi-ins.ca/ensi/index.html*

**PsychNet/American Psychological Association**
*http://www.apa.org/psychnet/*

**SocioSite: Feminism and Woman Issues**
*http://www.pscw.uva.nl/sociosite/TOPICS/Women.html*

Primary groups are small, intimate, spontaneous, and personal. In contrast, secondary groups are large, formal, and impersonal. Primary groups include the family, couples, gangs, cliques, teams, and small tribes or rural villages. Primary groups are the main sources that the individual draws upon in developing values and an identity. Secondary groups include most of the organizations and bureaucracies in a modern society and carry out most of its instrumental functions. Often primary groups are formed within secondary groups such as a factory, school, or business.

Urbanization, geographic mobility, centralization, bureaucratization, and other aspects of modernization have had an impact on the nature of groups, the quality of the relationships between people, and individuals' feelings of belonging. The family, in particular, has undergone radical transformation. The greatly increased participation of women in the paid labor force and their increased careerism have led to severe conflicts for women between their work and family roles.

The first subsection of this unit deals with marriage and family in the context of dramatic changes in the culture and the economy. Everyone seems to agree that the family is in trouble, but Stephanie Coontz challenges this viewpoint in the first article in this subsection. She takes issue with the data presented for the decline of marriage and the family thesis and offers evidence that marriage is strong today even though divorce is common. In fact, she argues that today's families are better than families of a century ago in many ways. According to Coontz "the biggest problem facing most families… is not that our families have changed too much but that our institutions have changed too little."

The next two articles look at the failure of marriage; the first analyzes why families are started outside of marriage and the second analyzes the impacts of marriages ending. In the first James Wilson explores why the "illegitimacy ratio" has risen to 33 percent. Using history and statistics he searches for the major causes. Wilson argues that welfare is a cause, although a small one. The big cause is cultural change, which has removed the stigma both of welfare and of unmarried motherhood. Cultural changes have also weakened the moral underpinnings of marriage. Since Wilson believes in the power of culture he also believes that it is very hard to change the situation. The next article, by Walter Kim, presents a fairly complete examination of the consequences of divorce on the children. He reviews the debate over whether a bad marriage or a divorce is more harmful for the children. The evidence shows that both are bad.

The next subsection focuses on sexual behavior and gender roles. In "Now for the Truth About Americans and Sex," Philip Elmer-Dewitt reviews a recent national survey of American sexual behavior and corrects many common misimpressions. He points out, among other things, that Americans are more sexually faithful to their spouses than is commonly perceived. In the next article, John Leland discusses the greater public acceptance of homosexual lifestyles but not of giving homosexual

marriages the status of heterosexual marriages. However, the legal recognition of gay marriages has become the main issue with gays today and they are not gaining headway on this battle. Gay marriages are still not recognized as legal in 49 states, and over two-thirds of the states have passed laws banning same-sex marriages. The next article discusses gender equality in marriages, which has increased greatly in the past several decades and has caused problems. For example, if the husband's career does not automatically come before the wife's, how do egalitarian couples work out extremely difficult career conflicts? Susan Caminiti discusses this question largely by telling stories about how numerous couples have dealt with conflicting issues.

The last subsection of unit 3 looks at cities and communities. The first article in the unit speculates on what might happen when within a half century no group will be a majority in America. Today this is true of Sacramento, California. The authors examine how this situation works out in America's most integrated city. Twenty percent of babies are multiracial and though racial tensions exist, they are relatively minor.

# THE AMERICAN FAMILY

**New research about an old institution challenges the conventional wisdom that the family today is worse off than in the past. Essay by Stephanie Coontz**

As the century comes to an end, many observers fear for the future of America's families. Our divorce rate is the highest in the world, and the percentage of unmarried women is significantly higher than in 1960. Educated women are having fewer babies, while immigrant children flood the schools, demanding to be taught in their native language. Harvard University reports that only 4 percent of its applicants can write a proper sentence.

## Things were worse at the turn of the last century than they are today. Most workers labored 10 hours a day, six days a week, leaving little time for family life.

There's an epidemic of sexually transmitted diseases among men. Many streets in urban neighborhoods are littered with cocaine vials. Youths call heroin "happy dust." Even in small towns, people have easy access to addictive drugs, and drug abuse by middle-class wives is skyrocketing. Police see 16-year-old killers, 12-year-old prostitutes, and gang members as young as 11.

America at the end of the 1990s? No, America at the end of the 1890s.

The litany of complaints may sound familiar, but the truth is that many things were worse at the start of this century than they are today. Then, thousands of children worked full-time in mines, mills and sweatshops. Most

workers labored 10 hours a day, often six days a week, which left them little time or energy for family life. Race riots were more frequent and more deadly than those experienced by recent generations. Women couldn't vote, and their wages were so low that many turned to prostitution.

DAHLSTROM COLLECTION/TIME INC.

**c. 1890** A couple and their six children sit for a family portrait. With smaller families today, mothers spend twice as much time with each kid.

In 1900 a white child had one chance in three of losing a brother or sister before age 15, and a black child had a fifty-fifty chance of seeing a sibling die. Children's-aid groups reported widespread abuse and neglect by parents. Men who deserted or divorced their wives rarely paid child support. And only 6 percent of the children graduated from high school, compared with 88 percent today.

LEWIS HINE/CULVER PICTURES

**1915** An Italian immigrant family gathers around the dinner table in an apartment on the East Side of New York City. Today, most families still eat together—but often out.

Why do so many people think American families are facing worse problems now than in the past? Partly it's because we compare the complex and diverse families of the 1990s with the seemingly more standard-issue ones of the 1950s, a unique decade when every long-term trend of the 20th century was temporarily reversed. In the 1950s, for the first time in 100 years, the divorce rate fell while marriage and fertility rates soared, crating a boom in nuclear-family living. The percentage of foreign-born individuals in the country decreased. And the debates over social and cultural issues that had divided Americans for 150 years were silenced, suggesting a national consensus on family values and norms.

Some nostalgia for the 1950s is understandable: Life looked pretty good in comparison with the hardship of the Great Depression and World War II. The GI Bill gave a generation of young fathers a college education and a subsidized mortgage on a new house. For the first time, a majority of men could support a family and buy a home without pooling their earnings with those of other family members. Many Americans built a stable family life on these foundations.

But much nostalgia for the 1950s is a result of selective amnesia—the same process that makes childhood memories of summer vacations grow sunnier with each passing year. The superficial sameness of 1950s family life was achieved through censorship, coercion and discrimination. People with unconventional beliefs faced governmental investigation and arbitrary firings. African Americans and Mexican Americans were prevented from voting in some states by literacy tests that were not ad-

ministered to whites. Individuals who didn't follow the rigid gender and sexual rules of the day were ostracized.

*Leave It to Beaver* did not reflect the real-life experience of most American families. While many moved into the middle class during the 1950s, poverty remained more widespread than in the worst of our last three recessions. More children went hungry, and poverty rates for the elderly were more than twice as high as today's.

Even in the white middle class, not every woman was as serenely happy with her lot as June Cleaver was on TV. Housewives of the 1950s may have been less rushed than today's working mothers, but they were more likely to suffer anxiety and depression. In many states, women couldn't serve on juries or get loans or credit cards in their own names.

And not every kid was as wholesome as Beaver Cleaver, whose mischievous antics could be handled by Dad at the dinner table. In 1955 alone, Congress discussed 200 bills aimed at curbing juvenile delinquency. Three years later, LIFE reported that urban teachers were being terrorized by their students. The drugs that were so freely available in 1900 had been outlawed, but many children grew up in families ravaged by alcohol and barbiturate abuse.

Rates of unwed childbearing tripled between 1940 and 1958, but most Americans didn't notice because unwed mothers generally left town, gave their babies up for adoption and returned home as if nothing had happened. Troubled youths were encouraged to drop out of high school. Mentally handicapped children were warehoused in institutions like the Home for Idiotic and Imbecilic Children in Kansas, where a woman whose sister had lived there for most of the 1950s once took me. Wives routinely told pollsters that being disparaged or ignored by their husbands was a normal part of a happier than-average marriage.

## Many of our worries today reflect how much better we want to be, not how much better we used to be.

Denial extended to other areas of life as well. In the early 1900s, doctors refused to believe that the cases of gonorrhea and syphilis they saw in young girls could have been caused by sexual abuse. Instead, they reasoned, girls could get these diseases from toilet seats, a myth that terrified generations of mothers and daughters. In the 1950s, psychiatrists dismissed incest reports as Oedipal fantasies on the part of children.

Spousal rape was legal throughout the period and wife beating was not taken seriously by authorities. Much of what we now label child abuse was accepted as a normal part of parental discipline. Physicians saw no reason to question parents who claimed that their child's broken bones had been caused by a fall from a tree.

MARGARET BOURKE-WHITE

**1937: The Hahn family sits in the living room of a working-class Muncie home, which rents for $10 a month. Class distinctions have eroded over 60 years.**

# American Mirror

Muncie, Ind. (pop. 67,476), calls itself America's Hometown. But to generations of sociologists it is better known as America's Middletown—the most studied place in the 20th century American landscape. "Muncie has nothing extraordinary about it," says University of Virginia professor Theodore Caplow, which is why, for the past 75 years, researchers have gone there to observe the typical American family. Muncie's averageness first drew sociologists Robert and Helen Lynd in 1924. They returned in 1935 (their follow-up study was featured in a LIFE photo essay by Margaret Bourke-White). And in 1976, armed with the Lynds' original questionnaires, Caplow launched yet another survey of the town's citizens.

Caplow discovered that family life in Muncie was much healthier in the 1970s than in the 1920s. No only were husbands and wives communicating more, but unlike married couples in the 1920s, they were also shopping, eating out, exercising and going to movies and concerts together. More than 90 percent of Muncie's couples characterized their marriages as "happy" or "very happy." In 1929 the Lynds had described partnerships of a drearier kind, "marked by sober accommodation of each partner to his share in the joint undertaking of children, paying off the mortgage and generally 'getting on.' "

Caplow's five-year study, which inspired a six-part PBS series, found that even though more moms were working outside the home, two thirds of them spent at least two hours a day with their children; in 1924 fewer than half did. In 1924 most children expected their mothers to be good cooks and housekeepers, and wanted their fathers to spend time with them and respect their opinions. Fifty years later, expectations of fathers were unchanged, but children wanted the same—time and respect—from their mothers.

This year, Caplow went back to survey the town again. The results (and another TV documentary) won't be released until December 2000.

—*Sora Song*

There are plenty of stresses in modern family life, but one reason they seem worse is that we no longer sweep them under the rug. Another is that we have higher expectations of parenting and marriage. That's a good thing. We're right to be concerned about inattentive parents, conflicted marriages, antisocial values, teen violence and child abuse. But we need to realize that many of our worries reflect how much better we *want* to be, not how much better we *used* to be.

Fathers in intact families are spending more time with their children than at any other point in the past 100 years. Although the number of hours the average woman spends at home with her children has declined since the early 1900s, there has been a decrease in the number of children per family and an increase in individual attention to each child. As a result, mothers today, including working moms, spend almost twice as much time with each child as mothers did in the 1920s. People who raised children in the 1940s and 1950s typically report that their own adult children and grandchildren communicate far better with their kids and spend more time helping with homework than they did—even as they complain that other parents today are doing a worse job than in the past.

Despite the rise in youth violence from the 1960s to the early 1990s, America's children are also safer now than they've ever been. An infant was four times more likely to die in the 1950s than today. A parent then was three times more likely than a modern one to preside at the funeral of a child under the age of 15, and 27 percent more likely to lose an older teen to death.

If we look back over the last millennium, we can see that families have always been diverse and in flux. In each period, families have solved one set of problems only to face a new array of challenges. What works for a family in one economic and cultural setting doesn't work for a family in another. What's helpful at one stage of a family's life may be destructive at the next stage. If there is one lesson to be drawn from the last millennium of family history, it's that families are always having to play catch-up with a changing world.

Take the issue of working mothers. Families in which mothers spend as much time earning a living as they do raising children are nothing new. They were the norm throughout most of the last two millennia. In the 19th century, married women in the United States began a withdrawal from the workforce, but for most families this was made possible only by sending their children out to work instead. When child labor was abolished, married women began reentering the workforce in ever large numbers.

For a few decades, the decline in child labor was greater than the growth of women's employment. The result was an aberration: the male-breadwinner family. In the 1920s, for the first time, a bare majority of American children grew up in families where the husband provided all the income, the wife stayed home full-time, and they and their siblings went to school instead of work. During the 1950s, almost two thirds of children grew up in such

MARK KAUFFMAN

**1955** A family poses in Seattle. Husbands today are doing more housework.

families, an all-time high. Yet that same decade saw an acceleration of workforce participation by wives and mothers that soon made the dual-earner family the norm, a trend not likely to be reversed in the next century.

What's new is not that women make half their families' living, but that for the first time they have substantial control over their own income, along with the social freedom to remain single or to leave an unsatisfactory marriage. Also new is the declining proportion of their lives that people devote to rearing children, both because they have fewer kids and because they are living longer. Until about 1940, the typical marriage was broken by the death of one partner within a few years after the last child left home. Today, couples can look forward to spending more than two decades together after the children leave.

The growing length of time partners spend with only each other for company has made many individuals less willing to put up with an unhappy marriage, while women's economic independence makes it less essential for them to do so. It is no wonder that divorce has risen steadily since 1900. Disregarding a spurt in 1946, a dip in the 1950s and another peak around 1980, the divorce rate is just where you'd expect to find it, based on the rate of

increase from 1900 to 1950. Today, 40 percent of all marriages will end in divorce before a couple's 40th anniversary. Yet despite this high divorce rate, expanded life expectancies mean that more couples are reaching that anniversary than ever before.

Families and individuals in contemporary America have more life choices than in the past. That makes it easier for some to consider dangerous or unpopular options. But it also makes success easier for many families that never would have had a chance before—interracial, gay or lesbian, and single-mother families, for example. And it expands horizons for most families.

Women's new options are good not just for themselves but for their children. While some people say that women who choose to work are selfish, it turns out that maternal self-sacrifice is not good for children. Kids do better when their mothers are happy with their lives, whether their satisfaction comes from being a full-time homemaker or from having a job.

Largely because of women's new roles at work, men are doing more at home. Although most men still do less housework than their wives, the gap has been halved since the 1960s. Today, 49 percent of couples say they share childcare equally, compared with 25 percent of 1985.

Men's greater involvement at home is good for their relationships with their parents, and also good for their children. Hands-on fathers make better parents than men who let their wives do all the nurturing and childcare: They raise sons who are more expressive and daughters who are more likely to do well in school, especially in math and science.

## The biggest problem is not that our families have changed too much but that our institutions have changed too little.

In 1900, life expectancy was 47 years, and only 4 percent of the population was 65 or older. Today, life expectancy is 76 years, and by 2025, about 20 percent of Americans will be 65 or older. For the first time, a generation of adults must plan for the needs of both their parents and their children. Most Americans are responding with remarkable grace. One in four households gives the equivalent of a full day a week or more in unpaid care to an aging relative, and more than half say they expect to do so in the next 10 years. Older people are less likely to be impoverished or incapacitated by illness than in the past, and they have more opportunity to develop a relationship with their grandchildren.

Even some of the choices that worry us the most are turning out to be manageable. Divorce rates are likely to remain high, but more non-custodial parents are staying in touch with their children. Child-support receipts are up. And a lower proportion of kids from divorced families are exhibiting problems than in earlier decades. Stepfamilies are learning to maximize children's access to supportive adults rather than cutting them off from one side of the family.

Out-of-wedlock births are also high, however, and this will probably continue because the age of first marriage for women has risen to an all-time high of 25, almost five years above what it was in the 1950s. Women who marry at an older age are less likely to divorce, but they have more years when they are at risk—or at choice—for a nonmarital birth.

Nevertheless, births to teenagers have fallen from 50 percent of all nonmarital births in the late 1970s to just 30 percent today. A growing proportion of women who have a nonmarital birth are in their twenties and thirties and usually have more economic and educational resources than unwed mothers of the past. While two involved parents are generally better than one, a mother's personal maturity, along with her educational and economic status, is a better predictor of how well her child will turn out than her marital status. We should no longer assume that children raised by single parents face debilitating disadvantages.

As we begin to understand the range of sizes, shapes and colors that today's families come in, we find that the differences *within* family types are more important than the differences *between* them. No particular family form guarantees success, and no particular form is doomed to fail. How a family functions on the inside is more important than how it looks from the outside.

The biggest problem facing most families as this century draws to a close is not that our families have changed too much but that our institutions have changed too little. America's work policies are 50 years out of date, designed for a time when most moms weren't in the workforce and most dads didn't understand the joys of being involved in childcare. Our school schedules are 150 years out of date, designed for a time when kids needed to be home to help with the milking and haying. And many political leaders feel they have to decide whether to help parents stay home longer with their kids or invest in better childcare, preschool and afterschool programs, when most industrialized nations have long since learned it's possible to do both.

So America's social institutions have some Y2K bugs to iron out. But for the most part, our families are ready for the next millennium.

# DIVORCE AND COHABITATION

## Why We Don't Marry

### JAMES Q. WILSON

Everyone knows that the rising proportion of women who bear and raise children out of wedlock has greatly weakened the American family system. This phenomenon, once thought limited to African Americans, now affects whites as well, so much so that the rate at which white children are born to an unmarried mother is now as high as the rate for black children in the mid-1960s, when Daniel Patrick Moynihan issued his famous report on the Negro family. For whites the rate is one-fifth; for blacks it is over one-half.

Almost everyone—a few retrograde scholars excepted—agrees that children in mother-only homes suffer harmful consequences: the best studies show that these youngsters are more likely than those in two-parent families to be suspended from school, have emotional problems, become delinquent, suffer from abuse, and take drugs. Some of these problems may arise from the economic circumstances of these one-parent families, but the best studies, such as those by Sara McLanahan and Gary Sandefur, show that low income can explain, at most, about half of the differences between single-parent and two-parent families. The rest of the difference is explained by a mother living without a husband.

And even the income explanation is a bit misleading, because single moms, by virtue of being single, are more likely to be poor than are married moms. Now that our social security and pension systems have dramatically reduced poverty among the elderly, growing up with only one parent has dramatically increased poverty among children. In this country we have managed to shift poverty from old folks to young folks. Former Clinton advisor William Galston sums up the matter this way: you need only do three things in this country to avoid poverty—finish high school, marry before having a child, and marry after the age of 20. Only 8 percent of the families who do this are poor; 79 percent of those who fail to do this are poor.

This pattern of children being raised by single parents is now a leading feature of the social life of almost all English-speaking countries and some European ones. The illegitimacy ratio in the late 1990s was 33 percent for the United States, 31 percent for Canada, and 38 percent for the United Kingdom.

Now, not all children born out of wedlock are raised by a single mother. Some, especially in Sweden, are raised by a man and woman who, though living together, are not married; others are raised by a mother who gets married shortly after the birth. Nevertheless, there has been a sharp increase in children who are not only born out of wedlock but are raised without a father. In the United States, the percentage of children living with an unmarried mother has tripled since 1960 and more than doubled since 1970. In England, 22 percent of all children under the age of 16 are living with only one parent, a rate three times higher than in 1971.

Why has this happened? There are two possible explanations to consider: money and culture.

Money readily comes to mind. If a welfare system pays unmarried mothers enough to have their own apartment, some women will prefer babies to husbands. When government subsidizes something, we get more of it. But for many years, American scholars discounted this possibility. Since the amount of welfare paid per mother had declined in inflation-adjusted terms, and since the amount paid in each state showed no correlation with each state's illegitimacy rate, surely money could not have caused the increase in out-of-wedlock births.

This view dominated scholarly discussions until the 1990s. But there are three arguments against it. First, the inflation-adjusted value of welfare benefits was not the key factor. What counted was the inflation-adjusted value of all the benefits an unmarried mother might receive—not only welfare, but also food stamps, public housing, and Medicaid. By adding these in, welfare kept up with inflation.

Second, what counted was not how much money each state paid out, but how much it paid compared with the cost of living in that state. As Charles Murray pointed out, the benefits for a woman in New Orleans ($654 a month) and those for one in San Francisco ($867 a month) made nearly identical contributions to the cost of living, because in New Orleans it cost about two-thirds as much to live as it did in San Francisco.

Third, comparing single-parent families and average spending levels neglects the real issue: how attractive is welfare to a low-income unmarried woman in a given locality? When economist Mark Rosenzweig asked this question of women who are part of the National Longitudinal Survey of Youth—a panel study of people that has been going on since 1979—he found that a 10 percent increase in welfare benefits made the chances that a poor young woman would have a baby out of wedlock before the age of 22 go up by 12 percent. And this was true for whites as well as blacks. Soon other scholars were confirming Rosenzweigs findings. Welfare made a difference.

## WELFARE CHILDREN

But how big a difference? AFDC began in 1935, but by 1960 only 4 percent of the children getting welfare had a mother who had never been married; the rest had mothers who were widows or had been separated from their husbands. By 1996 that had changed dramatically: now approximately two-thirds of welfare children had an unmarried mom, and hardly any were the offspring of widows.

Why this change? At least for blacks, one well-known explanation has been offered: men did not marry because there were no jobs for them in the big cities. As manufacturing employment sharply declined in the central cities, William Julius Wilson has argued, blacks were unable to move to the suburbs as fast as the jobs. The unemployed males left behind are not very attractive as prospective husbands to the women they know, and so more and more black women do without marriage.

The argument has not withstood scholarly criticism. First, Mexican Americans, especially illegal immigrants, live in the central city also, but the absence of good jobs has not mattered, even though many Mexicans are poorer than blacks, speak English badly, and if undocumented cannot get good jobs. Nevertheless, the rate of out-of-wedlock births is much lower among these immigrants than it is among African Americans, as W. J. Wilson acknowledges.

Second, Christopher Jencks has shown that there has been as sharp a decline in marriage among employed black men as among unemployed ones, and that the supply of employed blacks is large enough to provide husbands for almost all unmarried black mothers. For these people, as Jencks concludes, "marriage must... have been losing its charms for non-economic reasons."

Moreover, the argument that single-parent families have increased because black men have not been able to move to wherever factory jobs can be found does not explain why such families have grown so rapidly among whites, for whom moving around a city should be no problem. For these whites—and I suspect for many blacks as well—there must be another explanation.

To explain the staggering increase in unmarried mothers, we must turn to culture. In this context, what I mean by culture is simply that being an unmarried mother and living on welfare has lost its stigma. At one time living on the dole was shameful; now it is much less so. As this may not be obvious to some people, let me add some facts that will support it.

## STIGMA

Women in rural communities who go on welfare leave it much sooner than the same kind of women who take welfare in big cities, and this is true for both whites and blacks and regardless of the size of their families. The studies that show this outcome offer a simple explanation for it. In a small town, everyone knows who is on welfare, and welfare recipients do not have many friends in the same situation with whom they can associate. But in a big city, welfare recipients are not known to everyone, and each one can easily associate with other women living the same way. In the small town, welfare recipients tell interviewers the same story: "I always felt like I was being watched"; "they treat us like welfare cattle"; people make "nasty comments." But in a big city, recipients had a different story: Everyone "is in the same boat I am"; people "dont look down on you."

American courts have made clear that welfare laws cannot be used to enforce stigma. When Alabama tried in 1960 to deny welfare to an unmarried woman who was living with a man who was not her husband, the U.S. Supreme Court objected. Immorality, it implied, was an outdated notion. The states have no right to limit welfare to a "worthy person," and welfare belongs to the child, not the mother. If the state is concerned about immorality, it will have to rehabilitate the women by other means.

How did stigma get weakened by practice and undercut by law, when Americans—no less than Brits, Canadians, and Australians—favor marriage and are skeptical of welfare?

Let me suggest that beneath the popular support for marriage there has slowly developed, almost unnoticed, a subversion of it, which can be summarized this way: whereas marriage was once thought to be about a social union, it is now about personal preferences. Formerly, law and opinion enforced the desirability of marriage without asking what went on in that union; today, law and opinion enforce the desirability of personal happiness without worrying much about maintaining a formal relationship. Marriage was once a sacrament, then it became a contract, and now it is an arrangement. Once religion provided the sacrament, then the law enforced the contract, and now personal preferences define the arrangement.

The cultural change that made this happen was the same one that gave us science, technology, freedom, and capitalism: the Enlightenment. The Enlightenment—that extraordinary intellectual development that began in eighteenth-century England, Scotland, Holland, and Germany—made human reason the measure of all things, throwing off ancient rules if they fell short. What the king once ordered, what bishops once enforced, what tradition once required was to be set aside in the name of scientific knowledge and personal self-discovery. The Enlightenment's great spokesmen were David Hume, Adam Smith, and Immanuel Kant; its greatest accomplishment was the creation of the United States of America.

I am a great admirer of the Enlightenment. But it entailed costs. I take great pride in the vast expansion in human freedom that the Enlightenment conferred on so many people, but I also know that the Enlightenment spent little time worrying about those cultural habits that make freedom meaningful and constructive. The family was one of these.

## THE ENLIGHTENMENT

It was in the world most affected by the Enlightenment that we find both its good and bad legacies. There we encounter both remarkable science and personal self-indulgence. There we find human freedom and high rates of crime. There we find democratic governments and frequent divorces. There we find regimes concerned about the poor and a proliferation of single-parent families.

Single-parent families are most common in those nations—England, America, Canada, Australia, France, the Netherlands—where the Enlightenment had its greatest effect. Such families are far less common in Italy, Spain, Eastern Europe, Russia, the Middle East, China, and Japan. It was in the enlightened nations that nuclear rather than extended families became common, that individual consent and not clan control was the basis of a marriage contract, and that divorce first became legal.

But why did the Enlightenment have its greatest effect on the English-speaking world and on northwestern Europe? I think it was because life in those countries had for so long been arranged in ways that provided fertile ground in which human reason and personal freedom could take root and prosper. Alan Macfarlane, the great English anthropologist, has shown that land in England was individually owned as far back as the thirteenth century and possibly even earlier. There, and in similar countries in northwestern Europe, land ownership had established the basis for a slow assertion of human rights and legal defenses. If you own the land, you have a right to keep, sell, or bequeath it, and you have access to courts that will defend those rights and, in defending them, will slowly add more rights.

## LAND OWNERSHIP

Marriage depended on land. Until a young man inherited or bought a piece of property, he was in no position to take a wife. The rule was: no land, no marriage. As a result, English men and women married at a much older age than was true elsewhere. But with the rise of cities and the growth of industrialism, that began to change. Now a man and a woman, already defined by rights that were centuries old, could marry on an income, not on a farm, and so they married at a younger age.

English couples could get married on the basis of their individual consent, without obtaining the formal approval of their parents, though parents still might try to influence these decisions, and among the landed aristocracy such influence was often decisive. But for most people, the old rule of the Roman Catholic church was in force: no marriage was legitimate unless the man and woman freely consented. That rule found its widest observance in countries like England, where individual land ownership and personal rights reinforced it.

In Eastern Europe, to say nothing of the Middle and Far East, a different culture had been created out of a different system for owning land. In many parts of these regions, land lay in the control of families and clans. No individual owned it, and no individual could sell or bequeath it. One man might run the farm, but he did so not on the basis of ownership, but because of his seniority or skill, with the land itself remaining the property of an extended family.

In these places—where courts, unimportant in matters of real estate, tended to be unimportant in other respects as well—human rights were less likely to develop. In clan-based regimes, families often decided what man a woman might marry, and, since family labor worked family-owned land, men and women married at a young age, in hopes of adding many children to the common labor force.

The Enlightenment did not change the family immediately, because everyone took family life for granted. The most important Enlightenment thinkers assumed marriage and denounced divorce. That assumption—and in time that denunciation—slowly lost force, as people gradually experienced the widening of human freedom.

The laws, until well into the twentieth century, made it crystal clear that, though a child might be conceived by an unmarried couple, once born it had to have two parents. There was no provision for the state to pay for a single-parent child, and public opinion strongly and unanimously endorsed that policy.

But by the end of the nineteenth century and the early years of the twentieth, policies changed, and then, slowly, opinion changed. Two things precipitated the change: first, a compassionate desire to help needy children; and second, a determination to end the legal burdens under which women suffered. The first was a powerful force, especially since the aid to needy children was designed to help those who had lost their fathers owing to wars or accidents, as so many did as a consequence of the First World War and of industrial or mining accidents. Slowly, however, a needy child was redefined to include those of any mother without a husband, and not just any who had become a widow.

## EMANCIPATION OF WOMEN

The emancipation of women was also a desirable process. In America and England, nineteenth-century women already had more rights than those in most of Europe, but when married they still could not easily own property, file for a divorce, or conduct their own affairs. By the 1920s most of these restrictions had ended, and once women got the vote, there was no chance of these limitations ever being reinstated.

We should therefore not be surprised that the twenties were an enthusiastic display of unchaperoned dating, provocative dress, and exhibitionist behavior. Had it not been for a time-out imposed by the Great Depression and the Second World War, we would no longer be referring to the sixties as an era of self-indulgence; we would be talking about the legacy of the twenties.

The sixties reinstated trends begun half a century earlier, but now without effective opposition. No-fault divorce laws were passed throughout most of the West, the pill and liberalized abortion laws dramatically reduced the chances of unwanted pregnancies, and popular entertainment focused on pleasing the young. As a result, family law, in Carl Schneider's term, lost its moral basis. It was easier to get out of a marriage than a mortgage. This change in culture was made crystal clear by court decisions. At the end of the nineteenth century, the Supreme Court referred to marriage as a "holy estate" and a "sacred obligation." By 1965 the same court described marriage as "an association of two individuals."

People still value marriage; but it is only that value—and very little social pressure or legal obligation—that sustains it.

But there is another part of the cultural argument, and it goes to the question of why African Americans have such high rates of mother-only families. When black scholars addressed this question, as did W. E. B. DuBois in 1908 and E. Franklin Frazier in 1939, they argued that slavery had weakened the black family. When Daniel Patrick Moynihan repeated this argument in 1965, he was denounced for "blaming the victim."

An intense scholarly effort to show that slavery did little harm to African-American families followed that denunciation; instead, what really hurt them was migrating to big cities where they encountered racism and oppression.

## SLAVERY

It was an astonishing argument. Slavery, a vast and cruel system of organized repression that, for over two centuries, denied to blacks the right to marry, vote, sue, own property, or take an oath; that withheld from them the proceeds of their own labor; that sold them and their children on the auction block; that exposed them to brutal and unjust punishment: all this misery had little or no effect on family life, but moving as free people to a big city did. To state the argument is to refute it.

But since some people take academic nonsense seriously, let me add that we now know, thanks to such scholars as Orlando Patterson, Steven Ruggles, and Brenda E. Stevenson, that this argument was empirically wrong. The scholars who made it committed some errors. In calculating what percentage of black mothers had husbands, they accepted many women's claims that they were widows, when we now know that such claims were often lies, designed to conceal that the respondents had never been married. In figuring out what proportion of slaves were married, these scholars focused on large plantations, where the chance of having a spouse was high, instead of on small ones, where most slaves lived, and where the chance of having a spouse was low. On these small farms, only about one-fifth of the slaves lived in a nuclear household.

After slavery ended, sharecropping took its place. For the family, this was often no great improvement. It meant that it was very difficult for a black man to own property and thus hard for him to provide for the progress of his children or bequeath to them a financial start in life. Being a tenant farmer also meant that he needed help on the land, and so he often had many children, despite the fact that, without owning the land, he could not provide for their future.

The legacy of this sad history is twofold. First, generations of slaves grew up without having a family, or without having one that had any social and cultural meaning. Second, black boys grew up aware that their fathers were often absent or were sexually active with other women, giving the boys poor role models for marriage. Today, studies show that the African-American boys most likely to find jobs are those who reject, rather than emulate, their fathers; whereas for white boys, those most likely to find work are those who admire their fathers.

What is astonishing today is that so many African Americans are married and lead happy and productive lives. This is an extraordinary accomplishment, of which everyone should be proud. But it is an accomplishment limited to only about half of all black families, and white families seem to be working hard to catch up.

But there remains at least one more puzzle to solve. Culture has shaped how we produce and raise children, but that culture surely had its greatest impact on how educated people think. Yet the problem of weak, single-parent families is greatest among the least educated people. Why should a culture that is so powerfully shaped by upper-middle-class beliefs have so profound an effect on poor people? If some intellectuals have devalued marriage, why should ordinary people do so? If white culture has weakened marriage, why should black culture follow suit?

I suspect that the answer may be found in Myron Magnet's book *The Dream and the Nightmare*. When the haves remake a culture, the people who pay the price are the have-nots. Let me restate his argument with my own metaphor. Imagine a game of crack-the-whip, in which a line of children, holding hands, starts running in a circle. The first few children have no problem keeping up, but near the end of the line the last few must run so fast that many fall down. Those children who did not begin the turning suffer most from the turn.

There are countless examples of our cultural crack-the-whip. Heroin and cocaine use started among elites and then spread down the social scale. When the elites wanted to stop, they could hire doctors and therapists; when the poor wanted to stop, they could not hire anybody. The elites endorsed community-based centers to treat mental illness, and so mental hospitals were closed down. The elites hired psychiatrists; the poor slept on the streets. People who practiced contraception endorsed loose sexuality in writing and movies; the poor practiced loose sexuality without contraception. Divorce is more common among the affluent than the poor. The latter, who can't afford divorce, deal with unhappy marriages by not getting married in the first place. My only trivial quarrel with Magnet is that I believe these changes began a century ago and even then built on more profound changes that date back centuries.

Now you probably expect me to tell you what we can do about this, but if you believe, as I do, in the power of culture, you will realize that there is very little one can do. As a University of Chicago professor once put it, if you succeed in explaining why something is so, you have probably succeeded in explaining why it must be so. He implied what is in fact often the case: change is very hard.

The remarkable fact is that today so many Americans value marriage, get married, and want their children to marry. Many often cohabit, but when a child arrives most get married. The ones who don't make their children suffer. But to many people the future means more cohabitation—more "relationships"—and fewer marriages. Their goal is Sweden, where marriage is slowly going out of style.

The difficulty with cohabitation as opposed to marriage has been brilliantly laid out by Linda Waite and Maggie Gallagher in their book *The Case for Marriage*. In it they show that married people, especially men, benefit greatly from marriage: they are healthier, live longer, and are less depressed. But many young men today have not absorbed that lesson. They act as if sex is more important than marriage, worry more about scoring than dating, and are rewarded by their buddies when they can make it with a lot of young women. To them, marriage is at best a long-term benefit, while sex is an immediate preoccupation. This fact supplies us with a sober lesson: the sexual revolution—one that began nearly a century ago but was greatly hastened by the 1960s—was supposed to help make men and women equal. Instead it has helped men, while leaving many women unmarried spectators watching *Sex and the City* on HBO.

One could imagine an effort to change our culture, but one must recognize that there are many aspects of it that no one, least of all I, wants to change. We do not want fewer freedoms or less democracy. Most of us, myself included, do not want to change any of the gains women have made in establishing their moral and legal standing as independent actors with all the rights that men once enjoyed alone. We can talk about tighter divorce laws, but it is not easy to design one that both protects people from ending a marriage too quickly with an easy divorce and at the same time makes divorce for a good cause readily available.

The right and best way for a culture to restore itself is for it to be rebuilt, not from the top down by government policies, but from the bottom up by personal decisions. On the side of that effort, we can find churches—or at least many of them—and the common experience of adults that the essence of marriage is not sex, or money, or even children: it is commitment

---

*Mr. Wilson teaches at Pepperdine University. From "Why We Don't Marry," by James Q. Wilson,* City Journal, *Winter 2002, pages 46–55.*

Originally published in the June 2002 issue of *Current*, pp. 8-12. © 2002 by James Q. Wilson.

# SHOULD YOU STAY TOGETHER FOR THE KIDS?

A controversial book argues that the damage from divorce is serious and lasting, but many argue that the remedy of parents staying hitched is worse than the ailment

**By WALTER KIRN**

ONE AFTERNOON WHEN JOANNE WAS nine years old she came home from school and noticed something missing. Her father's jewelry box had disappeared from its usual spot on her parents' bureau. Worse, her mother was still in bed. "Daddy's moved out," her mother told her. Joanne panicked. She began to sob. And even though Joanne is 40 now, a married Los Angeles homemaker with children of her own, she clearly remembers what she did next that day. Her vision blurred by tears, she searched through the house that was suddenly not a home for the jewelry box that wasn't there.

Time heals all wounds, they say. For children of divorce like Joanne, though, time has a way of baring old wounds too. For Joanne, the fears that her parents' split unleashed—of abandonment, of loss, of coming home one day and noticing something missing from the bedroom—deepened as the years went by. Bursts of bitterness, jealousy and doubt sent her into psychotherapy. "Before I met my husband," she remembers, "I sabotaged all my other relationships with men because I as-

sumed they would fail. There was always something in the back of my head. The only way I can describe it is a void, unfinished business that I couldn't get to."

For America's children of divorce—a million new ones every year—unfinished business is a way of life. For adults, divorce is a conclusion, but for children it's the beginning of uncertainty. Where will I live? Will I see my friends again? Will my mom's new boyfriend leave her too? Going back to the early '70s—the years that demographers mark as the beginning of a divorce boom that has receded only slightly despite three decades of hand wringing and worry—society has debated these children's predicament in much the same way that angry parents do: by arguing over the little ones' heads or quarreling out of earshot, behind closed doors. Whenever concerned adults talk seriously about what's best for the children of divorce, they seem to hold the discussion in a setting—a courtroom or legislature or university—where young folks aren't allowed.

That's changing. The children are grown now, and a number are speaking up,

telling stories of pain that didn't go away the moment they turned 18 or even 40. A cluster of new books is fueling a backlash, not against divorce itself but against the notion that kids somehow coast through it. Stephanie Staal's *The Love They Lost* (Delacorte Press), written by a child of divorce, is part memoir and part generational survey, a melancholy volume about the search for love by kids who remember the loss of love too vividly. *The Case for Marriage* by Linda Waite and Maggie Gallagher (Doubleday) emphasizes the positive, arguing that even rocky marriages nourish children emotionally and practically.

The most controversial book, comes from Judith Wallerstein, 78, a therapist and retired lecturer at the University of California, Berkeley. In *The Unexpected Legacy of Divorce* (Hyperion) she argues that the harm caused by divorce is graver and longer lasting than we suspected. Her work raises a question that some folks felt was settled back in the days of *Love, American Style*: Should parents stay together for the kids?

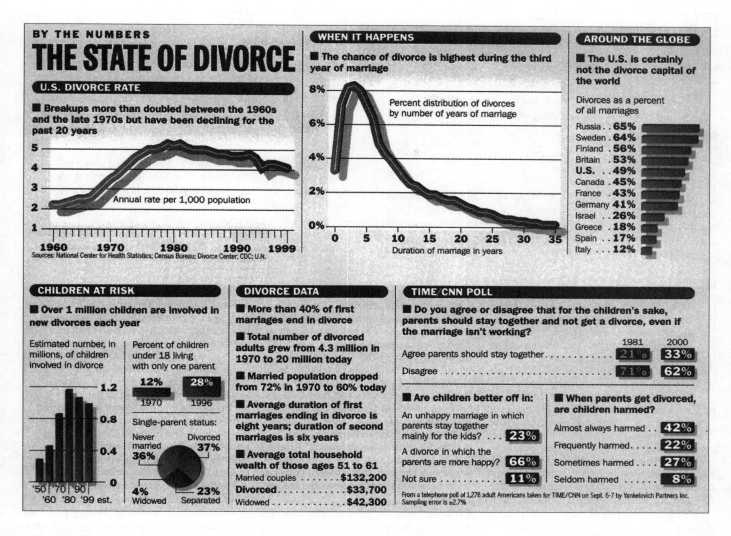

**BY THE NUMBERS**
# THE STATE OF DIVORCE

## U.S. DIVORCE RATE

■ Breakups more than doubled between the 1960s and the late 1970s but have been declining for the past 20 years

Annual rate per 1,000 population

Sources: National Center for Health Statistics; Census Bureau; Divorce Center; CDC; U.N.

## WHEN IT HAPPENS

■ The chance of divorce is highest during the third year of marriage

Percent distribution of divorces by number of years of marriage

Duration of marriage in years

## AROUND THE GLOBE

■ The U.S. is certainly not the divorce capital of the world

Divorces as a percent of all marriages

Russia . . 65%
Sweden . 64%
Finland . 56%
Britain . 53%
U.S. . . 49%
Canada . 45%
France . 43%
Germany 41%
Israel . . 26%
Greece . 18%
Spain . . 17%
Italy . . . 12%

## CHILDREN AT RISK

■ Over 1 million children are involved in new divorces each year

Estimated number, in millions, of children involved in divorce

Percent of children under 18 living with only one parent

12% (1970)  28% (1996)

Single-parent status:
Never married 36%
Divorced 37%
Widowed 4%
Separated 23%

## DIVORCE DATA

■ More than 40% of first marriages end in divorce

■ Total number of divorced adults grew from 4.3 million in 1970 to 20 million today

■ Married population dropped from 72% in 1970 to 60% today

■ Average duration of first marriages ending in divorce is eight years; duration of second marriages is six years

■ Average total household wealth of those ages 51 to 61
Married couples . . . . . . $132,200
**Divorced** . . . . . . . . . . . $33,700
Widowed . . . . . . . . . . . . $42,300

## TIME/CNN POLL

■ Do you agree or disagree that for the children's sake, parents should stay together and not get a divorce, even if the marriage isn't working?

|  | 1981 | 2000 |
|---|---|---|
| Agree parents should stay together | 21% | 33% |
| Disagree | 71% | 62% |

■ Are children better off in:

An unhappy marriage in which parents stay together mainly for the kids? . . . **23%**

A divorce in which the parents are more happy? **66%**

Not sure . . . . . . . . . . **11%**

■ When parents get divorced, are children harmed?

Almost always harmed . . **42%**
Frequently harmed . . . . . **22%**
Sometimes harmed . . . . **27%**
Seldom harmed . . . . . . **8%**

From a telephone poll of 1,278 adult Americans taken for TIME/CNN on Sept. 6-7 by Yankelovich Partners Inc. Sampling error is ±2.7%

---

Listening to children from broken families is Wallerstein's lifework. For nearly three decades, in her current book and two previous ones, she has compiled and reflected on the stories of 131 children of divorce. Based on lengthy, in-depth interviews, the stories are seldom happy. Some are tragic. Almost all of them are as moving as good fiction. There's the story of Paula, who as a girl told Wallerstein, "I'm going to find a new mommy," and as a young woman—too young, it turned out—impulsively married a man she hardly knew. There's Billy, born with a heart defect, whose parents parted coolly and amicably but failed to provide for his pressing medical needs.

It's the rare academic who can make a reader cry. Maybe that's why, with each new installment, Wallerstein's study has created shock waves, shaping public opinion and even the law. Her attention-getting style has proved divisive. For experts in the field of family studies (who tend to quarrel at least as bitterly as the dysfunc-

tional clans they analyze), she's a polarizing figure. To her admirers, this mother of three and grandmother of five, who has been married to the same man for 53 years, is a brave, compassionate voice in the wilderness. To her detractors, she's a melodramatic doomsayer, a crank.

What drew someone from such a stable background to the study of marital distress? At the end of the 1960s, Wallerstein, whose Ph.D. is in clinical psychology, moved from Topeka, Kans., in the ho-hum heartland, to swinging California. "Divorce was almost unheard of in the Midwest," she recalls. Not so on the Gold Coast, the state had just passed its pioneering no-fault divorce law. Wallerstein took a job consulting at a large community mental-health center in Marin County just as the social dam began to crack. "We started to get complaints," she says," from nursery school teachers and parents: 'Our children are having a very hard time. What should we do?'"

The prevailing view at the time, she says, was that divorce was no big deal for

kids. So much for the power of positive thinking. "We began to get all these questions," Wallerstein remembers. "The children were sleepless. The children in the nursery school were aggressive. They were out of control." When Wallerstein hit the library for answers, she discovered there were none. The research hardly existed, so she decided to do her own. She had a hunch about what she would learn. "I saw a lot of children very upset," she says, "but I fully expected that it would be fleeting."

Her hunch was wrong. Paradise for kids from ruptured families wasn't easily regained. Once cast out of the domestic garden, kids dreamed of getting back in. The result more often than not was frustration and anxiety. Children of divorce suffer depression, learning difficulties and other psychological problems more frequently than those of intact families. Some of Wallerstein's colleagues, not to mention countless divorced parents, felt they were being guilt-tripped by a square. They didn't want to hear this somber news.

## DIVORCE/THE DEBATE

"We have to pay attention to what Judy Wallerstein says... It's another reason not to be sanguine about what happens to children following divorce and not to cling to this 1970s opinion that it's no big deal, they'll bounce back, just be happy yourself."
—BARBARA DAFOE WHITEHEAD, *author of* The Divorce Culture: Rethinking Our Commitments to Marriage and Family

"I think [Wallerstein] is wonderful at seeing the trees, but sometimes she misses the forest. For the most part, kids from divorced families are resilient. They bounce back from all the stresses. Some kids are at risk, but the majority are functioning well."
—ROBERT EMERY, *director of the University of Virginia's Center for Children, Families and the Law*

"[My parents] tried to stick it out for an extra year. That year was horrible... It's really devastating when your parents divorce. But it doesn't automatically mean that I wish my parents were still together. People who haven't gone through parental divorce don't really understand that."
—STEPHANIE STAAL, *author of* The Love They Lost: Living with the Legacy of Our Parents' Divorce

"I think the kids are better off if divorce is handled intelligently—that is, if both parents talk to the kids, explain what it is. Let's say each party remarries. The children get the benefit of now four adults in their life, instead of two. If everything works well, the kids benefit."
—LARRY KING, *five-times-divorced TV talk-show host*

Every marriage waxes and wanes... So thinking about getting divorced when things are awful is in some ways a shortsighted view. You're cutting off your foot because you have an ingrown toenail."
—LINDA WAITE, *co-author of* The Case for Marriage: Why Married People Are Happier, Healthier and Better Off Financially

"I'm not suggesting that divorce be outlawed. But people move too quickly without trying to work through their problems in the relationship."
—MARSHALL HERSKOVITZ, *co-creator of TV's* Once and Again

"What most of the large-scale scientific research shows is that although growing up in a divorced family elevates the risk for certain kinds of problems, it by no means dooms children to having a terrible life. The fact of the matter is that most kids from divorced families do manage to overcome their problems and do have good lives."
—PAUL AMATO, *professor of sociology, Penn State University*

Now, decades later, some still don't want to hear her. For parents, her book's chief finding, to be sure, is hardly upbeat or very reassuring; children take a long time to get over divorce. Indeed, its most harmful and profound effects tend to show up as the children reach maturity and struggle to form their own adult relationships. They're gun-shy. The slightest conflict sends them running. Expecting disaster, they create disaster. "They look for love in strange places," Wallerstein says. "They make terrible errors of judgment in whom they choose."

Marcie Schwalm, 26, a Bloomington, Ill, legal secretary whose parents split when she was four, illustrates Wallerstein's thesis well. As a young woman she couldn't seem to stick with the same boyfriend. "I thought guys were for dating and for breaking up with a few weeks later," she says. "I would go into a relationship wondering how it was going to end." Finally, Marcie says, a college beau told her she had a problem. She's married now, and her feelings about divorce have a hard-line, 1950s tone: "Divorce is not something I am going to go through. I would do whatever it takes to keep the marriage together."

Kristina Herrndobler, 17, isn't so sure that harmony can be willed. Now a high

school student in Benton, Ill., she too was four when her parents called it quits. She says she has no memories of the trauma, just an abiding skepticism about marriage and a resolve to settle for nothing less than the ideal man. "I don't want my kids to wind up in a single-parent situation," she says. "And I don't want to have kids with a man I don't want to be married to forever. I don't believe in the fairy tale. I hope it exists, but I really don't believe it does."

And therein lies another problem, according to Wallerstein: the belief, quite common in children of divorce, that marriage is either a fairy tale or nothing. These jittery, idealistic children tend to hold out for the perfect mate—only to find they have a very long wait. Worse, once they're convinced they've found him, they're often let down. High romantic expectations tend to give way, Wallerstein reports, to bitter disillusionments. Children from broken families tend to marry later, yet divorce more often than those from intact homes.

So divorce often screws up kids. In itself, this isn't news, though many experts feel Wallerstein overstates the case. That divorce may screw them up for a long, long time and put them at risk for everything from drug abuse to a loveless, solitary old

age is more disturbing—and even more debatable. Christy Buchanan, a professor of psychology at Wake Forest University and co-author of *Adolescents After Divorce* (Harvard), is typical of Wallerstein's detractors. "I think the main drawback of the sort of research she does is that you can't necessarily generalize it to a broad population," Buchanan says. "The other caution I would put forth is that she has a group of divorced families but no comparison group of nondivorced families. [Perhaps in response to this longstanding complaint, Wallerstein also interviewed children of intact marriages for her new book.] There's some good research suggesting that many of the problems that have been attributed to divorce in children were actually present prior to the divorce."

Not rigorous enough. Too gloomy. Those are the leading raps against Wallerstein. Paul Amato, a sociology professor at Penn state, has researched divorce and children for 20 years, casting the sort of wide statistical net that hardheaded academics favor and Wallerstein eschews as too impersonal. While Amato agrees with her about divorce's "sleeper effect" on children—the problems that crop up only after they're grown—he finds her work a bit of a bummer. "It's a dismal kind of pic-

# Is Divorce Getting a Bum Rap?

KATHA POLLITT

Are Americans a nation of frivolous divorcers who selfishly pursue the bluebird of happiness, oblivious to their children's needs? Divorce opponents like Judith Wallerstein seem to think most parents see divorce as a marvelous opportunity for the whole family. How immature do they think people are? All over America, unhappy spouses lie awake at night wondering if they and their kids can afford divorce—financially, socially, emotionally. Where will they live, how will they pay the bills, will the kids fall apart, will there be a custody battle, what will their families say? The very fact that so many people leave their marriage for a future with so many pitfalls proves that divorce is anything but a whim. Most people I know who split up (not to mention my ex and me) spend years working up to it.

---

## SPLIT DECISIONS: "America doesn't need more 'good enough' marriages"

---

In her new book, Wallerstein argues that children don't care if their parents are happy—they just want the stability of a two-parent household, without which they would later flail through adulthood and have a hard time forming good relationships. This conclusion, like her other gloomy generalizations ("Parenting erodes almost inevitably at the breakup and does not get restored for years, if ever"), is based on a small, nonrepresentative sample of families who were going through divorce in 1971 in affluent Marin County, Calif. Wallerstein looks for evidence that divorce harms kids, and of course she finds it—now well into their mid-30s, her interviews still blame their parents' breakup for every rock on the path to fulfillment—but the very process of participating in a famous ongoing study about the effects of divorce encourages them to see their lives through that lens. What if she had spent as much time studying children whose parents had terrible marriages but stayed together for the kids? How many 35-year-old "children" would be blaming their problems on the nights they hid in their rooms while Mom and Dad screamed at each other in the kitchen? Wallerstein points out many children of divorce feel overly responsible for their parents' happiness. But what about the burden of knowing that one or both of your parents endured years of misery—for you?

As a matter of fact, we know the answer to that question. The baby boomers, who helped divorce become mainstream, were the products of exactly the kind of marriages the anti-divorcers approve of—the child-centered unions of the 1950s, when parents, especially Mom, sacrificed themselves on the altar of family values and the suburban respectability. To today's anti-divorcers those may seem like "good enough" marriages—husband and wife rubbing along for the sake of the children. The kids who lived with the silence and contempt said no thank you.

America doesn't need more "good enough" marriages full of depressed and bitter people. Nor does it need more pundits blaming women for destroying "the family" with what are, after all, reasonable demands for equality and self-development. We need to acknowledge that there are lots of different ways to raise competent and well-adjusted children, which—as according to virtually every family researcher who has worked with larger and more representative samples than Wallerstein's tiny handful—the vast majority of kids of divorce turn out to be. We've learned a lot about how to divorce since 1971. When Mom has enough money and Dad stays connected, when parents stay civil and don't bad-mouth each other, kids do all right. The "good enough" divorce—why isn't *that* ever the cover story?

*Katha Pollitt is an author and a columnist for* The Nation.

---

ture that she paints," he says. "What most of the large-scale, more scientific research shows is that although growing up in a divorced family elevates the risk for certain kinds of problems, it by no means dooms children to having a terrible life."

And what about children raised from the start by single moms? Last month, TIME ran a story about the challenges faced by single women having children of their own. But in all the coverage about how those women are coping, the impact on the kids is sometimes underplayed—and their issues are not that different from those of kids from divorced households. "Some studies have directly compared children who were raised by mothers who are continuously single with mothers who went through a divorce," says Amato. "In general, the outcomes for children seem to be pretty similar. It appears to increase the risk for some types of problems: in con-

duct, in school, in social relations. Neither one appears to be optimal for children."

Besides her conclusions on children's long-term prospects following divorce, Wallerstein makes another major point in her book—one that may result in talk-show fistfights. Here it is: children don't need their parents to like each other. They don't even need them to be especially civil. They need them to stay together, for better or worse. (Paging Dr. Laura!) This imperative comes with asterisks, of course, but fewer than one might think. Physical abuse, substance addiction and other severe pathologies cannot be tolerated in any home. Absent these, however, Wallerstein stands firm: a lousy marriage, at least where the children's welfare is concerned, beats a great divorce.

Them's fighting words.

The shouting has already started. Family historian Stephanie Coontz, author of

*The Way We Never Were: American Families and the Nostalgia Trap* (Basic) questions the value of papering over conflicts for the kids' sake. Sure, some parents can pull it off, but how many and for how long? For many couples," Coontz says, "things only get worse and fester, and eventually, five years down the road, they end up getting divorced anyway, after years of contempt for each other and outside affairs."

Coontz doesn't believe in social time travel. She doesn't think we can go back to *Leave It to Beaver* after we've seen *Once and Again*. Unlike Wallerstein, whose investigation is deep but rather narrow (the families in her original study were all white, affluent residents of the same Northern California county, including non-working wives for whom divorce meant a huge upheaval), Coontz takes a lofty, long view of divorce. "In the 1940s

BOOK EXCERPT

# Fear of Falling

A sense that love is doomed often haunts the offspring of divorce as they grow up and try to build relationships of their own, says a controversial new book based on a 25-year study of 131 children. Here we follow a young woman's painful search for love that can last

BY JUDITH WALLERSTEIN, JULIA LEWIS AND SANDRA BLAKESLEE

WHEN MOST PEOPLE HEAR THE WORD DIVORCE, THEY THINK IT means one failed marriage. The child of divorce is thought to experience one huge loss of the intact family, after which stability and a second, happier marriage comes along. But this is not what happens to most children of divorce. They experience not one, not two, but many more losses as their parents go in search of new lovers or partners. Each of these throws the child's life into turmoil and brings back painful reminders of the first loss.

Children observe their parents' courtships with a mixture of excitement and anxiety. For adolescents, the erotic stimulation of seeing their parents with changing partners can be difficult to contain. Several young teenage girls in the study began their own sexual activity when they observed a parent's involvement in a passionate affair. Children watch their parents' lovers with everything from love to resentment, hoping for some clue about the future. They participate actively as helper, critic and audience. They are not afraid to intervene. One mother returning home from a date found her school-age children asleep in her bed. Since they'd told her earlier that they didn't like her boyfriend, she took the hint. Many new lovers are attentive to the children, regularly bringing little gifts. But even the most charming lovers can disappear overnight. Second marriages with children are much more likely to end in divorce than first marriages.

The experience of Karen, whose identity I have concealed here, is typical of many I have seen. Her father's second wife, who was nice to the children, left without warning three years into the marriage. After she was gone, her father had four more girlfriends who caused him a great deal of suffering when they also left. Karen's mother had three unhappy love affairs prior to her remarriage, which ended after five years. The childhood of Karen and her siblings were filled with a history of new attachments followed by losses and consequent distress for both parents. Karen's brother, at age 30, told me: "What is marriage? Only a piece of paper and a piece of metal. If you love someone, it breaks your heart." In this study, only 7 of the 131 children experienced stable second marriages in which they had good relationships on both sides of the divorced family. Can we be surprised that so many children of divorce conclude that love is fleeting?

When I turn to the notes of my interview with Karen 15 years after her parents' divorce, the image of a young woman crying inconsolably enters my mind. Karen was sitting on the sofa in my old office, with her chin in her hands and elbows on her knees, telling me about her live-in relationship with her boyfriend Nick. "I've made a terrible mistake," she said, twisting a damp tissue into the shape of a rope. "I can't believe I've gotten myself into this. It's what I grew up dreading most and look what happened."

Karen gripped her fingers tightly until her knuckles shone like moons. "What's wrong?" I asked, as gently as I could. "Everything," she moaned. "He drinks beer. He has no ambition, no life goals, no education, no regular job. When I come home after work,

he's just sitting there in front of the TV and that's where he's been all day." Then Karen's voice dropped. "But he loves me," she said in anguish. "He would be devastated if I ever left him." Even in her great distress and anger she was intensely cognizant of her boyfriend's suffering. I thought to myself, this epitomizes Karen—she's always aware of other people's hurts and suffering.

"But then why did you move in with him?"

"I'm not sure. I knew I didn't love him. But I was scared of marriage. I was scared of divorce, and I'm terrified of being alone. When Nick asked me to live with him, I was afraid that I'd get older and that I wouldn't have another chance. I kept thinking that I'd end up lonely like my dad. And Mom."

I looked at this beautiful young woman and shook my head in disbelief. Could she really think that this was all she could hope for? Karen must have read my mind because she quickly said, "I know. People have been telling me how pretty I am since I was a child. But I don't believe it. And I don't care."

"How did you meet Nick?"

She sighed as she answered, "Well, we hardly knew each other in high school. I think that he had a crush on me from afar. Then in my junior year I broke my ankle and during the six weeks that I was hobbling around, he was very kind to me, carrying my stuff and visiting me. He was the only one who took any care of me. He also comes from a divorced family with lots of troubles. When he dropped out of school, I felt very sorry for him."

"Then how did he come back into your life?"

"I was having a real bad time. My brother was getting into serious trouble with the law and my dad wouldn't do anything to help. I was frantic and beginning to realize that all my efforts to hold my family together were wasted. So when Nick asked me to move in with him, I said yes. Anything to get away, even though I knew from the outset he had no plans for the future. After the first day, I said to myself, 'Oh, my God, what did I do?' But at least I knew he won't betray me. At least I'm safe from that."

"Karen, this fear of betrayal is pretty central to you. You keep mentioning it."

"It's been central to my life," she agreed. "Both my parents played around. I saw it all around me. They felt that if you are not getting what you want, you just look elsewhere." (I've never heard anyone put the alternative morality of our divorce culture so succinctly.)

Like a good caregiver child, Karen reinstalled her troubled relationships with her mother and father into her early relationships with men. As rescuers, most young women like Karen are used to giving priority to the needs of others. Karen confessed that she had never in her life thought about what would make her happy. "That would be like asking for the moon," she said. "I was always too worried about my family to ask for me."

*(continued)*

## Fear of Falling *(continued)*

What prompts so many children of divorce to rush into a cohabitation or early marriage with as much forethought as buying a new pair of shoes? Answers lie in the ghosts that rise to haunt them as they enter young adulthood. They live in fear that they will repeat their parents' history, hardly daring to hope that they can do better. Dating and courtship raise their hopes of being loved sky-high—but also their fears of being hurt and rejected. This amalgam of fear and loneliness can lead to multiple affairs, hasty marriages, early divorce, and—if no take-home lessons are gleaned from it all—a second and third round of the same.

Here's how it works: at the threshold of young adulthood, relationships move center stage. But for many that stage is barren of good memories of how an adult man and woman can life together in a loving relationship. The psychological scaffolding they need to construct a happy marriage has been badly damaged by the two people they depended on while growing up. Children learn all kinds of lessons at their parents' knees from the time they are born to the time they leave home. There is no more exciting image to the child than the frame that includes Mom and Dad kissing, fighting, conferring, frowning, crying, yelling or hugging. These thousand-and-one images are internalized, and they form the template for the child's view of how men and women treat each other, how parents and children communicate, how brothers and sisters get along.

Unlike children from intact families, children of divorce in our study spoke very little about their parents' interaction. Parents who divorce may think of their decision to end the marriage as wise, courageous and the best remedy for their unhappiness—indeed, it may be so—but for the child the divorce carries one meaning: the parents have failed at one of the central tasks of adulthood. Together and separately, they failed to maintain the marriage. This failure shapes the child's inner template of self and family. If they failed, I can fail too. And if, as happens so frequently, the child observes more failed relationships in the years after divorce, the conclusion is simple. *I have never seen a man and a woman together on the same beam. Failure is inevitable.*

When I talked with Karen again nine years later, at age 34, she told me on the phone that "I'm in a whole other place than our last meeting. It's all new." As she came through my front door, she looked radiant. I was suddenly aware that in all the years we've known each other, I had rarely seen her happy. She was dressed very simply in black wool slacks, white pullover and herringbone suit jacket. Her stunning blue eyes had a new twinkle that flashed as we greeted each other warmly.

I told her how lovely she looked and congratulated her on her forthcoming marriage. "Who's the lucky man?"

"We're both lucky," she said, settling on the sofa. "Gavin and I did everything differently compared to how I lived my life before." And she launched into her story. Within months of our last meeting, she had moved out of the apartment she shared with Nick and said goodbye. As she had anticipated, he was devastated, begged her to come back, and made her feel guiltier than ever.

"How were you able to leave?" I asked.

She answered slowly, her face pale. "I felt like I was dying. It has to be the hardest thing I've ever done and it took all my courage." She described how she would come home after work and find her partner lying on the couch, waiting for her to take charge. It was just like taking care of her mom. At that point, she realized she had to get out. Her escape took her to the East Coast, graduate school, and ultimately into a dream job—directing a regional public health program for handicapped children.

It was there that Karen met her fiancé, Gavin, an assistant professor of economics. As she told me about him, I smiled and said, "I remember when you thought you didn't have choices. It looks like you've made quite a few recently."

"I decided to take a chance, and I discovered what I want. And I finally figured out what I don't want. I don't want another edition of my relationships with my mom or dad. I don't want a man who is dependent on me."

"And you do want?"

"I want a lover and a husband. I'm no longer frantic to find just anybody because if I have to, I can live alone. I can stand on my own two feet. I'm no longer afraid." And then the sadness around her eyes returned. "But it's not really all behind me. Like I told you, part of me is always waiting for disaster to strike. It never really goes away, never."

In hearing story after story like Karen's, I realized that compared with children from intact families, children of divorce follow a different trajectory for growing up. *It takes them longer.* Their adolescence is protracted and their entry into adulthood is delayed. Children of divorce need more time to grow up because they have to accomplish more: they must simultaneously let go of the past and create mental models for where they are headed, carving their own way. Those who succeed deserve gold medals for integrity and perseverance. Having rejected their parents as role models, they have to invent who they want to be and what they want to achieve in adult life. This is far beyond what most adolescents are expected to achieve.

Children of divorce are held back from adulthood because the vision of it is so frightening. The fact that Karen and others were able to turn their lives around is very good news for all of us who have been worried about the long-term effects of divorce on children. It sometimes took many years and several failed relationships, but close to half of the women and over a third of the men in our study were finally able to create a new template with themselves in starring roles. They did it the hard way—by learning from their own experience. They got hurt, kept going, and tried again. Some had relatives, especially grandparents, who loved them and provided close-up role models. Some had childhood memories from before the divorce that gave them hope and self-confidence. Only a few had mentors, but when they came along they were greatly appreciated. One young man told me, "My boss has been like a father to me, the father that I always wanted and never had." Men and women alike were especially grateful to lovers who stood by them and insisted that they stick around for the long haul. Finally, a third of the men and women in our study sought professional help from therapists and found that they could establish a trusting relationship with another person and use it to get at the roots of their difficulties.

We now come to a final, critical question. What values does this generation hold regarding marriage and divorce? Their vote is clear. Despite their firsthand experience of seeing how marriages can fail, they sincerely want lasting, faithful relationships. No single adult in this study accepts the notion that marriage is going to wither away. They want stability and a different life for their children. They want to do things better than their parents.

REPRINTED FROM THE UNEXPECTED LEGACY OF DIVORCE: A 25 YEAR LANDMARK STUDY, BY JUDITH WALLERSTEIN, JULIA M. LEWIS AND SANDRA BLAKESLEE. © 2000 JUDITH WALLERSTEIN, JULIA LEWIS AND SANDRA BLAKESLEE, PUBLISHED BY HYPERION

# What If They Tough It Out?

**P**eople tend to believe that if a husband and wife are unhappy with each other, their children will also be unhappy. What's left out of the equation are the many families like Gary's, where the parents stay together and try to keep the peace. Gary (whose identity I've concealed) described with gusto his happy memories of childhood play, but had not revealed what he meant by the "indoor version" of his family. "What was that all about?" I asked.

"There was this feeling of tension that you could cut with a knife," Gary replied. "As things got worse between them, there were fewer words and more and more tension. My brother and sister and I spent as much time out of the house as we could."

"Things got pretty bad when I was in junior high school," he said. "One morning, after I knew Dad hadn't been home the night before, I was feeling really low. I guess I was seriously worried that he wouldn't come back. Mom had been all teary-eyed and silent during breakfast. I got on my bike to ride to school but I just couldn't face going. So I rode down to Dad's store. I thought I'd just peek in to see if he was there. He saw me looking and must've sensed something was wrong because he just left off helping a customer and came straight out to me. I remember he looked tired but he also looked kind of alarmed. He asked if anything was wrong at home and looked relieved when I told him there wasn't.

"So we went back into his office and we talked. He said he didn't know why Mom was so angry and suspicious but that sometimes he had to leave because it got to him and made him angry. He pointed to the old leather couch in the office and told me that when he did leave, this was where he slept.

"That was when I asked him if they might divorce. I'll always remember this part. His face went all saggy like he was going to cry, and he reached out and hugged me hard. 'Let me tell you something, Sport. Marriage is like a roller coaster. It has real highs and real lows. The lows have been worse than I thought, and the highs have been better than I thought. The big picture is that I love your mother, and you kids are the high point of our marriage. The picture right now is your mother and I are in a slump, but we'll work our way out of it. I know we will because we love you kids so much. Our marriage has been challenging, but it's been a good ride, and I'm hanging on till the end.'"

Gary was choking up as he recalled his father's words and blinking back tears. Finally, he said, "That was one of the most important conversations of my whole life."

"For me it was definitely better that they stayed together," he said. "But that's because they were great parents. My brother, sister and I never doubted that they loved us. My mom was lonely and, as I look back, probably depressed, but she continued to be very interested in us and our schoolwork and our activities. In other words, our world was protected. But if they *had* split up, I'd lay you bets that my father would have been remarried in a flash. And maybe had a couple more kids. We would have definitely lost out."

"How?"

"He wouldn't have been around for me. I doubt that my mom would have remarried, although who knows? It was better for me and my brother and sister, even if our folks missed out on some goodies of life. I know that's selfish of me."

"Why do you say that?"

"Because I have no idea how unhappy my parents were. After all, there are a lot of other things in life besides kids. Now that I'm an adult, I feel terribly sorry for both of them."

the average marriage ended with the death of the spouse," Coontz says. "But life expectancy is greater today, and there is more potential for trouble in a marriage. We have to become comfortable with the complexity and ambiguity of every family situation and its own unique needs."

That's just a lot of fancy, high-flown talk to Wallerstein and her followers. Ambiguity doesn't put dinner on the table or drive the kids to soccer practice or save for their college education. Parents do. And parents tend to have trouble doing these things after they get divorced. In observing what goes wrong for kids when their folks decide to split, Wallerstein is nothing if not practical. It's not just the absence of positive role models that bothers her, it's the depleted bank accounts, the disrupted play-group schedules, the frozen dinners. Parents simply parent better, she's found, when there are two of them. Do kids want peace and harmony at home? Of course. Still, they'll settle for hot meals.

Wallerstein didn't always feel this way. Once upon a time, she too believed that a good divorce trumped a bad marriage where children were concerned. "The central paradigm now that is subscribed to throughout the country," says Wallerstein, "is if at the time of the breakup people will be civil with each other, if they can settle financial things fairly, and if the child is able to maintain contact with both parents, then the child is home free." Wallerstein helped build this mode, she says, but now she's out to tear it down. "I'm changing my opinion," she says flatly.

The family-values crowd is pleased as punch with Wallerstein's change of heart. Take David Blankenhorn, president of the Institute for American Values. "There was a sense in the '70s especially, and even into the '80s, that the impact of divorce on children was like catching a cold: they would suffer for a while and then bounce back," he says. "More than anyone else in the country, Judith Wallerstein has shown that

that's not what happens." Fine, but does this oblige couples to muddle through misery so that Johnny won't fire up a joint someday or dump his girlfriend out of insecurity? Blankenhorn answers with the sort of certainty one expects from a man with his imposing title. "If the question is, If unhappily married parents stay together for the sake of their kids, will that decision benefit their children?, the answer is yes."

We can guess how the moral stalwarts will answer such questions. What about ordinary earthlings? Virginia Gafford, 56, a pet-product saleswoman in Pawleys Island, S.C., first married when she was 19. The marriage lasted three years. She married again, had a second child, Denyse, and divorced again. Denyse was 14. She developed the classic symptoms. Boyfriends jilted her for being too needy. She longed for the perfect man, who was nowhere to be found. "I had really high expectations," says Denyse. "I wanted Superman, so they wouldn't do what Dad had done." Denyse is in college now and getting fine grades, but her mother still has certain regrets. "If I could go back and find any way to save that marriage, I'd do it," she says. "And I'd tell anyone else to do the same."

For Wallerstein and her supporters, personal growth is a poor excuse for dragging the little ones through a custody battle that just might divide their vulnerable souls into two neat, separate halves doomed to spend decades trying to reunite. Anne Watson is a family-law attorney in Bozeman, Mont., and has served as an administrative judge in divorce cases. She opposes tightening divorce laws out of fear that the truly miserable—battered wives, the spouses of alcoholics—will lose a crucial escape route. But restless couples who merely need their space, in her opinion, had better think twice and think hard. "If people are divorcing just because of choices they want to make, I think it's pretty tough on the kids," Watson says. "Just because you're going to feel better, will they?"

That, of course, is the million-dollar question. Wallerstein's answer is no, they'll feel worse. They'll feel worse for quite a while, in fact, and may not know why until they find themselves in court, deciding where their own kids will spend Christmas. It's no wonder Wallerstein's critics find her depressing.

Does Wallerstein's work offer any hope or guidance to parents who are already divorced? Quite a bit, actually. For such parents, Wallerstein offers the following advice; First, stay strong. The child should be assured that she is not suddenly responsible for her parents' emotional well-being. Two, provide continuity for the child, maintaining her usual schedule of activities. Try to keep her in the same playgroup, the same milieu, among familiar faces and accustomed scenes. Lastly, don't let your own search for new love preoccupy you at the child's expense.

Her chief message to married parents is clear: Suck it up if you possibly can, and stick it out. But even if you agree with Wallerstein, how realistic is such spartan advice? The experts disagree. Then again, her advice is not for experts. It's directed at people bickering in their kitchen and staring up at the ceiling of their bedroom. It's directed at parents who have already divorced and are sitting alone in front of the TV, contemplating a second try.

The truth and usefulness of Wallerstein's findings will be tested in houses and apartments, in parks and playgrounds, not in sterile think tanks. Someday, assuming we're in a mood to listen, millions of children will give us the results.

*—Reported by Jeanne McDowell/*
*Los Angeles, Timothy Padgett/Miami,*
*Andrea Sachs/New York and*
*David E. Thigpen/Chicago*

# Now for the Truth About Americans and
# SEX

## The first comprehensive survey since Kinsey smashes some of our most intimate myths

PHILIP ELMER-DEWITT

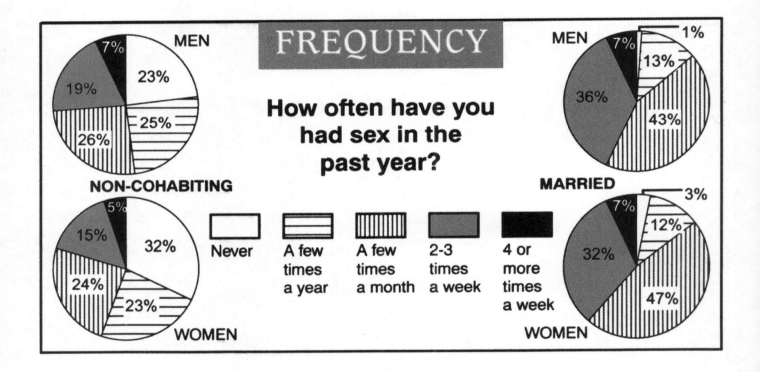

**FREQUENCY**

**How often have you had sex in the past year?**

MEN — NON-COHABITING: 7%, 23%, 25%, 26%, 19%

WOMEN: 5%, 32%, 23%, 24%, 15%

MEN — MARRIED: 7%, 1%, 13%, 43%, 36%

WOMEN: 7%, 3%, 12%, 47%, 32%

Never / A few times a year / A few times a month / 2-3 times a week / 4 or more times a week

IS THERE A LIVING, BREATHING ADULT WHO hasn't at times felt the nagging suspicion that in bedrooms across the country, on kitchen tables, in limos and other venues too scintillating to mention, other folks are having more sex, livelier sex, better sex? Maybe even that quiet couple right next door is having more fun in bed, and more often. Such thoughts spring, no doubt, from a primal anxiety deep within the human psyche. It has probably haunted men and women since the serpent pointed Eve toward the forbidden fruit and urged her to get with the program.

Still, it's hard to imagine a culture more conducive to feelings of sexual inadequacy than America in the 1990s. Tune in to the soaps. Flip through the magazines. Listen to Oprah. Lurk in the seamier corners of cyberspace. What do you see and hear? An endless succession of young, hard bodies preparing for, recovering from or engaging in constant, relentless copulation. Sex is every-

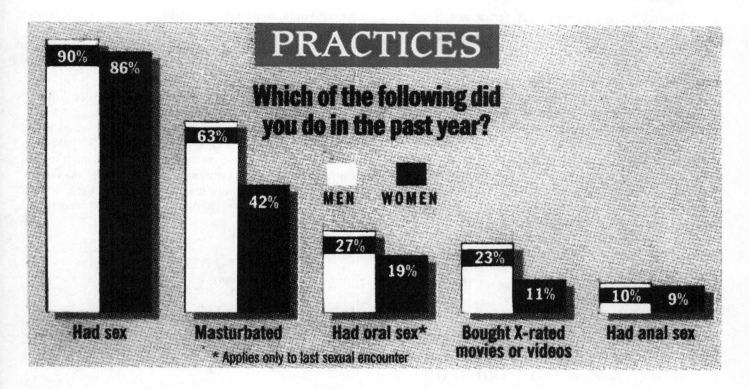

## PRACTICES

### Which of the following did you do in the past year?

**MEN** **WOMEN**

- Had sex — 90% / 86%
- Masturbated — 63% / 42%
- Had oral sex* — 27% / 19%
- Bought X-rated movies or videos — 23% / 11%
- Had anal sex — 10% / 9%

\* Applies only to last sexual encounter

where in America—and in the ads, films, TV shows and music videos it exports abroad. Although we know that not every ZIP code is a Beverly Hills, 90210, and not every small town a Peyton Place, the impression that is branded on our collective subconscious is that life in the twilight of the 20th century is a sexual banquet to which everyone else has been invited.

Just how good is America's sex life? Nobody knows for sure. Don't believe the magazine polls that have Americans mating energetically two or three times a week. Those surveys are inflated from the start by the people who fill them out: *Playboy* subscribers, for example, who brag about their sex lives in reader-survey cards. Even the famous Kinsey studies—which caused such a scandal in the late 1940s and early '50s by reporting that half of American men had extramarital affairs—were deeply flawed. Although Alfred Kinsey was a biologist by training (his expertise was the gall wasp), he compromised science and took his human subjects where he could find them: in boardinghouses, college fraternities, prisons and mental wards. For 14 years he collared hitchhikers who passed through town and quizzed them mercilessly. It was hardly a random cross section.

Now, more than 40 years after Kinsey, we finally have some answers. A team of researchers based at the University of Chicago has released the long-awaited results of what is probably the first truly scientific survey of who does what with whom in America and just how often they do it.

The findings—based on face-to-face interviews with a random sample of nearly 3,500 Americans, ages 18 to 59, selected using techniques honed through decades of po-

litical and consumer polling—will smash a lot of myths. "Whether the numbers are reassuring or alarming depends on where you sit," warns Edward Laumann, the University of Chicago sociologist who led the research team. While the scientists found that the spirit of the sexual revolution is alive and well in some quarters—they found that about 17% of American men and 3% of women have had sex with at least 21 partners—the overall impression is that the sex lives of most Americans are about as exciting as a peanut-butter-and-jelly sandwich.

Among the key findings:

- Americans fall into three groups. One-third have sex twice a week or more, one-third a few times a month, and one-third a few times a year or not at all.

- Americans are largely monogamous. The vast majority (83%) have one or zero sexual partners a year. Over a lifetime, a typical man has six partners; a woman, two.

- Married couples have the most sex and are the most likely to have orgasms when they do. Nearly 40% of married people say they have sex twice a week, compared with 25% for singles.

- Most Americans don't go in for the kinky stuff. Asked to rank their favorite sex acts, almost everybody (96%) found vaginal sex "very or somewhat appealing." Oral sex ranked a distant third, after an activity that many may not have realized was a sex act: "Watching partner undress."

- Adultery is the exception in America, not the rule. Nearly 75% of married men and 85% of married women say they have never been unfaithful.
- There are a lot fewer active homosexuals in America than the oft-repeated 1 in 10. Only 2.7% of men and 1.3% of women report that they had homosexual sex in the past year.

THE FULL RESULTS OF THE NEW SURVEY ARE SCHEDULED to be published next week as *The Social Organization of Sexuality* (University of Chicago; $49.95), a thick, scientific tome co-authored by Laumann, two Chicago colleagues—Robert Michael and Stuart Michaels—and John Gagnon, a sociologist from the State University of New York at Stony Brook. A thinner companion volume, Sex in America: A Definitive Survey (Little, Brown; $22.95), written with New York Times science reporter Gina Kolata, will be in bookstores this week.

# 54% of men think about sex daily. 19% of women do

But when the subject is sex, who wants to wait for the full results? Even before the news broke last week, critics and pundits were happy to put their spin on the study.

"It doesn't ring true," insisted Jackie Collins, author of *The Bitch, The Stud* and other potboilers. "Where are the deviants? Where are the flashers? Where are the sex maniacs I see on TV every day?"

"I'm delighted to hear that all this talk about rampant infidelity was wildly inflated," declared postfeminist writer Camille Paglia. "But if they're saying the sexual revolution never happened, that's ridiculous."

"Positively, outrageously stupid and unbelievable," growled *Penthouse* publisher Bob Guccione. "I would say five partners a year is the average for men."

"Totally predictable," deadpanned Erica Jong, author of the 1973 sex fantasy *Fear of Flying*. "Americans are more interested in money than sex."

"Our Puritan roots are deep," said *Playboy* founder Hugh Hefner, striking a philosophical note. "We're fascinated by sex and afraid of it."

"Two partners? I mean, come on!" sneered *Cosmopolitan* editor Helen Gurley Brown. "We advise our Cosmo girls that when people ask how many partners you've had, the correct answer is always three, though there may have been more."

Europeans seemed less surprised—one way or the other—by the results of the survey. The low numbers tend to confirm the Continental caricature of Americans as flashy and bold onscreen but prone to paralysis in bed. Besides, the findings were pretty much in line with recent studies conducted in England and France that also found low rates of homosexuality and high rates of marital fidelity. (The French will be gratified by what a comparison of these surveys shows: that the average Frenchman and -woman has sex about twice as often as Americans do.)

If the study is as accurate as it purports to be, the results will be in line with the experience of most Americans. For many, in fact, they will come as a relief. "A lot of people think something is wrong with them when they don't have sexual feelings," says Toby, a 32-year-old graduate student from Syracuse, New York, who, like 3% of adult Americans (according to the survey), has never had sex. "These findings may be liberating for a lot of people. They may say, 'Thank God, I'm not as weird as I thought.'"

**SEX ABROAD**

**In your lifetime how many sex partners have you had?**

From foreign studies cited in this survey

Scientists, on the whole, praise the study. "Any new research is welcome if it is well done," says Dr. William Masters, co-author of the landmark 1966 study Human Sexual Response. By all accounts, this one was very well done. But, like every statistical survey, it has its weaknesses. Researchers caution that the sample was too limited to reveal much about small subgroups of the population—gay Hispanics, for example. The omission of people over 59 is regrettable, says Shirley Zussman, past president of the American Association of Sex Educators, Counselors and Therapists: "The older population is more sexually active than a 19-year-old thinks, and it's good for both 19-year-olds and those over 59 to know that."

## PARTNERS

### How many sexual partners have you had since age 18?

MEN

WOMEN

3% HIGH SCHOOL GRADUATES (both sexes)

ALL COLLEGE GRADUATES (both sexes)

None  1  2-4  5-10  11-20  21 or more

The Chicago scientists admit to another possible defect: "There is no way to get around the fact some people might conceal information," says Stuart Michaels of the Chicago team, whose expertise is designing questions to get at those subjects people are most reluctant to discuss. The biggest hot button, he says, is homosexuality. "This is a stigmatized group. There is probably a lot more homosexual activity going on than we could get people to talk about."

## The 2nd most appealing sex act: seeing partner undress

It was, in large part, to talk about homosexual activity that the study was originally proposed. The project was conceived in 1987 as a response to the AIDS crisis. To track the spread of the AIDS virus—and to mount an effective campaign against it—government researchers needed good data about how much risky sexual behavior (anal sex, for example) was really going on. But when they looked for scientific data about sex, they found little besides Kinsey and Masters and Johnson.

So the National Institutes of Health issued a formal request for a proposal, tactfully giving it the bland title "Social and Behavioral Aspects of Fertility Related Behavior" in an attempt to slip under the radar of right-wing politicians. But the euphemism fooled no one—least of all Jesse Helms. In the Reagan and Bush era, any government funding for sex research was suspect, and the Senator from North Carolina was soon lobbying to have the project killed. The Chicago team redesigned the study

several times to assuage conservative critics, dropping the questions about masturbation and agreeing to curtail the interview once it was clear that a subject was not at high risk of contracting AIDS. But to no avail. In September 1991 the Senate voted 66 to 34 to cut off funding.

The vote turned out to be the best thing that could have happened—at least from the point of view of the insatiably curious. The Chicago team quickly rounded up support from private sources, including the Robert Wood Johnson, Rockefeller and Ford foundations. And freed of political constraints, they were able to take the survey beyond behavior related to AIDS transmission to tackle the things inquiring minds really want to know: Who is having sex with whom? How often do they do it? And when they are behind closed doors, what exactly do they do?

The report confirms much of what is generally accepted as conventional wisdom. Kids *do* have sex earlier now: by 15, half of all black males have done it; by 17, the white kids have caught up to them. There *was* a lot of free sex in the '60s: the percentage of adults who have racked up 21 or more sex partners is significantly higher among the fortysomething boomers than among other Americans. And AIDS *has* put a crimp in some people's sex lives: 76% of those who have had five or more partners in the past year say they have changed their sexual behavior, by either slowing down, getting tested or using condoms faithfully.

But the report is also packed with delicious surprises. Take masturbation, for example. The myth is that folks are more likely to masturbate if they don't have a sex partner. According to the study, however, the people who masturbate the most are the ones who have the most sex. "If you're having sex a lot, you're thinking about sex a lot," says Gagnon. "It's more like Keynes (wealth begets wealth) and less like Adam Smith (if you spend it on this, you can't spend it on that)."

Or take oral sex. Not surprisingly, both men and women preferred receiving it to giving it. But who would have guessed that so many white, college-educated men would have done it (about 80%) and so few blacks (51%)? Skip Long, a 33-year-old African American from Raleigh, North Carolina, thinks his race's discomfort with oral sex may owe much to religious teaching and the legacy of slavery: according to local legend, it was something slaves were required to do for their masters. Camille Paglia is convinced that oral sex is a culturally acquired preference that a generation of college students picked up in the '70s from seeing Linda Lovelace do it in *Deep Throat*, one of the first—and last—X-rated movies that men and women went to see together. "They saw it demonstrated on the screen, and all of a sudden it was on the map," says Paglia. "Next thing you knew, it was in *Cosmo* with rules about how to do it."

More intriguing twists emerge when sexual behavior is charted by religious affiliation. Roman Catholics are the most likely to be virgins (4%) and Jews to have the most sex partners (34% have had 10 or more). The women most likely to achieve orgasm each and every time (32%) are, believe it or not, conservative Protestants. But Catholics edge out mainline Protestants in frequency of intercourse. Says Father Andrew Greeley, the sociologist-priest and writer of racy romances: "I think the church will be surprised at how often Catholics have sex and how much they enjoy it."

## Among women 29% always had an orgasm during sex

But to concentrate on the raw numbers is to miss the study's most important contribution. Wherever possible, the authors put those figures in a social context, drawing on what they know about how people act out social scripts, how they are influenced by their social networks and how they make sexual bargains as if they were trading economic goods and services. "We were trying to make people think about sex in an entirely different way," says Kolata. "We all have this image, first presented by Freud, of sex as a riderless horse, galloping out of control. What we are saying here is that sex is just like any other social behavior: people behave the way they are rewarded for behaving."

Kolata and her co-authors use these theories to explain why most people marry people who resemble them in terms of age, education, race and social status, and why the pool of available partners seems so small—especially for professional women in their 30s and 40s. "You can still fall in love across a crowded room," says Gagnon. "It's just that society determines whom you're in the room with."

That insight, applied to AIDS, leads the Chicago team to a conclusion that is sure to get them into trouble. America's AIDS policy, they say, has been largely misdirected. Although AIDS spread quickly among intravenous drug users and homosexuals, the social circles these groups travel in are so rigidly circumscribed that it is unlikely to spread widely in the heterosexual population. Rather than pretend that AIDS affects everyone, they say, the government would be better advised to concentrate its efforts on those most at risk.

That's a conclusion that will not sit well with AIDS activists or with many health-policy makers. "Their message is shocking and flies against the whole history of this epidemic," says Dr. June Osborn, former chair of the National Commission on AIDS. "They're saying we don't have to worry if we're white, heterosexual adults. That gets the public off the hook and may keep parents from talking to their kids about sex. The fact is, teens are at enormous risk for experimentation."

## Of married people, 94% were faithful in the past year

Other groups will find plenty here to make a fuss about. Interracial couples are likely to take offense at the author's characterization of mixed-race marriages as unlikely to succeed. And right-to-life activists who believe abortion is widely used as a cruel form of birth control are likely to be unconvinced by the finding that 72% of the women who have an abortion have only one.

Elsewhere in the study, the perceptual gulf between the sexes is reminiscent of the scene in *Annie Hall* where Woody Allen tells his psychiatrist that he and Annie have sex "hardly ever, maybe three times a week," and she tells hers that they do it "constantly; I'd say three times a week." In the Chicago study, 54% of the men say they think about sex every day or several times a day. By contrast, 67% of the women say they think about it only a few times a week or a few times a month. The disconnect is even greater when the subject turns to forced sex. According to the report, 22% of women say they have been forced to do sexual things they didn't want to, usually by someone they loved. But only 3% of men admit to ever forcing themselves on women. Apparently men and women have very different ideas about what constitutes voluntary sex.

But the basic message of *Sex in America* is that men and women have found a way to come to terms with each other's sexuality—and it is called marriage. "Our study," write the authors, "clearly shows that no matter how sexually active people are before and between marriages... marriage is such a powerful social institution that, essentially, married people are all alike—they are faithful to their partners as long as the marriage is intact."

Americans, it seems, have come full circle. It's easy to forget that as recently as 1948, Norman Mailer was still

# HOMOSEXUALITY

MEN

2.7% In the past year

7.1% Since puberty

1.3%

3.8%

**Have you had sex with someone of your gender?**

**Are you sexually attracted to people of the same gender?**

6.2%

4.4%

WOMEN

using the word fug in his novels. There may have been a sexual revolution—at least for those college-educated whites who came of age with John Updike's swinging *Couples*, Philip Roth's priapic *Portnoy* and Jong's *Fear of Flying*—but the revolution turned out to have a beginning, a middle and an end. "From the time of the Pill to Rock Hudson's death, people had a sense of freedom," says Judith Krantz, author of *Scruples*. "That's gone."

It was the first survey—Kinsey's—that got prudish America to talk about sex, read about sex and eventually watch sex at the movies and even try a few things (at least once). Kinsey's methods may have been less than perfect,

but he had an eye for the quirky, the fringe, the bizarre. The new report, by contrast, is a remarkably conservative document. It puts the fringe on the fringe and concentrates on the heartland: where life, apparently, is ruled by marriage, monogamy and the missionary position. The irony is that the report Jesse Helms worked so hard to stop has arrived at a conclusion that should make him proud. And it may even make the rest of us a bit less anxious about what's going on in that bedroom next door.

**—Reported by Wendy Cole/Chicago, John F. Dickerson/New York and Martha Smilgis/Los Angeles**

# Shades of Gay

**With AIDS no longer an all-consuming crisis, the battle for tolerance
has moved to schools, churches, offices and the frontiers of family life.**

## By John Leland

IN THEIR SMALL TOWN IN CENTRAL PENNSYLVANIA, GARY and Greg, both in their late 30s, are known to neighbors simply as "the guys." The town is fairly conservative, and the two men thought twice before buying a house there. But Greg grew up nearby and trusted the people. In two years they've had few bad experiences. They call each other "honey" in the grocery store, and the children of their straight friends call them "uncle" and "uncle." At Gary's office, his straight co-workers tend to be more up on gay issues than he is, not to mention the plot lines from "Will & Grace." "They realize we have the same worries they do," says Gary. "Now in tax season, they'll say, 'That sucks that you can't put Greg on your return.'" Yet within this cocoon of small-town bonhomie, the two men and their friends straddle the paradox of gay life in 2000: with every increment of progress in politics, Hollywood and the workplace, there arise new nodes of friction.

No longer bracketed by the AIDS crisis or the daily thrum of over bigotry, gays and straights are engaging in each other's lives in more intimate ways than ever before, with a contradictory mixture of progress and resistance. In the following pages, NEWSWEEK explores the often-disorienting frontiers of a struggle no longer easily defined by protests or rabid rhetoric: the thorny play between gays and straights in the family, the schools, the military and the church.

Across the country, men and women like Gary and Greg negotiate lives that would have been hard to imagine just a few years ago. Open homosexuals cut an unprecedented profile in politics, on television and movies, and in the mundane vicissitudes of even small-town America. With role models like rock star Melissa Etheridge and her partner, Julie Cypher, more couples are having or adopting children, and so engaging in the civic life of schools, day-care centers and sports leagues. Employers are increasingly extending health benefits to same-sex partners. For gay teens, whose experience has often been one of dark isolation, about 700 high schools now have gay-straight alliances. And the Internet has be-

come a boundless mecca for gay social life. Even Republicans are taking at least cautious note of the rising political bloc. After some awkward sputtering, George W. Bush last week agreed to consider meeting with the gay Log Cabin Republicans, a tentative but landmark step for a party and candidate that actively court constituencies opposed to gay rights. "The anti-gay vote," says Democratic Rep. Barney Frank, who is openly gay, "is shrinking."

---

By many measures, tolerance has grown. In a NEWSWEEK Poll, **83%** of Americans say gays deserve job protection, up from **56%** in a 1977 survey.

Benefits are still controversial. Only **58%** think gay spouses are entitled to health insurance, and **54%** feel partners should get Social Security checks.

---

But this tide of good news describes only one half of the paradox. Last week California passed Proposition 22, becoming the 31st state to pass a new law banning same-sex marriages (Colorado will soon become the 32d). These are key losses in what has become one of the most contentious fronts of the gay-rights movement. Against the protest of gay groups, Paramount TV announced an upcoming show of Dr. Laura Schlessinger, whose radio broadcasts reach 20 million listeners, and who has called homosexuality a "biological error" and gay sex "deviant." Hate crimes like the murder of Matthew Shepard and Pfc. Barry Winchell, beaten to death in his bunk at Fort Campbell, Ky., last July, shatter the most deeply cherished notions of security. Gay people of color, in particular, often find themselves buffeted by competing biases. "Holding hands walking down the street?" asks Kevin McGruder, executive director of Gay Men of African Descent in New York. "That's not something I'd do in Harlem." For the first time, more gay and bisexual black and Latino men than whites were diagnosed with AIDS in 1998. For gays and lesbians, as well as their families and friends, this push-pull between progress and resistance cuts directly through their lives—how to live in a culture that loves Rupert Everett but kills Barry Winchell?

This ambivalence plays out in two new NEWSWEEK polls—one of the general public, the other of gays, lesbians and bisexuals—that draw strikingly different lines of perceived acceptance and discrimination. About two thirds of the general public say they have contact with openly gay people. This familiarity has brought a level of comfort. Fewer (46 percent, down from 54 percent in 1998) say they believe homosexuality is a sin, while a high percentage think gays should have equal rights in employment (83 percent) and housing (78 percent), and that gay spouses should get benefits from health insurance (58 percent) and Social Security (54 percent). A small majority of gays, lesbians and bisexuals (56 percent) say straight people are becoming more tolerant. Only 9 percent say straights are less tolerant. (Polling gays is notoriously tricky, and this sample, provided by a marketing company, is likely to be more upscale and openly gay than the larger gay and lesbian population.)

On more intimate questions, though, straight people are not always so comfortable. For all their expressed good will toward homosexuals, 57 percent are opposed to gay marriage; 50 percent say gays should not adopt; 35 percent oppose gays serving openly in the military; 36 percent say gays should not teach elementary school. Six in 10 gay men and women perceive "a lot" of discrimination against homosexuals. "Gays and lesbians as a group are still among the most despised minorities," says Columbia University researcher Alan Yang, who has analyzed a wide array of nonpartisan polls. For all the process of recent years, he says, the public still ranks gays on a par with undocumented immigrants.

In her home in conservative Orange County, Calif., last week, Denise Penn, 40, felt the bitter sting of this contradiction. Penn, who is bisexual, has always felt comfortable in her community. "In my home life," she says, "I'm a mom and people I meet just treat me that way. When some dykey-looking women come over to my house, my neighbors just casually wave hi." But the battle over Proposition 22, the ban on gay marriage, shook her. Neighbors displayed a sea of blue and yellow signs reading PROTECT MARRIAGE. She wanted to put up a red sign opposing the initiative, but her 15-year-old son worried. "He's afraid people will hurt me," she says.

The courts and the political arena reflect the conflicted instincts of the nation at large. As California and Colorado were moving to ban gay marriage, Vermont's House Judiciary Committee earlier this month approved a bill

# A Force to Be Reckoned With at the Polls

Increasingly affluent and politically involved, openly gay voters are wielding more power, and state legislatures are toughening up protections for gay citizens.

**Election turnout**
PERCENTAGE OF SELF-IDENTIFIED GAY, LESBIAN AND BISEXUAL VOTERS

| 1990 | 92* | 94 | 96* | 98 |
|------|-----|----|-----|-----|
| 1.3 | 2.2 | 1.6 | 5.0 | 4.2 |

*PRESIDENTIAL ELECTIONS

**Comparable clout**
PERCENTAGE OF TOTAL ELECTORATE

| Union households | 22.7% |
|------------------|-------|
| Senior citizens (65+) | 19.6 |
| African-Americans | 10.2 |
| Latinos | 5.3 |
| Gays/lesbians/bisexuals | 4.2 |
| Jews | 2.6 |
| Asian-Americans | 1.2 |

**Hate-crimes laws expand across the nation (Dec. 1999)**

SEXUAL ORIENTATION AND GENDER  |  SEXUAL ORIENTATION  |  DO NOT HAVE LAWS BASED ON SEXUAL ORIENTATION  |  DO NOT HAVE HATE-CRIMES LAWS

SOURCES: VOTER NEWS SERVICE; "OUT AND VOTING II," BY ROBERT W. BAILEY; NATIONAL GAY AND LESBIAN TASK FORCE

that would recognize same-sex "civil unions" (the bill must still go before the whole House and Senate). The state's auditor, Ed Flanagan, is now running to become the first openly gay man elected to the U.S. Senate. His eight-year career in office, he maintains, has been neither helped nor hurt by his sexual orientation. "The most significant thing about coming out [in 1995]," he says, "was that there really was no change."

On a Sunday afternoon in Pennsylvania, Gary and Greg and their friends grapple with their mixed fortunes. Instead of rhetorical fury, they alternate between casual ease and an edge of nuanced grievance. They mention a mutual friend—goodhearted, straight, liberal. "But he doesn't think gay people should adopt," says Barbie Sunderlin, 37, a courier for Federal Express. "Ed," a dentist, says his brother and sister accept him, but don't want their kids to know he's gay. "I guess there must be something wrong with what I am," he says. Peggy Lichty, 41, who runs a small business, complains that her local Blue Cross/Blue Shield underwriter doesn't offer a plan that would enable her to cover her employees' domestic partners. Even acceptance, says Sunderlin, echoing a lament from the civil-rights movement, has come at the cost of self-censorship. "We make our in-roads in society because we purposely make ourselves mainstream. Not that you deny your individuality or your sexuality. But you don't automatically say what you think."

These are the subtle conflicts that shape life in the diminuendo of the AIDS crisis. Until very recently, the framework for such struggles didn't even exist. Just six years ago, says Beatrice Dohrn, legal director of the Lambda Legal Defense and Education Fund, "the gay-marriage project… was considered on the loony fringes of the movement. Judges would say children shouldn't be in the custody of gay couples and that's it. Now, having children is a serious option. It's a sea change." Such are the growing pains of a maturing movement. Three decades

after the Stonewall Riots in New York's Greenwich Village, it's these intimate battles, the home fires, that have become the fire this time.

*With* DEBRA ROSENBERG, NADINE JOSEPH, VICTORIA SCANLAN STEFANAKOS *and* MICHAEL CRONIN

FOR THIS NEWSWEEK POLL, PRINCETON SURVEY RESEARCH ASSOCIATES INTERVIEWED 1,303 ADULTS MARCH 3-10. THE MARGIN OF ERROR WAS + /- 5 PERCENTAGE POINTS. THE NEWSWEEK POLL © 2000 BY NEWSWEEK, INC.

# When CAREERS Collide

## More and more couples are grappling with a modern dilemma: How do you reconcile conflicts in a union of equals in the business world?

By Susan Caminiti

CARLEY RONEY AND HER HUSBAND, David Liu, probably spend more time talking about weddings than any other couple in America. Co-founders of the on-line wedding site theknot.com, theirs is a world consumed with bridal gowns, honeymoons, and china patterns. Yet on the subject of their own union, silence reigned. "We've always wanted to keep it a secret that we're married, but eventually it came out," says Roney from theknot.com's offices in Manhattan's bustling Soho district.

> **"There are no easy answers when it comes to figuring out who will be the high–flier and who will sit back."**

While she admits that it might appear a little strange for the founders of the premier wedding spot on the Web to have hidden their own marriage, the 32-year-old Roney makes no bones about their reasoning. "It's considered a business risk," she says matter-of-factly. If you think she's

paranoid, consider the grilling the pair got from potential investors during their pre-IPO road show in November 1999. "Basically they were asking, 'If one of you had to fire the other one, could you do it? Or if we had to fire one of you, would the other one be able to deal with it?'" Roney recounts.

Theknot.com's founders and potential backers all implicitly understood a fact of modern life that is rarely acknowledged, at least out loud: Two-career couples are more likely than ever to be on a collision course. "When both people are firmly invested in their careers, there are no easy answers when it comes to figuring out who will be the high-flier and who will sit back," says Jane Bermont, a senior consultant at WFD, a Watertown, Massachusetts, firm that specializes in work/life issues.

Not so long ago, when couples spoke of career conflict, it usually meant he had the career, she had the conflict. Even if the wife had a job, the husband was probably the primary breadwinner, and if sacrifices had to be made at work, she would make them. But today a woman is likely to be just as invested in her career as a man is. In 1990, 303,000 women earned more than $75,000 a year. In 1999, more than 1.7 million women reached that mark. And 23 percent of wives outearn their husbands, according to the most recent data from the U.S. Bureau of Labor Statistics.

But while the notion that a woman is serious about her career may not raise eyebrows anymore, it does raise some sticky situations. And we're not just talking about who will take care of the kids (although that's part of it). Today, couples find themselves trying to decide how to live together while working for business competitors, or whether they can live together at all after one of them is offered a transfer to another city. They deal with issues that can arise when a wife makes more money than her husband or with the perception that a woman is riding her husband's coattails if both are successful in the same industry.

Couple by couple, case by case, men and women are trying to sort out what has become a very millennial dilemma: How do you reconcile conflicts in a union of two equals in the business world?

"In the last five years we've had a lot of couples dealing with this," says Cecile Burzynski, vice president and COO of LeaderSource, a Minneapolis-based career coaching firm. "Many people don't know how to start or how they are going to solve it." Burzynski and her staff sit down with couples, first individually and then together, to get them talking about what they value. Some come to LeaderSource on their own, others are sent by an employer, but the common denominator, she says, is that they are at a loss as to how to resolve these kinds of issues in a fair way. "If they have a committed relationship, they find a way to work it out," Burzynski says. "If not, they've found an easy out."

At ITS WORST, a career conflict can be devastating. To take one recent example, Jeanine Pirro, district attorney for New York State's Westchester County, had her career knocked off track by her husband's poor judgment. In 1998 DNA tests revealed that Albert Pirro, a prominent businessman, was the father of a teenage girl whose mother has sued for child support. Last May he was convicted, along with his brother, of federal tax fraud. Jeanine Pirro herself hasn't been charged with any wrongdoing, but political experts say the upheaval was one of the primary reasons she wasn't tapped to run for the U.S. Senate against Hillary Clinton when New York Mayor Rudolph Giuliani dropped out of the race.

"Clearly Jeanine Pirro was one of the stars of the Republican Party in the state," says George Arzt, a New York political strategist. "Her future was unlimited. I think it's much more difficult for her now." Shades of Geraldine Ferraro, whose political career was never the same after her husband was accused of shady business dealings back in the 1980s.

This kind of high-profile career conflict might be eye-catching, but more benign strife often lurks in the subtext of the news. When Christiane Amanpour, the hard-hitting war reporter for CNN, was transferred to London in 1997, her husband, James Rubin, left his post as Madeleine Albright's right-hand man at the State Department to write and be a part-time caretaker to their newborn son. Willow Bay, co-anchor of CNN's *Moneyline,* has called the issue of working through career conflict "the defining challenge of our generation." She should know—when her husband, Bob Iger, got the job as president and COO of Disney last February, she had to persuade her bosses at CNN to allow her to work from the West Coast.

> # "We didn't argue, but it was strange. I honestly don't know if he thought I'd never actually be offered the job."

Of course, most couples don't have the star wattage to command such a solution. Five years ago, Joan Overlock was working for a large New York advertising agency and living in the city with her husband, Bo, an entertainment marketing consultant. Looking for something new, she was receptive when a headhunter called about a senior marketing position at The Limited clothing company—even though the job was in Columbus, Ohio. "I told Bo I was going out to Columbus to talk to [The Limited CEO] Les Wexner and he basically said, 'Go for it,'" Overlock recalls.

That interview turned into a series of meetings over several months with various Limited senior executives. "I was really excited about the opportunity at this point, but I wanted to know from Bo if I should keep pursuing it or just drop it now," she says. He never indicated that he wasn't ready to pack it all up and go. But when the offer came through—and she accepted—he was shocked. "We didn't argue about it, but it was strange. I honestly don't know if Bo thought I'd never actually be offered the job, or that I would [never] actually take it," Overlock says. "I think somehow he was thinking, 'She's a New Yorker. She'll never move to Ohio.'"

Would she have taken the job if he'd refused to move? There's a long pause before Overlock answers the question, a pause that makes it clear that no wasn't really an option. "I would have tried to convince him that this was the right move," she says evenly. "There would have been further conversations."

Bo supervised the construction of their new home in Columbus rather than look for work for the first year. With the house complete, however, he found his job search rather dismal. "Jobs in the entertainment industry just don't exist in Columbus," he says. "It definitely put a wedge in our marriage," Joan acknowledges. "I was completely immersed in this new job for the first year, and even though Bo was working on our house, I know he felt abandoned. It was almost like a reversal of how it used to be when the husband got transferred and the wife had to create this new social life. But it's easier for a woman. Women can get into socialization easier with things like schools, churches, etc. But this just didn't provide what he needed to feel fulfilled."

Eventually, things got so tense that the couple began seeing a marriage counselor. "His frustration with our situation was translating into anger, and that anger was directed at me," Joan says. "We just stopped communicating. I think at that point we both knew he couldn't stay in Columbus." After widening his search, Bo landed a job with Radiowave.com, a Chicago company that provides Internet streaming service to radio stations and record labels. Whenever possible he flies from Columbus to Chicago on Monday morning and returns home Thursday night. In Chicago he has an apartment within walking distance of his office, but "not much of a social life," he says. "I do this because I'm a real believer in water-cooler dynamics, that you have to show your face at work to stay in the loop."

Transferring a married employee puts a strain not only on the relationship, but on the company as well. According to a recent study by corporate relocation consulting firm Forward Mobility, 13 percent of employees who relocated left their jobs in the first year, more than three times the average national attrition rate. When the transferee is a woman and the husband receives no career assistance—and only 38 percent do, according to the latest annual Atlas Van Lines Corporate Relocation Survey—Forward Mobility reports that the annual attrition rate leaps to 18 percent.

Today, when Bo rejoins the family on the weekends, he and Joan take their dogs for long walks and use the time to talk about whatever is on their minds. Eventually Joan believes she, Bo, and their 12-year-old daughter Hannah will live together again full-time. "The growth and rewards I've had since joining The Limited I never would have experienced had I stayed where I was in New York," she says. "So it's important that we all try to make this arrangement work. But I know this isn't something you can do indefinitely."

FOR OTHER COUPLES, the trouble isn't too much distance, it's too little. Annika Pergament and Michael O'Looney have been husband and wife since 1996. Before they were married, they were competitors: She was an anchor/reporter for local cable news outlet NY1, he a more seasoned general assignment reporter for New York's CBS affiliate. When they would cross paths at a press conference or a raging fire, Pergament felt his experience far surpassed her own. "Michael never did anything to make me feel like I wasn't doing a good job. It was all in my head," she says. "But I used to tell him that I hated seeing him at sites. It made me so nervous."

A few years ago, for example, the pair were both assigned to cover the story of a police officer in the Bronx who had been shot. Pergament started her shift after the story had been unfolding and found herself trying to catch up. "The NY1 truck and the CBS truck were parked side by side and Michael and I were both doing live shots for the morning news," she recalls. "Since I wasn't there from the beginning I didn't have a lot of the facts and it was just aw-

ful. I told him, 'I can't stand this.' I mean, can you imagine anything worse than being nervous to begin with, but then I'm standing next to my boyfriend, who's very good at what I'm trying to do?"

> **"I think that compromise breeds resentment: You're giving up what you want to make the other person happy. But delayed gratification—that's different."**

Last January, when Pergament joined the CBS affiliate's news department to cover the consumer reporter beat and breaking news, new issues arose. On the whole, she's glad they work at the same station, and even on the same story at times, but the hours can be a problem—she works 9 AM to 6 PM, he from 3 PM to about 11 PM—and sometimes shoptalk seems unavoidable. "We have so much else to talk about, but somehow it always gets back to who we saw that week, or the stories we've been working on," she says.

Pergament says that despite the gap in experience, she doesn't feel like she's in his shadow at the station. "If he was doing well and I wasn't, that would be hard, I think. But I don't think CBS looks at the two of us and says there can be only one rising star with this couple. We have different names and separate agents and I think our work has to speak for itself. New York is too important a market for them to keep me on if I wasn't doing a good job, no matter who I'm married to."

COMMUNICATION, self-confidence, clear boundaries—experts say that the same strategies that work in solving many problems in a marriage should be brought to bear in career conflicts as well. When the issue is a deadlock that allows only one career can move ahead, for example, the answer may depend on the couple's goals. If it's money or security, they may choose to push the career that brings in the most income; if one person is facing a once-in-a-lifetime opportunity, pay may be less of an issue.

The saving grace for many couples is remembering that today's decision doesn't have to be the last word. The career leader can switch off several times. "The key to the whole thing is negotiability and flexibility. You have to revisit and renegotiate," says Tina Tessina, a psychotherapist who counsels couples and individuals in Long Beach, California. "I think compromise breeds resentment: You're giving up what you want to make the other person happy. But delayed gratification—that's different."

Tessina says of the 10 or so couples she sees each week, two or three are struggling with these kinds of problems. "I have been seeing more of it," she says. "During the past 15 years it's been constantly on the rise."

While some couples solve their dilemmas by haggling over the kitchen table or talking it through with therapists like Tessina, others are turning to programs specifically created to help with career conflict. Jane Bermont's firm has held a handful of seminars at major corporations over the past few years designed for high-potential dual-career couples. For a day and a half, participants talk about the benefits and challenges of being in such a relationship, aiming to define what's important to each participant as an individual, as one half of a couple, and as a professional. For the sponsoring company, the exercise not only eases tension among employees, it helps the corporation understand what it needs to do to keep both of the people happy.

"I wish them well," says consultant Azriela Jaffe, who's spoken with hundreds of men and women for the on-line newsletter she writes for couples, many of whom work together (azriela.com). As the author of several books on relationships and business—including *Honey, I Want to Start My Own Business,* a guide for entrepreneur couples—Jaffe has written about the issue for years. She says that the temptation for corporations to "tie things up in neat little H.R. packages" assumes that there are concrete solutions.

"The truth is, there aren't. A company can say it's designed a program to put a couple on an equal track. But then what happens when one spouse gets a promotion halfway around the world?" she says. "All bets are off. And it's up to the couple to figure out how to make it work, not the company."

---

SUSAN CAMINITI interviewed Heidi Miller in the September issue of WORKING WOMAN.

# Where Everyone's a MINORITY

**Welcome to SACRAMENTO, America's most integrated city.
What's life like in this melting pot, and why is there still racial tension?**

## By RON STODGHILL and AMANDA BOWER

SACRAMENTO

Sequoia Way is easy for travelers to overlook. Nestled in the middle-class neighborhood of Village Park on the south side of Sacramento, Calif., it is an unremarkable stretch of single-story frame houses. But if you stroll a bit along the winding road and visit Sequoia Way's residents, you will quickly realize there's something extraordinary about this street.

You will meet Tom and Debra Burruss, who moved onto the street a couple of years ago. He's black and she's white, but on Sequoia the interracial union doesn't stand out. The Burrusses' next-door neighbors are also minorities, a Vietnamese couple named Ken Wong and Binh Lam. Living directly across are the Cardonas, a Hispanic-and-white couple. And nearby are the Farrys, a Japanese- and-white pair. In fact, sprinkled throughout the street are more flavors than you can get at Baskin-Robbins—Mexicans, African Americans, East Indians, Asians, you name it.

Now head downtown to William Land Elementary School. Here the classrooms are so ethnically diverse that teachers are considering switching from celebrating individual cultural holidays, like Black History Month, Cinco de Mayo and Chinese New Year, to holding a multiethnic festival. Of Land's 347 kids, 189 speak a language other than English at home. Immigrant parents are so common in Sacramento's public schools that one child volunteered that her father is also a foreigner—he's from New York.

Or go over to Downtown Plaza mall and chat with teenage couples like Kayla, 17, and Gerald, 18. Kayla's mother is white, and her father is black; Gerald's mother is Japanese, and his dad is black. As they munch pizza in a bustling food court as diverse as a U.N. cafeteria, Kayla shrugs her shoulders at the notion of same-race friendships. "Personally, it doesn't matter what color you are," she says. "I am mixed, he is mixed, and most everybody is mixed."

So it goes in America's most integrated city, as determined in research for TIME by the Civil Rights Project at Harvard University (*see box on next page*). In Sacramento everyone's a minority—including whites. Of the city's inhabitants, 41% are non-Hispanic white, 15.5% are black, 22% are Hispanic and 17.5% are Asian/Pacific Islander. Although many cities are diverse (think New York City or Los Angeles), in Sacramento people seem to live side by side more successfully. The city got that way thanks in part to affordable real estate for middle-class households (the black population has dropped in the Bay Area but increased in Sacramento over the past 10 years) as well as innovative housing programs for low-income families. In addition, state-government agencies and college campuses are sprinkled throughout the city, providing stable, well-paid, equal-opportunity employment.

But while Sacramento approaches an ideal for integration, it certainly isn't paradise. Beneath the multicolored surface, the city's 407,018 inhabitants vacillate between racial harmony and ethnic tension. You see a Sikh casually strolling into a Mexican restaurant for takeout, an Eskimo and a white punk hanging out together downtown. But you also see black and Hispanic parents outraged because their kids' test scores lag behind those of whites and Asians in integrated schools. And you hear Anne Gayles-White, the N.A.A.C.P. chapter president, saying "There's still too much hatred and racism in a city like this."

Sacramento's Crayola culture is no statistical anomaly. Indeed, it may well be a sign of the times. Non-Hispanic whites still account for 69% of the U.S. population and maintain a predominant share of the nation's fiscal and political power. But by 2059 at the latest, according to U.S. Census figures, there will no longer be a white majority in America. Sacramento, then, provides perhaps the clearest view into the nation's future—a glimpse into what our neighborhoods, schools, churches and police forces may look like just a few decades from now.

## 70 LANGUAGES, ONE SYSTEM

Three weeks ago, Yun Qian (Cindy) Zhong, a sixth-grader assigned to Randy Helms' homeroom, walked into William Land Elementary School for the first time. She had all the gifts of a model student—intelligence, friendliness and an eagerness to learn. There was just one problem: Zhong, an immigrant from Canton, China, didn't speak a word of English.

Helms didn't panic. His students and their parents hail from as far away as Vietnam, Mexico, Germany, Portugal, Panama and, fortunately, China. By the end of Zhong's second week,

Helms, with help from the Cantonese-speaking students in his class, had taught Zhong to count past 10 as well as to answer yes and no to questions translated for her.

A William Land education doesn't come easy. The school is located in a poor community downtown (90% of Land's kids qualify for free lunch), the classes are big (Helms alone teaches 32 students) and language barriers are routine (many kids' parents speak no English). Kids are tested for English proficiency within 30 days of enrolling; most score from 1 to 5 out of a maximum of 10. Across Sacramento, educators face similar challenges. How does a school district of 53,400 students communicate with a parent group that speaks more than 70 languages? And perhaps even more pressing, how much do cultural differences contribute to the fact that Latino and African-American children do not perform as well on standardized tests as white and Asian kids in the city's integrated schools?

Take John F. Kennedy High School, which at first blush is a picture of integration, with 21% white students, 22% black, 35% Asian and 16% Latino (the remainder are primarily Pacific Islanders, Filipinos and American Indians). J.F.K. routinely ships top graduates to Ivy League schools. But while the typical Asian kid has a 3.01 grade-point average, African-American kids score 1.85. What's going on? School district superintendent Jim Sweeney attributes the gap to class differences. J.F.K. students come from two neighborhoods—a middle-class area known as the Pocket, and a low-income, predominantly black and Hispanic part of town called Meadowview. Lower-income parents, he says, are often less able to spend time helping their kids with homework and encouraging them to learn. "Some surveys say poor children actually hear a million less words a year in the formative years," he says.

That explanation is too simplistic for Patricia Gándara, a University of California at Davis professor of education and Sacramento resident. She believes that teachers and administrators stereotype students on the basis of race. There are plenty of examples—from the teacher who asked a Latino boy if his parents had jobs (his mother was a school principal) to the Mexican child in an advanced-placement class who was asked whether she was Asian (her classmates couldn't imagine that a Latina could perform so well). "The schools make assumptions along class lines about which parents care and which don't, and parents and children begin to read those signs very early," Gándara says.

The district is making some progress in closing the gap. One effective method: home visits, which foster a relationship between teachers and parents and encourage working together to meet a child's needs. Suggested by a parent in 1998, the program helped boost reading scores in the district's elementary schools 36% and math scores 73% (reading and math scores are still only at the 46th and 59th national percentile, respectively).

## THE MOST SEGREGATED HOUR

IT IS SUNDAY MORNING IN SACRAMENTO'S Meadowview community, and hundreds of Russian-speaking immigrants—men in dark suits, women in traditional head scarves, children excited about the latest X-box game—are thronging into the First Slavic Evangelical Baptist Church. A couple of blocks away, African

---

## WHY SACRAMENTO?

In determining Sacramento to be the most integrated major U.S. city, the Civil Rights Project at Harvard University, using raw data from the U.S. Census Bureau. focused on metropolitan areas that have at least half the national population share of the three main minority groups (not less than 6.3% African American, 2.1% Asian, 6.2% Hispanic). Using a measure known as the "dissimilarity index," researchers looked at the integration of those three groups with each other and with whites, then weighted the scores to account for specific minorities' varied histories. Black-white integration, in this analysis, is assigned more value than Asian-white. Places where the military is a major employer were eliminated, because barracks and military housing skew results. Last, experts compared the ethnic makeup of local public schools with that of the overall school-age population (a close match suggests that integration is stable).

---

Americans fill the sanctuary at Twenty-Fourth Street Baptist Church to listen to the Rev. Samuel Mullinax preach the same Gospel. An hour later, Latinos begin filing into the pews of nearby St. Anne's Catholic Church for a Spanish-language Mass. Meadowview residents live together, but many pray separately.

More than 30 years ago, Martin Luther King Jr. famously said that "the 11 o'clock hour on Sunday is the most segregated hour in American life." It's an indictment that still carries weight today, as an estimated 90% of Americans worship primarily with members of their race or ethnicity. Yet Sacramento's complex social tapestry challenges conventional notions that racial segregation in worship is a failure of America's national ideal of equality. Sometimes segregation is driven not by bigotry but by language barriers and cultural heritage.

When Ukrainian immigrant Tamila Demyanik says, through an interpreter, that "the church is the major part of my life," it is no understatement. To the Demyaniks, First Slavic is a lifeline in a foreign land. Her husband buys bread at First Slavic and checks its bulletin board and a Russian phone book for community information. Longtime church members accustomed to America provide emotional support to newcomers and help them negotiate thickets of red tape in health care, housing and more.

Kevin Armstrong, a United Methodist pastor and director of the Religion and Public Teaching Project, based in Indianapolis, Ind., concedes that segregation, whether voluntary or compulsory, seems at odds with religious ideals. But he argues that the outcome often justifies the practice, particularly in immigrant communities. "They preserve their tradition," Armstrong explains, "sing in their native language, eat the food of their own culture, [and are] with people who remember what their land looks like and who their people are."

## SHADES OF BLUE

CRUISING DEL PASO HEIGHTS in an unmarked police car, Chou Vang, 33, gestures toward a section of tired apartment houses

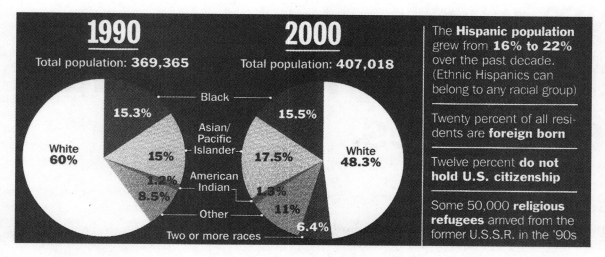

**1990**
Total population: **369,365**

White 60%
Black 15.3%
Asian/Pacific Islander 15%
American Indian 1.2%
Other 8.5%

**2000**
Total population: **407,018**

White 48.3%
Black 15.5%
Asian/Pacific Islander 17.5%
American Indian 1.3%
Other 11%
Two or more races 6.4%

The **Hispanic population** grew from **16% to 22%** over the past decade. (Ethnic Hispanics can belong to any racial group)

Twenty percent of all residents are **foreign born**

Twelve percent **do not hold U.S. citizenship**

Some 50,000 **religious refugees** arrived from the former U.S.S.R. in the '90s

and talks about gang violence. "Back in Laos, the Hmong are a minority ethnic group," he explains, "and the ethnic Lao ruled and ran the country. They have carried their old tensions to this country."

Vang is a police officer with the Sacramento police department, assigned to the problem-oriented policing unit. He is also a Laos-born member of the Hmong. The combination—his cop instincts and Hmong sensibility—enables Vang to be an effective negotiator in Hmong cases, including recurring episodes of gang violence between north-side teens and another Hmong gang in the southern part of town. Vang works on cases of all types, and frequently they involve drugs. In Del Paso Heights methamphetamines are the drug of choice. In Sacramento just last week federal authorities indicted 10 people on charges of importing *yaba*, a candy-flavored amphetamine.

The Sacramento police department has had difficulty attracting immigrant officers and people of color. White men still make up 46% of the department's staff; women swell the Caucasian ranks to 70%. Hispanics of any race account for 12%, blacks 8% and Asians 8%. Concern about racial profiling led the department to launch a study of its practices in 2000, and its first report found that 27% of drivers stopped by police were African American although African Americans make up only 15.5% of the local population. Despite such controversies, Vang feels he made the right move in signing up. "Occasionally someone will tell me to go back to my own country," he says. "But for the most part, I don't think they see me as an Asian. They just see me as a police officer."

## ALL OF ME

WHEN MARIKO FERRONATO WAS 3 YEARS OLD, she would regularly quiz her mother about which half of her was white and which was Japanese. "I thought there was a physical line that divided the Japanese me from the Caucasian me," says Ferronato,

now 18 and a high school senior. A soccer goalie who plays the violin and has her eye on pre-med studies, Ferronato says her racial identity developed in stages. At her mostly white elementary school, she considered herself a white person "who happened to eat a lot of sticky rice." But in the ninth grade at her diverse high school, another student, who is white, called her a "cheating Jap." It hit hard. "I then tried to focus primarily on my Japanese side, completely ignoring my white side, as if to make up for all those years," she says.

In the 2000 U.S. Census, 24 in 1,000 people said they were multiracial (it's the first time Census pollers asked the question). It's often said with pride. While people of mixed race were once portrayed as tragic figures in movies, such as 1934's *Imitation of Life*, its 1959 remake and 1960's *I Passed for White*, today's pop-culture scene is bursting with mixed-race heroes, from movie tough guys Vin Diesel and The Rock to golfer Tiger Woods and rising tennis star James Blake to singers like Alicia Keys and Norah Jones. Sacramento is ahead of the curve; 2 of every 10 babies born here are multiracial. When those babies grow up and start marrying—a national survey shows more than 90% of today's teens approve of interracial marriage—the numbers will climb even higher.

It took time—and a feeling of not quite belonging at an Asian students' club—for Ferronato to finally realize that she is neither Japanese nor white. She is both. "Now I believe in the theory of hybrid vigor," she says. "A specimen derived from two different species has the strongest traits of both sides."

BUT PEOPLE ARE NOT PLANTS, AND THEORIES are not proofs. Sacramento, as a city, is still searching to find its best self, its strongest traits. Single-race parents of mixed-race children can offer guidance to their kids but not always full understanding. Sacramento is on a similar, unchaperoned journey. Will hybrid theory hold? Who can tell? But the blossoms will be something to see.

# UNIT 4

# Stratification and Social Inequalities

## Unit Selections

## Key Points to Consider

- Explain why you believe that technology could reduce or increase social inequalities.

- What inequalities do you find unacceptable and what inequalities do you find acceptable?

- Why is stratification such an important theme in sociology?

- Which social groups are likely to rise in the stratification system in the next decade? Which groups will fall? Why?

- How does stratification along income lines differ from stratification along racial or gender lines?

- Do you think women and blacks are treated fairly in America? Are changes needed in the policies that deal with discrimination? Why or why not?

 **Links: www.dushkin.com/online/**
These sites are annotated in the World Wide Web pages.

**Americans With Disabilities Act Document Center**
*http://www.jan.wvu.edu/links/adalinks.htm*

**American Scientist**
*http://www.amsci.org/amsci/amsci.html*

**Give Five**
*http://www.independentsector.org/give5/givefive.html*

**Joint Center for Poverty Research**
*http://www.jcpr.org*

**NAACP Online: National Association for the Advancement of Colored People**
*http://www.naacp.org*

**Patterns of Variability: The Concept of Race**
*http://www.as.ua.edu/ant/bindon/ant270/lectures/race/race1.htm*

**The Urban Institute**
*http://www.urban.org/welfare/overview.htm*

People are ranked in many different ways—by physical strength, education, wealth, or other characteristics. Those who are rated highly often have power over others, special status, and prestige. The differences among people constitute their life chances, the probability that an individual or group will be able to obtain the valued and desired goods in a society. These differences are referred to as stratification, the system of structured inequalities in social relationships.

In most industrialized societies, income is one of the most important divisions among people. Karl Marx described stratification in terms of class rather than income. For him social class referred mainly to two distinct groups: those who control the means of production and those who do not. This section examines the life chances of the rich and the poor and of various disadvantaged groups, which best demonstrates the crucial features of the stratification system in the United States.

The first subsection of this unit deals with the differences between classes and income levels. Inequality of income has increased, but so has equality of opportunity. Isabel Sawhill, in her article "Still the Land of Opportunity?" presents an up-to-date picture of inequality in America with special emphasis on the degree of equality of opportunity. The changes in the past decade are mixed. In the last article, Geoffrey Colvin explains why executive compensation has risen to absurd levels that are often unrelated to performance. He also explains why this absurdity will continue.

The American welfare system is addressed in the second subsection of unit 4. The first article describes the generous welfare system for the rich, and the next describes the stingy and disappearing welfare system for the poor. First, Donald Barlett and James Steele explain how corporations milk federal, state, and local governments of billions of dollars. It comes as no surprise to a student of society that the political economy is set up to benefit the upper class and the powerful but the extent of that bias, when pointed out, can shock us anyway. The next article on welfare reviews the research analyzing the results of the 1996 welfare reform. Caseloads have declined over 50 percent, and 60 percent of those who leave welfare are working, but much of this change may be due to the economy. Isabel Sawhill concludes that the reform has had positive impacts in moving welfare mothers to the labor force, but she also reviews many concerns about its effects in the current recession.

The most poignant inequality in America is the gap between blacks and whites. Recently there has been considerable good news that the gap has been closing and many indicators that quality of life has improved for blacks. In the next article both Ed Marciniak and Don Wycliff discuss changes in racism. Marciniak argues that racism has very mild consequences today while Wycliff argues that even though blacks have made wonderful progress since the mid-sixties, nevertheless, racism continues and will not be eliminated as long as both blacks and whites keep griping about unfairness. A cooperative spirit is needed. In the next article, the authors demonstrate the prevalence of prejudice and hatred in America and how quickly hatred toward a group can evolve. Since September 11, 2001, hatred toward Muslims has erupted despite calls for tolerance from President George Bush and other public leaders. One explanation of hatred and prejudice against entire groups is social identity theory. People have a powerful drive to divide people into groups, identify with one group, and develop negative views of some of the out groups. Fortunately, "people who are concerned about their prejudices have the power to correct them." The next article discusses the problem of integrating different groups in the context of massive immigration into the United States. Can so many newcomers be assimilated into American culture? According to Anne Wortham, the United States has been quite successful in assimilating immigrants, most of whom want what America stands for when they come. They support democracy and other American institutions and are willing to work hard to get ahead. Relatively high and rising intermarriage rates demonstrate increasing assimilation, but continuing housing segregation is one indicator of impediments to assimilation.

The last subsection of unit 4 deals with sex inequalities. In the first article of the section, Judy Olian documents the many forms of sex inequality. She also explains why the inequality persists. Besides discrimination, she blames quite different formative experiences for boys and girls and the different attitudes that result from them, as well as several factors that operate in adult life. In the next article, Toni Nelson describes the worldwide oppression of women and the frequent violence done to them. Some of these injustices result from pure greed and exploitation. Female genital mutilation (FGM) is one aspect of unequal rights for women that has come to the attention of the American public, because some women have sought political asylum in the United States to escape this practice.

The articles in this unit portray tremendous differences in wealth and life chances among people. Systems of inequality affect what a person does and how he or she does it. An important purpose of this unit is to help you become more aware of how stratification operates in social life.

# Still the land of opportunity?

## ISABEL V. SAWHILL

This article is based, in part, on *Getting Ahead: Economic and Social Mobility in America*, by Daniel P. McMurrer and Isabel V. Sawhill, Urban Institute Press, Washington, D.C., 1998.

AMERICA is known as "the land of opportunity." But whether it deserves this reputation has received too little attention. Instead, we seem mesmerized by data on the distribution of incomes which show that incomes are less evenly distributed than they were 20 or 30 years ago. In 1973, the richest 5 percent of all families had 11 times as much income as the poorest one-fifth. By 1996, they had almost 20 times as much. But it is not only the distribution of income that should concern us. It is also the system that produces that distribution.

Indeed, I would argue that one cannot judge the fairness of any particular distribution without knowing something about the rules of the game that gave rise to it. Imagine a society in which incomes were as unequal as they are in the United States but where everyone had an equal chance of receiving any particular income—that is, in which the game was a completely unbiased lottery. Although some, especially those who are risk adverse, might blanch at the prospect of losing, and might wish for a more equal set of outcomes a priori (as most fatuously argued by John Rawls), others might welcome the chance to do exceedingly well. But—and this is the important point—no one could complain that they hadn't had an equal shot at achieving a good outcome. So the perceived fairness of the process is critical, and the rules governing who wins and who loses matter as much as the outcomes they produce.

In talking about this issue, we often invoke the phrase "equal opportunity," but we seldom reflect on what we really mean by "opportunity," how much of it we really have, and what we should do if it's in short supply. Instead, we have an increasingly sterile debate over income equality. One side argues for a redistribution of existing incomes, through higher taxes on the wealthy and more income support for the poor. The other side argues that inequality reflects differences in individual talent and effort, and as such is a spur to higher economic growth, as well as just compensation for unequal effort and skill. If there is any common ground between these two views, it probably revolves around the idea of opportunity and the measures needed to insure that it exists.

## Opportunity first

The American public has always cared more about equal opportunity than about equal results. The commitment to provide everyone with a fair chance to develop their own talents to the fullest is a central tenet of the American creed. This belief has deep roots in American culture and American history and is part of what distinguishes our public philosophy from that of Europe. Socialism has never taken root in American soil.

Public opinion is only one reason to refocus the debate. Another is that the current emphasis on income inequality begs the question of how much inequality is too much. Virtually no one favors a completely equal distribution of income. Inequality in rewards encourages individual effort and contributes to economic growth. Many would argue that current inequalities far exceed those needed to encourage work, saving, and risk taking, and further that we need not worry about the optimal degree of inequality in a society that has clearly gone beyond that point. But the argument is hard to prove and will not satisfy those who believe that inequality is the price we pay for a dynamic economy and the right of each individual to retain the benefits from his or her own labor. In light of these debates, if any public consensus is to be found, it is more likely to revolve around the issue of opportunity than around the issue of equality.

A final reason why opportunity merits our attention is that it gets at the underlying processes that produce inequality. It addresses not just the symptoms but the causes of inequality. And a deeper understanding of these causes can inform not only one's sense of what needs to be done but also one's sense of whether the existing distribution of income is or is not a fair one.

## Three societies

Consider three hypothetical societies, all of which have identical distributions of income as conventionally measured. The first society is a meritocracy. It provides the most income to those who work the hardest and have the greatest talent, regardless of class, gender, race, or other characteristics. The second one, I will call a "fortune-cookie society." In this society, where one ends up is less a matter of talent or energy than pure luck. The third society is class-stratified. Family background in this society is all important, and thus you need to pick your parents well. The children in this society largely end up where they started, so social mobility is small to nonexistent.

The United States and most other advanced countries are a mixture of these three ideal types. Given a choice between the three, most people would probably choose to live in a meritocracy. Not only do the rules determining success in a meritocracy produce greater social efficiency but, in addition, most people consider them inherently more just. Success is dependent on individual action. In principle, by making the right choices, anyone can succeed, whereas in a class-stratified or fortune-cookie society, people are buffeted by forces outside their control. So, even if the distribution of income in each case were identical, most of us would judge them quite differently. We might even prefer to live in a meritocracy with a less equal distribution of income than in a class-stratified or fortune-cookie society with a more equal distribution. Indeed, social historians have found this to be the case. The American public accepts rather large disparities in income and wealth because they believe that such disparities are produced by a meritocratic process. Even those at the bottom of the distribution believe that their children will do better than they have. It is this prospect, and the sense of fairness that accompanies it, that has convinced the American body politic to reject a social-welfare state.

For the last 25 years, the top one-fifth of the population has been improving their prospects while the other 80 percent has lagged behind. Yet no one has rebelled. The many have not imposed higher taxes on the few. (Small steps in this direction were taken in 1993, but the Democratic president who proposed them later apologized to a group of wealthy donors for doing so.) Even welfare recipients tell survey researchers that they consider the new rules requiring them to work at whatever job they can get fair. They plan on "bettering themselves." Such optimism flies in the face of studies suggesting that women on welfare (and those similar to them) will earn poverty-level wages for most of their lives. But it is an optimism that is characteristically, if in this case poignantly, American.

Several points need to be made about our purported meritocracy. The first is that even a pure meritocracy leaves less room for individual agency than is commonly believed. Some of us are blessed with good genes and good parents while others are not. The second is that the United States, while sharing these inherent flaws with other meritocracies, remains a remarkably dynamic and fluid society. Although it is not a pure meritocracy, it has moved closer to that ideal than at any time in its past. The third point is that, in the past, a rapid rate of economic growth provided each new generation with enhanced opportunities. It was this fact, in large part, that contributed to our image as the land of opportunity. But a mature economy cannot count on this source of upward mobility to leaven existing disparities; it needs instead to repair its other two opportunity-enhancing institutions: families and schools. The remainder of this essay elaborates on each of these points.

## The inherent limits of a meritocracy

In a meritocracy, one would expect to find considerable social and economic fluidity. In such a system, the abler and more ambitious members of society would continually compete to occupy the top rungs. Family or class background, per se, should matter little in the competition while education should matter a lot.

The social-science literature contains a surprising amount of information on this topic. Based on my own reading of this literature, I would argue that social origins or family background matter a good deal. Not everyone begins the race at the same starting line. The kind of family into which a child is born has as much or more influence on that child's adult success than anything else we can measure. Yes, education is important too, but when we ask who gets a good education, it turns out to be disproportionately those from more advantaged backgrounds. Well-placed parents are much more likely to send their children to good schools and to encourage them to succeed academically. In short, although not as evident as in a class-stratified society, even in a meritocracy one had better pick one's parents well.

Why do families matter so much? There are at least three possibilities. The first is that well-placed parents can pass on advantages to their children without even trying: They have good genes. The second is that they have higher incomes, enabling them to provide better environments for their children. The third is that they are simply better parents, providing their children an appropriate mix of warmth and discipline, emotional security and intellectual stimulation, and preparation for the wider world.

It has proved difficult to discover which of these factors is most important. However, as Susan Mayer demonstrates in her recent book, *What Money Can't Buy*, the role of material resources has probably been exaggerated.

Most studies have failed to adjust for the fact that parents who are successful in the labor market have competencies that make them good parents as well. It is these competencies, rather than the parents' income, that help their children succeed. I don't want to leave the impression that income doesn't matter at all. It enables families to move to better neighborhoods; it relieves the stresses of daily living that often produce inadequate parenting; and, most obviously, it enables parents to purchase necessities. Still, additional income assistance, although possibly desirable on other grounds, is not likely to produce major changes in children's life prospects.

Genes clearly matter. We know this from studies of twins or siblings who have been raised apart. However, IQ or other measures of ability are at least somewhat malleable, and differences in intelligence only partially explain who ends up where on the ladder of success. Good parenting and an appropriate home environment are much harder to measure, but studies suggest that they may explain a substantial portion of the relationship between family background and later success in school or in the labor market. In addition, children with two parents fare much better than those with only one, in part because they have higher incomes but also because the presence of a second parent appears, according to all of the evidence, to be beneficial in and of itself.

So, for whatever reason, families matter. Unless we are willing to take children away from their families, the deck is stacked from the beginning. And even if one could remove children from their homes, there would still be the pesky little matter of differences in genetic endowments. Since a meritocracy has no good way of dealing with these two fundamental sources of inequality, it is a pipe dream to think that it can provide everyone with an equal chance. If we want a society in which there is less poverty and more equality, we will have to work harder and more creatively to compensate for at least some of these initial advantages and disadvantages.

## How much social mobility?

Whatever its flaws, a meritocracy is clearly better than some of the alternatives. Although economic and social mobility may be inherently limited, it exists. But just how much of it do we actually have in the United States? Do families matter so much that children can rarely escape their origins? Do people move up and down the economic ladder a little or a lot? Before attempting to answer these questions, let us consider a simple example of a society consisting of only three individuals: Minnie, Mickey, and Mighty.

Assume that Minnie, Mickey, and Mighty start with incomes (or other valued goods) of $20,000, $30,000, and $40,000 respectively. Now imagine that Minnie's children do extremely well, moving from an income of $20,000 to one of $40,000. Mighty's children, by contrast, fall in status or well-being from $40,000 to $20,000. Mickey's situation doesn't change. This is the sort of social mobility we would expect to find in a meritocracy. It is a story of rags to riches (or the reverse) in a generation. *Note that the distribution of income, as conventionally measured, has not changed at all.* As Joseph Schumpeter once put it, the distribution of income is like the rooms in a hotel—always full but not necessarily with the same people.

This same rags-to-riches story can occur over a lifetime as well as between generations. Those at the bottom of the income scale often move up as they accumulate skills and experience, add more earners to the family, or find better jobs. Those at the top may move down as the result of a layoff, a divorce, or a business failure. Thus any snapshot of the distribution of incomes in a single year is unlikely to capture the distribution of incomes over a lifetime. For example, in a society in which everyone was poor at age 25 but rich at age 55, the distribution of annual incomes for the population as a whole would be quite unequal, but everyone would have the same lifetime incomes!

Now note that it is theoretically possible for the distribution of income to become more unequal at the same time that the Minnies of the world are improving their status. Is this what happened over the last few decades in the United States? The answer is yes and no. On the one hand, we know that there is a lot of income mobility within the population. Every year, about 25 percent or 30 percent of all adults move between income quintiles (say, from being in the bottom one-fifth of the income distribution to being in the second lowest fifth.) This rate increases with time, approaching 60 percent over a 10-year period. So there is considerable upward and downward movement. A lot of the Minnies in our society move up, and a lot of the Mightys move down. A few of the Minnies may even trade places with the Mightys of the world, as in our example. On the other hand, most people don't move very far; many remain stuck at the bottom for long periods; and some apparent moves are income reporting errors. (These are particularly large among the very poor and the very wealthy whose incomes tend to come from unearned sources that are difficult to track and that they may be reluctant to reveal.) Most importantly, from the data we have, there is no suggestion of more mobility now than there was 20 or 30 years ago. So one can't dismiss complaints about growing income inequality with the argument that it has been accompanied by *more* opportunity than in the past for everyone to share in the new wealth.

But what about Minnie's and Mighty's children? Suppose we look at mobility across generations instead of looking at it across their own life cycles? Here, the news is much more positive. Social mobility in America appears to have increased, at least since 1960, and probably going back to the middle of the last century (though the data for measuring such things is much better for the more recent period). This conclusion is based on studies done by Michael Hout, David Grusky, Robert Hauser,

David Featherman, and others—studies that show less association between some measure of family background and eventual adult career success now than in the past. This association has declined by as much as 50 percent since the early 1960s, according to Hout.

What has produced this increase in social mobility? The major suspects are a massive broadening of educational opportunities, the increased importance of formal education to economic success, and more meritocratic procedures for assigning workers to jobs (based on "what you know rather than who you know"). In addition, the extension of opportunities to some previously excluded groups—most notably women and blacks—has produced greater diversity in the higher, as well as the lower, ranks.

## How much economic mobility?

Now return to our three-person society and consider a second scenario. In this one, the economy booms, and Minnie, Mickey, and Mighty all double their initial incomes from $20,000, $30,000, and $40,000 to $40,000, $60,000, and $80,000. Clearly, everyone is better off, although the relative position of each (as well as the distribution of income) is exactly the same as before. It is this sort of economic mobility, rather than social mobility per se, that has primarily been responsible for America's reputation as the land of opportunity. In other words, the growth of the economy has been the most important source of upward mobility in the United States; it is the reason that children tend to be better off than their parents. In a dynamic economy, a farmer's son can become a skilled machinist, and the machinist's son a computer programmer. Each generation is better off than the last one even if there is no social mobility. (Class-based differentials in fertility aside, social mobility—as distinct from economic mobility—is, by definition, a zero-sum game.)

But, as important as it was historically, economic mobility has been declining over the past few decades for the simple reason that the rate of economic growth has slowed. Young men born after about 1960, for example, are earning less (in inflation-adjusted terms) than their fathers' generation did at the same age. It would be nice to assume that a higher rate of growth is in the offing as we enter a new century. Certainly, new technologies and new markets abroad make many observers optimistic. But whatever the force of these developments, they haven't yet improved the fortunes of the youngest generation.

In sum, both these factors—the increase in social mobility and the decline in economic mobility—have affected prospects for the youngest generation. The good news is that individuals are increasingly free to move beyond their origins. The bad news is that fewer destinations represent an improvement over where they began. For those concerned about the material well-being of the youngest generation, this is not a welcome message. But for those concerned about the fairness of the process, the news is unambiguously good.

## Class stratification

Not only has economic growth slowed but its benefits now accrue almost entirely to those with the most education. Simply being a loyal, hard-working employee no longer guarantees that one will achieve the American dream. Whatever progress has been made in extending educational opportunities, it has not kept pace with the demand. Men with a high-school education or less have been particularly hard hit. The combination of slower growth and a distribution of wage gains that have favored women over men and the college educated over the high-school educated since the early 1970s has hurt poorly educated men. Their real incomes are less than one-half what they otherwise would have been in 1995. Education is, to put it simply, the new stratifying variable in American life. This, of course, is what one would hope for in a meritocracy, but only if everyone has a shot at a good education.

It is said that Americans would rather talk about sex than money. But they would rather talk about money than class, and some would rather not talk about the underclass at all. Many people consider the label pejorative, but research completed in the past decade suggests that such a group may indeed exist. Its hallmark is its lack of mobility. This group is not just poor but persistently poor, often over several generations. It is concentrated in urban neighborhoods characterized by high rates of welfare dependency, joblessness, single parenthood, and dropping out of school. It is disproportionately made up of racial and ethnic minorities. Although still relatively small (a little under three million people in 1990, according to an Urban Institute analysis of Census data), it appears to be growing. Anyone who doubts the existence of such a group need only read the detailed first-hand portrayals of ghetto life in Alex Kotlovitz's *There are No Children Here*, Leon Dash's *Rosa Lee*, or Ron Suskind's *A Hope in the Unseen*. These accounts suggest that dysfunctional families, poor schools, and isolation from mainstream institutions are depriving a significant segment of our youth of any prospect of one day joining the middle class.

All of this is by way of a caution: Whatever the broader trends in economic and social mobility, there may be enclaves that get left behind. Moreover, one can argue that it is this subgroup—and their lack of mobility—that should be our main concern. The very existence of such a group threatens our sense of social cohesion and imposes large costs on society. Its nexus with race is particularly disturbing.

## What to do?

If families and education matter so much, we had best look to them as sources of upward mobility for all Americans—and especially for those stuck at the bottom of the economic ladder. Imagine a world in which everyone graduated from high school with the basic competencies needed by most employers—a world in which no one had a child before they were married and all had a reasonably decent job. Even if these parents held low-wage jobs, and one of them worked less than full-time, they would have an income sufficient to move them above the official poverty line (about $12,000 for a family of three in 1995). The entry-level wage for a male high-school graduate in 1995 was $15,766. If his wife took a half-time job at the minimum wage, they could earn another $5,000 a year. No one should pretend that it is easy to live on $20,000 a year, especially in an urban area. Rent, utilities, and work-related expenses alone can quickly gobble up most of this amount. It would make enormous sense, in my view, to supplement the incomes of such families with an earned income tax credit, subsidized health care, and subsidized child care.

What does not make sense is to insist that the public continue to subsidize families started by young unwed mothers. As of 1990, 45 percent of all first births were to women who were either teenagers, unmarried, or lacking a high-school degree. Add in all those with high-school diplomas that are worthless in the job market, and the picture is even grimmer. *There is no public-policy substitute for raising a child in a home with two parents who are adequately educated.*

Of course, poorly educated parents are nothing new. In fact, the proportion of mothers who are high-school graduates is higher now than it has ever been. But bear in mind that in the past mothers were not expected to work (in part because far more of them were married), that the economy didn't require people of either sex to have nearly as much education, and that the proportion of children in single-parent families was a fraction of what it is today. Because of increases in divorce and especially out-of-wedlock childbearing, we now have a situation in which three-fifths of all children will spend time in a fatherless family. Almost one-third of all children are born out of wedlock in the United States, and the proportion exceeds one-half in such cities as New York, Chicago, Philadelphia, Detroit, and Washington, D.C. One needn't be an advocate of more traditional family values to be worried about the economic consequences of such social statistics. In fact, the growth of never-married mothers can account for almost all of the growth in the child poverty rate since 1970.

Where does the cycle stop? Urban schools that half a century ago may have provided the children of the poor a way into the middle class are now more likely to lock them into poverty. More than half of fourth and eighth graders in urban public schools fail to meet even minimal standards in reading, math, or science, and more than half of students in big cities will fail to graduate from high school. How can America continue to be the land of opportunity under these circumstances? If families and schools are critical to upward mobility, these children have little chance of success. We have no choice but to address both of these issues if we want to provide opportunities for the next generation.

## Strengthening families

Despite all the talk about the deterioration of the family, no one knows quite what to do about the problem. Welfare reform, which has not only eliminated AFDC as a permanent source of income for young mothers but also made young fathers more liable to pay child support, may well deter some out-of-wedlock childbearing. The next step should be to make the Earned Income Tax Credit (EITC) more marriage friendly. Today, as a result of the credit, a working single parent with two children can qualify for almost $4,000 a year. But if she marries another low-wage earner, she stands to lose most or all of these benefits. Congress should consider basing the credit on individual, rather than family, earnings. (A requirement that couples split their total earnings before the credit rate was applied would prevent benefits from going to low-wage spouses in middle-income families.) Such a revised EITC would greatly enhance the incentive to marry.

Equally important, we should find top-quality child care for those children whose mothers are required to work under the new welfare law. Indeed, such care might provide them with the positive experiences that they often fail to get within the home. Such intervention, if properly structured to accomplish this goal, can pay rich dividends in terms of later educational attainment and other social outcomes. The research on this point is, by now, clear. Although early gains in IQ may fade, rigorous studies have documented that disadvantaged children who receive a strong preschool experience are more likely to perform well in school.

Some argue that out-of-wedlock childbearing is the result of a lack of jobs for unskilled men. Although I don't think the evidence backs this view, it may have some merit. If so, we should offer jobs to such men in a few communities and see what happens. But we should tie the offer of a job to parental responsibility or give preference to men who are married.

Finally, I am convinced that messages matter. Many liberals argue that young women are having babies out of wedlock because they or their potential spouses are poor and face bleak futures. It is said that such women have no choice but to become unwed mothers. As an after-the-fact explanation, this may be partly true, but it is often accompanied by too ready an acceptance of early, out-of-wedlock childbearing by all concerned. Such fatalistic expectations have a way of becoming self-fulfilling. Just as it is wrong to presume that poor children can't excel in school, so too it is wrong to suggest to young women from disadvantaged backgrounds that early, out-of-wedlock childbearing is their only option. The fact remains that education and deferred childbearing, preferably within marriage, are an almost certain route out of poverty. Perhaps if more people were willing to deliver this message more forcefully, it would begin to influence behavior. Though the question needs to be studied more closely, it would appear that the decline in welfare caseloads since 1993 was triggered, in part, by a new message. Moreover, the new emphasis on conservative values may have contributed to the decrease in teen pregnancy and early childbearing since 1991. These new values can explain as much as two-thirds of the decline in sexual activity among males between 1988 and 1995, according to an Urban Institute study.

## Fixing urban schools

We must stem the tide of early, out-of-wedlock births for one simple reason: Even good teachers cannot cope with large numbers of children from poor or dysfunctional homes. And equally important, children who are not doing well in school are more likely to become the next generation of teenage mothers. This is a two-front war in which success on one front can pay rich dividends on the other. Lose the battle on one front, and the other is likely to be lost as well.

That many schools, especially those in urban poor neighborhoods, are failing to educate their students is, I think, no longer in dispute. What is contested is how to respond. Some say that the solution lies in providing vouchers to low-income parents, enabling them to send their children to the school of their choice. Others argue that school choice will deprive public schools of good students and adequate resources. They favor putting more money into the public schools. But choice programs have the potential to provide a needed wake up call to these same schools. Too many people are still defending a system that has shortchanged the children of the poor. Public schools are not about to disappear, and no one should believe that choice programs alone are a sufficient response to the education crisis. We should be equally attentive to the new choice programs and to serious efforts to reform the public schools.

In Chicago, for example, a new leadership team took over the school system in 1995–96 and instituted strong accountability measures with real consequences for schools, students, and teachers. Failure to perform can place a school on probation, lead to the removal of a principal, or necessitate that a student repeat a grade. New supports, such as preschool programs, home visiting, after-school and summer programs, and professional development of teachers, are also emphasized. Early indications are that these efforts are working to improve Chicago's public schools.

## A more equal chance

I began with a plea that we focus our attention less on the distribution of income and more on the opportunity each of us has to achieve a measure of success, recognizing that there will always be winners and losers but that the process needs to be as fair and open as possible. It can be argued that the process is, to one degree or another, inherently unfair. Children do not have much opportunity. They do not get to pick their parents—or, for that matter, their genetic endowments. It is these deepest of inequalities that have frustrated attempts to provide a greater measure of opportunity. Education is supposed to be the great leveler in our society, but it can just as easily reinforce these initial inequalities.

Thus any attempt to give every child the same chance to succeed must come to terms with the diversity of both early family environments and genetic endowments. In policy terms, this requires favoring the most disadvantaged. Numerous programs from Head Start to extra funding for children in low-income schools have attempted to level the playing field. But even where such efforts have been effective, they have been grossly inadequate to the task of compensating for differences in early environment. Assuming we are not willing to contemplate such radical solutions as removing children from their homes or cloning human beings, we are stuck with a certain amount of unfairness and inequality.

The traditional liberal response to this dilemma has been to redistribute income after the fact. It is technically easy to do but likely to run afoul of public sentiment in this country, including the hopes and dreams of the disadvantaged themselves. They need income; but they also want self-respect. In my view, we must find ways to strengthen families and schools in ways that give children a more equal chance to compete for society's prizes. To do otherwise runs counter to America's deepest and most cherished values.

---

ISABEL V. SAWHILL is a senior fellow at the Brookings Institution and author (with Daniel P. McMurrer) of *Getting Ahead: Economic and Social Mobility in America* (Urban Institute Press).

Reprinted with permission from *The Public Interest*, No. 135 (Spring 1999), pp. 3-17. © 1999 by National Affairs, Inc.

# The great CEO pay heist

Executive compensation has become highway robbery—we all know that. But how did it happen? And why can't we stop it? The answers lie in the perverse interaction of CEOs, boards, consultants, even the feds.

## BY GEOFFREY COLVIN

SANDY WEILL, WHO got a pay package worth some $151 million for running Citigroup last year, was a Brooklyn teenager back in the summer of 1950, preparing to return to Peekskill Military Academy. Jack Welch, whose pay for managing GE last year totaled about $125 million, was caddying at a golf course near his home in Massachusetts, having completed his freshman year at Salem High School. In Chicago, Larry Ellison—2000 pay as Oracle's chief: $92 million—was an ordinary 6-year-old. There's no reason any of them would have given the least bit of attention to events in Washington that summer, let alone suspected that what was going on there would change their lives and the life of virtually every future American CEO.

But that's what happened. After weeks of horsetrading, Congress sent President Truman the Revenue Act of 1950, and on Sept. 23 he signed it into law. Buried deep within that bill was a section amending the tax code. And that change, scarcely remarked upon at the time, made it legal and practical for companies to pay employees with an interesting form of currency called the stock option.

Thus began the madness. If you want to understand America's out-of-control CEO pay machine—including Steve Jobs' recent $872 million options grant, by far the largest ever—start there. The machine is worth understanding because it has begun churning out dollar amounts so mammoth that even hardened professionals grope for words. "Outrageous in many cases and unrelated to services rendered," says Charles Elson, a director of three publicly held corporations who runs the University of Delaware's Center for Corporate Governance. "In many cases, outside the charts," says Joseph Bachelder, the New York lawyer who has probably negotiated more top CEO pay contracts than anyone else. "Grossly high—astronomical," says Richard Koppes, a well-known governance expert with the Jones Day Reavis & Pogue law firm. "I've generally worried these guys weren't getting paid enough," says Harvard Business School professor Michael Jensen, who has written some of the

most influential work on CEO pay. "But now even I'm troubled."

What they and many others find so stunning are recent gargantuan pay packages unlike any seen before. Maybe you recall being shocked by the numbers of about a decade ago, when Time Warner's Steve Ross got a $75 million package, and Heinz's Anthony O'Reilly received four million options worth some $40 million. Such amounts marked the top end of the scale through the boom times of the mid-'90s. But suddenly, in recent years, pay has ballooned into nine-figure totals, almost defying comprehension. Consider:

• The No. 1 earners in each of the past five years got packages valued cumulatively at nearly $1.4 billion (see chart), or $274 million on average. Yet far from delivering the superb results investors might have expected from the world's highest-priced management, four of the five companies have been marginal to horrible performers. They are Walt Disney, Cendant, Computer Associates, and Apple Computer.

• Apple's Steve Jobs got last year's mightiest pay package, valued by FORTUNE at $381 million. (For the purposes of calculating his 2000 package, we have valued his monstrous options grant at one-third the exercise price of the shares optioned. And, of course, we've included the $90 million Gulfstream the Apple board gave him.) How big is that? The last time the public got furious over CEO pay was in 1992, when reports of huge numbers for 1991 sparked a flurry of reform efforts. Yet the 14 highest-paid CEOs then, including such legendary mega-earners as Coca-Cola's Roberto Goizueta, Philip Morris' Hamish Maxwell, GE's Welch, and ITT's Rand Araskog, together earned less than Steve Jobs did last year all by himself (even without the plane!). Yes, it's true that Jobs has paid himself only $1 a year since he returned to Apple as CEO in 1997. And, yes, he deserves to be rewarded—handsomely—for bringing Apple back from the dead. But *still*...

• Dell CEO Michael Dell received more than 38 million options from 1996 through 1998, though as the company's sole

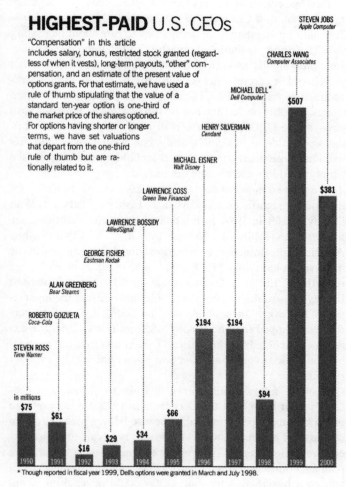

## HIGHEST-PAID U.S. CEOs

"Compensation" in this article includes salary, bonus, restricted stock granted (regardless of when it vests), long-term payouts, "other" compensation, and an estimate of the present value of options grants. For that estimate, we have used a rule of thumb stipulating that the value of a standard ten-year option is one-third of the market price of the shares optioned. For options having shorter or longer terms, we have set valuations that depart from the one-third rule of thumb but are rationally related to it.

STEVEN JOBS
Apple Computer

CHARLES WANG
Computer Associates

MICHAEL DELL*
Dell Computer

HENRY SILVERMAN
Cendant

MICHAEL EISNER
Walt Disney

LAWRENCE COSS
Green Tree Financial

LAWRENCE BOSSIDY
AlliedSignal

GEORGE FISHER
Eastman Kodak

ALAN GREENBERG
Bear Stearns

ROBERTO GOIZUETA
Coca-Cola

STEVEN ROSS
Time Warner

in millions

$507
$381
$194
$194
$94
$75
$66
$61
$34
$29
$16

1990 1991 1992 1993 1994 1995 1996 1997 1998 1999 2000

* Though reported in fiscal year 1999, Dell's options were granted in March and July 1998.

Fortune Chart/Source: Executive Compensation Advisory Services; Fortune

founder he already owned 353 million shares. Similarly, Oracle CEO Larry Ellison got a huge 20-million-share options grant, accounting for virtually all his pay last year, even though he already owned nearly 700 million company shares outright. What could possibly have been the point? "If they weren't already motivated enough to protect the owners' interests, then their shareholders are in worse trouble than they think," says shareholder activist Nell Minow.

The largest pay component in virtually all these cases is the stock option, which has mushroomed from modest use in the 1950s to a source of breathtaking CEO wealth today. A big reason for its runaway popularity is the insane way accounting authorities let companies treat options in financial statements—a way that's great for executives and awful for shareholders.

More broadly, pay is out of control because many board compensation committees, which set CEO pay, aren't doing their job. Why not? That's always been a bit of a mystery, because the comp committee code of silence is sort of like the Mob's *omertà*, only stricter. Nonetheless, FORTUNE's Carol Loomis persuaded some high-powered comp committee members to tell, anonymously, what goes on behind those doors. The picture isn't pretty.

There's no simple explanation for the latest extraordinary pay figures. Today's roaring CEO pay machine is a giant device of many parts, built up over decades. Besides options, other important pieces have come from compensation consultants, economic developments, social trends, even government; indeed, the government's occasional attempts to restrain CEO pay have almost always had the opposite effect. What's so remarkable about the machine is that through all the ups and downs of business, the waxing and waning of corporate fortunes, it turns in only one direction—and faster all the time.

It wasn't always so. Through the '50s, the '60s, and part of the '70s, CEO pay actually grew more slowly than the pay of average workers. Most CEOs were publicly invisible and liked it that way. Adjusted for inflation, pay packages were much smaller than today's. They included options, though by modern standards the grants were pitiful; 20,000 shares were a big deal. Pay didn't seem tied particularly tightly to performance, yet stocks performed well: The S&P 500 advanced 11.3% a year on average in the low-inflation era from 1950 to 1964.

That golden age ended abruptly when stocks entered a long coma in 1964—and we soon began to see the early stirrings of today's opulent reward system. Since the market was going nowhere, options weren't paying off and substantial raises seemed hard to justify. So compensation consultants—yes, they were around back then—began cooking up the creative pay-enhancing gimmicks they have continued to devise ever since. Indeed, consultants play a critical role as the pay machine's expert mechanics. They understand every gear and sprocket and can always find a way to make the machine go faster. That's exactly what they do, in their utterly conflicted position—paid by management to advise management on how management should be paid.

The consultants' most inspired creation in the days of the stock market doldrums was a device called performance shares, which rewarded CEOs if they could increase earnings per share by a given amount in a given period—and never mind that EPS could be manipulated in a thousand unholy ways. What's important is the logic. You might have expected it to go like this: The stock isn't moving, so the CEO shouldn't be rewarded. But it was actually the opposite: The stock isn't moving, so we've got to find some other basis for rewarding the CEO. That difference, which persists to this day, is one of the keys to understanding megapay.

Another important element of today's CEO pay developed soon after. "An awful lot of CEOs should honor Curt Flood," says Michael Halloran of compensation firm SCA Consulting. Flood was the St. Louis Cardinals outfielder who in 1969 challenged the reserve clause in baseball players' contracts; though he lost his case in the Supreme Court, his quest inspired developments that made scores of players free agents by the late 1970s. Soon 20-year-old shortstops were making more than CEOs, and CEOs hated it. Surely they were worth more! And through that argument they started getting more. The counterargument—that athletes' pay, unlike CEOs', was determined in a brutally competitive open market—didn't get much airtime in the boardroom.

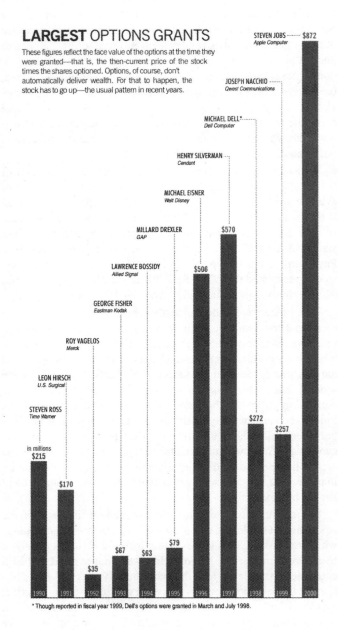

## LARGEST OPTIONS GRANTS

These figures reflect the face value of the options at the time they were granted—that is, the then-current price of the stock times the shares optioned. Options, of course, don't automatically deliver wealth. For that to happen, the stock has to go up—the usual pattern in recent years.

STEVEN JOBS ---- $872
*Apple Computer*

JOSEPH NACCHIO ----
*Qwest Communications*

MICHAEL DELL* --------
*Dell Computer*

HENRY SILVERMAN ----
*Cendant*

MICHAEL EISNER
*Walt Disney*

MILLARD DREXLER ----
*GAP*

LAWRENCE BOSSIDY
*Allied Signal*

GEORGE FISHER
*Eastman Kodak*

ROY VAGELOS
*Merck*

LEON HIRSCH
*U.S. Surgical*

STEVEN ROSS
*Time Warner*

in millions

$215 | $170 | $35 | $67 | $63 | $79 | $506 | $570 | $272 | $257 | $872

1990 1991 1992 1993 1994 1995 1996 1997 1998 1999 2000

\* Though reported in fiscal year 1999, Dell's options were granted in March and July 1998.

Fortune Chart/Source: Executive Compensation Advisory Services; Fortune

Meanwhile, in a radical shift, CEOs were becoming celebrities. As business became glamorized in the 1980s, CEOs realized that being famous was more fun than being invisible. Compensation consultants who were around at the time report a startling phenomenon: Instead of being embarrassed by their appearance near the top of published CEO pay rankings, many CEOs began to consider it a badge of honor. That societal change is another key part of today's CEO pay machine.

Though stock options have been available since 1950, today's options culture began in the bull market of the 1980s. This makes perfect sense, of course; since stocks essentially went nowhere from 1964 to 1982, options during that era didn't exactly make a CEO's heart beat faster. But once stocks took off, options suddenly became an excellent vehicle for getting rich, and companies began delivering them in truckloads.

Besides, corporate raiders like Boone Pickens were arguing, rightly, that most CEOs didn't have enough skin in the game—they didn't own enough company stock to care about increasing the share price. Institutional investors and shareholder activists were pressing the same case. It was a classic demonstration that you should be careful what you wish for. Companies quickly responded by handing the CEO tons more options and restricted shares. Trouble was, that came on top of already generous cash pay—so the CEO's interest wasn't *really* aligned with that of the shareholders. Besides, if the stock went down, the CEO wouldn't lose money the way shareholders did. He or she simply wouldn't exercise the options.

We pause a moment now to recognize a couple of CEOs for historically significant roles. Michael Eisner signed on as Walt Disney's chief in 1984 with a contract that changed the game for all who followed. Written by Graef S. Crystal—then America's preeminent compensation consultant, now one of the most vehement critics of CEO pay—the contract offered huge rewards if Eisner delivered great profits. Crystal advised Disney's board that the contract could make Eisner the highest-paid CEO ever. Understood, said the board. Eisner then performed as hoped for, and his pay—$57 million in 1989, for example—ratcheted the numbers up a giant notch. (That contract has long since expired, and last year Eisner got big pay for poor performance.)

Eisner's fellow trailblazer was Roberto Goizueta, Coca-Cola's chief from 1981 until his death in 1997. He turned Coke into a champion performer, and because he was paid heavily in options and restricted stock, he apparently became the first executive billionaire: the first person to amass assets worth more than $1 billion as a hired hand, without having founded or financed a business. After that, CEOs could never think about their pay in the same way again.

The pay machine's newest pieces appeared in a flurry in the early 1990s. The forces of the previous decade—the bull market, the huge options grants, the Eisner-and-Goizueta effect—combined to produce a slew of mammoth pay packages. The public became furious—so furious that Washington had to act.

So in 1993 Congress created section 162(m) of the tax code, which prevents companies from taking a tax deduction for CEO salaries over $1 million a year; pay that varies on the basis of performance remains fully deductible. Compensation consultants agree that this change, far from restricting CEO pay, probably helped increase it. Many salaries that were below $1 million now rose to that level, since it was virtually government-endorsed.

Around the same time, the SEC required companies to report CEO pay in far greater detail, the better to inform shareholders. Ambitious CEOs now knew better than ever what their peers were getting—and could push for packages that were superior in every particular.

And with that, the main elements of today's megapay machine were in place. How does it work? Let's take a look:

1. A poorly performing company, under pressure from active investors, fires its CEO and seeks to bring in a highly touted outsider. The outsider has tons of options from his current em-

ployer that he'll forfeit if he leaves or joins a competitor. So the new employer has to make him whole by paying a massive signing bonus. Most egregious example: Conseco last year paid former GE Capital chief Gary Wendt a signing bonus of $45 million—cash—to forfeit his GE options and become CEO.

2. The ousted CEO was probably earning a lot—it's all public info—so the new guy argues, logically, that if the old CEO was getting so much for doing a lousy job, he, the presumed savior, should get a great deal more. He probably does, and the details are reported in the proxy statement.

3. The comp consultants duly enter that mammoth signing bonus and pay package into their databases, and the median pay in that industry jumps.

4. Every comp committee in that industry, when determining the chief's pay, is now looking at higher median levels. Since comp consultants report that virtually all committees believe their CEO ranks at the 75th percentile or above, they will almost certainly award packages that raise the median even further.

5. The typical underperforming CEO whose stock falls receives even more options and perhaps restricted stock. Inevitably, the publicly stated reason is that this gives him greater incentive to get the stock up. The actual logic is that since his old options are worthless—and because it would look profligate to take a tax hit by raising his salary above its current $1 million and a bonus increase would look terrible in light of recent poor performance—the only way to give him more money is to grant a big slug of new options at today's lower price, plus restricted stock, which will pay off no matter what.

6. Those mushrooming stock awards are cited by other comp committees as justification for handing lots more stock to their own CEOs.

7. When an underperformer finally gets canned, he leaves behind a formidable pay package, and the company may have to entice an outsider to give up his own giant package. Return to Step 1.

On and on this wondrous machine turns, cranking out bigger numbers with every revolution. Logical question: If all the machine's parts were installed by 1993, why is it only now that we're hearing such outrage over the results? Answer: The American public isn't angered by big pay. It's angered by perceived injustice. The last major outcry, in 1991 and 1992, arose from huge CEO pay at a time of recession and widespread lay-

offs. Pay kept right on rocketing after that, but when the economy got back on track and the stock markets caught fire, who cared? This time the backdrop is a dragging economy and a market collapse that hurt millions of people. Like the last crisis, this, too, shall pass.

And then what? Three facts combine to create the fuel that keeps the American CEO pay machine spinning at today's furious clip. First and most fundamental, the managers and directors, who control the corporation day by day, are not the owners, who bear the cost of what the managers and directors do. Shareholders may be incensed by their CEO's pay, but doing something about it is so cumbersome that it almost never happens. That separation of ownership from control, and the potential for mischief it creates, have been apparent for 70 years. We accept it because it's the price we pay for a system of broad-based capitalism that has enabled the funding of the world's largest and most successful enterprises.

Second, the American culture celebrates wealth and fame above almost all else. "Even if a CEO is worth it, should he take it?" asks Ken West of TIAA-CREF, America's largest private pension fund. In many countries a nine-figure pay package, and the attention it attracts, would be just too far outside social bounds. Not here.

Third, we're in a revolutionizing global economy where the difference between the right CEO and the wrong one is all the difference in the world. Many will fail. Demand for winners is huge, the supply small. In that environment the best CEOs will cost more than ever, and—who knows?—may be worth it.

Now, what are the odds that those facts will change anytime soon? Not good, it would seem. On the other hand, the chances that the economy will pick up and the public will feel better by next proxy season are excellent. That's why, despite this year's mind-blowing numbers and the outraged reaction they've provoked, a hard-headed realist would have to say that America's CEO pay machine looks well oiled and finely tuned, with a whole lot of life in it still.

---

REPORTER ASSOCIATES *Ann Harrington, Paola Hjelt*

---

FEEDBACK: *gcolvin@fortunemail.com*

# CORPORATE WELFARE

**A TIME investigation uncovers how hundreds of companies get on the dole—and why it costs every working American the equivalent of two weeks' pay every year**

**By Donald L. Barlett and James B. Steele**

HOW WOULD YOU LIKE TO PAY ONLY A QUARTER OF THE REAL ESTATE TAXES you owe on your home? And buy everything for the next 10 years without spending a single penny in sales tax? Keep a chunk of your paycheck free of income taxes? Have the city in which you live lend you money at rates cheaper than any bank charges? Then have the same city install free water and sewer lines to your house, offer you a perpetual discount on utility bills—and top it all off by landscaping your front yard at no charge?

Fat chance. You can't get any of that, of course. But if you live almost anywhere in America, all around you are taxpayers getting deals like this. These taxpayers are called corporations, and their deals are usually trumpeted as "economic development" or "public-private partnerships." But a better name is corporate welfare. It's a game in which governments large and small subsidize corporations large and small, usually at the expense of another state or town and almost always at the expense of individual and other corporate taxpayers.

Two years after Congress reduced welfare for individuals and families, this other kind of welfare continues to expand, penetrating every corner of the American economy. It has turned politicians into bribery specialists, and smart business people into con artists. And most surprising of all, it has rarely created any new jobs.

While corporate welfare has attracted critics from both the left and the right, there is no uniform definition. By TIME's definition, it is this: any action by local, state or federal government that gives a corporation or an entire industry a benefit not offered to others. It can be an outright subsidy, a grant, real estate, a low-interest loan or a government service. It can also be a tax break—a credit, exemption, deferral or deduction, or a tax rate lower than the one others pay.

The rationale to curtail traditional welfare programs, such as Aid to Families with Dependent Children and food stamps, and to impose a lifetime limit on the amount of aid received, was compelling: the old system didn't work. It was unfair, destroyed incentive, perpetuated dependence and distorted the economy. An 18-month TIME investigation has found that the same indictment, almost to the word, applies to corporate welfare. In some ways, it represents pork-barrel legislation of the worst order. The difference, of course, is that instead of rewarding the poor, it rewards the powerful.

And it rewards them handsomely. The Federal Government alone shells out $125 billion a year in corporate welfare, this in the midst of one of the more robust economic periods in the nation's history. Indeed, thus far in the 1990s, corporate profits have totaled $4.5 trillion—a sum equal to the cumulative paychecks of 50 million working Americans who earned less than $25,000 a year, for those eight years.

**During one of the most robust economic periods in our nation's history, the Federal Government has shelled out $125 billion in corporate welfare, equivalent to all the income tax paid by 60 million individuals and families.**

That makes the Federal Government America's biggest sugar daddy, dispensing a range of giveaways from tax abatements to price supports for sugar itself. Companies get government money to advertise their products; to help build new plants, offices and stores; and to train their workers. They sell their goods to foreign buyers that make the acquisitions with tax dollars supplied by the U.S. government; engage in foreign transactions that are insured by the government; and are excused from paying a portion of their income tax if they sell products overseas. They pocket lucrative government contracts to carry out ordinary business operations, and government grants to conduct research that will improve their profit margins. They are extended partial tax immunity if they locate in certain geographical areas, and they may write off as business expenses some of the perks enjoyed by their top executives.

The justification for much of this welfare is that the U.S. government is creating jobs. Over the past six years, Congress appropriated $5 billion to run the Export-Import Bank of the United States, which subsidizes companies that sell goods abroad. James A. Harmon, president and chairman, puts it this way: "American workers… have higher-quality, better-paying jobs, thanks to Eximbank's financing." But the numbers at the bank's five biggest beneficiaries—AT&T, Bechtel, Boeing, General Electric and McDonnell Douglas (now a part of Boeing)—tell another story. At these companies, which have accounted for about 40% of all loans, grants and long-term guarantees in this decade, overall employment has fallen 38%, as more than a third of a million jobs have disappeared.

The picture is much the same at the state and local level, where a different kind of feeding frenzy is taking place. Politicians stumble over one another in the rush to arrange special deals for select corporations, fueling a growing economic war among the states. The result is that states keep throwing money at companies that in many cases are not serious about moving anyway. The companies are certainly not reluctant to take the money, though, which is available if they simply utter the word relocation. And why not? Corporate executives, after all, have a fiduciary duty to squeeze every dollar they can from every locality waving blandishments in their face.

State and local governments now give corporations money to move from one city to another—even from one building to another—and tax credits for hiring new employees. They supply funds to train workers or pay part of their wages while they are in training, and provide scientific and engineering assistance to solve workplace technical problems. They repave existing roads and build new ones. They lend money at bargain-basement interest rates to erect plants or buy equipment. They excuse corporations from paying sales and property taxes and relieve them from taxes on investment income.

There are no reasonably accurate estimates on the amount of money states shovel out. That's because few want you to know. Some say they maintain no records. Some say they don't know where the files are. Some say the information is not public. All that's certain is that the figure is in the many billions of dollars each year—and it is growing, when measured against the subsidy per job.

In 1989 Illinois gave $240 million in economic incentives to Sears, Roebuck & Co. to keep its corporate headquarters and 5,400 workers in the state by moving from Chicago to suburban Hoffman Estates. That amounted to a subsidy of $44,000 for each job.

In 1991 Indiana gave $451 million in economic incentives to United Airlines to build an aircraft-maintenance facility that would employ as many as 6,300 people. Subsidy: $72,000 for each job.

In 1993 Alabama gave $253 million in economic incentives to Mercedes-Benz to build an automobile-assembly plant near Tuscaloosa and employ 1,500 workers. Subsidy: $169,000 for each job.

And in 1997 Pennsylvania gave $307 million in economic incentives to Kvaerner ASA, a Norwegian global engineering and construction company, to open a shipyard at the former Philadelphia Naval Shipyard and employ 950 people. Subsidy: $323,000 for each job.

This kind of arithmetic seldom adds up. Let's say the Philadelphia job pays $50,000. And each new worker pays $6,700 in local and state taxes. That means it will take nearly a half-century of tax collections from each individual to earn back the money granted to create his or her job. And that assumes all 950 workers will be recruited from outside Philadelphia and will relocate in the city, rather than move from existing jobs within the city, where they are already paying taxes.

All this is in service of a system that may produce jobs in one city or state, thus fostering the illusion of an uptick in employment. But it does not create more jobs in the nation as a whole. Market forces do that, and that's why 10 million jobs have been created since 1990. But most of those jobs have been created by small- and medium-size companies, from high-tech start-ups to franchised cleaning services. FORTUNE 500 companies, on the other hand, have erased more jobs than they have created this past decade, and yet they are the biggest beneficiaries of corporate welfare.

To be sure, some economic incentives are handed out for a seemingly worthwhile public purpose. The tax breaks that companies receive to locate in inner cities come to mind. Without them, companies might not invest in those neighborhoods. However well intended, these subsidies rarely produce lasting results. They may provide short-term jobs but not long-term employment. And in the end, the costs outweigh any benefits.

And what are those costs? The equivalent of nearly two weekly paychecks from every working man and woman in America—extra money that would stay in their pockets if it didn't go to support some business venture or another.

If corporate welfare is an unproductive end game, why does it keep growing in a period of intensive government cost cutting? For starters, it has good p.r. and an army of bureaucrats working to expand it. A corporate-welfare bureaucracy of an estimated 11,000 organizations and agencies has grown up, with access to city halls, statehouses, the Capitol and the White House. They conduct seminars, conferences and training sessions. They have their own trade associations. They publish their own journals and newsletters. They create attractive websites on the Internet. And they never call it "welfare." They call it "economic incentives" or "empowerment zones" or "enterprise zones."

Whatever the name, the result is the same. Some companies receive public services at reduced rates, while all others pay the full cost. Some companies are excused from paying all or a portion of their taxes due, while all others must pay the full amount imposed by law. Some companies receive grants, low-interest loans and other subsidies, while all others must fend for themselves.

In the end, that's corporate welfare's greatest flaw. It's unfair. One role of government is to help ensure a level playing field for people and businesses. Corporate welfare does just the opposite. It tilts the playing field in favor of the largest or the most politically influential or most aggressive businesses.…

# From Welfare to Work

## Making Welfare a Way Station, Not a Way of Life

BY ISABEL SAWHILL

In 1996 Congress reformed a welfare system that was deeply unpopular with the American public. Although Republicans pushed hard for reform, many Democrats—led by former President Bill Clinton—went along, and in the end both parties took credit for the new law. The system was transformed from one that handed out cash to one that required work and penalized with a loss of benefits those who failed to comply with the requirement. What had been called Aid to Families with Dependent Children (AFDC) became Temporary Assistance for Needy Families (TANF). The use of the word "temporary" was noteworthy. Welfare was to be a way station, not a way of life.

Although most politicians supported these changes, many scholars and advocates for the poor complained that the new law was a voyage into uncharted waters—an experiment with the lives of some of the nation's most vulnerable citizens and their children. Noncitizens who were legal residents of the United States were dealt an even bigger blow, as they and their children lost many benefits previously available to them. In this special issue of the *Brookings Review*, our contributors assess the results of the experiment to date and reflect on next steps, including what modifications may be needed when Congress reau-

thorizes the law in 2002 and what directions all this suggests for antipoverty policy in the United States. This introductory essay builds on their insights but contains my own assessment as well.

### Is Welfare Reform Working?

Not surprisingly, the answer to the question of whether welfare reform is working depends on whom you ask. That said, even the law's critics point to at least some successes while its supporters acknowledge some limitations.

All our contributors agree that caseloads have declined far more than expected (from 5 million families in 1994 to 2.2 million in June 2000), that about 60 percent of those who have left welfare are working, that employment rates among single mothers have increased dramatically, and that child poverty has declined. They also agree that a substantial minority of mothers who have left the rolls are not working and that many of those who remain on the rolls may have difficulty finding or keeping jobs because of poor schooling, substance abuse, depression, or other barriers to employment. Finally, those who are working tend to earn low wages (about $7.00 an hour on average) making it hard for them to support their families.

Another concern, noted by Wendell Primus, Mark Greenberg, and Tom Downey in particular, is that the poverty rate has not fallen as much as the caseload. Fewer poor children are receiving assistance. In addition, the incomes of the poorest one-fifth of single-parent families have continued to fall, many families remain in deep poverty, and according to some reports, requests for emergency assistance have grown. Overall, 700,000 families were significantly worse off in 1999 than their counterparts in 1995.

Because welfare reform was implemented during an unprecedented economic expansion, questions also must be raised about how much of the good news should be attributed to the 1996 law and how much to a strong economy or to the growth of other programs such as the earned income tax credit (EITC) over this same period. Research on this question doesn't permit firm answers, but almost everyone agrees that all three have been important. In his essay, Ron Haskins compares the 1990s with the 1980s, when employment also expanded strongly but without comparable declines in caseloads. The data he cites suggest that welfare reform played an important, and probably a critical, role.

Still, many people remain uneasy about what will happen should the economy sink into a prolonged recession. An economic downturn would not only swell the caseload, according to this view, but strain state budgets, perhaps forcing some states to cut benefits. At a minimum, states would likely reduce spending on an array of supportive services for those making the transition from welfare to work and for other low-income families.

Mickey Kaus considers the longer-term implications of welfare reform. He notes that reform was at least partially motivated by a view that the old system of no-strings entitlements had encouraged the growth of an urban underclass, characterized by idleness and out-of-wedlock childbearing. For many, dismantling this system is the key to reconnecting an isolated and stigmatized group of the poor to work and marriage. Even if the short-term result were to make this group worse off, Kaus argues, these longer-term goals should be pursued. The major purpose of the 1996 law, after all, was not to end poverty or improve material well-being, but to end dependency and encourage the formation of stable two-parent, married families. Although the family formation goals have not yet been achieved, some signs are encouraging. Teen pregnancy and birth rates have plummeted, and the proportion of children born outside marriage has leveled off. Lack of more definitive progress in family formation should not be surprising, for such cultural changes are deep-seated and likely to be decades in the making. In the meantime, the dramatic increase in employment among never-married mothers has had one unintended consequence: by creating greater sympathy for their lives, it has made new supports for this group politically feasible and thereby transformed the debate about poverty. No longer is the debate primarily about how much cash assistance and support services to provide to mothers who stay home with their children; it is about how much assistance to give them once they are working to support these same children.

One important feature of the new law was the enormous discretion it gave the states. Several contributors (Richard Nathan and Tom Gais, Mark Greenberg, and Bruce Katz and Katherine Allen) address the question of devolution and how welfare reform has played out differently in various parts of the country. Most states have embraced the goal of getting recipients into jobs as quickly as possible, a strategy that appears more cost-effective than providing substantial up-front education and training. But it is also a strategy dictated in large measure by federal rules that require states to place an increasing fraction of their caseloads in jobs and that reward them for doing so by freeing up funds for other, related purposes. Many states also supplement the limited earnings of those moving into jobs by allowing them to keep a portion of their welfare check. And as Gordon Berlin notes, these efforts to make work pay, although more costly than mandating work alone, can produce more positive effects not only on employment and earnings but also on some measures of child well-being. A key issue for the future will be whether welfare reform is about improving the lives of families and children or about ending dependency and saving money for taxpayers. Thus far, different states have adopted different approaches, with Minnesota, for example, emphasizing making work pay while Texas and Wisconsin have put more emphasis on ending dependency. And whatever formal policy choices states may make, local practices vary substantially not only from one state to another but even from one county to another within a state.

For these and other reasons, caseloads have declined unevenly. On average nationwide they have dropped by more than half, but that average reflects sharp variations—from 90 percent in Wyoming and 79 percent in Wisconsin to 46 percent in California and 26 percent in Hawaii between January of 1994 and June of 2000. And as Katz and Allen note, declines have been slower in the cities than outside of them, so that more and more of the caseload is concentrated in urban counties.

Not surprisingly, states are happy with their new role and are likely to want a simple extension of the law when it is reauthorized in 2002. But the wide latitude given states by the law must be balanced against the need for accountability. Today policymakers lack good information about what states are doing, where federal funds are being spent, who is receiving what services, and what happens to families after they leave welfare. Data on such matters have never been adequate, but as Nathan and Gais, as well as Greenberg, note, devolution has entailed real losses in information.

## Does the Law Need to Be Changed?

Vin Weber observes that neither of the political parties in Washington is advocating major changes in welfare law.

Both are more likely to fine-tune or modify it in ways that build on, rather than reverse, its current thrust. From a local perspective as well, some stability could be useful; too much change at the federal level makes life difficult for those with day-to-day responsibility for implementing the law.

Nonetheless, debates will undoubtedly arise about funding as well as other matters. Conservatives may argue that states no longer need so much money in the face of falling caseloads while liberals will want to expand funding to serve both those who remain on the rolls and a broader group of low-income working families. Currently, states receive $16.5 billion a year from Washington to assist needy families with children. States are required to maintain their own spending at 75–80 percent of what they spent during the early 1990s, or around $11 billion a year. Because caseloads have declined sharply, states have reaped a windfall and now have much more to spend per family on welfare than they did before 1996. But if caseloads should rise again in response to a recession, states are likely to need more than the small contingency fund now available for this purpose. Because the allocation of federal funds among states is based on commitments that historically favored high-benefit states, another issue is the fairness of providing more than twice as much federal money for a poor child in a wealthy state as for one in a poorer state.

One of the new law's most contentious issues has always been its five-year limit on the time families may receive federally funded benefits. Because the time limit will not begin to kick in until this coming fall, its full effects have not yet been felt. Should states start implementing it in the midst of a recession, the resulting harm to families could produce an outcry that might well change the debate. But states have other options. They may use their own funds to keep families on the rolls longer or may put families into community service jobs. Federal rules already allow states to exempt 20 percent of their caseload from the limit, and states may ask Washington to liberalize those rules.

The issues of funding and time limits will almost surely be linked to a broader debate about the purposes of the law. Once the goal of welfare reform is broadened beyond providing cash assistance to needy families to include encouraging marriage, making work pay, and helping families with problems ranging from substance abuse to mental health, the adequacy of any particular level of resources is unclear. Indeed, one danger is that funding will be set based on historical experience while the objectives expand in new directions. In particular, several contributors argue that the law should give much more attention to reducing poverty and finding strategies and performance measures that relate to this larger goal.

## Beyond Welfare: The Unfinished Agenda
Certainly, the new welfare law, and any modifications to it in 2002, will not end the debate about poverty in the United States. That debate is ongoing and will always in-

volve disputes about the balance between individual and social responsibility. In 2002 the reauthorization of TANF and related legislation, such as food stamps and the child care block grant, will provide an opportunity to reengage that debate.

I would argue that the three most important aspects of that broader debate are what society owes to those who work but remain poor; what, if anything, can be done to reduce childbearing outside of marriage; and how to break the cycle of poverty for children growing up in low-income communities.

Supports for the working poor have expanded over the past two decades, especially since 1990. The earned income tax credit is now the nation's largest antipoverty program by far. Future debates are likely to center on whether it can be further expanded to encourage work and marriage while minimizing error and fraud. Other support strategies likely to be discussed are subsidized child care or health insurance for low-income adults, a higher minimum wage, refundable tax credits for children in families that work, or cash supplements paid through the welfare system for those in low-paid jobs. Concerns about whether the least skilled will be able to find work in a less robust economy may also be addressed. Although few states have chosen to back up the work requirement in the new welfare law with community service jobs for those unable to find jobs in the private sector, linking the two has broad appeal. Liberals have always liked the idea of guaranteeing a job to those unable to find work and conservatives have come to understand that last-resort jobs in the public sector make a tough work requirement more politically acceptable as well as easier to enforce.

## The key challenges now are to provide greater supports for low-wage work, reduce childbearing outside of marriage, and ensure that more children have a good start in life.

Reducing childbearing outside of marriage is a more daunting challenge. Not only is there less consensus about this as a goal, but also there are far fewer workable remedies. Nonetheless, reducing out-of-wedlock childbearing was a key goal of the 1996 legislation and for good reason. The growth of single-parent families, driven almost entirely by out-of-wedlock childbearing in recent years, has substantially worsened child poverty. Wade Horn suggests that public policy might encourage marriage by reducing the marriage penalty in the EITC, by helping fathers earn enough to support their children, and by funding programs that enhance the marital and parenting skills of high-risk families. But he admits that such strategies may not change people's behavior. The fact that many women in these communities begin childbearing at a very early age—typically in their teens—suggests the need to prevent early sex and pregnancy. The 1996 law provided funding for abstinence education programs whose efficacy remains unproven. Bearing in mind that the typical teenager spends about 7 hours a day watching television, surfing the Internet, and reading popular magazines, reaching them through these popular media may be far more cost-effective than school or community-based programs regardless of whether the message is abstinence or safer sex. In short, emphasis needs to be placed as much on changing cultural norms through creative use of the media as on offering more sex education programs. And with so many mothers now working, and some evidence that this has created problems for their adolescent children, more after-school programs may be needed as well.

Breaking the cycle of child poverty is a high priority for many but often gets lost in discussions of the welfare system. To the extent it is discussed, it is usually in the context of providing child care for mothers leaving welfare for work. Most observers recognize that the children of these mothers will need some sort of care, but they cannot agree whether the available care is adequate and whether improving it could be one way to break the cycle of poverty. Thus far, there is little evidence that requiring mothers to work has harmed their children. But the goal of leaving no child behind goes beyond doing no harm. In fact, many believe that if every young child of a mother leaving welfare had access to Head Start or another high-quality early education program, more children would reach school age ready to learn and, with appropriate follow-up in the elementary grades, go on to greater success as adults.

## Looking Ahead

Welfare reform has been far more successful than most people anticipated. Caseloads are down, employment among single mothers is up, and poverty rates have fallen. In the absence of a major recession that reverses all this good news, it is unlikely that the direction of current policy will be reversed or that major features of the 1996 law will be modified. That doesn't mean there won't be some changes and that reauthorization won't or shouldn't catalyze a broader debate about antipoverty policy in the United States. The most important challenges in this regard are to provide greater supports for low-wage work, to reduce childbearing outside of marriage, and to ensure that more children have a good start in life.

*Isabel Sawhill is a senior fellow in the Brookings Economic Studies program and a co-director of the Brookings Welfare Reform & Beyond Initiative.*

From *Brookings Review*, Summer 2001, pp. 4-7. © 2001 by The Brookings Review.

# RACISM ISN'T WHAT IT USED TO BE

## But not everyone has noticed

### Ed Marciniak

A new vocabulary is surfacing to assess the state of race relations in the United States. The operative words and approaches signal remarkable changes.

In the 1960s our racial language was dominated by "civil rights," "integration," "desegregation," "prejudice," "discrimination," "colored," and "Negroes." Nowadays, the comparable words and ideas have become: "racism," "diversity," "hate crimes," "racial profiling," "redlining," "reparations," "blacks," and "African Americans."

We are in transition, striving to find a racial vocabulary appropriate to today's society and culture. This is a touchy, controversial endeavor.

The 1960s, furthermore, emphasized equality of treatment—in employment, voting, housing, and government services. In the new millennium the stress has shifted to equality of results. Now the assumption of some is that ethnic and racial groups should be proportionately represented in occupations, incomes, wealth, college graduations, achievements, and failures. On the other hand, black athletes now dominate the nation's sports, such as track, basketball, football, and baseball (almost). Inequality is not the same as inequity.

The variations in language reflect the notable developments in race relations since 1963 when Martin Luther King Jr. gave his "I Have a Dream" speech to two hundred thousand people, culminating the March on Washington. Or since 1964 when Congress enacted the U.S. Civil Rights Act. Consider only a few of the changes:

In 1966, 42 percent of American blacks had incomes below the official poverty line. Recently, the U.S. Census Bureau reported that 24 percent of the nation's blacks were under that poverty line. At the same time, the poverty rate for whites was 8 percent.

Nationwide, the count of black elected officials zoomed from some 100 in the 1960s to 9,000 in the new millennium. In political jurisdictions where the voting majority is of one race, candidates of another continue to gain office.

We now have a national holiday in January honoring a black minister who preached and practiced nonviolence. And it can no longer be claimed that 11 A.M. on Sunday is the nation's most segregated hour of the week.

Affirmative-action programs originally intended for blacks now embrace Hispanics, Asians, women, and/or gays. Some university affirmative-action programs give priority to students in poverty.

The reading public has come to realize that Toni Morrison is black and a writer. But she is not a black writer.

Hispanics will soon overtake blacks as the largest "minority." Meanwhile, efforts to create ongoing coalitions among blacks, Hispanics, and Asians have not been successful.

A growing number of blacks who have "made it" want to be seen as having arrived there by their own ability rather than affirmative action. In California, Florida, Michigan, and Texas, for example, affirmative-action programs based on race in college admissions have been challenged by whites, and also by some blacks.

These racial changes since the 1960s—and others too numerous to highlight—have encouraged a new generation of black leaders to recommend that priority also be given to those social problems that only tortuously can be linked solely to racism. They point, for example, to the prevalence of black-on-black crime, absentee fathers, the disproportion of AIDS among blacks compared to whites, the large number of single-parent black households in public-housing projects, and the poorly performing public schools in those neighborhoods. The victims of black crime are predominantly black.

That is why in Chicago last year, U.S. Representative Bobby Rush (D-Ill.) convened a summit on black-on-black crime and asked the attendees to "find alternatives to the culture of gun violence. It is critical we teach by example the true method of conflict resolution... " At about the same time, James T. Meeks, vice president of Jesse Jackson's Rainbow/Push coalition, appealed to fellow blacks: "Let's stop blaming everybody else for the problems of black men and start doing something for ourselves. Yes, white folks have treated us wrong. Yes, there is an injustice, but we're doing a whole lot of stuff to ourselves. To black America, if you want to help, we've got to start in our own house."

Several years ago, the need for such self-scrutiny was dramatically summarized in the *Economist* (March 7, 1998):

> Black unemployment in desperate ghettos is not obviously the result of racism. Most of the worst-stricken cities are run by black mayors, after all; and social services that might once have ignored the plight of blacks are also run by blacks. Black entrepreneurs as well as white ones have fled the inner cites for the suburbs.... A bigger cause of black poverty is that 70 percent of all black children are born out of wedlock.... During the Depression, poverty was acute but families were more cohesive.

In spite of an era of high prosperity, the persistence of child poverty among blacks (and whites), can be attributed, in the main, to the decline in marriage and to the tide of single-parent households. Statistics for 1999 from the U.S. Census Bureau confirmed this conclusion: 50 percent of black children under six in families without a father lived in poverty, while only 9 percent of those in a two-parent family were poor.

While the new black leaders may echo the *Economist*'s devastating overview, they do not deny that racism exists. For them, however, racism as *the* reason for the durability of black poverty has become more difficult to substantiate. Consequently, they search for new ways to eradicate disparities in income, seeking additional means of uprooting black poverty. They struggle to have their voices heard and their proposals implemented. In doing so, they play down white guilt and black helplessness.

On the other hand, the racial gains since the 1960s, the disturbing social conditions within some black communities, and the calls for self-help initiatives have put traditional civil-rights leaders on the defensive. Disinclined to air "dirty linen" in public, they continue viewing the world through the prism of race. As a result, the civil-rights establishment now strives even harder to keep racism high on the nation's agenda and conscience. How? By shunning the more favorable data about black achievement. They publicize instead anecdotal data about racism's presence to garner support for their contention that the nation's 34 million blacks are still the victims and that racism is omnipresent.

In their eagerness, hyperbole often suffuses their arguments. Alabama's Southern Poverty Law Center recently claimed in a fund-raising letter: "I'm sure that you are well aware that our schools are racked with racial strife and intolerance against those who are different. Some call it a national crisis. Our communities are seething with racial violence. African Americans, Hispanics, and Asian Americans are assaulting each other."

In their tug of war with the venerable civil-rights establishment, new—and increasingly influential—black leaders no longer seek to divide (victimizers vs. victims). Instead, they hope to unite blacks and whites so that together they will address the serious social problems that beset inner-city neighborhoods. Their first priority goes to reducing urban poverty. In the new millennium, a new civil-rights agenda is being fashioned to promote two-parent families, curb street violence, improve public schools, reduce dependency on drugs, and uproot poverty. These objectives may prove to be more difficult to achieve than the equal-opportunity goals of the civil-rights movement in the 1960s, but they are no less worthy of pursuit.

---

**Ed Marciniak** *is president of the Institute of Urban Life at Loyola University, Chicago.*

---

# Don Wycliff

Ed Marciniak is absolutely right when he says we are struggling for a new way to talk intelligently and usefully about race. But what inhibits such conversation, I think, is less the lack of a new vocabulary than the persistence of an old one: the vocabulary of racial guilt and innocence. Our whole racial "dialogue" has become a contest to establish or escape guilt, and, as a result, is shot through with dishonesty.

Most white people—or what appears to me to be most—seem intent mainly on establishing their personal innocence: innocence of racial bias, of discrimination, of any connection to or benefit from slavery. Not only is this beside the point, it's also impossible. One cannot escape the personal implications of membership in a society, no matter how personally blameless one may be. Where race in America is concerned, there are no innocents.

For their part, black people—or at least black leaders—seem more intent than ever on pressing the issue of white personal guilt: for slavery, for segregation, for lingering discrimination, for whatever deficits African Americans still suffer. More than three decades into the nation's effort to pay off that promissory note Martin Luther King Jr.

spoke of in his "I Have a Dream" speech, black leaders seem intent on denying that anything at all has changed, determined not to "let the white man off the hook." As a black man, a Christian, and a person who has required the forgiveness and forbearance of others more than once in his life, I am deeply troubled by this particular gambit. The notion of acting as moral prosecutor and judge of a fellow human being strikes me as odious. I take seriously the scriptural admonition against judging others, "for the measure by which you measure is the measure by which you will be measured." There is nothing more foolish and unbecoming, it seems to me, than to go about peering into the eyes of others in search of motes.

(I am reminded in this connection of an e-mail sent me by a black friend of about my age, fifty-four, after the recent deadly school shooting in San Diego. It was a newspaper column in which the writer, a white man, urged other whites to face up to the fact that this kind of behavior was a white kid's malady. My friend underscored that point in his accompanying note. I didn't reply to him, but if I had I would have told him you could bet that, before this terrible phenomenon runs its course, there'll be a black kid somewhere who will do the same thing. There is no racial immunity to the sort of demons that possess children and propel them to such murderous lunacy. To think such immunity exists is to succumb to the pride that goes before a fall—and an embarrassment.)

Not only is such moral prosecution foolish and unbecoming, it's ineffective. Increasingly over the last two decades, white people have given evidence that they have hardened to this sort of thing, that they're through feeling racial guilt—whether they ought to be or not. Obviously, not all take this attitude, but a growing number that now seem to be a majority do. This refusal of guilt first manifested itself in the election of Ronald Reagan and has continued ever since—even through the two Clinton administrations. Paralleling this change has been another: the loss by blacks of the moral high ground that goes along with victim status. Frankly, given the very real and dramatic progress African Americans have made over the last three and one-half decades, it is hard to sustain the argument that we remain, as a group, victims of a relentless and unyielding societal racism. To be sure, racism persists and continues to distort lives. Probably in no area is its effect greater than in law enforcement and criminal justice. The ruinous rates of black unwed motherhood to which Marciniak refers are not unrelated to the depressing rates of arrest and incarceration of black men, so many of whom are thereby rendered "unmarriageable."

But to contend, as some black spokesmen do, that racism remains the defining fact of black life in this country, that "a black man just can't get ahead," is simply, demonstrably false. There are too many exceptions, too many success stories, for that to be true. Such exceptions are now, arguably, the rule. But it wasn't just a general perception of steadily increasing black progress that eroded the notion of blacks as victims and changed the moral equation on race. Had that been the case, I don't think there would be the raw edginess to race relations that is so much in evidence now. No, there was one very specific and singular event that, I believe, sealed the change. That event was the trial of O.J. Simpson and the reaction of black people to it.

It appeared to many whites—and I hear this every time a hot racial issue is aired in the newspaper—that a black man got away with murder in this high-profile case by portraying himself as a victim of police racism. Not only did blacks on the Simpson jury let him get away, but the black community at large applauded it, demonstrating thereby that racial solidarity was more important than justice. Or so the thinking goes. I don't think it was fully appreciated at the time what a watershed in race relations the Simpson verdict was. Indeed, grotesque as the idea may seem, the Simpson case is emblematic of what many white and black conservative critics consider the grievous defect of affirmative action and other programs of racial redress: a black man escaped responsibility for the killing of two white persons so that society could make redress for his supposed victimization by a social institution, the police. Take away the homicidal element and these critics see the same principle at work in, for example, the University of Michigan affirmative-action cases: In an attempt to redress historical social wrongs, less-deserving minority applicants are favored over more-deserving white ones. It's an argument that, it appears, the Supreme Court is ready to buy.

So if there is unfinished business in the area of racial equality and the old vocabulary of racial guilt and innocence have become impediments, what's to be done? We could do far worse, I think, than go back to Martin Luther King Jr. for instruction and example. King and his "dream" are invoked so frequently and wantonly nowadays that I have almost grown tired of them. I know that's heresy, but there is a treacly quality to so much of the talk about King and his dream that it is like an overdose of candy. However, the fact is that King preached hard truths and he was not a man to take the easy road. He entered by the narrow gate—the gate of nonviolent direct action. You almost never hear anyone talk about that anymore. The genius of his approach was manifold. It involved direct action, an active challenge to injustice. But it was nonviolent, a refusal to use what he considered immoral means to achieve a moral end. It put the onus on those maintaining the system of injustice to respond—and to live with themselves afterward. It forced them to confront their consciences, not to listen to moral harangues.

That last fact is critical, especially in our over-the-top, in-your-face, finger-wagging age, when nobody feels any compunction about calling attention to the faults and failures of others. King had the grace and the good sense not to go about acting as moral prosecutor of his fellow humans—even if he may privately have considered them monsters. That may have been a tactical decision—like leaving room in a diplomatic negotiation for one's rival to gracefully back down, to save face. I like to think his belief in nonviolence was an expression of real grace, the result of King's having received forgiveness for his sins and thereby being inclined to forgive others. But whether King's attitude was tactical or something more—or something else entirely—I don't see any contemporary black leader who behaves that way. And that's a real loss because King's approach is the only way whites can be rendered receptive again to the need to exert themselves to rectify what remains of racism in American society.

We in the United States have made an amazing racial revolution over the last three and one-half decades. There may be another nation that has done as much, but if there is, I don't know of it. We must tell our people—black, white, brown, red, yellow—all about that revolution. We need to give ourselves a big round of applause. Then we must challenge ourselves—without condemning—to finish the job. And we must do it in terms that will cause people to nod "yes" instead of turning away in disgust. I personally am fond of those words from the preamble to the Constitution, the ones about creating "a more perfect union." Where is the Martin Luther King of our age, or the Abraham Lincoln, or the Lyndon Johnson, or the Cesar Chavez, who can speak those words in a way that will move us to the next stage of the struggle for American union?

**Don Wycliff** *is public editor of the* Chicago Tribune.

From *Commonweal*, June 1, 2001, pp. 12-14. © 2001 by Commonweal Foundation. Reprinted by permission. For subscriptions, call toll-free: 1-888-495-6755.

# WHY WE HATE

**We may not admit it, but we are plagued with xenophobic tendencies. Our hidden prejudices run so deep, we are quick to judge, fear and even hate the unknown.**

By Margo Monteith, Ph.D. and Jeffrey Winters

**BALBIR SINGH SODHI WAS SHOT TO DEATH ON** September 15 in Mesa, Arizona. His killer claimed to be exacting revenge for the terrorist attacks of September 11. Upon his arrest, the murderer shouted, "I stand for America all the way." Though Sodhi wore a turban and could trace his ancestry to South Asia, he shared neither ethnicity nor religion with the suicide hijackers. Sodhi—who was killed at the gas station where he worked—died just for being different in a nation gripped with fear.

For Arab and Muslim Americans, the months after the terrorist attacks have been trying. They have been harassed at work and their property has been vandalized. An Arab San Francisco shop owner recalled with anger that his five-year-old daughter was taunted by name-callers. Classmates would yell "terrorist" as she walked by.

Public leaders from President George W. Bush on down have called for tolerance. But the Center for American-Islamic Relations in Washington, D.C., has tallied some 1,700 incidents of abuse against Muslims in the five months following September 11. Despite our better nature, it seems, fear of foreigners or other strange-seeming people comes out when we are under stress. That fear, known as xenophobia, seems almost hardwired into the human psyche.

Researchers are discovering the extent to which xenophobia can be easily—even arbitrarily—turned on. In just hours, we can be conditioned to fear or discriminate against those who differ from ourselves by characteristics as superficial as eye color. Even ideas we believe are just common sense can have deep xenophobic underpinnings. Research conducted this winter at Harvard reveals that even among people who claim to have no bias, the more strongly one supports the ethnic profiling of Arabs at airport-security checkpoints, the more hidden prejudice one has against Muslims.

But other research shows that when it comes to whom we fear and how we react, we do have a choice. We can, it seems, choose not to give in to our xenophobic tendencies.

## THE MELTING POT

America prides itself on being a melting pot of cultures, but how we react to newcomers is often at odds with that self-image. A few years ago, psychologist Markus Kemmelmeier, Ph.D., now at the University of Nevada at Reno, stuck stamped letters under the windshield wipers of parked cars in a suburb of Detroit. Half were addressed to a fictitious Christian organization, half to a made-up Muslim group. Of all the letters, half had little stickers of the American flag.

Would the addresses and stickers affect the rate at which the letters would be mailed? Kemmelmeier wondered. Without the flag stickers, both sets of letters were mailed at the same rate, about 75 percent of the time. With the stickers, however, the rates changed: Almost all the Christian letters were forwarded, but only half of the Muslim letters were mailed. "The flag is seen as a sacred object," Kemmelmeier says. "And it made people think about what it means to be a good American."

In short, the Muslims didn't make the cut.

Not mailing a letter seems like a small slight. Yet in the last century, there have been shocking examples of xenophobia in our own back yard. Perhaps the most famous in American history was the fear of the Japanese during World War II. This particular wave of hysteria lead to the rise of slurs and bigoted depictions in the media, and more alarmingly, the mass internment of 120,000 people of Japanese ancestry beginning in 1942. The internments have become a national embarrassment: Most of the Japanese held were American citizens, and there is little evidence that the imprisonments had any real strategic impact.

Today the targets of xenophobia—derived from the Greek word for *stranger*—aren't the Japanese. Instead, they are Muslim immigrants. Or Mexicans. Or Chinese. Or whichever group we have come to fear.

Just how arbitrary are these xenophobic feelings? Two famous public-school experiments show how easy it is to turn one "group" against another. In the late 1960s, California high school history teacher Ron Jones recruited students to participate in an exclusive new cultural program called "the Wave." Within weeks, these students were separating themselves from others and aggressively intimidating critics. Eventually, Jones confronted the students with the reality that they were unwitting participants in an experiment demonstrating the power of nationalist movements.

## Sonam Wangmo:
**"Am I fearful of Arab men in turbans? No, I am not. I was born and raised in India, and I am familiar with other races. I have learned to be attuned to different cultures. I find that there are always new, positive things to be learned from other people; it brings out the best in us."**

A few years later, a teacher in Iowa discovered how quickly group distinctions are made. The teacher, Jane Elliott, divided her class into two groups—those with blue eyes and those with brown or green eyes. The brown-eyed group received privileges and treats, while the blue-eyed students were denied rewards and told they were inferior. Within hours, the once-harmonious classroom became two camps, full of mutual fear and resentment. Yet, what is especially shocking is that the students were only in the third grade.

### SOCIAL IDENTITY

The drive to completely and quickly divide the world into "us" and "them" is so powerful that it must surely come from some deep-seated need. The exact identity of that need, however, has been subject to debate. In the 1970s, the late Henri Tajfel, Ph.D., of the University of Bristol in England, and John Turner, Ph.D., now of the Australian National University, devised a theory to explain the psy-

chology behind a range of prejudices and biases, not just xenophobia. Their theory was based, in part, on the desire to think highly of oneself. One way to lift your self-esteem is to be part of a distinctive group, like a winning team; another is to play up the qualities of your own group and denigrate the attributes of others so that you feel your group is better.

## Terry Kalish:
**"I am planning a trip to Florida, and I'm nervous about flying with my kids; I'm scared. If an Arab man sat next to me, I would feel nervous. I would wonder, 'Does he have explosives?' But then I feel ashamed to think this way. These poor people must get so scrutinized. It's wrong."**

Tajfel and Turner called their insight "social identity theory," which has proved valuable for understanding how prejudices develop. Given even the slenderest of criteria, we naturally split people into two groups—an "in-group" and an "out-group." The categories can be of geopolitical importance—nationality, religion, race, language—or they can be as seemingly inconsequential as handedness, hair color or even height.

Once the division is made, the inferences and projections begin to occur. For one, we tend to think more highly of people in the in-group than those in the out-group, a belief based only on group identity. Also, a person tends to feel that others in the in-group are similar to one's self in ways that—although stereotypical—may have little to do with the original criteria used to split the groups. Someone with glasses may believe that other people who wear glasses are more voracious readers—even more intelligent—than those who don't, in spite of the fact that all he really knows is that they don't see very well. On the other hand, people in the out-group are believed to be less distinct and less complex than are cohorts in the in-group.

Although Tajfel and Turner found that identity and categorization were the root cause of social bias, other researchers have tried to find evolutionary explanations for discrimination. After all, in the distant past, people who shared cultural similarities were found to be more genetically related than those who did not. Therefore, favoring the in-group was a way of helping perpetuate one's genes. Evolutionary explanations seem appealing, since they rely on the simplest biological urges to drive complicated behavior. But this fact also makes them hard to prove. Ironically, there is ample evidence backing up the "softer" science behind social identity theory.

# HIDDEN BIAS

Not many of us will admit to having strong racist or xenophobic biases. Even in cases where bias becomes public debate—such as the profiling of Arab Muslims at airport-security screenings—proponents of prejudice claim that they are merely promoting common sense. That reluctance to admit to bias makes the issue tricky to study.

To get around this problem, psychologists Anthony Greenwald, Ph.D., of the University of Washington in Seattle, and Mahzarin Banaji, Ph.D., of Harvard, developed the Implicit Association Test. The IAT is a simple test that measures reaction time: The subject sees various words or images projected on a screen, then classifies the images into one of two groups by pressing buttons. The words and images need not be racial or ethnic in nature—one group of researchers tested attitudes toward presidential candidates. The string of images is interspersed with words having either pleasant or unpleasant connotations, then the participant must group the words and images in various ways—Democrats are placed with unpleasant words, for instance.

## Rangr:
"For the months following 9/11, I had to endure my daily walk to work along New York City's Sixth Avenue. It seemed that half the people stared at me with accusation. It became unbearable. Yet others showed tremendous empathy. Friends, co-workers and neighbors, even people I had never met, stopped to say, 'I hope your turban has not caused you any trouble.' At heart, this is a great country."

The differences in reaction time are small but telling. Again and again, researchers found that subjects readily tie in-group images with pleasant words and out-group images with unpleasant words. One study compares such groups as whites and blacks, Jews and Christians, and young people and old people. And researchers found that if you identify yourself in one group, it's easier to pair images of that group with pleasant words—and easier to pair the opposite group with unpleasant imagery. This reveals the underlying biases and enables us to study how quickly they can form.

Really though, we need to know very little about a person to discriminate against him. One of the authors of this story, psychologist Margo Monteith, Ph.D., performed an IAT experiment comparing attitudes toward two sets of made-up names; one set was supposedly "American,"

the other from the fictitious country of Marisat. Even though the subjects knew nothing about Marisat, they showed a consistent bias against it.

While this type of research may seem out in left field, other work may have more "real-world" applications. The Southern Poverty Law Center runs a Web version of the IAT that measures biases based on race, age and gender. Its survey has, for instance, found that respondents are far more likely to associate European faces, rather than Asian faces, with so-called American images. The implication being that Asians are seen as less "American" than Caucasians.

Similarly, Harvard's Banaji has studied the attitudes of people who favor the racial profiling of Arab Muslims to deter terrorism, and her results run contrary to the belief that such profiling is not driven by xenophobic fears. "We show that those who endorse racial profiling also score high on both explicit and implicit measures of prejudice toward Arab Muslims," Banaji says. "Endorsement of profiling is an indicator of level of prejudice."

# BEYOND XENOPHOBIA

If categorization and bias come so easily, are people doomed to xenophobia and racism? It's pretty clear that we are susceptible to prejudice and that there is an unconscious desire to divide the world into "us" and "them." Fortunately, however, new research also shows that prejudices are fluid and that when we become conscious of our biases we can take active—and successful—steps to combat them.

Researchers have long known that when observing racially mixed groups, people are more likely to confuse the identity of two black individuals or two white ones, rather than a white with a black. But Leda Cosmides, Ph.D., and John Tooby, Ph.D., of the Center for Evolutionary Psychology at the University of California at Santa Barbara, and anthropologist Robert Kurzban, Ph.D., of the University of California at Los Angeles, wanted to test whether this was innate or whether it was just an artifact of how society groups individuals by race.

To do this, Cosmides and her colleagues made a video of two racially integrated basketball teams locked in conversation, then they showed it to study participants. As reported in the *Proceedings of the National Academy of Sciences*, the researchers discovered that subjects were more likely to confuse two players on the same team, regardless of race, rather than two players of the same race on opposite teams.

Cosmides says that this points to one way of attacking racism and xenophobia: changing the way society imposes group labels. American society divides people by race and by ethnicity; that's how lines of prejudice form. But simple steps, such as integrating the basketball teams, can reset mental divisions, rendering race and ethnicity less important.

This finding supports earlier research by psychologists Samuel Gaertner, Ph.D., of the University of Delaware in Newark, and John Dovidio, Ph.D., of Colgate University in Hamilton, New York. Gaertner and Dovidio have studied how bias changes when members of racially mixed groups must cooperate to accomplish shared goals. In situations where team members had to work together, bias could be reduced by significant amounts.

Monteith has also found that people who are concerned about their prejudices have the power to correct them. In experiments, she told subjects that they had performed poorly on tests that measured belief in stereotypes. She discovered that the worse a subject felt about her performance, the better she scored on subsequent tests. The guilt behind learning about their own prejudices made the subjects try harder not to be biased.

This suggests that the guilt of mistaking individuals for their group stereotype—such as falsely believing an Arab is a terrorist—can lead to the breakdown of the belief in that stereotype. Unfortunately, such stereotypes are reinforced so often that they can become ingrained. It is difficult to escape conventional wisdom and treat all people as individuals, rather than members of a group. But that seems to be the best way to avoid the trap of dividing the world in two—and discriminating against one part of humanity.

## READ MORE ABOUT IT:

*Nobody Left to Hate: Teaching Compassion After Columbine,* Elliot Aronson (W.H. Freeman and Company, 2000)
*The Racist Mind: Portraits of American Neo-Nazis and Klansmen,* Madonna Kolbenschlag (Penguin Books, 1996)

*Margo Monteith, Ph.D., is an associate professor of psychology at the University of Kentucky. Jeffrey Winters is a New York-based science writer.*

# THE MELTING POT

## Part I: Are We There Yet?

*Anne Wortham*

In the years following the American Revolution the expectation developed that over time the best traditions of Europe would be blended or amalgamated into a dynamic unity; that Englishmen, Germans, Italians, Irishmen, and Russians[1] would all become Americans, a new group that would be different from any of the original groups but also a combination of them all.[2] This was the vision of a young French nobleman, Michel Guillaume Jean de Crèvecoeur (1735–1813), who immigrated to the United States in 1759 and in 1782 published a book on life in America entitled *Letters From an American Farmer*. "What, then, is the American, this new man?" asked Crèvecoeur. "He is neither an European nor the descendant of an European; hence that strange mixture of blood which you will find in no other country…. Here individuals of all nations are melted into a new race of men whose labor and posterity will one day cause great changes in the world."[3]

> *"What, then, is the American, this new man?" asked Crèvecoeur. "He is neither an European nor the descendant of an European; hence that strange mixture of blood which you will find in no other country…. Here individuals of all nations are melted into a new race of men whose labor and posterity will one day cause great changes in the world."*

Crèvecoeur's image of the United States as a melting pot had little basis in fact. For one thing, by restricting his application of the melting pot to whites, he omitted American Indians and Negroes, who made up about 20 percent of the total colonial population. Extensive cultural diversity had been characteristic of the aboriginal North American peoples long before European colonialization.[4] Crèvecoeur's model also ignored the cultural and regional differences among the diverse Europeans who immigrated to the New World in the seventeenth century: they were no more homogeneous than the indigenous people of many cultures who already populated the land.

In contrast to Crèvecoeur's vision, which reflected his romanticized perception of his times, Ralph Waldo Emerson (1803–1882) saw the melting pot as a promise to be fulfilled in the future. Unlike Crevecoeur, he included Negroes in the mix. For Emerson the United States was the "asylum of all nations," and he predicted that "the energy of Irish, Swedes, Poles, and Cossacks, and all the European tribes—of the Africans, and of the Polynesians, will construct a new race, a new religion, a new state, a new literature, which will be as vigorous as the new Europe which came out of the smelting-pot of the Dark Ages, or that which earlier emerged from Pelasgic and Etruscan barbarism."[5]

## MORE MELTING POT VISIONS

Yet another melting-pot vision was promoted by the influential historian Frederick Jackson Turner (1861–1932). In 1893, Turner argued that American identity was not Anglo-Saxon in origin and was forged in the Middle West, which he saw as "a newer and richer civilization" from which "a new product, which held the promise of world brotherhood" had emerged. The frontier had been the catalyst that had already fused the immigrants into a composite new national stock, argued Turner.[6] But his model was an inaccurate depiction of frontier reality. As Vincent Parrillo points out, "The pioneers did adapt to their new environment but the culture remained Anglo-American in form and content. Furthermore, in many areas of the Middle West Turner speaks about, culturally homogeneous settlements of Germans or Scandinavians often maintained distinct subcultures for generations."[7]

Perhaps the most quoted melting-pot idealist is Israel Zangwill (1864–1926), a British-born Jew, whose 1908 play *The*

*My grandmother came from Russia
A satchel on her knee
My grandfather had his father's cap
He brought from Italy.
They'd heard about a country
Where life might let them win
They paid the fare to America
And there they melted in*

*Lovely Lady Liberty
With her book of recipes
And the finest one she's got
Is the great American melting pot.
The great American melting pot.*

*America was founded by the English,
But also by the Germans,
Dutch and French.
The principle still sticks;
Our heritage is mixed.
So any kid could be the president.*

*You simply melt right in,
It doesn't matter what your skin.
It doesn't matter where you're from,
Or your religion, you jump right in
To the great American melting pot.
The great American melting pot.
Ooh, what a stew, red, white and blue.*

*America was the New World*

*And Europe was the Old,
America was the land of hope,
Or so the legend told.
On steamboats by the millions,
In search of honest pay,
Those nineteenth-century immigrants sailed
To reach the U.S.A.
Lovely Lady Liberty
With her book of recipes
And the finest one she's got
Is the great American melting pot.
What good ingredients,
Liberty and immigrants.*

*They brought the country's customs,
Their language and their ways.
They filled the factories, tilled the soil,
Help build the U.S.A.
Go on and ask your grandma,
Hear what she has to tell
How great to be an American
And something else as well.*

*Lovely Lady Liberty
With her books of recipes
And the finest one she's got
Is the great American melting pot.
The great American melting pot.*

*The great American melting pot.
The great American melting pot.*

The lyrics above are from the television and video-tape feature *The Great American Melting Pot* developed by SchoolHouse Rock, which uses animation and music to teach lessons to children.* Even the most cursory reading of the lyrics cannot avoid their non sequiturs and resulting half-truths and inaccuracies. What the feature represents as "melting in" can be more accurately described as patterns of assimilation and pluralism. Furthermore, it betrays the perspectives of early melting-pot visionaries who restricted the process to European immigrants. There never was a melting pot, there is not now a melting pot, and we are not headed toward a melting pot, at least not in the sense meant by its early proponents. Yet "The Great American Melting Pot" illustrates how powerful an image the melting pot continues to be in American life.

Part I of this examination of the melting-pot ideal will show that despite its continued academic and popular usage, the concept has limited theoretical utility and little basis in reality. Pluralism is both the reality and drama of American society. However, as ethnically diverse as the nation is, it nevertheless has a cultural core that immigrants are expected to assimilate. Part II* will identify the key elements of that cultural core, with particular emphasis on their origins and their functions.

—A.W.

*"Great American Melting Pot" from *American Rock* [video recording], Stanford, CT: Capital cities/ABC video Pub., 1995.

*Melting Pot* portrayed America as "God's crucible, the great melting pot where all the races of Europe are melting and reforming!" To the immigrants entering Ellis Island, Zangwill's protagonist exhorted: "A fig for your feuds and vendettas! German and Frenchman, Irishman and Englishman, Jews, Russians—into the crucible with you all! God is making the American... He will be the fusion of all the races, the coming superman."[8] The politician William Jennings Bryan (1860–1925) echoed Zangwill's sentiments: "Great has been the

Greek, the Latin, the Slav, the Celt, the Teuton, and the Saxon; but greater than any of these is the American, who combines the virtues of them all."[9]

Reflecting on the plausibility of the melting-pot ideal, Milton Gordon notes that, given a population drawn from many nations, "was it not possible then, to think of the evolving American society not simply as a slightly modified England but rather as a totally new blend, culturally and biologically, in which the stocks and folkways of Europe were, figuratively speaking, indiscriminately mixed in the political pot of the emerging nation and melted together by the fires of American influence and interaction into a distinctly new type?"[10]

---

*It became apparent during the decades before World War I that immigrants were not giving up the ways of their origins as the price of assimilation and were not mixing together in the great crucible to form the new American.*

---

This frame of mind was certainly plausible, but the vision itself could not be realized. When it became apparent during the decades before World War I that immigrants were not giving up the ways of their origins as the price of assimilation and were not mixing together in the great crucible to form the new American, the melting-pot idea as a natural laissez-faire process was abandoned. At the turn of the twentieth century, the policy of coerced assimilation, known as "Americanization," was inaugurated. Public schools, patriotic societies, chambers of commerce, women's clubs, public libraries, social settlements, and even industrial plants were enlisted to divest the immigrant of his foreign heritage, suppress his native language, teach him English, make him a naturalized citizen, and inject into him a loyalty to American institutions.[11]

The Americanization movement was coercive, condescending, and suppressive; it implied that American culture was a finished product, in an Anglo-Saxon pattern, that it was superior to all others, and that immigrants should adapt to Anglo-American culture as fast as possible. Immigrants were under no illusion; they knew that Americanization was the precondition for access to better jobs, higher education, political participation, and other opportunities. Nevertheless, the policy fell into disrepute. The most celebrated opponent of the melting pot and Americanization was the philosopher Horace Kallen, who developed the theory of cultural pluralism. The real meaning of American history, argued Kallen, was cultural pluralism, freedom, and unity through group diversity.[12]

Since the appearance of Kallen's theory, most of the major studies of American minority groups have been alternately guided by the theories of assimilation and cultural pluralism. Yet the failure of the melting-pot thesis to become policy has not prevented it from being of great ideological influence, becoming the utopian lens through which Americans view their society.

## MELTING-POT THEORY

Theoretically, the melting-pot model is one of several answers to the question: What is the best way of integrating disparate peoples into a single nation? The form of this question is as old as questions posed by the founders of Western philosophy; but in modern thought it dates back to Thomas Hobbes' question: How and why is society possible? The issue, known as the Hobbesian "problem of order," was central in the thought of eighteenth- and nineteenth-century social philosophers and sociologists. It was no less the preoccupation of the framers of the American nation, whose particular concern was the creation of one nation out of thirteen colonies: Would the United States be politically one nation, or would it not? Their answer is represented in the motto on the face of the Great Seal of the United States: *E pluribus unum* (out of many, one).[13] Although *E pluribus unum* shares with the melting-pot metaphor the same species (the problem of social organization), they are of different genera. The former expresses the political ideal of fashioning one nation out of many states, and is more appropriate to today's federal system; the latter refers to the biological and cultural amalgamation of groups into a new group.

---

*In the extreme form of cultural assimilation, the previously distinct cultural groups would lose all their distinguishable behavior and values.*

---

Although technically the concept of the melting pot refers to the amalgamation of groups, it is also used variously to refer to two different patterns of assimilation: (1) unidimensional, one-way assimilation, or Anglo-conformity, by which immigrants relinquish their own culture in favor of the dominant culture and are remade according to the idealized Anglo-Saxon mold;[14] and (2) reciprocal assimilation or acculturation, which may involve either direct social interaction or exposure to other cultures by means of mass media. As the outcome of such contact, the dominant group adopts some traits of minorities while the cultural patterns of the dominant group are taken over by minority groups. An example of Anglo-conformity is learning the English language; acculturation can be seen in the Americanization of foreign cuisine.

Suppose the plausibility of the melting-pot model. Given a structural environment of democratic political institutions, voluntary association, and a relatively free and open economic system, exactly what attitudes and behavior would be necessary to realize the blending, melting, and fusing processes portrayed by melting-pot visionaries? Gordon has identified subprocesses of assimilation that, when linked together, could theoretically produce a culturally and biologically amalgamated people. Foremost among these processes would be "the complete mixture of the various stocks through intermarriage—in other words, *marital* assimilation, or amalgamation."[15] *Cultural* assimilation or acculturation would involve the intermixing of cultural traits (language, values, religion, everyday norms, dress, diet) of various groups to "form a blend somewhat different from the cultures of any one of the groups separately." This is the process by which Italians become Italian Americans, Poles become Polish Americans, and Haitians become Haitian

Americans. In the extreme form of cultural assimilation, the previously distinct cultural groups would lose all their distinguishable behavior and values.

Large-scale intermarriage presupposes *structural* assimilation of immigrants; that they have "entered into cliques, clubs, and other primary groups, and institutions of the host society and, in addition, placed their own impress upon these social structures to some extent." Melting would most certainly require *identificational* assimilation "in the form of all groups merging their previous sense of peoplehood into a new and larger ethnic identity which, in some fashion, honors its multiple origins at the same time that it constitutes an entity distinct from them all." Individuals would no longer see themselves as distinctive and would stake their personal identities to participation and success in the mainstream institutions of the society; they may maintain what Herbert Gans calls "symbolic ethnicity," which can be taken on or off without any real social cost to the individual, but they would think of themselves as Americans.[16]

---

*When the melting-pot vision is measured against these combined processes that are the necessary conditions of its creation, it has no basis in reality.*

---

Since, as a consequence of amalgamation, there would not be any identifiably separate groups to be a target, attitude-receptional assimilation would be evident in the absence of prejudicial attitudes and stereotyping on the part of both dominant and minority ethnic groups. Behavioral-receptional assimilation would be apparent in the absence of intentional discrimination against groups. Finally, civic assimilation would have taken place, "since disparate cultural values are assumed to have merged and power conflict between groups would be neither necessary nor possible."

An example of assimilation using these dimensions is as follows. An immigrant arrives in the United States, takes on American customs, and learns to speak flawless English (cultural assimilation). She encounters no prejudice from neighbors or employers (*attitude-receptional* assimilation), and is able to live and work where she pleases (behavioral-receptional assimilation). She observes that no political or social issues separate her group from the host society (civic assimilation). Increasingly she no longer thinks of herself as an immigrant, or as having ties to "the old country," but sees herself as an American (identificational assimilation). She marries a member of the dominant group (marital assimilation) and joins bridge clubs, professional societies, and sororities that are composed entirely of core society members (structural assimilation).[17]

Such a detailed account of the subprocesses of assimilation indicates just how difficult assimilation is for an individual, let alone an entire ethnic group, particularly racially visible groups such as Negroes, Indians, and Asians. When the melting-pot vi-

Black slaves on the deck of the bark *Wildfire*. Its arrival into Key West, Florida, on April 30, 1860, violated the 1809 law prohibiting the importation of slaves.

sion is measured against these combined processes that are the necessary conditions of its creation, it has no basis in reality. If all the assimilation processes that the melting pot entails were completed, says Martin Marger, the result would be a homogeneous society

> in which ethnicity plays no role in the distribution of wealth, power, and prestige. This does not mean, of course, that other forms of social differentiation and stratification such as age, sex, and class would not exist; it means only that the ethnic forms would no longer be operative. In essence, a society in which all groups have perfectly assimilated is no longer a multiethnic society. However, this complete form of assimilation is rarely achieved, either for the society as a whole or for specific groups and individuals. Instead, assimilation takes different forms and is evident in different degrees.[18]

Sociologist Seymour Martin Lipset believes that the melting pot is validated by intermarriage statistics, which, as he surmises, "indicate that majorities of Catholics, Jews, Italians, Irish, and Japanese Americans marry out of their ancestral groups."[19] Indeed, demographic data also show greater tolerance for black-white intermarriages, although they are the least common form of racial intermarriage for whites.[20] However, while some degree of amalgamation occurs between groups in a pluralistic society, it is not often a total societal process in the sense meant by the melting-pot theory. As for the emergence of a distinct new national culture evolving from elements of all other cultures, Marger notes: "Ideologically, societies may advocate some kind of ethnic melting pot wherein all groups contribute in proportionate amounts to form a new social system, but such a cultural and, particularly, structural fusion is a chimera."[21]

## ASSIMILATION IMPEDIMENTS

An example of the demographic and socioeconomic variability with which groups assimilate is Frances Fitzgerald's description of the impact of the movement of ethnic groups to the suburbs. When members of European ethnic communities left the cities in the wake of the flight of manufacturing, they did not "melt" into the white middle class; rather, instead of a melting pot, what they experienced was "a centrifuge that spun them around and distributed them out again across the landscape according to new principles: families with incomes of, say, thirty to sixty thousand dollars a year went to one suburb; families with incomes of, say, sixty to a hundred thousand dollars went to another; and young, single people were flung, en masse, into the recently vacated downtown neighborhoods." Ethnicity, class, and lifestyle were no longer correlated. Many of the young people came from blue-collar backgrounds but were college educated and did not think of themselves as hyphenated Americans. "By the mid-sixties the whole deck of white middle-class society had been reshuffled, and the old cards of identity—Italian-American, WASP, Russian Jewish-American— had lost much of their meaning."[22]

The situation for lower-class minorities in the central cities— where ethnicity, class, and lifestyle remain highly correlated— has been just the opposite of the suburbanization experience of the white ethnics Fitzgerald describes. Data from a study of seventy-four of the country's largest cities and metropolitan areas from 1970 to 1990 show that despite an increase in employment opportunities and a decline in formal discrimination in the wake of civil rights legislation, low wages and lack of access and opportunity continue to plague minorities concentrated in central cities. The housing patterns of minorities, particularly blacks, have not kept pace with the movement of employment to the suburbs. The percent of employment in the suburbs has been rising faster than the percent of population moving to the suburbs.[23] William Julius Wilson refers to this trend in which minorities live where the jobs aren't as "spatial mismatch."[24] The situation is exacerbated by the lack of rail and bus lines that accommodate commuting from the city to the suburbs.

Housing segregation such as this means that minorities lack the social networks and resources that are conducive to fostering entry into the mainstream. It illustrates the difficulty of achieving structural assimilation, particularly to the degree that is necessary for the realization of the other processes of assimilation. Yet, despite the assimilation problems of inner-city minorities, demographic data show modest declines in racial residential segregation in most metropolitan areas, and the growing suburbanization of blacks, Hispanics, and Asians matches the broad shift in attitudes on residential integration and openness to racial mixing in neighborhoods.

*In the 1970s scholars found that although there had been considerable "melting" of ideas and cultural attributes, the ethnics themselves had proved "unmeltable" in any ultimate sense.*

In the 1970s scholars found that although there had been considerable "melting" of ideas and cultural attributes, the ethnics themselves had proved "unmeltable" in any ultimate sense. Not only had ethnic belonging survived, but so had the subjective evaluations of ethnic categories in the community. A decade later, as noted above, Fitzgerald observed that for later-generation white ethnics, ethnicity was not something that influenced their lives unless they wanted it to. Mary Waters, who has studied patterns of "optional ethnicity," writes that "for an increasing number of European-origin individuals whose parents and grandparents have intermarried, the ethnicity they claim is largely a matter of personal choice as they sort through all of the possible combinations of groups in their genealogies."[25]

But the situation is quite different for visible minorities. Waters writes that the freedom to include or exclude ancestries in one's identification is not the same for those defined racially in American society. Racially defined minorities "are constrained to identify with the part of their ancestry that has been socially defined as the 'essential' part. African Americans, for example, have been highly socially constrained to identify as blacks, without other options available to them, even when they know that their forebears included many people of American Indian or European background."[26]

Being a white ethnic is not entirely unproblematic. That researchers do not include them among "racially-defined groups" does not mean that they are not racially defined by others and that there are no negative consequences for being so defined. While the ethnic components of white identity are receding with each generation's increased distance from its immigrant ancestors, the racial component of their identity is a handicap for many. As Michael Omni and Howard Winant point out, whites have been racialized in the post-civil rights movement era, and "now, the very meaning of 'white' has become a matter of anxiety and concern."[27]

In a study of racial diversity at the University of California at Berkeley, students expressed several themes and dilemmas of contemporary white identity. Lacking a sense of ethnic identity, one student said, "I think that I may be missing something that other people have, that I am not experiencing." Another identified the disadvantages of being white with respect to the distribution of resources: "Being white means that you're less likely to get financial aid…. It means that there are all sorts of tutoring groups and special programs that you can't get into, because you're not a minority." Said another: "If you want to go with stereotypes, Asians are the smart people, the blacks are great athletes, what is white? We're just here. We're the oppressors of the nation."[28]

---

*Caribbean-American immigrants even push their children to adopt strategies, such as invoking their accents or other references to French or British colonial culture, to differentiate themselves from U.S.-born blacks and avoid the stigma of "blackness."*

---

As the authors point out, although white Americans have not been immune to the process of racialization, unlike "people of color," they are prohibited from asserting their racial identity in political life.[29] In the aftermath of the civil rights movement, a double standard developed by which the reification of racial identity was deemed appropriate for everyone but whites. Blacks, Hispanics, and American Indians are expected to assert racial and ethnic pride, and whites are expected to concede their collective culpability for the plight of minorities, accept their stigma without protest, and to applaud minorities for resisting their stigma.

The stereotyping of *white* to mean "oppressor" and "racist" causes identity problems for colored minorities as well—ironically, because "white" is also associated with rationality, the work ethic, and intellectual achievement. Min Zhou describes how it plays out in the generational conflict between immigrant parents and their U.S.-born children in the Asian-American and Caribbean-American communities. "Ironically, the parent generation consciously struggles to push children to become 'white' by moving their families to white neighborhoods, sending their children to white schools, and discouraging their children from playing basketball and mimicking hip-hop culture. But becoming 'white' is politically incorrect, and thus unacceptable for the U.S.-born generation."[30]

Caribbean-American immigrants even push their children to adopt strategies, such as invoking their accents or other references to French or British colonial culture, to differentiate themselves from U.S.-born blacks and avoid the stigma of "blackness."[31] A common concern among Haitians in south Florida is that their children will adopt the attitudes of the inner city's underclass. Vietnamese parents in New Orleans often try to keep their children immersed in their ethnic enclave, discouraging them from assimilating too fast.[32]

The absurdity of this kind of stereotyping extends to high-achieving native black children, especially college students, who feel they must camouflage their strivings and achievements to avoid the stigma of "whiteness."

The definition of *American* to mean "white," which can be traced to the writings of melting-pot visionaries like Crèvecoeur, also has a negative impact on the identificational assimilation of "people of color." In a study of children of Haitians, Cubans, West Indians, Mexicans, and Vietnamese in south Florida and Southern California, the researchers asked repondents how they identified themselves. Most chose categories of hyphenated Americans, few chose "American" as their identity. Asked if they believed the United States was the best country in the world, most of them answered no.[33]

On the other hand, as Min Zhou points out, U.S.-born children and grandchildren of Asian and Hispanic ancestry find that although they are already assimilated and think of themselves as American, their American identity is often questioned because they look like the contemporary influx of "colored" immigrants. "Suddenly they are confronted with the renewed image of themselves as 'foreigners'," notes Zhou. "Harassment of a Mexican American accused of being an undocumented immigrant, or comments about a third-generation Japanese American's 'good English' are frequently reported."[34]

## THE PLURALIST REALITY

As the sources of tension and conflict in intergroup relations indicate, assimilation is not an inevitable outcome of immigration. Most groups in America are incompletely assimilated. Although there has been widespread cultural assimilation in American society—due, in part, to mass communications, mass transportation, and education— structural assimilation has not yet occurred on a grand scale. Gordon stresses that structural assimilation is more difficult to achieve than cultural assimilation because it involves penetration into the close interactions and associations of dominant ethnic groups. Even when members of ethnic groups penetrate secondary and formal organizational structures—schools, workplaces, and political arenas—they may still lack more primary and personal ties with members of dominant ethnic groups.

Nathan Glazer and Daniel Moynihan were among the first to emphasize that even as many of their customs are replaced with those of the dominant American society, white ethnic groups continue to reveal residential, behavioral, organizational, and cultural patterns that mark their distinctive ethnic identity, one that subtly separates them from the middle-class, American Protestant core.[35] They think of themselves as Americans sharing one national culture and as members of distinct groups with distinctive ways of life.

America has always been a pluralistic society. In its rejection of ethnic exclusivity and denial of the political recognition or formal status of ethnic groups, the American political system has made ethnic-group formation and maintenance a voluntary matter. Despite many policies of exclusivism, the history of American society has been such that the structural basis for ethnic preservation has been progressively undermined by a system of justice based on individual rights and the demands of a market economy. However, while ethnicity (as a sense of peoplehood) has been undermined by the forces of modernization and transformed by acculturation, and while social mobility has taken members of ethnic groups across boundaries of the ethnic structural network, ethnic belonging has persisted and considerable structural pluralism exists along racial and religious lines.

*This reality of regional differentiation as well as national origin has been totally ignored by the U.S. Census Bureau's lumping together persons from Central America, Mexico, Puerto Rico, and Cuba into a superethnic group called "Hispanics."*

Gordon attempted to capture the complexity of simultaneous assimilation and pluralism by focusing on ethnic group subcultures that are to some extent organized within subsocieties. While assimilation takes place within economic, political, and educational institutions, ethnic subsocieties are maintained in the institutional areas of religion, family, and recreation. It is in this sense that Gordon sees both assimilation and cultural pluralism occurring. Moreover, while race, religion, and nationality are important determinants of these subsocieties, these three variables are intersected by three others: social class, urban-rural residence, and regional residence. The various combinations of these dimensions of differentiation create what Gordon calls "ethclasses." Examples of such ethclasses include southern, lower-class, Protestant, rural blacks; northern, upper-class, white, urban Jews; northern, lower-class, white, urban, Catholics; and western, middle-class, suburban, third-generation Japanese.[36]

Viewing the assimilation process from the vantage point of the ethclass reveals that immigrants do not assimilate American culture in general; rather, they tend to adopt the folkways of the regions in which they settle. So it is, for instance, that there are Yankee Jews, Philadelphia Jews, southern Jews, and backslapping Texas Jews in cowboy boots and ten-gallon hats. Such cases of regional assimilation illustrate the fact that assimilation is itself pluralistic. This reality of regional differentiation as well as national origin has been totally ignored by the U.S. Census Bureau's lumping together persons from Central America, Mexico, Puerto Rico, and Cuba into a superethnic group called "Hispanics." The ethclass also casts light on the multidimensional nature of intergroup relations in America. For instance, the factors of social class, urban-rural residence, and regional residence enable us to understand that groups that are the object of prejudice and discrimination vary according to those differences. The experiences of blacks in the South vary from those of blacks and Puerto Ricans in the North, and their experiences differ from those of Mexican Americans in the Southwest or Vietnamese in the West.

Because of the prevalence of incomplete assimilation—of the simultaneous integration into the societal mainstream and retention of ethnic group identification—it is more accurate to apply the model of pluralism in understanding American intergroup relations. The general meaning of pluralism is the coexistence and mutual toleration of groups that retain their separate identities. There are three dimensions of the generic pluralist model of intergroup relations: cultural, structural, and political. At the cultural level, each group is free to maintain and develop its own culture, not totally separated but voluntarily segregated to a considerable degree. At the structural level, groups participate in different institutions and informal arrangements rather than in the same ones. Political pluralism is the distribution of political power among various interest groups and organizations, not equally, but with equal rights to organize or join coalitions to influence political decisions that have bearing on their perceived interests.[37]

## AMERICA'S PLURALIST PARADOX

In these definitions, the concept of pluralism has a sociological connotation. Pluralism also refers to an ideological position that takes the view that the cultures and identities of different groups ought to be preserved.

In his monumental study of American race relations, Gunnar Myrdal concluded that a key characteristic of American life was the contradiction between the political ideals of the American creed, which call for just treatment of all people, regardless of race, creed, or color, and the practices of prejudice and differential treatment of people on the basis of race.[38] In the six and one-half decades since Myrdal's report, the United States has clearly moved a considerable distance toward implementing the implications of the American creed for race relations. However, in the aftermath of the civil rights and immigration legislation of the mid-1960s, America has been facing what Gordon calls a new dilemma that "is oriented toward a choice of the kinds of group pluralism which American governmental action and the attitudes of the American people will foster and encourage."[39]

The question for Gordon is "which type of pluralist society is most appropriate and most beneficial for a nation composed of many ethnic groups." America has always been a pluralistic society. What causes the current dilemma of choice, says Gordon, is "the role of government in racial and ethnic relations, together with ethical and philosophical issues revolving around just rewards and whether to treat persons as individuals or as members of a categorically defined group." Nathan Glazer characterizes the situation as follows:

> We have a complex of education, culture, law, administration, and political institutions which has deflected us onto a course in which we publicly establish ethnic and racial categories for differential treatment, and believe that by so doing we are establishing a just and good society.... But this has meant that we abandon the first principle of a liberal society, that the individual's interests and good and welfare are the test of a

**114**

good society, for we now attach benefits and penalities to individuals simply on the basis of their race, color, and national origin. The implications of the new course are an increasing consciousness of the significance of group membership, increasing divisiveness on the basis of race, color, and national origin, and a spreading resentment against the favored groups.[40]

---

*Liberal pluralism seeks equality between individuals, inequality of result, and unity out of group diversity by means of individual rights.*

---

It is these issues that point to the competing frameworks of pluralism that he distinguishes as *liberal* pluralism and *corporate* pluralism. Liberal pluralism seeks equality between individuals, inequality of result, and unity out of group diversity by means of individual rights. Corporate pluralism seeks equality between groups, equality of result, and unity out of group diversity by means of group rights. The conflict between liberal and corporate pluralism arises in part out of what Peter Berger calls "the concurrence of modernizing and demodernizing impulses in the contemporary situation." The modernizing impulse entails an aspiration for liberation from restrictive solidarities of collective life and ideologies. The demodernizing impulse, whether it looks backward into the past or forward into the future, seeks a reversal of the modern trends that its adherents believe have alienated the individual. Their aim is to liberate the individual from what they believe are the dehumanizing excesses of individualism, capitalism, and democracy.[41]

## WHERE ARE WE?

Gordon ended his essay on the conflicting models of pluralism with the prediction that "what the American people decide about this patterned complex of issues in the last twenty years of the twentieth century will have much to do with determining the nature, shape, and destiny of racial and ethnic relations in America in the twenty-first century." Lipset thinks of the future of American ethnicity in terms of an ongoing conflict between two different perspectives of equality expressed in the mass behavior of average Americans on the one hand, and in the discussions and proposals of intellectuals and the ideological Left on the other.

Lipset insists that for the masses, the melting-pot image "remains as appropriate as ever."[42] By melting pot, Lipset means American universalism, the desire to incorporate groups into one culturally unified whole, [which] is inherent in the founding ideology—the American Creed."[43] Although melting pot is not technically the term that describes what Lipset means, it is clearly a vision that is consistent with the option of liberal pluralism that Gordon identifies. (My qualification of Lipset rests

on the understanding of melting pot to mean a biologically and/or culturally amalgamated whole, whereas Lipset's usage refers to a culturally unified whole, which he understands to be a democratic pluralistic society.)

The liberal pluralistic society that Gordon proposes (and that Lipset calls universalistic pluralism) is characterized by David Sears as

a "cosmopolitan liberal" society in which diverse groups comfortably coexist, tolerating each other's modest differences but sharing a strong bond of loyalty to the superordinate nation. This universalist traditional ideal of American integration is perhaps most often captured in the idea of the 'melting pot.' To its adherents, the melting pot means the intermingling of varied cultural streams in the crucible of American life. Immigrants enrich popular culture without threatening the distinctive core of national identity, a Lockean commitment to individual rights shared by all citizens. In principle, though less fully in practice, this conception of American identity is ethnically inclusive, its adherents believing that American society could assimilate all newcomers.[44]

---

*Indeed, what might be called "identity politics" goes beyond ethnicity to include such groups as women, gays, and the disabled.*

---

The second option of corporate pluralism, which Lipset asserts is promoted by intellectuals and the ideological Left, is "particularism, the preservation of subnational group loyalties," which entails the right of ethnic groups to cultural survival.[45] "The emphasis on univeralism has declined in political discourse, while particularism—described by some as multiculturalism—has become more important," says Lipset. In the vision of multiculturalism, writes David Sears, "the differences between groups are not appreciated but institutionalized, in formal power-sharing coalitions." The term *multiculturalism* was first advanced in Canada. Its guiding political principles "are the recognition of and respect for individuals' cultural identity, the primacy of ethnic identity in defining political interests, the idea of communal representation, and the importance of public policies that respond to the claims of subordinate cultural groups. In that sense, multiculturalism is a redistributive ideology that justifies the claims of subordinate groups to a greater share of society's goods. It does so by invoking the notion of group rather than individual rights."

Multiculturalism, which Sears calls the "'hard' particularistic version" of pluralism, "asserts the viability and merit of multiple cultures within a society and advocates government action to maintain these equally worthy cultures. As an ideal image of society, multiculturalism rejects the assimilationist ethos of the melting pot in favor of the mosaic, which typically consists of differently colored tiles isolated from each other by impenetrable grout. It construes racial or ethnic identity as the preferred choice of self-definition." Although its roots are in the black civil rights movement, Sears notes that "multiculturalism extends the model of blacks' struggle for equality in two senses. First, it regards all the distinct cultures within the country as morally and intellectually equal, most notably including the new immigrants from Latin America and Asia. Indeed, what might be called 'identity politics' goes beyond ethnicity to include such groups as women, gays, and the disabled. Second, it advocates official action to achieve equality for all groups."[46]

---

*Clearly, it is toward mutality and respect for differences that we should be headed, not toward melting or politicized "diversity."*

---

The success of the multiculturalists in promoting their vision is indicated by Aguirre and Turner's observation that "it is now politically incorrect to question pluralism or, worse, to extol the virtues of integration of ethnics into an Anglo-Saxon cultural core—at least within academia. But if there is no cultural core to which each wave of immigrants adjusts, or if ethnic populations of any size refuse or cannot adjust, then societal integration will be tenuous."[47] This is not a rejection of the reality of ethnic pluralism but recognition of the requirement of a democratic republic (and capitalism) that ethnic pluralism revolve around weak ethnic identification.

Public opinion research indicates that the vast majority of Americans believe that this is still the land of opportunity, where meritorious achievement is possible. Their opposition to government-enforced pluralism should be seen as a reflection of loyalty to an idealized and seemingly threatened civic culture in which individual equality was enshrined as a core democratic principle. Omni and Winant believe that culture, which was espoused across the political and cultural spectrum as a central ideal, seems to many Americans to be a receding ideal. Yet, they argue, "Avoiding racial polarization in our society may well depend on resuscitating and rearticulating that very vision so as to go beyond race-specific demands to a society of greater social justice for all."[48] There is some hope in the paradoxical reality, as Marger points out, that "while groups extoll the need to retain an ethnic culture and encounter declining resistance to its retention from the dominant group, societal trends continue to erode those cultural differences," compressing cultural singularities into common forms.[49] We may also hope that the erosion of cultural differences will reveal the unique "Americanness" that is a key component of our cultural core. It has the capacity to facilitate the universalism of the American creed.

Denying the existence of the melting pot leaves much to be explained. No denial has been made here of the existence of a metaphorical "pot," only that the processes occurring within amount to a universal "melting." Australian author and art critic Robert Hughes correctly argues that it is too simplistic to say that America is, or ever was, a melting pot. "But it is also too simple to say none of its contents actually melted," writes Hughes. "No single metaphor can do justice to the complexity of cultural crossing and perfusion in America."[50] To be sure, there is some melting (marital and cultural assimilation); however, as pointed out, there is also unevenly spread structural, identificational, attitude-receptional, behavior-receptional, and civic assimilation.

For utopians who dream of a unified, monoethnic, homogenous society, the lack of universal melting is a pathological situation that must be overcome. For realists, to say universal melting is not occurring is not to claim an unnecessary failure but to assert that the facts of human nature, history, and voluntary human association preclude universal melting. However, this is not to deny the possibility of cohesion and unity. Peace, harmony, prosperity, and unity do not require homogeneity, but they do require cohesion. What many Americans experience, and some resist, is not melting but mutuality—a mutuality that, as Hughes points out, "has no choice but to live in recognition of difference."[51] Whether differences persist as distinctions, or are intermingled or merged into something unlike the original form, is no threat to social order so long as mutuality is maintained and distinctions are not used as political clubs of tribal warfare. If mutuality is destroyed, however, differences become the "cultural ramparts" of the current cultural wars. Clearly, it is toward mutuality and respect for differences that we should be headed, not toward melting or politicized "diversity."

## NOTES

1. Actually numerous waves of immigrants came from many nations to America, including but not confined to these.
2. William Newman, American Pluralism: *A Study of Minority Groups and Social Theory* (New York: Harper & Row, 1973), 63.
3. J. Hector St. John (Michel-Guillaume-Jean de Crèvecoeur), *Letters From an American Farmer* (New York: Fox, Duffield & Co., 1904), 54–55.
4. Vincent Parrillo, *Diversity in America* (Thousand Oaks, California: Pine Forge Press, 1996), 18.
5. *The Journals and Miscellaneous Notebooks of Ralph Waldo Emerson*, ed. Ralph Orth and Alfred Ferguson (Cambridge: Belknap, 1971), 9; 299–300.
6. Frederick Jackson Turner, *The Frontier in American History* (New York: Henry Holt, 1920), 3–4.
7. Vincent Parrillo, *Strangers to These Shores*, 5th ed. (Boston: Allyn and Bacon, 1997), 11.
8. Israel Zangwill, *The Melting Pot* (New York: Macmillan, 1909).
9. As quoted in Peter Rose, *They and We: Racial and Ethnic Relations in the United States*, 3rd ed. (New York: Random House, 1981), 64.
10. Milton Gordon, *Assimilation in American Life* (New York: Oxford University Press, 1964), 115.
11. Brewton Berry, *Race and Ethnic Relations*, 3rd ed. (Boston: Houghton Mifflin, 1965), 212–13.

12. Horace Kallen, "Democracy Versus the Melting Pot," *The Nation*, 25 Feb., 1915, 220.

13. The phrase, which can be traced back to Horace's *Epistles*, was suggested by the designer of the Great Seal, Philadelphia artist and painter Pierre Eugene Du Simitiere, who became a naturalized citizen in 1769. Du Simitiere was consultant to Benjamin Franklin, John Adams, and Thomas Jefferson, members of the first committee for the selection of the seal. The official motto of the United States is "In God We Trust," adopted on July 30, 1956.

14. The term "Anglo-conformity" was introduced by Stewart G. Cole and Mildred Wise Cole, *Minorities and the American Promise* (New York: Harper & Row, 1937).

15. This quotation and those that follow in this paragraph are from Gordon, *Assimilation in American Life*, 124–26.

16. Herbert Gans, "Symbolic Ethnicity: The Future of Ethnic Groups and Cultures in America," *Ethnic and Racial Studies* 2 (January 1979): 1–20.

17. From Richard Schaefer, *Racial and Ethnic Groups* (Boston: Little, Brown, 1979), 40–41.

18. Martin Marger, *Race and Ethnic Relations: American and Global Perspectives*, (Belmont, California: Wadsworth Publishing, 1985), 71.

19. Seymour Martin Lipset, *American Exceptionalism: A Double-Edged Sword* (New York: W.W. Norton, 1996), 249. See also Seymour Martin Lipset and Earl Raab, *Jews and the New American Scene* (Cambridge: Harvard University Press, 1995); Stanley Lieberson and Mary Waters, *From Many Strands: Ethnic and Racial Groups in Contemporary America* (New York: Russell Sage Foundation, 1989); and Mary Waters, *Ethnic Options*: Choosing Identities in America (Berkeley: University of California Press, 1990).

20. Lawrence Bobo, "Racial Attitudes and Relations," in *America Becoming: Racial Trends and Their Consequences*, vol. I, ed. Neil Smelser, William Wilson, and Faith Mitchell (Washington, D.C.: National Academy Press, 2001), 295.

21. Marger, *Race and Ethnic Relations*, 78.

22. Frances Fitzgerald, *Cities on a Hill: A Journey Through Contemporary American Cultures* (New York: Simon & Schuster, 1981), 16–17, 387.

23. Manuel Pastor Jr. "Geography and Opportunity," in *America Becoming*, 435–67. See also Douglas Massey, "Residential Segregation and Neighborhood Conditions in U.S. Metropolitan Areas," in *America Becoming*, 391–434.

24. William Julius Wilson, *The Truly Disadvantaged: The Inner City, the Underclass, and Public Policy* (Chicago: University of Chicago Press, 1987).

25. Mary Waters, "Optional Ethnicities: For Whites Only?" in *Origins and Destinies: Immigration, Race and Ethnicity in America*, ed. Silvia Pedraza and Ruben G. Rumbaut (Belmont, California: Wadsworth, 1996), 447.

26. Waters, "Optional Ethnicities."

27. Michael Omni and Howard Winant, "Contesting the Meanings of Race in the Post-Civil Rights Movement Era," in *Origins and Destinies*.

28. Omni and Winant, "Contesting the Meaning of Race."

29. Omni and Winant, "Contesting the Meaning of Race."

30. Min Zhou, "Immigration and the Dynamics of Race and Ethnicity," *America Becoming*, 222–23.

31. Alejandro Portes and A. Stepick, *City on the Edge: The Transformation of Miami* (Berkeley: University of California Press, 1993).

32. William Booth, "The Myth of the Melting Pot, Part 1: One Nation, Indivisible: Is It History?" *Washington Post*, February 22, 1998.

33. Alejandro Portes and Rubin Rumbaut, *Immigrant America: A Portrait*, 2nd ed. (Berkeley: University of California Press, 1996).

34. Zhou, "Immigration and the Dynamics of Race and Ethnicity."

35. Nathan Glazer and Daniel Moynihan, *Beyond the Melting Pot*, 2nd ed. (Cambridge: MIT Press, 1970).

36. Gordon, *Assimilation in American Life*, 18–54.

37. F. James Davis, *Minority-Dominant Relations: A Sociological Analysis* (Arlington Heights, Illinois: AHM Publishing, 1979), 152–54.

38. Gunnar Myrdal, *An American Dilemma* (New York: Harper and Brothers, 1944).

39. Milton Gordon, "Models of Pluralism: The New American Dilemma," *Annals of the American Academy of Political and Social Science*, March 1981.

40. Nathan Glazer, *Affirmative Discrimination: Ethnic Inequality and Public Policy* (New York: Basic Books, 1976), 220.

41. Peter Berger, Brigitte Berger, and Hansfried Kellner, *The Homeless Mind* (New York: Vintage, 1974), 196.

42. Lipset, *American Exceptionalism*, 249–50.

43. Seymour Martin Lipset, "Historical Traditions and National Characteristics: A Comparative Analysis of Canada and the United States," in *Patterns of Modernity, Volume I: The West*, ed. S.N. Eisenstadt, (New York: New York University Press, 1987), 77–78.

44. David Sears, Jack Citrin, Sharmaaine Cheleden, and Colette van Laar, "Cultural Diversity and Multicultural Politics: Is Ethnic Balkanization Psychologically Inevitable?" in *Cultural Divides: Understanding and Overcoming Group Conflict*, ed. Deborah Prentice and Dale Miller, (New York: Russell Sage Foundation, 1999), 35–79.

45. Lipset, "Historical Traditions and National Characteristics."

46. Sears et al., "Cultural Diversity and Multicultural Politics."

47. Adalberto Aguirre Jr. and Jonathan Turner, *American Ethnicity: The Dynamics and Consequences of Discrimination*, 2nd ed. (Boston: McGraw- Hill, 1998), 247.

48. Omni and Winant, "Contesting the Meaning of Race," 476.

49. Marger, *Race and Ethnic Relations*, 290–91.

50. Robert Hughes, *Culture of Complaint: The Fraying of America* (New York: Oxford University Press, 1993), 12–13.

51. Hughes, *Culture of Complaint*, 12–13.

*Anne Wortham is associate professor of sociology at Illinois State University.*

*\* Part II of this article [was] published in a subsequent issue.*

From *The World & I*, September 2001, pp. 261–281. © 2001 by The World & I, a publication of The Washington Times Corporation. Reprinted by permission.

# The Past and Prologue

## FEMALE EXECUTIVES AND PROFESSIONALS

Address by JUDY OLIAN, *Dean of Penn State's Smeal College of Business Administration*
*Delivered to the Penn State Professional Women's Network, New York city, New York, February 7, 2001*

Thanks so much for this warm invitation to this terrific group of women. It's not a topic I talk much about. I usually contemplate the future of business, networked organizations, or the Smeal College, and I haven't taken much time to collect the information or to introspect about women's professional or executive careers. If I were to do that, I probably would have been tempted to reflect on female professional experiences by extrapolating from my own, and from my friends' and acquaintances' personal work histories. And, if I were to generalize from the power concentrated in this room, all is well among female professional America! There are many extraordinarily successful women here tonight whose expertise and professionalism have propelled them to the senior ranks of public and private organizations. Is that the whole story? I'm not sure.

This invitation prompted me to dig a little, so if you'll forgive me, I'll present a lot of numbers, I'll probably flood you with numbers and survey results as ingredients in shaping this story. Each of us will stir this pot of ingredients and see probably a slightly different picture or taste a slightly different dish, to use the metaphor. I'd be especially interested in hearing these differences in perception as we open the floor up for discussion. Let me start with a few factoids about the state of women in business in the year 2000.

In the year 2000:

46.5% of the workforce is female

29.5% of the managerial and professional specialty positions are held by women

12.5% of corporate officers are women among Fortune 500

11.7% of Fortune 500 members of the Board of Directors are women

That's 419 of the Fortune 500 who have female Board members, slightly down from the prior year

6.2% of the highest titled in the Fortune 500 are women

4.1% of the top earners are women, and I remind you that as a baseline, 46.5% of the workforce is female

2 of the Fortune 500 CEOs are women, 1 less than in the prior year

The only indicator that seems to go up consistently in the Fortune 500 is the number of companies with more than 3 female directors (it's now 45, up from 34 companies the prior year). I'll talk later about tokenism issues, and whether there's a minimum threshold, a small critical mass of people before one can break a dominant pattern. Interestingly, there seem to be more successes among the Fortune 500 than among the Fortune 501–1,000, perhaps because of the concerted public efforts and visibility of the Fortune 500.

If I compare the Fortune 500 to the Fortune 501–1000:

11.7% of the Fortune 500 versus 8.5% of the Fortune 501–1000 Board seats are held by women

16% of the Fortune 500 versus 38% of the Fortune 501 to 1000 companies have zero women on the Board, that is, the Fortune 500 are more than twice as likely to have female board members

84% of the Fortune 500 have at least one woman on the Board, compared to 62% among Fortune 501–1000. So, the numbers are far less attractive in the Fortune 501 to 1000.

Those are just the raw numbers on the "state of the world"—for professional women in the U.S. What accounts for this story in the year 2001—37 years after passage of Title VII of the Civil Rights Act of 1964 which assured equal opportunity for both men and women? My hypothesis, is that three areas account for the critical path differences between men and women:

Formative experiences
Career take-off experiences

Career experiences

1. Let's start with formative experiences. What happens pre-entry into business school careers is not equal between the genders:

Looking at pre-career experiences, boys choose computer sciences or computer engineering 5 times more frequently than girls, even though both agree on the importance of computer skills. That's from an Arthur Anderson survey of 650, 15–18 year olds, [C] 2000.

Boys are twice as likely to want to be CEO of tech company, versus girls aspiring to a career in health services, to be CEO of a clothing company, teacher, or small business owner (Anderson survey).

92% of girls report the need for female role models, but don't see enough of them (Anderson survey).

Today, overall, 48% of business students are women at the undergraduate level, and at the MBA level in top Business Schools that declines to 30% who are women.

From a Catalyst survey of 888 women and 796 males who are MBA alumni of top Business Schools (© 2000), the biggest reported reason for the relative scarcity of women in MBA programs is the absence of female role models. We saw that in the statistics presented earlier among business corporations, boards and CEO's. That is true also for Business Schools—22% of faculty across all B Schools are women, 7% of deans across all B Schools are women and certainly fewer among the major business schools.

Female MBAs report lower confidence in their math abilities.

Male freshmen report double the confidence in their computer skills than women, even though there is virtually identical computer use (from a UCLA survey of 400,000 incoming freshmen in 2000).

Women are less likely to be in feeder careers for MBAs—25% of males getting MBAs have engineering backgrounds vs. 9% of female MBAs; conversely, 23% of females getting MBAs are from the arts and humanities compared to 14% of males.

Both males and females see business careers as incompatible with work and life balance. But, women MBAs rate free time and relaxation as very important, more so than do men (60% women vs. 47% men who rate this as very important).

Few women view wealth accumulation as very important to them, 15% women vs. 22% men (GMAC).

These pre-business differences in self-confidence factors, aspirations, and feeder entry points into MBA programs account for some differences in the likelihood of getting an MBA, and the expectations about pay-offs from a business career. Undoubtedly that affects the extent to which women pursue MBAs, and what they aspire to do afterwards.

My second hypothesis is that the difference in the population of male and female professional demographics is attributable to early career take-off experiences.

When women accept jobs post-business education, they are more likely to be affected by location preferences (50% of women versus 35% of men indicate location as key), perhaps because women have more mobility constraints.

Women's choices after their business education are much more likely to be affected by their perception of jobs' contribution to society (14% of women say that's very important vs. 7% for men—GMAC).

Women are much more likely to be affected by the availability of family friendly benefits in their first job (8% vs. 2% for men—GMAC survey).

Among B School graduates, men are much more likely to start in management positions (36% vs. 27% of women—GMAC survey).

More men are in line positions post MBA (45% vs. 37% among women); more women are in staff positions post MBA (40% women vs. 30% men).

Men are more likely to work in Finance and General management; women are more likely to work in consulting.

Men are generally more satisfied with their career advancement.

Even when women take global assignments which is critical for their subsequent career progression, they appear to make their decision with more constraints. They are more likely to be single than are men, and if they are married, they are twice as likely than men to have a fully employed working spouse. So, there is a greater likelihood of making this choice because they are single rather than married, or if they are married they are more constrained than men because of a less movable spouse.

The third conjecture for why the world looks different for professional women is that they experience different career outcomes, and make different career decisions based on their career experiences.

When men change employers during the course of their career, their average salary increase is $25,000 compared to an average salary increase for women of $10,000. This figure controls for job tenure and any other job differences between the men and women. Why? The authors of this study just recently published by the Academy of Management suggest it has to do with more extensive social net works past men have, and pure discrimination.

Women report significantly more time out of their careers over the course of their first ten years post-MBA—an average of 22 months out of the workforce versus 10 months for men. The reasons for women are much more likely to be family related—birth/adoption, childcare, versus for men it's attributed to company mergers, company dissolutions, or reorganizations.

Women MBA graduates are much more likely to work part-time than male MBA graduates (27% vs. 5%), mainly again for childcare and birth/adoption reasons.

Among graduates of MBA programs, women are more likely than men to cite flexibility, lifestyle issues as reasons to start their own business, compared to male entrepreneurs who cite market, financial, and personality reasons such as independence to start their own businesses.

Women entrepreneurs are more likely to own small businesses (71% of female entrepreneurs have businesses of less than $250,000 in revenues a year, compared to 22% of male entrepreneurs); however bigger entrepreneurs with more than $1M in revenues a year are much more likely to be men (62% vs. 17% among women).

Men are much more likely to work continuously post MBAs (61% vs. 29% among women), and the differences are more extreme among MBA grads with children, where women are more likely to disrupt their career.

Interestingly, men and women are dissatisfied with their work/life balance (25% of men and 33% of women). The dissatisfaction with work/life balance goes up linearly, the more hours the person works.

Males and females use flex-time and telecommuting similarly, but again, women are much more likely to resort to part-time work, leave, or compressed work weeks in response to these difficulties.

Among MBA graduates from the Catalyst survey, the top three reasons cited by female executives as barriers to their advancement at work are:

Stereotyping and preconceptions (partially a function of whom they report to, and who reports to them)

Exclusion from informal networks—whether it's golf, sports, spectator events or late night drinking

Inhospitable corporate environments. In fact, just last week, in the Chronicle of Higher Education, I was looking at a statement coming out of the top eight universities in the country. The statement acknowledged mistreatment of female faculty in the sciences and engineering and described various steps that they are going to take to remedy that mistreatment—a public acknowledgement of the in-hospitability of those corporate environments.

Based on this factual "dump" of survey and demographic data, what overarching conclusions can we reach regarding women professionals as a group? Any generalized conclusions, of course, overlook huge individual differences, as is evident in this room.

There are similarities between male and female career experiences.

There are very few differences between men and women regarding their satisfaction with career and job opportunities post MBA.

There are few differences between men and women regarding risk preferences and personal investment decisions.

More women than men are "CEOs at home"—62% of women vs. 38% of men manage their home checking account, 53% women vs. 38% men create the family budget, 46% of women vs. 42% of men make the family's savings and investment decisions (WingspanBank.com survey)

Both are dissatisfied with work/home imbalances

But there are also some real differences:

The cultures of our upbringing, preparatory experiences and self concepts create differences in confidence factors that are critical to choice of business careers especially true of men and women's self concepts true of their math and computer skills and aspirations.

Women make, or are channeled into, initial career choices that are not natural feeders into graduate business education or business careers.

Once into a career women choose, or are assigned, non-line positions or functional areas which are not as visible or natural springboards for promotion.

If in global positions, they're either single, or have less flexibility because of the complexity of a working spouse.

Women appear to respond (by choice or situation) in different ways than men to the extreme stresses associated with work/home imbalances. They respond by reducing or withdrawing entirely from their work involvement.

As entrepreneurs, they go for more modest ventures than men.

The low numbers in female enrollment in MBA Programs (and actually that's a modest decline relative to more recent years), is not due to their entrepreneurial ventures. It's more due to perceived lack of role models, lack of hospitality of the work environment, and balance challenges.

Knowing what we know about female executive styles, how do women fit with the changing workplace, merged global markets and the transformation to a technology based economy? In a nutshell, today's and tomorrow's organizations are going to be global, churning and changing, flat, relying very heavily on networked technologies that empower through knowledge sharing and through various options for work arrangements. Tomorrow's organizations offer opportunities for entrepreneurship in yet to be founded industries, with rewards for creativity and risk taking.

Is that good news or bad news for women? I think it's both.

The bad news is that organizations without boundaries, that are so porous between work and non-work, pose huge challenges for personal balance. The absence of boundaries between work and non-work means that people are tethered all the time, and if they're tethered, that exacerbates the challenges of balance between work and personal lives. Women may suffer even more given their unequal burden regarding family care, at least to date.

Women are also more prone to make choices to avoid competition and conflict. That's based on the work of Deborah Tannen and Judy Rosener and various developmental psychologists. Fighting for scarce resources in competitive situations creates conflict, often inevitable in leadership positions. Women have to make those choices, and sometimes play those roles, despite their disposition against such behaviors (again, ignoring individual differences).

We know, also from developmental psychologists, that women are less likely to be self-promoting and are more deferential, not a recipe for leadership and visibility enhancement. Women may not network as well, especially when they're in predominantly male corporations and functions. Churning organizations that repeatedly change configurations through mergers, acquisitions, and reorganizations place an even greater premium on networking, and whom you know.

Women may not be as good as men at creating a network around them that supports their leadership, that is, others who handle conflict and deliver the bad news on their behalf, and therefore protect their leadership position.

And, women still cite as barriers the stereotypes and attributions made by others—colleagues, superiors and subordinates—that reflect others' discomfort with their power and leadership, which may lead to disadvantage. This may not be intentional discrimination, but merely discomfort with their role as leaders, resulting in exactly the same kind of disadvantage in promotion or placement.

The good news, and I think it's very good news, is that knowledge organizations do place a premium on functioning without a formal power base. Women do that better, according again to developmental psychologists, Deborah Tannen, Judy Rosener and others. Women tend to be more interactive and transformational leaders, and tend not to lead through command, control, reward, and punishment. Women tend to derive their power from their personal charisma, from their work record and accomplishments, and from personal relationships, not from hierarchy, title, and position. In today's flat, organizations that really fits well.

Women tend also to be more comfortable with sharing power and inviting participation, perfect for today's flat, knowledge-based organization. And they tend to recognize and enhance the self-worth of others, again suited to today's flat, knowledge-based organization.

The fiber optically networked workplace does create more options on how to work—when, where, how much—so that it may, over time, reduce the disadvantaged choices that women are making. Over time, virtual workplace structures may alleviate the juggling played between work and non-work and the difficulties both men and women confront because of the balance challenges. But women will especially benefit because, at this point, the data demonstrate that they assume the disproportionate burden.

The other piece of good news is that once women become more than a token, and the threshold of "the first one" is crossed, it seems to get a little easier (e.g., Boards of Directors with 3 or more women).

In sum, this is a mixed view and a set of conjectures that I propose to you. I presented a mind boggling set of numbers and survey data and I'm interested in your reactions on the basis of experience, or your insights into survey data. Thank you for your patience. I genuinely appreciated the opportunity to introspect, through you, more than you can imagine.

From *Vital Speeches of the Day*, April 15, 2001, pp. 398-401. © 2001 by City News Publishing Company, Inc.

# VIOLENCE AGAINST WOMEN

It may be the biggest human rights issue in the world—and it is certainly one of the least discussed. Yet increasingly, women are finding ways to fight the mutilation, rape, beating, and murder that have been their lot.

**Toni Nelson**

## A GIRL IS MUTILATED IN EGYPT

It is not a ritual that many people would expect—much less want—to witness. Yet in the fall of 1994, the television network CNN brought the practice of female genital mutilation (FGM) into living rooms around the world, by broadcasting the amputation of a young Egyptian girl's clitoris. Coinciding with the United Nations International Conference on Population and Development in Cairo, the broadcast was one of several recent events that have galvanized efforts to combat the various forms of violence that threaten women and girls throughout the world. The experience suffered by 10-year-old Nagla Hamza focused international attention on the plight of the more than 100 million women and girls in Africa victimized by FGM. In doing so, it helped spur conference delegates into formulating an official "Programme of Action" that condemned FGM and outlined measures to eliminate the practice.

Euphemistically referred to as female circumcision, FGM encompasses a variety of practices ranging from excision, the partial or total removal of the clitoris and labia minora, to infibulation, in which all the external genitals are cut away and the area is restitched, leaving only a small opening for the passage of urine and menstrual blood. Nagla's mutilation, performed by a local barber without anesthesia or sanitary precautions, was typical. Although the physical and psychological consequences of FGM are severe and often life-threatening, the practice persists due to beliefs that emerged from ancient tribal customs but which have now come to be associated with certain major religions. In Israel, for instance, FGM is practiced by Jewish migrants from the Ethiopian Falasha community; elsewhere in Africa, it is found among Christian and Islamic populations. But FGM has no inherent association with any of these religions. Although some Islamic scholars consider it an important part of that religion, FGM actually predates Islam, and neither the Qur'an, the primary source for Islamic law, nor the Hadith, collections of the Prophet Mohammed's lessons, explicitly require the practice.

Justifications for FGM vary among the societies where it occurs (FGM is practiced in 28 African nations, as well as in scattered tribal communities in the Arabian Peninsula and various parts of South Asia). But most explanations relate in some way to male interest in controlling women's emotions and sexual behavior. One of the most common explanations is the need to lessen desire so women will preserve their virginity until marriage. The late Gad-Alhaq Ali Gad-Alhaq, Sheik of Cairo's al-Azhar Islamic University at the time of the CNN broadcast, explained it this way: the purpose of FGM is "to moderate sexual desire while saving womanly pleasures in order that women may enjoy their husbands." For Mimi Ramsey, an anti-FGM activist in the United States who was mutilated in her native Ethiopia at age six, FGM is meant to reinforce the power men have over women: "the reason for my mutilation is for a man to be able to control me, to make me a good wife." Today, migrants are bringing FGM out of its traditional societies and into Europe, North America, and Australia. Approximately 2 million girls are at risk each year.

As in other countries where the practice is commonplace, Egypt's official policy on FGM has been ambiguous. Although a Ministry of Health decree in 1959 prohibited health professionals and public hospitals from performing the procedure, and national law makes it a crime to permanently mutilate anyone, clitoridectomies and other forms of FGM are not explicitly prohibited. An estimated 80 percent of Egyptian women and girls, or more than 18 million people, have undergone some form of FGM, which is often carried out by barbers in street booths on main squares of both small towns and large cities.

Before the CNN broadcast, Egyptian public opinion seemed to be turning against the practice. In early 1994, activists founded the Egyptian Task Force Against Female Genital Mutilation. Later that year, during the population conference, Population and Family Welfare Minister Maher Mahran vowed to delegates that "Egypt is going to work on the elimination of female genital mutilation." Plans were even laid for legislation that would outlaw FGM. But some members of Egypt's religious community saw the broadcast as a form of Western imperialism and used it to challenge both the secular government of Hosni Mubarak and the conference itself.

In October 1994, Sheik Gad-Alhaq ruled that FGM is a religious obligation for Muslims. The same month, Minister of Health Dr. Ali Abdel Fattah issued a decree permitting the practice in selected government hospitals. The Minister's directive came just 10 days after a committee of experts convened by him condemned FGM and denied that it had any religious justification. Fattah affirmed his personal opposition, but insisted that the decree was necessary to "save those victimized girls from being 'slaughtered' by unprofessionals."

In the wake of the Minister's decision, plans for the bill outlawing FGM were postponed. Contending that Fattah had effectively legalized the procedure, national and international nongovernmental organizations sought to reverse the decision through petition drives, public education initiatives, and lawsuits. And on October 17, 1995, Fattah reversed his decision, and the Ministry of Health once again banned FGM in public hospitals. The anti-FGM legislation, however, remains on hold.

## VIOLENCE IS A UNIVERSAL THREAT

Egypt's confused and ambivalent response to FGM mirrors in many ways the intensifying international debate on all forms of violence against women. And even though FGM itself may seem just a grotesque anomaly to people brought up in cultures where it isn't practiced, FGM is grounded in attitudes and assumptions that are, unfortunately, all too common. Throughout the world, women's inferior social status makes them vulnerable to abuse and denies them the financial and legal means necessary to improve their situations. Over the past decade, women's groups around the world have succeeded in showing how prevalent this problem is and how much violence it is causing—a major accomplishment, given the fact that the issue was not even mentioned during the

first UN Women's Conference in 1975 or in the 1979 UN Convention on All Forms of Discrimination Against Women. But as the situation in Egypt demonstrates, effective policy responses remain elusive.

Violence stalks women throughout their lives, "from cradle to grave"—in the judgment of *Human Development Report 1995*, the UN's annual assessment of social and economic progress around the world. Gender-specific violence is almost a cultural constant, both emerging from and reinforcing the social relationships that give men power over women. This is most obvious in the implicit acceptance, across cultures, of domestic violence—of a man's prerogative to beat his wife. Large-scale surveys in 10 countries, including Colombia, Canada, and the United States, estimate that as many as one-third of women have been physically assaulted by an intimate male partner. More limited studies report that rates of physical abuse among some groups in Latin America, Asia, and Africa may reach 60 percent or more.

Belying the oft-cried cliché about "family values," studies have shown that the biggest threat to women is domestic violence. In 1992, the *Journal of the American Medical Association* published a study that found that women in the United States are more likely to be assaulted, injured, raped, or murdered by a current or former male partner than by all other types of attackers combined. In Canada, a 1987 study showed that 62 percent of the women murdered in that year were killed by an intimate male partner. And in India, the husband or in-laws of a newly married woman may think it justified to murder her if they consider her dowry inadequate, so that a more lucrative match can be made. One popular method is to pour kerosene on the woman and set her on fire—hence the term "bride burning." One in four deaths among women aged 16 to 24 in the urban areas of Maharashtra state (including Bombay) is attributed to "accidental burns." About 5,000 "dowry deaths" occur in India every year, according to government estimates, and some observers think the number is actually much higher. Subhadra Chaturvedi, one of India's leading attorneys, puts the death toll at a minimum of 12,000 a year.

The preference for sons, common in many cultures, can lead to violence against female infants—and even against female fetuses. In India, for example, a 1990 study of amniocentesis in a large Bombay hospital found that 95.5 percent of fetuses iden-

tified as female were aborted, compared with only a small percentage of male fetuses. (Amniocentesis involves the removal of a sample of amniotic fluid from the womb; this can be used to determine the baby's sex and the presence of certain inherited diseases.) Female infanticide is still practiced in rural areas of India; a 1992 study by Cornell University demographer Sabu George found that 58 percent of female infant deaths (19 of 33) within a 12-village region of Tamil Nadu state were due to infanticide. The problem is especially pronounced in China, where the imposition of the one-child-per-family rule has led to a precipitous decline in the number of girls: studies in 1987 and 1994 found a half-million fewer female infants in each of those years than would be expected, given the typical biological ratio of male to female births.

Women are also the primary victims of sexual crimes, which include sexual abuse, rape, and forced prostitution. Girls are the overwhelming target of child sexual assaults; in the United States, 78 percent of substantiated child sexual abuse cases involve girls. According to a 1994 World Bank study, *Violence Against Women: The Hidden Health Burden*, national surveys suggest that up to one-third of women in Norway, the United States, Canada, New Zealand, Barbados, and the Netherlands are sexually abused during childhood. Often very young children are the victims: a national study in the United States and studies in several Latin American cities indicate that 13 to 32 percent of abused girls are age 10 and under.

Rape haunts women throughout their lives, exposing them to unwanted pregnancy, disease, social stigma, and psychological trauma. In the United States, which has some of the best data on the problem, a 1993 review of rape studies suggests that between 14 and 20 percent of women will be victims of completed rapes during their lifetimes. In some cultures, a woman who has been raped is perceived as having violated the family honor, and she may be forced to marry her attacker or even killed. One study of female homicide in Alexandria, Egypt, for example, found that 47 percent of women murdered were killed by a family member following a rape.

In war, rape is often used as both a physical and psychological weapon. An investigation of recent conflicts in the former Yugoslavia, Peru, Kashmir, and Somalia by the international human rights group, Human Rights Watch, found that "rape of women civilians has been deployed as a tactical weapon to terrorize civilian communities or to achieve 'ethnic cleansing.'" Studies suggest that tens of thousands of Muslim and Serbian women in Bosnia have been raped during the conflict there.

A growing number of women and girls, particularly in developing countries, are being forced into prostitution. Typically, girls from poor, remote villages are purchased outright from their families or lured away with promises of jobs or false marriage proposals. They are then taken to brothels, often in other countries, and forced to work there until they pay off their "debts"—a task that becomes almost impossible as the brothel owner charges them for clothes, food, medicine, and often even their own purchase price. According to Human Rights Watch, an estimated 20,000 to 30,000 Burmese girls and women currently work in brothels in Thailand; their ranks are now expanding by as many as 10,000 new recruits each year. Some 20,000 to 50,000 Nepalese girls are working in Indian brothels. As the fear of AIDS intensifies, customers are demanding ever younger prostitutes, and the age at which girls are being forced into prostitution is dropping; the average age of the Nepalese recruits, for example, declined from 14–16 years in the 1980s, to 10–14 years by 1994.

## THE HIDDEN COSTS OF VIOLENCE

Whether it takes the form of enforced prostitution, rape, genital mutilation, or domestic abuse, gender-based violence is doing enormous damage—both to the women who experience it, and to societies as a whole. Yet activists, health officials, and development agencies have only recently begun to quantify the problem's full costs. Currently, they are focusing on two particularly burdensome aspects of the violence: the health care costs, and the effects on economic productivity.

The most visible effects of violence are those associated with physical injuries that require medical care. FGM, for example, often causes severe health problems. Typically performed in unsterile environments by untrained midwives or barbers working without anesthesia, the procedure causes intense pain and can result in infection or death. Long-term effects include chronic pain, urine retention, abscesses, lack of sexual sensitivity, and depression. For the approximately 15 percent of mutilated women who have been infibulated, the health-related consequences are even

worse. Not only must these women be cut and stitched repeatedly, on their wedding night and again with each childbirth, but sexual dysfunction and pain during intercourse are common. Infibulated women are also much more likely to have difficulties giving birth. Their labor often results, for instance, in vesico-vaginal fistulas— holes in the vaginal and rectal areas that cause continuous leakage of urine and feces. An estimated 1.5 to 2 million African women have fistulas, with some 50,000 to 100,000 new cases occurring annually. Infibulation also greatly increases the danger to the child during labor. A study of 33 infibulated women in delivery at Somalia's Benadir Hospital found that five of their babies died and 21 suffered oxygen deprivation.

Other forms of violence are taking a heavy toll as well. A 1994 national survey in Canada, for example, found that broken bones occurred in 12 percent of spousal assaults, and internal injuries and miscarriages in 10 percent. Long-term effects may be less obvious but they are often just as serious. In the United States, battered women are four to five times more likely than non-battered women to require psychiatric treatment and five times more likely to attempt suicide. And even these effects are just one part of a much broader legacy of misery. A large body of psychological literature has documented the erosion of self-esteem, of social abilities, and of mental health in general, that often follows in the wake of violence. And the problem is compounded because violence tends to be cyclical: people who are abused tend to become abusers themselves. Whether it's through such direct abuse or indirectly, through the destruction of family life, violence against women tends to spill over into the next generation as violence against children.

Only a few studies have attempted to assign an actual dollar value to gender-based violence, but their findings suggest that the problem constitutes a substantial health care burden. In the United States, a 1991 study at a major health maintenance organization (a type of group medical practice) found that women who had been raped or beaten at any point in their lifetimes had medical costs two-and-a-half times higher during that year than women who had not been victimized. In the state of Pennsylvania, a health insurer study estimated that violence against women cost the health care system approximately $326.6 million in 1992. And in Canada, a 1995 study of violence against women,

which examined not only medical costs, but also the value of community support services and lost work, put the annual cost to the country at Cdn $1.5 billion (US $1.1 billion).

One important consequence of violence is its effect on women's productivity. In its World Development Report 1993, the World Bank estimated that in advanced market economies, 19 percent of the total disease burden of women aged 15 to 44— nearly one out of every five healthy days of life lost—can be linked to domestic violence or rape. (Violence against women is just as pervasive in developing countries, but because the incidence of disease is higher in those regions, it represents only 5 percent of their total disease burden.) Similarly, a 1993 study in the United States showed a correlation between violence and lower earnings. After controlling for other factors that affect income, the study found that women who have been abused earn 3 to 20 percent less each year than women who have not been abused, with the discrepancy depending on the type of sexual abuse experienced and the number of perpetrators.

Violence can also prevent women from participating in public life—a form of oppression that can cripple Third World development projects. Fear may keep women at home; for example, health workers in India have identified fear of rape as an impediment to their outreach efforts in rural sites. The general problem was acknowledged plainly in a UN report published in 1992, Battered Dreams: Violence Against Women as an Obstacle to Development: "Where violence keeps a woman from participating in a development project, force is used to deprive her of earnings, or fear of sexual assault prevents her from taking a job or attending a public function, development does not occur." Development efforts aimed at reducing fertility levels may also be affected, since gender-based violence, or the threat of it, may limit women's use of contraception. According to the 1994 World Bank study, a woman's contraceptive use often depends in large part on her partner's approval.

A recurrent motive in much of this violence is an interest in preventing women from gaining autonomy outside the home. Husbands may physically prevent their wives from attending development meetings, or they may intimidate them into not seeking employment or accepting promotions at work. The World Bank study relates a chilling example of the way in which violence can be used to control women's behavior: "In a particularly gruesome example of male backlash, a female leader of the highly successful government sponsored Women's Development Programme in Rajasthan, India, was recently gang raped [in her home in front of her husband] by male community members because they disapproved of her organizing efforts against child marriage." The men succeeded in disrupting the project by instilling fear in the local organizers.

## WOMEN BREAK THE SILENCE

"These women are holding back a silent scream so strong it could shake the earth." That is how Dr. Nahid Toubia, Executive Director of the U.S.-based anti-FGM organization RAINBO, described FGM victims when she testified at the 1993 Global Tribunal on Violations of Women's Human Rights. Yet her statement would apply just as well to the millions of women all over the world who have been victims of other forms of violence. Until recently, the problem of gender-based violence has remained largely invisible. Because the stigma attached to many forms of violence makes them difficult to discuss openly, and because violence typically occurs inside the home, accurate information on the magnitude of the problem has been extremely scarce. Governments, by claiming jurisdiction only over human rights abuses perpetrated in the public sphere by agents of the state, have reinforced this invisibility. Even human rights work has traditionally confined itself to the public sphere and largely ignored many of the abuses to which women are most vulnerable.

But today, the victims of violence are beginning to find their voices. Women's groups have won a place for "private sphere" violence on human rights agendas, and they are achieving important changes in both national laws and international conventions. The first major reform came in June 1993, at the UN Second World Conference on Human Rights in Vienna. In a drive leading up to the conference, activists collected almost half a million signatures from 124 countries on a petition insisting that the conference address gen-

der violence. The result: for the first time, violence against women was recognized as an abuse of women's human rights, and nine paragraphs on "The equal status and human rights of women" were incorporated into the Vienna Declaration and Programme of Action.

More recently, 18 members of the Organization of American States have ratified the Inter-American Convention on the Prevention, Punishment and Eradication of Violence Against Women. Many activists consider this convention, which went into effect on March 5, 1995, the strongest existing piece of international legislation in the field. And the Pan American Health Organization (PAHO) has become the first development agency to make a significant financial commitment to the issue. PAHO has received $4 million from Sweden, Norway, and the Netherlands, with the possibility of an additional $2.5 million from the Inter-American Development Bank, to conduct research on violence and establish support services for women in Latin America.

National governments are also drawing up legislation to combat various forms of gender violence. A growing number of countries, including South Africa, Israel, Argentina, the Bahamas, Australia, and the United States have all passed special domestic violence laws. Typically, these clarify the definition of domestic violence and strengthen protections available to the victims. In September 1994, India passed its "Pre-natal Diagnostic Techniques (Regulation and Prevention of Misuse) Act," which outlaws the use of prenatal testing for sex-selection. India is also developing a program to eradicate female infanticide. FGM is being banned in a growing number of countries, too. At least nine European countries now prohibit the practice, as does Australia. In the United States, a bill criminalizing FGM was passed by the Senate in May, but had yet to become law. More significant, perhaps, is the African legislation: FGM is now illegal in both Ghana and Kenya.

It is true, of course, that laws don't necessarily translate into real-life changes. But it is possible that the movement to stop FGM will yield the first solid success in the struggle to make human rights a reality for women. Over the past decade, the Inter-

African Committee on Traditional Practices Affecting the Health of Women and Children, an NGO dedicated to abolishing FGM, has set up committees in 25 African countries. And in March 1995, Ghana used its anti-FGM statute to arrest the parents and circumciser of an eight-year-old girl who was rushed to the hospital with excessive bleeding. In Burkina Faso, some circumcising midwives have been convicted under more general legislation. These are modest steps, perhaps, but legal precedent can be a powerful tool for reform.

In the United States, an important precedent is currently being set by a 19-year-old woman from the nation of Togo, in west Africa. Fleeing an arranged marriage and the ritual FGM that would accompany it, Fauziya Kasinga arrived in the United States seeking asylum in December 1994. She has spent much of the time since then in prison, and her request for asylum, denied by a lower court, is at the time of writing under appeal. People are eligible for asylum in the United States if they are judged to have a reasonable fear of persecution due to their race, religion, nationality, political opinions, or membership in a social group. However, U.S. asylum law makes no explicit provision for gender-based violence. In 1993, Canada became the world's first country to make the threat of FGM grounds for granting refugee status.

Whichever way the decision on Kasinga's case goes, it will be adopted as a binding general precedent in U.S. immigration cases (barring the passage of federal legislation that reverses it). But even while her fate remains in doubt, Kasinga has already won an important moral victory. Her insistence on her right *not* to be mutilated—and on the moral obligation of others to shield her from violence if they can—has made the threat she faces a matter of conscience, of politics, and of policy. Given the accumulating evidence of how deeply gender-based violence infects our societies, in both the developing and the industrialized countries, we have little choice but to recognize it as the fundamental moral and economic challenge that it is.

Toni Nelson is a staff researcher at the Worldwatch Institute.

From *World Watch*, July/August 1996, pp. 33–38. © 1996 by the Worldwatch Institute. Reprinted by permission.

# UNIT 5

# Social Institutions: Issues, Crises, and Changes

## Unit Selections

## Key Points to Consider

- Discuss whether or not it is important to preserve some continuity in institutions.

- How can institutions outlive their usefulness?

- Why are institutions so difficult to change? Cite examples where changes are instituted from the top down and others where they are instituted from the bottom up. Do you see a similar pattern of development for these types of changes?

- Is it possible to reform the political system to greatly reduce the corrupting role of money in politics? Why or why not?

- What basic changes in the economic system are evident in the things that you observe daily?

- How should issues like abortion and genetic engineering be decided?

 **Links: www.dushkin.com/online/**
These sites are annotated in the World Wide Web pages.

**Center for the Study of Group Processes**
*http://www.uiowa.edu/~grpproc/*

**International Labour Organization (ILO)**
*http://www.ilo.org*

**IRIS Center**
*http://www.iris.umd.edu*

**Marketplace of Political Ideas/University of Houston Library**
*http://info.lib.uh.edu/politics/markind.htm*

**National Center for Policy Analysis**
*http://www.ncpa.org*

**National Institutes of Health (NIH)**
*http://www.nih.gov*

Social institutions are the building blocks of social structure. They accomplish the important tasks of society—for example, regulation of reproduction, socialization of children, production and distribution of economic goods, law enforcement and social control, and organization of religion and other value systems.

Social institutions are not rigid arrangements; they reflect changing social conditions. Institutions generally change slowly. At the present time, however, many of the social institutions in the United States and many other parts of the world are in crisis and are undergoing rapid change. Eastern European countries are literally transforming their political and economic institutions. Economic institutions, such as stock markets, are becoming truly international, and when a major country experiences a recession, many other countries feel the effects. In the United States, major reform movements are active in political, economic, family, medical, and educational institutions.

The first subsection of unit 5 examines American political institutions. In the first article, G. William Domhoff examines the power structure of the American political system and finds it dominated by the corporate community. But how does his view account for democracy and the power that it gives the average person? What about the evident influence of workers, liberals, environmentalists, and challenge groups? Domhoff argues that these forces may get media coverage, but they cannot prevent the corporate community from controlling the federal government on basic issues of income, wealth, and economic power. Moreover, he shows how this community exercises its power.

The next article is one of those uncommon accounts of successful government actions that serve the public good. Several policies dealing with the environment, health, and safety have greatly benefited American citizens.

The following subsection deals with major problems and issues of the economy. In the first article Jerry Useem discusses the recent plague of corporate scandals and the response of the corporate world. Pressure from investors is causing corporations to clean up their act. CEOs are being scrutinized more and granted less autonomy. Accounting practices are being cleaned up and governance structures being revised to improve corporate accountability. A reformation is occurring in the business world. The next article examines how and why work "is taking over our lives—invading our homes, haunting our holidays, showing up for dinner." An important theme that Mark Hunter develops is that "the distinction between work and leisure no longer exists."

The social sphere is also in turmoil, as illustrated by the articles in the last subsection. A key issue for many parents and children is the quality of education, and the public's perception is rather negative. James Comer reviews many suggested solutions to the failure of American schools and finds them deficient because they are not based on sound principles of child development. The real solution requires powerful positive social interactions between students and teachers. Another important social issue is the possibility of genetically engineering future generations. The next article deals with issues that DNA research has opened up. The beneficial possibilities are enormous but so are the potential dangers and moral questions. For exam-

ple, society must now decide whether to continue to leave the creation of humans to providence and/or evolution or to genetically engineer our offspring. In his article, Colin Tudge presents the issues, options, and debates.

Another prominent and highly contested social issue is abortion, and in the next report, Frederica Mathewes-Green tries to find areas of agreement and compromise in this field of battle. She finds that no one thinks that abortion is a positive event; for some people, however, it is better than the alternatives. Why not improve the alternatives and make abortion unnecessary, she asks.

The next article is full of pain and death for it deals with the worldwide epidemic of AIDS with its focus on sub-Saharan Africa where 70 percent of those infected with HIV/AIDS reside. Of course we would expect the various governments to do everything in their power to stop the epidemic and help the victims and for the friends and relatives of the victims to have compassion. Unfortunately the true story is quite ugly. The shocking failure of many societies in the AIDS crisis reveals their fragility. The unbelievable brutality of the treatment of the AIDS victims by relatives and others reveals the depths of the evil that many people are capable of when they are afraid. In the final article, Andrew Greeley shows that the predicted decline of religion with the advance of science has never happened. Indeed, he shows that religion is strong and vibrant in America and has a bright future. He also describes many interesting changes in religious and moral beliefs and attitudes in the United States.

# Who Rules America?

## G. William Domhoff

## Power and Class in the United States

*Power* and *class* are terms that make Americans a little uneasy, and concepts like *power elite* and *dominant class* immediately put people on guard. The idea that a relatively fixed group of privileged people might shape the economy and government for their own benefit goes against the American grain. Nevertheless,... the owners and top-level managers in large income-producing properties are far and away the dominant power figures in the United States. Their corporations, banks, and agribusinesses come together as a *corporate community* that dominates the federal government in Washington. Their real estate, construction, and land development companies form *growth coalitions* that dominate most local governments. Granted, there is competition within both the corporate community and the local growth coalitions for profits and investment opportunities, and there are sometimes tensions between national corporations and local growth coalitions, but both are cohesive on policy issues affecting their general welfare, and in the face of demands by organized workers, liberals, environmentalists, and neighborhoods.

As a result of their ability to organize and defend their interests, the owners and managers of large income-producing properties have a very great share of all income and wealth in the United States, greater than in any other industrial democracy. Making up at best 1 percent of the total population, by the early 1990s they earned 15.7 percent of the nation's yearly income and owned 37.2 percent of all privately held wealth, including 49.6 percent of all corporate stocks and 62.4 percent of all bonds. Due to their wealth and the lifestyle it makes possible, these owners and managers draw closer as a common social group. They belong to the same exclusive social clubs, frequent the same summer and winter resorts, and send their children to a relative handful of private schools. Members of the corporate community thereby become a *corporate rich* who create a nationwide *social upper class* through their social interaction.... Members of the growth coalitions, on the other hand, are *place entrepreneurs,* people who sell locations and buildings. They come together as local upper classes in their respective cities

and sometimes mingle with the corporate rich in educational or resort settings.

The corporate rich and the growth entrepreneurs supplement their small numbers by developing and directing a wide variety of nonprofit organizations, the most important of which are a set of tax-free charitable foundations, think tanks, and policy-discussion groups. These specialized nonprofit groups constitute a *policy-formation network* at the national level. Chambers of commerce and policy groups affiliated with them form similar policy-formation networks at the local level, aided by a few national-level city development organizations that are available for local consulting.

Those corporate owners who have the interest and ability to take part in general governance join with top-level executives in the corporate community and the policy-formation network to form the *power elite,* which is the leadership group for the corporate rich as a whole. The concept of a power elite makes clear that not all members of the upper class are involved in governance; some of them simply enjoy the lifestyle that their great wealth affords them. At the same time, the focus on a leadership group allows for the fact that not all those in the power elite are members of the upper class; many of them are high-level employees in profit and nonprofit organizations controlled by the corporate rich....

The power elite is not united on all issues because it includes both moderate conservatives and ultraconservatives. Although both factions favor minimal reliance on government on all domestic issues, the moderate conservatives sometimes agree to legislation advocated by liberal elements of the society, especially in times of social upheaval like the Great Depression of the 1930s and the Civil Rights Movement of the early 1960s. Except on defense spending, ultraconservatives are characterized by a complete distaste for any kind of government programs under any circumstances—even to the point of opposing government support for corporations on some issues. Moderate conservatives often favor foreign aid, working through the United Nations, and making attempts to win over foreign enemies through patient diplomacy, treaties, and trade agreements. Historically, ultraconservatives have opposed most forms of foreign involvement, although they have become more tolerant of foreign trade agreements over the past thirty or forty years. At the same time, their hostility to the United Nations continues unabated.

Members of the power elite enter into the electoral arena as the leaders within a *corporate-conservative coalition,* where they are aided by a wide variety of patriotic, antitax, and other single-issue organizations. These conservative advocacy organizations are funded in varying degrees by the corporate rich, direct-mail appeals, and middle-class conservatives. This coalition has played a large role in both political parties at the presidential level and usually succeeds in electing a conservative majority to both houses of Congress. Historically, the conservative majority in Congress was made up of most Northern Republicans and most Southern Democrats, but that arrangement has been changing gradually since the 1960s as the conservative Democrats of the South are replaced by even more conservative Southern Republicans. The corporate-conservative coalition also has access to the federal government in Washington through lobbying and the appointment of its members to top positions in the executive branch....

Despite their preponderant power within the federal government and the many useful policies it carries out for them, members of the power elite are constantly critical of government as an alleged enemy of freedom and economic growth. Although their wariness toward government is expressed in terms of a dislike for taxes and government regulations, I believe their underlying concern is that government could change the power relations in the private sphere by aiding average Americans through a number of different avenues: (1) creating government jobs for the unemployed; (2) making health, unemployment, and welfare benefits more generous; (3) helping employees gain greater workplace rights and protections; and (4) helping workers organize unions. All of these initiatives are opposed by members of the power elite because they would increase wages and taxes, but the deepest opposition is toward any government support for unions because unions are a potential organizational base for advocating the whole range of issues opposed by the corporate rich....

# Where Does Democracy Fit In?

...[T]o claim that the corporate rich have enough power to be considered a dominant class does not imply that lower social classes are totally powerless. *Domination* means the power to set the terms under which other groups and classes must operate, not total control. Highly trained professionals with an interest in environmental and consumer issues have been able to couple their technical information and their understanding of the legislative and judicial processes with well-timed publicity, lobbying, and lawsuits to win governmental restrictions on some corporate practices. Wage and salary employees, when they are organized into unions and have the right to strike, have been able to gain pay increases, shorter hours, better working conditions, and social benefits such as health insurance. Even the most powerless of people—the very poor and those discrim-

inated against—sometimes develop the capacity to influence the power structure through sit-ins, demonstrations, social movements, and other forms of social disruption, and there is evidence that such activities do bring about some redress of grievances, at least for a short time.

More generally, the various challengers to the power elite sometimes work together on policy issues as a *liberal-labor coalition* that is based in unions, local environmental organizations, some minority group communities, university and arts communities, liberal churches, and small newspapers and magazines. Despite a decline in membership over the past twenty years, unions are the largest and best-financed part of the coalition, and the largest organized social force in the country (aside from churches). They also cut across racial and ethnic lines more than any other institutionalized sector of American society....

The policy conflicts between the corporate-conservative and liberal-labor coalitions are best described as *class conflicts* because they primarily concern the distribution of profits and wages, the rate and progressivity of taxation, the usefulness of labor unions, and the degree to which business should be regulated by government. The liberal-labor coalition wants corporations to pay higher wages to employees and higher taxes to government. It wants government to regulate a wide range of business practices, including many that are related to the environment, and help employees to organize unions. The corporate-conservative coalition resists all these policy objectives to a greater or lesser degree, claiming they endanger the freedom of individuals and the efficient workings of the economic marketplace. The conflicts these disagreements generate can manifest themselves in many different ways: workplace protests, industrywide boycotts, massive demonstrations in cities, pressure on Congress, and the outcome of elections.

Neither the corporate-conservative nor the liberal-labor coalition includes a very large percentage of the American population, although each has the regular support of about 25–30 percent of the voters. Both coalitions are made up primarily of financial donors, policy experts, political consultants, and party activists....

*Pluralism.* The main alternative theory [I] address.... claims that power is more widely dispersed among groups and classes than a class-dominance theory allows. This general perspective is usually called *pluralism,* meaning there is no one dominant power group. It is the theory most favored by social scientists. In its strongest version, pluralism holds that power is held by the general public through the pressure that public opinion and voting put on elected officials. According to this version, citizens form voluntary groups and pressure groups that shape public opinion, lobby elected officials, and back sympathetic political candidates in the electoral process....

The second version of pluralism sees power as rooted in a wide range of well-organized "interest groups" that are often based in economic interests (e.g., industrialists, bankers, labor unions), but also in other interests as well (e.g., environmental, consumer, and civil rights groups). These interest groups join together in different coalitions depending on the specific issues. Proponents of this version of pluralism sometimes concede that public opinion and voting have only a minimal or indirect influence, but they see business groups as too fragmented and antagonistic to form a cohesive dominant class. They also claim that some business interest groups occasionally join coalitions with liberal or labor groups on specific issues, and that business-dominated coalitions sometimes lose. Furthermore, some proponents of this version of pluralism believe that the Democratic Party is responsive to the wishes of liberal and labor interest groups.

In contrast, I argue that the business interest groups are part of a tightly knit corporate community that is able to develop classwide cohesion on the issues of greatest concern to it: opposition to unions, high taxes, and government regulation. When a business group loses on a specific issue, it is often because other business groups have been opposed; in other words, there are arguments within the corporate community, and these arguments are usually settled within the governmental arena. I also claim that liberal and labor groups are rarely part of coalitions with business groups and that for most of its history the Democratic Party has been dominated by corporate and agribusiness interests in the Southern states, in partnership with the growth coalitions in large urban areas outside the South. Finally, I show that business interests rarely lose on labor and regulatory issues except in times of extreme social disruption like the 1930s and 1960s, when differences of opinion between Northern and Southern corporate leaders made victories for the liberal-labor coalition possible....

## How the Power Elite Dominates Government

This [section] shows how the power elite builds on the ideas developed in the policy-formation process and its success in the electoral arena to dominate the federal government. Lobbyists from corporations, law firms, and trade associations play a key role in shaping government on narrow issues of concern to specific corporations or business sectors, but their importance should not be overestimated because a majority of those elected to Congress are predisposed to agree with them. The corporate community and the policy-formation network supply top-level governmental appointees and new policy directions on major issues.

Once again, as seen in the battles for public opinion and electoral success, the power elite faces opposition from a minority of elected officials and their supporters in labor unions and liberal advocacy groups. These opponents are sometimes successful in blocking ultra-conservative initiatives, but most of the victories for the liberal-labor coalition are the result of support from moderate conservatives....

## Appointees to Government

The first way to test a class-dominance view of the federal government is to study the social and occupational backgrounds of the people who are appointed to manage the major departments of the executive branch, such as state, treasury, defense,

and justice. If pluralists are correct, these appointees should come from a wide range of interest groups. If the state autonomy theorists are correct, they should be disproportionately former elected officials or longtime government employees. If the class-dominance view is correct, they should come disproportionately from the upper class, the corporate community, and the policy-formation network.

There have been numerous studies over the years of major governmental appointees under both Republican and Democratic administrations, usually focusing on the top appointees in the departments that are represented in the president's cabinet. These studies are unanimous in their conclusion that most top appointees in both Republican and Democratic administrations are corporate executives and corporate lawyers—and hence members of the power elite....

## Conclusion

This [section] has demonstrated the power elite's wide-ranging access to government through the interest-group and policy-formation processes, as well as through its ability to influence appointments to major government positions. When coupled with the several different kinds of power discussed in earlier [sections] this access and involvement add up to power elite domination of the federal government.

By *domination*, as stated in the first [section], social scientists mean the ability of a class or group to set the terms under which other classes or groups within a social system must operate. By this definition, domination does not mean control on each and every issue, and it does not rest solely on involvement in government. Influence over government is only the final and most visible aspect of power elite domination, which has its roots in the class structure, the corporate control of the investment function, and the operation of the policy-formation network. If government officials did not have to wait for corporate leaders to decide where and when they will invest, and if government officials were not further limited by the general public's acceptance of policy recommendations from the policy-formation network, then power elite involvement in elections and government would count for a lot less than they do under present conditions.

Domination by the power elite does not negate the reality of continuing conflict over government policies, but few conflicts, it has been shown, involve challenges to the rules that create privileges for the upper class and domination by the power elite. Most of the numerous battles within the interest-group process, for example, are only over specific spoils and favors; they often involve disagreements among competing business interests.

Similarly, conflicts within the policy-making process of government often involve differences between the moderate conservative and ultraconservative segments of the dominant class. At other times they involve issues in which the needs of the corporate community as a whole come into conflict with the needs of specific industries, which is what happens to some extent on tariff policies and also on some environmental legislation. In neither case does the nature of the conflict call into question the domination of government by the power elite.

...Contrary to what pluralists claim, there is not a single case study on any issue of any significance that shows a liberal-labor victory over a united corporate-conservative coalition, which is strong evidence for a class-domination theory on the "Who wins?" power indicator. The classic case studies frequently cited by pluralists have been shown to be gravely deficient as evidence for their views. Most of these studies reveal either conflicts among rival groups within the power elite or situations in which the moderate conservatives have decided for their own reasons to side with the liberal-labor coalition....

More generally, it now can be concluded that all four indicators of power introduced in [the first section] point to the corporate rich and their power elite as the dominant organizational structure in American society. First, the wealth and income distributions are skewed in their favor more than in any other industrialized democracy. They are clearly the most powerful group in American society in terms of "Who benefits?" Second, the appointees to government come overwhelmingly from the corporate community and its associated policy-formation network. Thus, the power elite is clearly the most powerful in terms of "Who sits?"

Third, the power elite wins far more often than it loses on policy issues resolved in the federal government. Thus, it is the most powerful in terms of "Who wins?" Finally, as shown in reputational studies in the 1950s and 1970s,... corporate leaders are the most powerful group in terms of "Who shines?" By the usual rules of evidence in a social science investigation using multiple indicators, the owners and managers of large income-producing properties are the dominant class in the United States.

Still, as noted at the end of the first [section], power structures are not immutable. Societies change and power structures evolve or crumble from time to unpredictable time, especially in the face of challenge. When it is added that the liberal-labor coalition persists in the face of its numerous defeats, and that free speech and free elections are not at risk, there remains the possibility that class domination could be replaced by a greater sharing of power in the future.

Excerpted from G. William Domhoff, *Who Rules America? Power and Politics in the Year 2000,* 3rd ed. (Mayfield, 1997). Copyright © 1997 by Mayfield Publishing Company. Reprinted by permission. Notes omitted.

# Where the Public Good prevailed

## Lessons from Success Stories in Health

### BY STEPHEN L. ISAACS AND STEVEN A SCHROEDER

Many Americans know, all too well, what is wrong with health care. Ask the single mother who waits half a day in a crowded clinic for a five-minute visit with a harried physician, or the unemployed worker who has been downsized out of his job and his health insurance. Their experience tells a devastating tale about our system's shortcomings.

But there is another, equally important story that concerns the problems we don't see anymore—at least not in the numbers of the past young victims of polio, mumps, and measles; preschoolers with neurological problems caused by lead poisoning; people in the prime of life dying prematurely from tuberculosis and influenza; hordes of patients with rotting teeth. While we need to address persistent inequities, we also need to understand the basis of victories in public health—not just to keep up our hopes, but to learn how research, advocacy, public discussion, and policy fit together in successful campaigns for change.

## GETTING THE LEAD OUT

Children in America today carry far less lead in their blood than they did just 20 years ago. The origins of that change go back nearly a century to 1904, when Australian pediatrician J. Lockhart Gibson found that lead paint caused lead poisoning of children in Queensland. A decade later, reports linking neurological damage in American children to lead began to appear. Mounting evidence of the metal's harmful effects led to sporadic local efforts to prevent poisoning caused by lead paint.

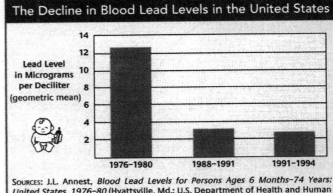

The Decline in Blood Lead Levels in the United States

Lead Level in Micrograms per Deciliter (geometric mean)

SOURCES: J.L. Annest, *Blood Lead Levels for Persons Ages 6 Months–74 Years: United States, 1976–80* (Hyattsville, Md.: U.S. Department of Health and Human Services, 1984); J.L. Pirkle et al., "Exposure of the U.S. Population to Lead, 1991–1994," *Environmental Health Perspectives* 106, no. 11 (1998): 745–750.

The single greatest source of lead, however, came from automobile engines. Leaded gasoline was introduced in the American market in 1923, less than a year after Thomas Midgely and his co-workers at the General Motors Research Corporation in Dayton, Ohio, discovered that adding tetraethyl lead to gasoline as an antiknock agent gave cars more zip and allowed them to go farther on a tank of gas. The potential health effects of tetraethyl lead became known shortly after its discovery. In 1924 a fire in Standard Oil's lead processing plant in Bayway, New Jersey, led to five deaths and caused severe tremors, psychosis, hallucinations, and other symptoms of serious lead poisoning in 35 injured workers.

The next year, the U.S. surgeon general convened a conference on the safety of lead in gasoline. Although public-health advocates testified in opposition to the release of a poison—lead—into the air, the lead, automotive, and chemical industries dominated the conference. Representing Standard Oil of New Jersey, Frank Howard said, "We have an apparent gift of God—tetraethyl lead" and accused opponents of standing in the way of progress. The surgeon general concluded that there were no good grounds for prohibiting the use of leaded gasoline as a motor fuel.

So matters stood until the 1960s, when a new generation of scientists began challenging the assertion that lead was harmless. Dr. Herbert Needleman, who became an advocate for efforts to lower lead levels, revealed that extremely low amounts could damage a child's nervous system. At hearings on air pollution chaired by Senator Edmund Muskie in 1966, Clair Patterson, a highly respected California Institute of Technology geochemist, testified that the amount of lead in the air was 100 times what it had been in the 1930s. The Muskie hearings led, ultimately, to passage of the Clean Air Act of 1970, which required automakers to reduce hazardous emissions drastically.

In fulfilling the mandate of the Clean Air Act, the newly formed Environmental Protection Agency began issuing standards for the maximum level of lead in gasoline. These regulations were consistently challenged by the lead and petroleum-refining industries. For example, in 1973 the EPA issued its initial lead standard—one that was to be phased in over five years beginning in 1975. The Ethyl Corporation promptly went to court. The lawsuit, ultimately resolved in the EPA's favor by the U.S. Court of Appeals, delayed implementation of the standard for two years.

Next-came a challenge from another direction. In the anti-regulation climate of the 1980s, Vice President George Bush's Task Force on Regulatory Relief pressured the EPA to roll back its lead standard. Activists from the Natural Resources Defense Council, the Environmental Defense Fund, Consumers Union, and other organizations fought back, and the press jumped on the story. "Incredibly, the Reagan administration appears willing to risk the health of hundreds of thousands of anonymous preschoolers, just so the oil companies can make a few bucks" wrote influential columnist Jack Anderson. At congressional hearings, witnesses presented new evidence demonstrating the effects of even very low levels of lead on the nervous systems of children.

At about this time, the U.S. Centers for Disease Control analyzed the results of the second National Health and Nutrition Examination Survey (NHANES). The survey showed that levels of lead in Americans' blood had dropped 37 percent between 1976 and 1980, largely because of reduced lead in gasoline. In the face of these data, plus all the negative publicity it was receiving, the EPA backed down. Instead of weakening the lead standard, it toughened it.

By the early 1990s, Congress was again involved. The 1990 amendments to the Clean Air Act banned the manufacture, sale, or introduction after 1992 of any engine requiring leaded gasoline. Congress also prohibited the use of all leaded gasoline for highway use after 1995. Since 1996, an outright ban on leaded gasoline has been in effect. These actions complemented laws that ban lead in paint, food containers, and solder joints. While lead-based paint continues to be a serious health hazard in inner-city buildings, legal restrictions have eliminated most new sources of lead poisoning. The results have been impressive. The third NHANES found that the average blood lead level in the United States had dropped by 78 percent between 1976 and 1994, largely because lead had virtually disappeared from gasoline—and because researchers and policy makers had overcome entrenched industry opposition in order to improve the public's health.

## GETTING THE FLUORIDE IN

Sometimes the obstacle to better health isn't an economic interest but public hysteria. Fluoridation has proved to be one of the cheapest, most effective public-health measures of the past century. Yet during the Red Scare of the 1950s, it faced strenuous opposition from groups who feared that it was part of a communist plot to poison Americans.

The origins of fluoridation also go back a century, to 1901, when Frederick McKay opened a dental practice in Colorado Springs, Colorado, and noticed that many of his patients had chocolate-like stains on their teeth. Even stranger, few of these patients had cavities. Dr. McKay spent the next 40 years investigating why some people developed what came to be known as Colorado Brown Stain. By 1931 scientists had established a link between fluorine and mottled teeth, and attention turned to whether fluorine protected against tooth decay.

Enter the U.S. government. H. Trendley Dean, director of dental research at the National Institutes of Health, collected water samples and examined children's teeth throughout the country; and in 1943, he concluded that children exposed to minuscule amounts of fluorine in water developed few or no cavities and avoided brown teeth. The next step for the Public Health Service was to test this conclusion. In January 1945, Grand Rapids, Michigan, became the first community to add fluoride, a compound of the element fluorine, to its drinking water, while residents of neighboring Muskegon, who continued to drink unfluoridated water, served as the comparison group. Three other communities began testing fluoride in the water shortly thereafter. The results were dramatic. In the four demonstration communities, cavities fell by 40 percent to 60 percent. Even as results were coming in, activists were campaigning to have fluoride added to the water supply. Wisconsin was the hotbed of dental activism; 50 communities in the state fluoridated their water by 1950. That year, under intense pressure from pro-fluoridation advocates, the Public Health Service and the American Dental Association endorsed fluoridation.

Then came Joe McCarthy and the backlash. In 1949, Stevens Point, Wisconsin, became the first community to

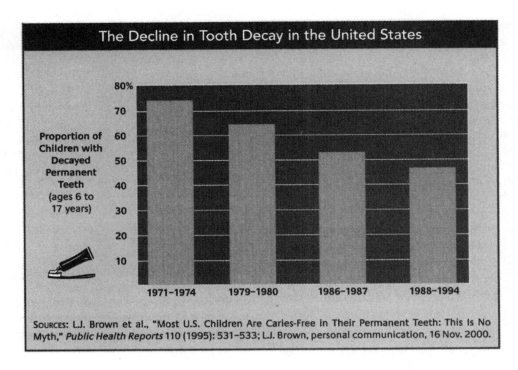

The Decline in Tooth Decay in the United States

Proportion of Children with Decayed Permanent Teeth (ages 6 to 17 years)

1971–1974    1979–1980    1986–1987    1988–1994

SOURCES: L.J. Brown et al., "Most U.S. Children Are Caries-Free in Their Permanent Teeth: This Is No Myth," *Public Health Reports* 110 (1995): 531–533; L.J. Brown, personal communication, 16 Nov. 2000.

reject fluoridation of the community's water supply. Opposition in other communities followed. At the height of the Cold War, opponents linked fluoridation to a perceived communist threat and spread tales of dead fish washing up on the shores of fluoridated reservoirs.

Those in favor of fluoridation struck back. The endorsements of major dental and medical organizations, supported by ongoing research, provided persuasive support for the safety of water fluoridation. When opponents went to court, they invariably lost as judges upheld local decisions to fluoridate water as a legitimate exercise of governmental authority. Of the 50 largest cities in the United States, 43 presently have fluoridated water systems. Some 62 percent of Americans live in communities with fluoridated water supplies. Cavities in children have dropped significantly (although the oral health of poor children is worse than that of well-to-do children). In the years 1971–1974, 74 percent of children six to 17 years old had one or more cavities in their permanent teeth. By the period 1988–1994, the percentage had dropped to 46 percent.

## THE AUTO-SAFETY CRUSADE

Public-health progress has often had to overcome the belief that nothing can be done about a problem until individuals improve their behavior. From the time of the nation's first automobile fatality, conventional wisdom had it that traffic accidents were the fault of bad drivers, not of the automobile itself. This viewpoint was articulated pithily by Harry Barr, Chevrolet's chief engineer: "We feel our cars are quite safe and reliable.... If drivers did everything they should, there wouldn't be any accidents."

By the 1950s, however, a respectable body of thought began to challenge the conventional wisdom. The medical profession—most particularly physicians who treated crash victims—weighed in early. By the mid-1950s, both the American Medical Association and the American College of Surgeons were recommending that automobile manufacturers design their cars for better passenger safety and equip them with safety belts. Triggered by concerns about the mounting toll of highway deaths, Senator Abraham Ribicoff of New York convened hearings that began in 1965 and continued into 1966. A 32-year-old lawyer named Ralph Nader was the star witness. Nader's book *Unsafe at Any Speed*, published in 1965, lambasted the automobile industry for its lack of concern about safety, singling out General Motors for selling the Chevrolet Corvair, an automobile produced with a defective and dangerous gas tank. The rest is the stuff of legend: GM hired private detectives to tail Nader and come up with dirt about his personal life, which they failed to do. When the attempted smear campaign came to light in March 1966, Nader became an instant national hero and used his new celebrity as a platform to promote auto safety.

The publicity galvanized public opinion and provided the impetus for Congress to pass the National Traffic and Motor Vehicle Safety Act and the Highway Safety Act in 1966. These laws established the National Highway Safety Bureau, the precursor of today's National Highway Traffic Safety Administration, and gave it the authority to set automobile safety standards.

As in the case of lead, new legislation precipitated legal and regulatory battles about how the law should be interpreted and carried out. Proposed federal regulations required that cars come equipped with padded instrument

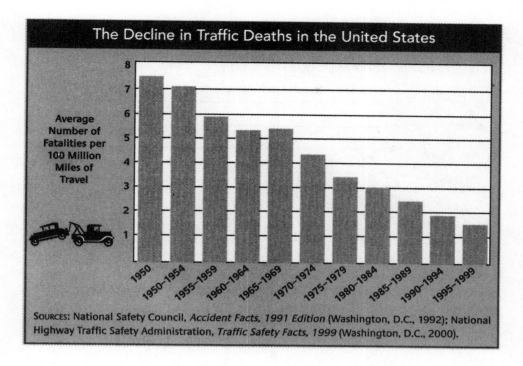

The Decline in Traffic Deaths in the United States

Average Number of Fatalities per 100 Million Miles of Travel

1950 | 1950–1954 | 1955–1959 | 1960–1964 | 1965–1969 | 1970–1974 | 1975–1979 | 1980–1984 | 1985–1989 | 1990–1994 | 1995–1999

SOURCES: National Safety Council, *Accident Facts, 1991 Edition* (Washington, D.C., 1992); National Highway Traffic Safety Administration, *Traffic Safety Facts, 1999* (Washington, D.C., 2000).

panels and seat belts, among other safety features. These rules were challenged by automobile manufacturers as unrealistic and by consumer safety advocates as weak and ineffectual. The battle over seat belts and, later, air bags lasted nearly a decade. Now, of course, they are both standard equipment.

During the late 1970s and early 1980s, an extraordinary grass-roots movement took shape across the nation. Doris Aiken founded Remove Intoxicated Drivers (RID) in 1978 after a drunk driver ran over and killed a teenager in her hometown of Schenectady, New York. Candy Lightner organized Mothers Against Drunk Driving (MADD) in 1980 after her daughter was run over and killed by a man who had been drinking. Aiken and Lightner cultivated the media, who responded by regularly featuring the speeches and activities of the anti-drunk-driving activists, particularly those of the charismatic Lightner. Hundreds of newspapers and magazine articles reported on the victims of drunk driving and their families. Drunk driving was the subject of television specials and dramatizations. Activists formed chapters of RID, MADD, and SADD (Students Against Driving Drunk) in communities around the country and began telling their stories though the media, providing victims' services, lobbying government officials, and monitoring the courts.

The effect of this grass-roots movement on public policy was stunning. Between 1981 and 1985 alone, state legislatures passed 478 laws to deter drunk driving. In 1982 Congress passed the Alcohol Traffic Safety Act, which provided extra funds to states that enacted stricter drunk-driving laws. To be eligible, a state had to require that a blood alcohol level of .10 percent was conclusive evidence of drunkenness. (The permissible alcohol level was lowered to .08 in 2000.) Two years later, in 1984, Congress stepped

in again and passed a law requiring states to enact a minimum drinking age of 21 or lose some of their federal highway funds. All states eventually complied.

Since the 1970s, public attitudes have changed remarkably. Drunk driving is no longer tolerated in a way it once was; even the liquor and beer industry recommends that drinkers give their car keys to a "designated driver" (a term that would not have been understood two decades ago). Behavior has changed, too. Between 1982 and 1999, deaths from alcohol-related crashes dropped by 37 percent. Safer cars, improved highways, better emergency medical services, and a decline in drunk driving have sent the nation's traffic fatality rate tumbling. On average in 1950, 7.6 individuals were killed for every 100 million vehicle miles traveled. By 1999 that statistic had plummeted to 1.6 persons—a decrease of more than 75 percent.

## AN UNFINISHED CRUSADE

Not very long ago, a movie star drawing slowly on a cigarette was considered the height of sophistication; medical-society meetings took place in rooms clouded with tobacco smoke; R.J. Reynolds and Philip Morris were considered so powerful that few dared to challenge them.

How things have changed! Planes are now smoke-free, as are many restaurants and offices; Joe Camel has been put out to pasture; and the $246-billion settlement between the tobacco companies and the states made front-page headlines. Americans have given up smoking in record numbers, and many of those who continue are trying to kick the habit. The percentage of adult male smokers in the United States dropped from a high of more than 50 percent in 1965 to about 26 percent in 1998. The percentage of adult fe-

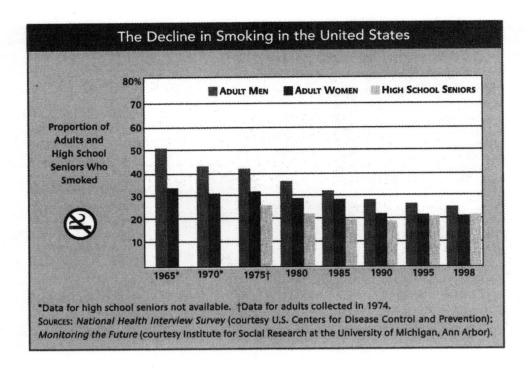

The Decline in Smoking in the United States

Proportion of Adults and High School Seniors Who Smoked

ADULT MEN    ADULT WOMEN    HIGH SCHOOL SENIORS

1965*    1970*    1975†    1980    1985    1990    1995    1998

*Data for high school seniors not available. †Data for adults collected in 1974.
SOURCES: *National Health Interview Survey* (courtesy U.S. Centers for Disease Control and Prevention);
*Monitoring the Future* (courtesy Institute for Social Research at the University of Michigan, Ann Arbor).

male smokers fell from its high of 34 percent in 1965 to 22 percent in 1998. Teenagers present more of a mixed picture. Although the percentage of American high school seniors who smoke daily decreased from a high of 29 percent in 1976 to a low of 17 percent in 1990, it then rose to 22 percent in 1998, before dropping slightly, to 21 percent, in 2000. Research, advocacy, media coverage, public education, politics, and government contributed to this unexpected transformation.

While the dangers of tobacco have long been recognized (in 1604 King James I branded the tobacco habit as "a loathsome custom to the Eye, Harmfull to the Braine, and dangerous to the lungs"), the scientific community ignored smoking until the last half of the twentieth century. As late as 1948, the *Journal of the American Medical Association (JAMA)* wrote, "More can be said on behalf of smoking as a form of escape from tension than against it."

Only two years later, in May 1950, *JAMA* published two articles linking smoking and lung cancer. In one of them, Ernst Wynder (who remained an anti-tobacco activist until his death in 1999) and Evarts Graham reported that of the more than 600 lung cancer patients they interviewed, 97 percent were moderately heavy to very heavy smokers. From there, the evidence mushroomed. By the late 1980s, some 60,000 studies had made it abundantly clear that tobacco causes cancers, stroke, and heart disease.

From published research to public awareness, however, there is often a long journey. In the case of smoking, the federal government played a critical role in narrowing the distance. In 1964 Surgeon General Luther Terry's widely publicized report woke up the nation to the dangers of tobacco. And in 1986, C. Everett Koop, surgeon general during the Reagan administration, reported that secondhand smoke caused cancers and other life-threatening illnesses—a finding that legitimized local, state, and federal efforts to limit smoking in public places.

Public-health advocates challenged the tobacco industry and kept the issues alive. Among the leaders were John Banzhaf, a Georgetown University law professor, whose organization ASH (Action on Smoking and Health) brought lawsuits and petitioned regulatory agencies, and Stanton Glantz, a University of California professor, whose advocacy groups Californians for Nonsmokers' Rights and, later, Americans for Nonsmokers' Rights, fought for the enactment of local and state anti-tobacco measures. Long-established organizations also joined the fray. The American Cancer Society, the American Lung Association, and the American Heart Association were relatively early participants. In 1982 these three organizations formed the Coalition on Smoking and Health, directed by Matt Myers, another longtime antismoking activist. The American Medical Association was the last to come to the table. Long ambivalent about smoking, the AMA ultimately proved to be an influential ally through its *Journal* articles and its work to organize antismoking coalitions.

Although some media organizations were slow to publicize the dangers of smoking (tobacco ads are a significant source of advertising revenues), others played an important early role. In December of 1952, *Reader's Digest* ran an article entitled "Cancer by the Carton." In it the most widely read magazine of its day reported, in plain English, the link between smoking and lung cancer and accused the tobacco industry of a cover-up. From then on, despite the best efforts of the tobacco industry, the danger of tobacco has become increasingly well known.

Laws and regulations have long been the backbone of antismoking efforts. A week after the release of the surgeon general's report in 1964, the Federal Trade Commission proposed that cigarette packages and advertising carry a strong warning label. In response the tobacco industry cried foul and tried to sabotage the legislation, a scenario that was to be replayed many times in the succeeding years. Ultimately, in 1965, over the fierce opposition of the tobacco industry, Congress passed a law requiring that cigarette packs and ads carry a watered-down warning. This was the first of many federal laws and regulations aimed at reducing smoking. Equally if not more important were local ordinances and state laws banning smoking in public places and making the sale of cigarettes to minors illegal. As Victor Crawford, a former Tobacco Institute lobbyist who became an anti-tobacco advocate after developing lung cancer, recalled, "We [the tobacco lobby] could never win at the local level. The reason is that all the health advocates are local activists who run the little political organizations. On the local level, I couldn't compete with them."

While Americans' attitudes toward smoking have changed, the tobacco industry remains a formidable force. Cigarettes and spit tobacco are still attractive to young people, and the commitment of the Bush administration to tobacco-control measures is, at best, uncertain. While the victories won so far in the national effort against tobacco are a cause for cheering, it is too early to celebrate them as permanent.

## INGREDIENTS OF SUCCESS

Cavities, lead poisoning, traffic fatalities, smoking—although serious health concerns remain, each of these examples involves a success story. These experiences are not triumphs of medical technology; rather—and this may explain why they are unappreciated—they are the result of social and behavioral change. Four elements shared by these quiet victories offer lessons for shaping public policy.

**1. Highly credible scientific evidence can persuade policy makers and withstand attack from those whose interests are threatened.** Tobacco is the clearest example. The evidence linking smoking with cancer and other deadly illnesses was so strong and so consistent that—over the legal and scientific objections of the tobacco companies—it provided a scientific basis for legislation, regulations, and judicial decisions; ultimately, it was persuasive enough to move public opinion. Similarly, well-structured comparative trials provided convincing evidence that moderate amounts of fluoride added to the water supply reduced tooth decay. The federal government's National Health and Nutrition Examination Surveys gave the EPA the foundation on which to base regulations—strongly challenged by the gasoline and lead lobbies—that eventually eliminated lead from the nation's gasoline supply.

**2. Public-health campaigns need advocates who are passionately committed to their cause, who have the inner resources to withstand the tremendous pressure applied by the industries whose practices they are criticizing, and who continue to fight even at the risk of their professional reputations.** Ralph Nader, Candy Lightnet, Herbert Needleman, and other crusaders have had a tremendous effect on social policy. But advocacy from outside the system is rarely enough. When government agencies and their leaders speak out, new ideas about public health become more acceptable to the mainstream media and the populace. Similarly, campaigns for change gain legitimacy from the backing of authoritative groups outside government, notably professional societies—such as the American Medical Association on seat belts, the American Dental Association on fluoridated water, and the American Cancer Society on tobacco.

**3. Public awareness and discussion depend on a partnership with the media. Advocates need the media to reach the public, and the media, looking for good stories, also need the advocates.** "Behind virtually every public-health-and-safety measure enacted in this half-century has been a media advocacy campaign to dramatize both the risks and the public-policy solution" says the Advocacy Institute's Michael Pertschuk. As a result of the media, few now doubt that smoking is bad for health, that drinking and driving is a lethal combination, that seat belts save lives, and that fluoridated water prevents cavities.

> For all our country's achievements, the United States still ranks 24th in measures of national health, according to the World Health Organization

**4. Law and regulation, often at the federal level, have been critical elements in focusing Americans' attention on health concerns, providing policy direction, and setting standards that have led to improvement in the public's health.** Despite all the criticism they have received, federal laws and regulations have vastly improved people's health. They have been—and continue to be—the underpinning that protects the health of the American public.

Because of the Clean Air Act, the Lead-Based Paint Act, and federal regulations that reduced or eliminated other sources of lead contamination, lead poisoning has been significantly reduced as a health concern. Because of highway safety laws and federal regulations mandating the use of seat belts and other safety features, drivers and their passengers are now much safer. Because of congressionally mandated warning labels on cigarette packs, bans on cigarette advertising, and similar legislation, plus lawsuits by state attorneys general and local ordinances banning smoking in public places, the nation is moving toward kicking the nicotine habit. Even at a time when many people are disillusioned with government, its role in protecting the health of the public cannot be underestimated.

As impressive as these victories appear, the United States still has a long way to go even to catch up with the rest of the developed world. For all our achievements, we still rank 24th in measures of national health, according to the World Health Organization. Imagine what we could do if we had social movements against homicide, HIV infection, unhealthy foods, and physical inactivity that could match what public-health initiatives have achieved in such areas as lead and tobacco. Without the energy of such social movements, the United States will be doomed to suffer from inferior health, no matter how much we invest in basic

biomedical research or cutting-edge medical technologies. Yet if we put that research to positive use in the public arena, combine it with committed advocacy, and follow up with intelligent policy-making, we can do much to improve America's health—not with miracles but with just hard work.

*For more on success stories in public health, see the links to this article at www.prospect.prg.*

STEPHEN L. ISAACS is the president of Health Policy Associates in San Francisco. STEVEN A. SCHROEDER is the president of the Robert Wood Johnson Foundation.

In Corporate America,

# It's Cleanup Time

## UNDER PRESSURE, A SLEW OF COMPANIES ARE NOW CHANGING THE WAY THEY DO BUSINESS. WILL IT LAST?

Jerry Useem

ADDITIONAL REPORTING BY MELANIE WARNER

Even at a time when hunting for the "next Enron" has become a national sport, Krispy Kreme Doughnuts would seem a highly unlikely target. The North Carolina-based purveyor of crullers and Hot Original Glazed has long enjoyed a sweet reputation with customers and investors. But early this year some shareholder questions turned sour. In particular, why was Krispy Kreme using a "synthetic lease" to finance a mixing factory—an off-balance-sheet practice that carried a whiff of Enron-style finance? CEO Scott Livengood felt the criticism was undeserved, and that his company was already a model of transparency. "It was guilt by association," he says. "But in this new environment, it was shoot first and ask questions later."

So Livengood formed a governance committee of independent board members, which recommended a hasty overhaul of governance and accounting practices. Krispy Kreme's synthetic lease is toast. All inside board members, save Livengood, will eventually be replaced with outsiders. Corporate loans to executives have been banned. And the top five executives can now sell their stock only in preplanned, immediately disclosed blocks.

To avoid even a passing resemblance to Enron's notorious partnerships, furthermore, the company has terminated a mutual fund that let executives invest directly in Krispy Kreme franchises—and it returned only the initial, unappreciated sums the executives had invested. "I really regret the things that have put us in this position," says Livengood. "But there's been a tremendous amount of damage done to the credibility of honest people."

It's cleanup time in corporate America, and a new set of rules is in force. Some of those rules are, of course, literal, such as those proposed by the New York Stock Exchange or contained in Congress's Sarbanes-Oxley Act. But some are taking hold as a result of fear—fear of disgusted, distrustful investors and their various avengers, including SEC investigators and New York State attorney general Eliot Spitzer. "You've got a totally disaffected individual investor community, and they're angry," says former Securities and Exchange Commission chairman Arthur Levitt. "They're going to differentiate between companies that stand with them and companies that don't."

## "THE ERA OF THE DOMINANT CEO DIED A QUICK AND PAINFUL DEATH, AND IT WILL BE A LONG TIME BEFORE IT COMES BACK."

This is a huge change of heart that has come remarkably fast. Between 1992 and 1999, the number of companies beating First Call estimates by exactly one penny quadrupled—and investors rewarded those companies for what was seen as great reliability. Now, says Baruch Lev, an accounting professor at New York University, "there will be suspicion of exactly meeting estimates, or beating them by a penny"—the presumption being that those companies could be accused of cooking their books. Corporate executives feel the heat. In a poll taken by Kennedy Information, publisher of *Shareholder Value* magazine, 46% said the wave of scandals had harmed the way investors viewed their companies, while 43% were changing the way they did business.

The most visible change has been a stampede to expense stock options; as of press time, 81 companies had announced they would treat stock options as a cost of doing business. But the cleanup has extended to insider selling, financial disclosure, even CEO pay—all issues that fed the image of corporate corruption. "Hopefully, this

# THE MASH NOTE EVERY CEO WANTS

What are the most coveted words in corporate America today? That's simple: "Sincerely, Warren."

With companies competing to clean up their act, a letter of praise from super-investor Warren Buffett has become the ultimate Good Housekeeping Seal of Approval. General Electric got one for announcing it would expense stock options. "For long, GE has brought good things to life," Buffett wrote. "Now GE has brought good things to accounting."

Standard & Poor's got one, too, for its new "core earnings" measure. "Your move is both courageous and correct," Buffett wrote in his letter, which S&P liked enough to post on its website. "In the future, investors will look back at your action as a milestone event." Other lucky recipients have included Bank One and Amazon.

"He's the only person or entity out there that still has an unblemished reputation," says S&P analyst Robert Friedman. Well, a few other voices still command credibility, such as John Bogle, the outspoken founder of Vanguard Group. But how did Bogle know that a speech about corporate accountability went over well? "[Buffett] gave me a very nice note after reading that speech," he says.

will convince my mother that companies are serious and that the numbers can be trusted," says Peggy Foran, vice president for corporate governance at Pfizer.

At Citigroup, under fire for its financing of Enron and WorldCom, CEO Sandy Weill is adopting what Prudential analyst Mike Mayo sarcastically calls "just-in-time corporate governance." Besides doing an about-face on the issue of expensing all stock options, Weill has set up a special governance committee, pledged to avoid any deals involving hidden off-balance-sheet transactions, and reaffirmed a "blood oath" never to sell more than 25% of his Citigroup stock.

Coca-Cola CFO Gary Fayard has had a road-to-Damascus conversion on stock options. "When Enron hit, I said, 'It's an anomaly,'" he recalls. "When the scandals came flooding out, I was floored. I couldn't believe it was that endemic." Foreseeing increased scrutiny of corporate accounting—and prodded by board member Warren Buffett—he and CEO Doug Daft decided to bite the bullet and expense options. Even Cendant, a company whose excessive pay packages have long been ridiculed, is trying to ride the reform train: It slashed CEO Henry Silverman's pay in half—to a mere $15 million—by getting rid of his annual options package.

Among corporate governance activists, long used to measuring their gains in inches, there's a giddy sense of suddenly having run the field. "I've never seen a debate end this quickly," bubbles Charles Elson, a governance expert at the University of Delaware. "The era of the dominant CEO died a very quick and painful death. It will be a long time before it comes back."

Indeed, both the Sarbanes law and the NYSE proposals would turn the corporation into a less imperial, more constitutional place. Boards will need a majority of independent directors; a more powerful audit committee led by a "financial expert"; and the chance to meet without management present. "The old ceiling is the new floor," says Patrick McGurn, vice president at Institutional Shareholder Services.

FOR MOST PUBLIC-COMPANY CEOS AND CFOS, IT was signing those papers that provided the most concrete reminder of how life has changed. At 8:30 on the morning of Aug. 13, one day before the executives of 947 American corporations had to swear, so help them God, that their financial statements were true, 15 people piled into a conference room on the 22nd floor of Pfizer's Manhattan headquarters. Awaiting them on the table were 300-page binders containing a year's worth of financial statements and detailed explanations—what is considered revenue, how Pfizer accounts for capital expenditures, how data come in from distant locations to headquarters, and so on. CFO David Shedlarz asked the two KPMG auditors a simple question: "If you were me, would you prepare the statements differently?" No, they replied.

Shedlarz signed off. For Pfizer the two-hour ceremony was largely perfunctory, because the company already thinks of itself as one of the good guys: It doesn't report *pro forma* earnings, doesn't pay auditors for consulting work, maintains a 15-person governance department, and is regularly praised for the independence of its board. "We had no hesitation whatsoever," says CEO Hank McKinnell, who also certified the numbers.

Other companies, though, fretted. "Obviously no CEO is going to be able to go out and count the actual beans," noted Lou Thompson, president of the National Investor Relations Institute. So at John Hancock Financial Services in Boston, CEO David D'Alessandro refused to put his John Hancock on the line until his underlings had signed too. Those who balked, he announced, could look for another job. Alan Hassenfeld, CEO of toymaker Hasbro, didn't have such reservations. "Look, if I had an office in Uzbekistan where somebody messed up on something, I might not know," he says. "But more than anything, a CEO has got to be the guardian. If you're going to abdicate that responsibility, then you don't belong here."

Still, many companies are taking unusual steps to ensure their numbers don't hide surprises. At car-parts chain AutoZone (which doesn't have to certify its financials until November, since its fiscal year ends in August),

CEO Steve Odland plans to turn a regular meeting of managers into a "roll-up certification." The 40 chieftains will huddle to pore over financials and sign 40 separate statements. Diebold, a maker of ATM machines, has an online "hot line" to give would-be Sherron Watkinses a chance to express concerns anonymously. And at discount brokerage Charles Schwab, co-CEO David Pottruck acknowledges that the Jeff Skilling defense—how was I supposed to know?—won't fly.

"In the past, we would take some things for granted—that our CFO has integrity, that there are systems for issues to get escalated [up the chain of command]," says Pottruck. "You can't presume anything now. You have to look everybody in the eye and make sure nobody is reluctant to speak up. And the question to ask is not 'Did you live by the letter of the law?' but 'Did you live by the spirit of the law?' Signing off on these certifications makes all the sense in the world. I'm amazed that some CEOs think this is a bad idea. Right now there's nothing more important than restoring investor confidence in the captains of the ship."

Companies that have discovered unpleasant surprises, meanwhile, find themselves between a rock and a hard place. Concealing those surprises now carries criminal penalties—while revealing them carries penalties of a different sort. "The market is so sensitive right now [that] investors get the slightest sniff of the word 'restatement,' and they put their sell order in," says Mark Bergman, head of the securities group at law firm Paul Weiss Rifkind Wharton & Garrison. The stock of advertising conglomerate Interpublic, for instance, tanked 24% when the company said it needed an extra week to sort out its numbers—even though the restatement turned out to be a relatively modest $68.5 million. "What was our choice?" asks Frank Borelli, head of the Interpublic board's audit committee. "The market did punish [the company], but at the end of the day [we] did the right thing."

Complicating the situation is widespread confusion over some points of the Sarbanes law. What, for instance, does the ban on loans to executives mean? Does it apply to something as trivial as travel advances? Relocation loans? And why does the law include not one but two overlapping certification requirements? (Did some Capitol Hill staffer forget to take one out at the last minute?) "Right now companies are going crazy because we don't have regulations on any of this stuff," says Pfizer's Peggy Foran, who, like everyone else, is awaiting clarification from the SEC. "Everybody's paranoid."

That paranoia is partly of the shareholder-lawsuit variety. While it's not clear that certifying their financials will make executives more liable in such actions, no one doubts that plaintiffs lawyers are sharpening their knives. "Lawsuits are undoubtedly going to increase," says Toby Myerson, a lawyer at Paul Weiss. "The CEO has now been held up as a target."

WHILE MOST CEOS ARE STICKING TO THE SCRIPT OF praising the legislation and solemnly declaring the importance of "restoring investor confidence," not everyone has lined up behind the new economic correctness. In Silicon Valley, where the issue of expensing stock options is read as a searing attack on technological innovation, dissent is the loudest. "This is going to be crappy for Silicon Valley," says Jean Kovacs, CEO of Comergent, a four-year-old software startup. "It's such a fabric of the way we do business out here, it seems unfair to make this a universal thing."

Among tech companies, only Amazon, Computer Associates, and USA Interactive have volunteered to expense options. But it's not just the stock-options issue that riles the Valley's libertarians. It's the broad, impulsive nature of the regulation pouring out of Washington. "There's this huge rush to do stuff, and it hasn't been thought through," says David Roux of private-equity fund Silver Lake Partners. "What you really need is a bunch of people's heads on stakes to satisfy the lynch mob."

At a recent board meeting of a tech company, Roux was handed a 300-page notebook. "There's one memo from the firm's outside law firm, another from the auditors, and a third from the company's general counsel, explaining all the signed, pending, and proposed rules, regulations, and laws being laid down by FASB, the SEC, Nasdaq, and the NYSE. There are four columns telling you everything everyone says you need to do. And there's four different definitions of what constitutes an independent director. It's dizzying," says Roux. He wonders where companies will find the slew of dedicated, financially literate people needed to serve as outside directors. "It will be difficult for many companies to meet the new standards for their boards," predicts Tom Neff, U.S. chairman of executive recruiter Spencer Stuart. "We're currently doing 130 board searches. There's a lot more people saying no." Some experts believe the changes will have other unforeseen consequences. "The costs of being a public company in the U.S. are going to go up, and that's going to affect the decision whether to go public, or whether you're going to list in the U.S. if you're a foreign issuer," says Karl Groskaufmanis, a lawyer at Fried Frank Harris Shriver & Jacobson.

Silicon Valley isn't the only node of resistance. On one issue—adhering to a high, common standard of financial reporting—corporate America is digging in its heels. Companies won't easily give up their addiction to *pro forma* numbers, the highly stylized versions of earnings derided as "earnings before bad stuff." Last year companies' *pro forma* numbers were 53% higher on average than their GAAP numbers, up from a 12% disparity the year before. "You would think companies would bend over backward to do the right thing," says Chuck Hill, director of research at Thomson First Call. "That didn't happen."

Many companies, for example, continue to rely on pension-fund credits to pad earnings. According to Vanguard Group founder John Bogle, even during this bear market the average S&P 500 company is assuming a hefty 9.75% annual pension return when 4.5% would be more like it. Such rosy assumptions lifted GE's earnings 7% last year and boosted Northrop Grumman's by 41%, according to a Merrill Lynch study. "We must demand realistic assumptions about the future returns, and we must also demand full reporting of past returns," Bogle said in a scolding speech entitled "Just When We Need It Most...Is Corporate Governance Letting Us Down?"

Part of the problem, many acknowledge, are the rules themselves. Generally Accepted Accounting Principles have allowed the fuzzy pension accounting since 1987, and in any case, "GAAP is so complicated that it's very difficult to know what is within GAAP or what violates it," says Baruch Lev, the NYU accounting professor. "We're ten months into the Enron thing, and I *still* don't know whether they violated GAAP."

Rather than await snail-paced accounting reform, a few companies have simply decided to hold themselves to a higher standard. AMB Property, a San Francisco real estate investment trust that was the first company this year to announce it would expense stock options, operates on what CEO Hamid Moghadam calls "principle-based"—as opposed to "rule-based"—accounting. "We try to understand the principle behind the guideline and live by it," Moghadam says. It's all predicated on the assumption, difficult to prove, that investors will pay a premium for such behavior. "It's not a sense of wanting to change the world or wanting to go to heaven," he says. "You want to make yourself attractive to the people who supply you with capital."

WHICH BRINGS US TO THE BIG QUESTION: IS ALL this change for real? Will the current spate of reforms permanently change the rules of the game? Or will companies revert to their old ways once the corporate scandals have been pushed off the front pages? The answer will depend mightily on big institutional investors. Traditionally they have been skittish about attacking the CEOs of companies whose pensions and 401(k) plans they often manage.

But now that "conspiracy of silence" may be cracking. The reason is simple: Fund managers fear that disillusionment with the financial system will lead the average investor to pull even more money out of the market. So instead of merely voting with their feet—by dumping stocks of shoddily run companies—money managers are getting into the arm-twisting business. After supporting management 100% in 2001, Bill Miller of Legg Mason Value Trust has refused to vote for six director slates this year, including those of MBNA and Starwood Hotels. Fidelity Investments has signaled its intention to take a tougher line against excessive executive compensation. And in a recent letter to CEOs, Vanguard warned that it

had voted against 64% of stock-based compensation proposals this year.

All this has helped make the 2002 proxy season a record setter. According to the Investor Responsibility Research Center, 83 shareholder proposals out of approximately 200 have received majority votes this year, compared with 66 out of 272 for all of 2001. One big winner: proposals to ban or limit companies from paying consulting fees to auditors, which forced changes at Walt Disney, Apple Computer, Bristol-Myers Squibb, and Johnson & Johnson. Also popular: caps on executive compensation, especially golden-parachute provisions.

## "THERE'S NOTHING MORE IMPORTANT THAN RESTORING INVESTOR CONFIDENCE IN THE CAPTAINS OF THE SHIP."

When proxy votes (which tend to be nonbinding) aren't enough, some fund managers are happy to make their feelings known directly. Tom Marsico, chairman of Denver's Marsico Capital Management, which manages $14 billion in assets, has been leaning on executives to ease up on their use of stock options and pay higher dividends to prove their earnings aren't fictitious. Not all executives are charmed. "The level of questioning definitely has changed," he says, "and they don't like it."

That's why Linda Selbach, manager of corporate governance at Barclays Global Investors in San Francisco, which manages $770 billion, has changed her home phone number several times. She's tired of executives calling her to complain that Barclays opposes their pay packages. "Some people are polite and gentlemanly," she says, "and some are surprisingly out of control."

Other CEOs are learning to live with the scrutiny. "Every question is fair game," declares Kenneth Freeman of Quest Diagnostics, a lab testing company based in Teterboro, N.J. When Marsico began interrogating Freeman about his stock-options package this summer, Freeman patiently walked him through the ins and outs of his compensation plan, even offering to let him meet with an internal pay specialist. Marsico came away satisfied. "[Freeman] said that going forward, this was a concern of his, too, and he didn't want to be pulled into the cauldron of CEOs whose compensation is considered to be excessive," says Marsico.

Some fund managers want to ratchet up the pressure tactics. Since April, a group of industry heavies including Bill Miller, Vanguard's Bogle, and the Davis Funds' Chris Davis have been working to form a Federation of Long-Term Investors. The goal is to assemble a group that controls up to $1 trillion, or nearly 10% of the stock market. Warren Buffett has lent his support, and the group is preparing a list of standards it could wield as a cudgel against deviant companies.

# ANDY GROVE **SPEAKS OUT**

**What's your view of the new regulations coming out of Washington?** Well, one part—attestation of financial reports—is a real pain in the ass. At Intel, we had an 11-hour financial meeting. I sat through it and learned a bunch of things about how we put together a statement. I met a bunch of the people responsible for the actual work; not the comptrollers, whom we normally deal with. It was very useful. Would we have done that without the SEC regulation? No. Should we have done it? Yes.

**Businesspeople of all stripes are being vilified. What's that like for someone who's spent his life building a company?** Very uncomfortable. You go to dinner, you feel the questioning eyes of people who have known you for a while, and it doesn't sit very well. The assumption of collective guilt is wearing. This may be self-serving, but I think on the whole it's undeserved.

**Do business leaders as a class need to answer back?** Yeah. I wish more of them did. To a fair extent my colleagues in business seem frozen at the stick—paralyzed by the unstated and unspecific accusation of us as a class. And sure, you can be ridiculed, singled out, attacked. But if you don't tell your side of the story, who will?

**You've been outspoken on the issue of expensing stock options, which has led to some heated exchanges between you and Warren Buffett. Have the two of you resolved any of your differences?** The godforsaken stock-option expensing issue… he and I finally agreed to disagree. We still correspond, but a little less heatedly. I don't think I have a chance to change his mind, and I don't know how I can change mine.

It's an accounting issue that shouldn't be resolved by our yelling, that shouldn't be political, that shouldn't be settled in op-ed columns—it should settled by FASB going away on a deserted island and thinking about it. A lot of emotion has blocked this rational accounting issue. A lot of what people are pissed about is executive compensation. The distinction between executive compensation and option expensing kind of gets lost.

**Arthur Levitt told us Silicon Valley companies "will be the last to fall because they believe they're special, and the rules for them should be different."** I take offense to that. And I think he's right. In some areas, we drank our own Kool-Aid. On the other hand, the employee and management practices pioneered by Hewlett and Packard and Noyce and Moore are increasingly appropriate ways to deal with employees.

**How can corporate America regain public trust?** No single act can do it. But a collection of things—reporting requirements, corporate governance, a move away from the imperial CEO—will add up. If you put CEOs on the right, boards of directors in the middle, and shareholders on the left, this whole thing is shifting power from the right to the left.

**What effect will this shift have on companies?** Every cure creates its own problems. We are transferring power to the left, which in principle is good. But if shareholders are less and less long-term oriented, we are putting power to ratify corporate decisions in the hands of day traders. Do day traders value good corporate governance and disclosure? I don't think so.

**Where does this leave directors?** That job has gotten dramatically more complicated. There are something like 100,000 to 150,000 board members in this country. If you gave a mass quiz—like a driver's license test—and asked rudimentary questions of those 100,000 people, I really wonder how many would pass. So if boards are really going to accept more responsibility, we need to educate them on the new requirements.

**Is the current reform a temporary run for cover, or is it a long-lasting change?** For our generation of business managers, it's a wakeup call that's going to last a while.

"The key here," says Arthur Levitt, "is whether the great institutions of America are willing to exercise the power they have to force responsible corporate behavior." On that score, he says, "the ground is moving. A board member is crazy if he doesn't respond to these events."

For Krispy Kreme's Scott Livengood, it's no longer a matter of "if." "I think these changes will be real, and they will be lasting," he says, "and all they're doing is getting us back to where we should have been all along."

---

REPORTER ASSOCIATE Eric Dash

---

FEEDBACK juseem@fortunemail.com

# Work Work Work **Work!**

It's taking over our lives—invading our homes, haunting our holidays, showing up for dinner. **Should we care?**

### by Mark Hunter

YOU'VE HEARD THE JOKE BY NOW, BUT IT RINGS so true that it bears retelling: A guy reads a headline saying "Clinton creates 8 million jobs", and he cracks wearily, "Yeah, and I got three of 'em."

That gag may be the epitaph of the 1990s. In a very real sense, all of us—not just the 13 percent of us working two or three part-time jobs to survive—have three jobs. There's the work we do for a living, the work we do for ourselves (in many cases, to make sure we still can make a living tomorrow), plus the combination of housework and caregiving. Researchers differ on how much time we put into each of these categories, but most agree on one crucial point: The total keeps growing. As my brother Richard, a vice president of the Gartner Group, a high-tech advisory company, puts it: "It's like trying to fit a size 12 into a size eight shoe."

By far the biggest chunk of our time still goes to the work we do for a living. A survey of some 3,000 employees nationwide by the Families and Work Institute (FWI), a New York nonprofit organization that addresses work and family issues, discovered that over the past two decades, the average time spent at a full-time job has risen from 43.6 to 47.1 hours per week. Over a year, that comes to about four extra weeks—the same figure that Juliet B. Schor arrived at in her controversial 1991 study, *The Overworked American*, one of the first books to document what she called "the decline of leisure."

This fact hit home for me when I returned to the U.S. in 1996 after a decade abroad. I began to notice that not one of the other seven people in my office left their desks at lunchtime, the way folks used to. Throw in that traditional half-hour lunch break, and that's another two-and-a-half hours every week that many people give to work—or about three more weeks per year. Likewise, the Bureau of Labor Statistics reports that since 1985 paid vacation time has declined, and so has the average time that workers take off sick. Not surprisingly, more than one third of

the people in the FWI survey said that they "often or very often feel used up at the end of the workday." It's true that some researchers, like John Robinson, a sociology professor at the University of Maryland, argue that it's mainly the well-off among us who are working more, as a matter of choice, and that on average our leisure time has increased. But that's not what I see all around me.

Simultaneously, the old line between work life and private life is vanishing. In trying to understand why employees often refused to take advantage of maternity leave and flex-time, sociologist Arlie Hochschild, author of *The Time Bind*, discovered, to her amazement, that work has become a form of 'home' and home has become 'work.' "She reports that many people now see their jobs as a more appreciative, personal sort of social world" compared with their homes, where in the age of divorce and double careers, "the emotional demands have become more baffling and complex." When I interviewed 40 men about their work-life tradeoffs, every one of them said that it was easier to be a success on the job than in his personal relationships. Is it just a coincidence that hit TV shows like *Taxi* or *Murphy Brown* substituted the workplace "family" for the domestic setting of *The Brady Bunch*?

Work has penetrated the home in another potent way, notes market researcher Judith Langer, who has interviewed several hundred people on this subject over the past ten years: "People feel that what they're required to do at work has spilled over into the rest of their lives—reading, keeping up with trends in their fields, keeping up with e-mail and voice mail. We had a guy come into a focus group carrying all the publications that had hit his desk that day and complain, 'Monday weighs 20 pounds.'"

Personal technology has turned what once were hobbies into jobs: When my brother goes home from the office, he fires up his PC and checks the online orders for his self-produced harmonica records. And when the one third of Americans with managerial or professional jobs leave home, work follows them on a cell phone, pager, or modem. This past winter I received numerous business-related e-mail messages from an executive who was on a hiking trip deep in the mountains of Utah. (Emergency rescue crews have reported finding stranded hikers in the wilderness who had filled their backpacks with a portable computer, but forgotten to bring enough food and water.) The next time a cell phone rings in a restaurant at dinnertime, notice how many people automatically reach for theirs, because it might be a business call. In the 1960s and 1970s, stress experts called this kind of thing multiphasic behavior, otherwise known as doing several tasks at once. Nowadays we call it efficiency.

## The distinction between work and leisure no longer exists

Ironically, the Baby Boomers, who came of age shouting their contempt for the man in the gray flannel suit, have done more than any other generation to erase the line between work and private life. Among the first to spot this paradox was Alvin Toffler in his 1980 futurist manifesto, *The Third Wave*. While most observers took those in the hippie movement for a bunch of unwashed, lazy bums, Toffler realized that they were really the prototype of a new kind of worker, the "prosumer"—people who, like frontier farmers, produce a share of what they consume, from home medicine to clothing (my fiancee creates a wardrobe every two years) to home-baked bread, instead of buying it all in the marketplace. "Once we recognize that much of our so-called leisure time is in fact spent producing goods and services for our own use," he noted, "then the old distinction between work and leisure falls apart."

Just as they turned the home into a workplace, Boomers redefined the ideal workplace as a playground. At the end of the 1970s, pollster Daniel Yankelovich found that this "New Breed" of Americans believed that work should be first and foremost a means to self-fulfillment—unlike their parents, who were taught by the Depression that any job that pays a secure wage was worth keeping. When Catalyst, a New York nonprofit organization that seeks to advance women in business, surveyed more than 800 members of two-career couples about what mattered most to them on the job, at the top of the list were emotional benefits such as supportive management, being able to work on their own, and having control over their product.

Our careers now start earlier and end later, reversing a trend that reached its peak after World War II, when child labor virtually disappeared and retirement became a right. These days, so many teenagers have jobs—and as a result are cutting back on sleep, meals, and homework—that the National Research Council has called for strict new limits on the hours they're allowed to work. At the same time, the number of people 55 and older who still are in the labor force has increased by 6 million since 1950, and most of that increase is women. The Department of Labor projects that this number is going to grow by another 6 million by the year 2006.

None of this was supposed to happen. Only a generation ago, the conventional wisdom among economists was that America was turning into an "affluent society", in which ever more efficient technology would produce an abundance of wealth that we could enjoy with less and less labor. Science-fiction novelists like Kurt Vonnegut imagined a society in which a tiny elite ran the show, while everyone else sat around bored. In their vision, work would no longer be a burden, but a privilege for the happy few.

There are a lot of reasons why things didn't turn out quite that way. One is the Vietnam War, which heated the American economy to the boiling point just as the oil shocks of the 1970s arrived—a combination that led to double-digit inflation and sapped the value of wages. Then successive waves of recession, mergers, and downsizing crashed through the American economy during the '80s. With few exceptions, one of the surest ways to raise a company's stock price—and along with it the value of its executives' stock options—was to fire a piece of its workforce. (Fortunately, downsizing appears to be losing steam, as Wall Street begins to suspect it as a desperate attempt to make a company's bottom line look good in the short term.) Gradually, overtime pay replaced wage increases as the main way to stay ahead of the bills.

The Baby Boom played a role here, too. With so many Boomers competing for jobs, they became cheap for employers: "For the first time in recent American history," marvels Landon Y. Jones in *Great Expectations: America and the Baby Boom Generation*, "the relative earnings of college graduates *declined*." In order to maintain or, in many cases to surpass, the lifestyles of their parents—more Baby Boomers now own homes and, on average, bigger homes than Americans did in the 1950s—they have gone deeply into debt. About one fourth of the average family's income now goes to pay various creditors, more than in any previous generation.

Just as the feminist revolution was urging women to do something with their lives besides raise kids and clean house, it became difficult for the average family to make ends meet without two incomes. Today, in nearly four out of five couples—compared with one out of five in 1950—both partners are in the labor force, with women working nearly as many hours for pay as men. One positive result is that since the late 1970s men have taken over a steadily growing (though still smaller) share of the childcare and household chores—nearly two hours' worth per day that used to be considered women's work.

Yet even visionary feminists like Dorothy Dinnerstein, who predicted this shift in her landmark 1976 book, *The Mermaid and the Minotaur*, did not foresee that it would also have a negative impact on our intimate lives. The Internet site BabyCenter recently polled roughly 2,000 of its new-mother visitors on whether they did or would return to work after their child was born. Two out of three survey participants said that they would go back to work within six months, but only one out of six said that she found the move "satisfying"; twice as many called it "wrenching." Men are also feeling the pinch." I have absolutely no time for myself or my friends," a married male executive and father complained to a Catalyst researcher. "Not enough time for us as a couple, and even the extended family say they don't see us enough."

## Work is focusing us to constantly learn new ways of working

In previous decades, surveys showed that the biggest source of problems for married couples was money; now, when both partners are asked what is the biggest challenge they face, the majority of two-career couples answer "too little time." Not surprisingly, a growing number of leading-edge companies now offer working couples flexible schedules, expanded parental leave, and other benefits that allow their employees to reconcile their jobs with their personal lives.

Paradoxically, the same technology that was supposed to make us all wealthy loafers has contributed to the work-life squeeze. Computers and the changes they wrought have eliminated entire categories of jobs—when was the last time, for example, you talked to a human operator, instead of an automated phone tree, when you called a big company? In his book *The End of Work*, Jeremy Rifkin warned that this trend would end by puffing nearly all of us out of a job—a neat Doomsday inversion of the old "affluent society" prophecy. But many economists argue that new jobs will be created by new technology, just as they always have been. Perhaps, but the pressures to adapt to these rapid technological changes are greater than ever.

Computers have even changed the rhythm of our work, giving us more of a say in how the job is done because technology-savvy frontline personnel become responsible for decisions that managers used to make, as they constantly feed information up and down the line. The same applies to managers, whose desktop PCs, equipped with software that does everything from keeping appointments to formatting business letters and writing contracts, have largely replaced personal secretaries. We get more control—which happens to be one of the key measures of job satisfaction—but in return we end up giving more of ourselves to the job.

Beyond requiring us to put in longer hours for fear of losing our jobs, work is changing us in positive ways. In particular, it is literally forcing us to expand beyond the limits of what we previously thought we could accom-

plish, to constantly learn new ways of working. A lifelong career now means lifelong retraining. As the Radcliffe Public Policy Institute in Cambridge, Massachusetts, reports, "The qualities that once nearly guaranteed lifelong employment—hard work, reliability, loyalty, mastery of a discrete set of skills—are often no longer enough." That message has come through loud and clear. About one out of 12 Americans moonlights from his or her principal job in order to learn new skills or weave a "safety net" in case that job is lost. And American universities, starved for students only a few years ago as the Baby Boom grew up and out of the classrooms, have found a burgeoning new market in older workers. Census data show that by 1996 an incredible 468,000 college students were age 50 and older—an increase of 43 percent since 1990.

I don't have to look far to see that trend at work. My brother's wife earned her degree as a geriatric nurse in her late 40s, and it's now her part-time career. My mother, who runs her own public-relations agency, is working toward a degree as an English-language teacher, which will become her post-"retirement" career. And I'm riding that same train. This year I began teaching myself to write code for the Internet, just like my friend Randy, a former magazine editor who spent years of evenings learning to make Web pages in order to support his family. Why? Because by the year 2006 there will be fewer jobs for journalists, according to the Department of Labor. Like everyone else, I've got a choice between moving up—or out.

And there's real excitement in acquiring fresh skills—including the joy of proving wrong the adage that old dogs can't learn new tricks. But many older workers are not getting a chance to share in that excitement: They are being shunted aside from the retraining they will need to stay in the labor market at a moment when they are the fastest-growing share of the labor force. And the point at which a worker on the rise becomes a worker who's consigned to history is coming earlier in people's careers, usually around age 44, according to the Bureau of Labor Statistics. This situation persists at a time when a 77-year-old astronaut named John Glenn just went back into space—and while the minimum age for receiving Social Security benefits is rising.

Perhaps more managers should look at the hard science on this question. In a survey of the available research, Paula Rayman, director of the Radcliffe Public Policy Institute notes that there are "at least 20 studies showing that vocabulary, general information, and judgment either rise or never fall before age 60." Despite these results, they found that managers "consistently made different hiring, promotion, training, and discipline decisions based *solely* [my emphasis] on the age of the workers."

A recent survey of 405 human-resources professionals found that only 29 percent of them make an active effort to attract and/or retain older workers. Among those employers who have made such efforts, establishing opportunities for advancement, skills training, and part-time

# six survival tips

THE RULES OF THE GAME MAY HAVE CHANGED, BUT midcareer and older workers still hold a number of aces—among them experience, wisdom, and adaptability. Here's some expert advice on how to play your cards and strengthen your hand for the future, gleaned from John Thompson, head of IMCOR, an interim executive placement firm in Stamford, Connecticut; Peter Cappelli, professor of management at The Wharton School in Philadelphia and author of *The New Deal at Work* (Harvard Business School Press 1999); and management gurus N. Fredric Crandall and Marc J. Wallace, authors of *Work and Rewards in the Virtual Workplace* (AMACOM, 1998)

**LEARN WHILE YOU EARN** If your company will pay for you to attend college-level courses to up-grade your skills, great. If not, take them anyway. Anything computer-related is a good bet. Microsoft offers training programs via organizations such as AARP.

**FLEX YOUR MUSCLES** By offering to work hours that younger workers may shun because of family and other commitments, you set yourself apart, especially in the eyes of employers in service industries who need 24-hour or seven-a-day week staffing. Employers such as the Home Shopping Network now rely on mature workers to fill a variety of positions.

**CAST A WIDE NET** The World Wide Web has radically changed the employment scene. A growing selection of jobs are being posted there, and so are résumés. Take a look at the Working Options section on AARP's Web site at www.aarp.org/working_options/home.html for career guidance and links to resources, including America's Job Bank.

**BECOME AN MVP** Do something to make yourself invaluable. For example, consider becoming a mentor to a young, up-and-coming manager who may need just the kind of guidance an experienced hand can offer. Another option: Seek out projects that matter to your boss and allow you to showcase your talents.

**TEST THE WATERS** Temporary workers are the fastest-growing segment of the labor force, for good reason. Companies faced with budget-cutting pressures are loathe to add full-time, permanent workers who drive up salary and benefit costs. It gives you an opportunity to try out an alternate career to see if it really fits. And temporary work often is the pathway to a permanent gig.

**BE A COMEBACK KID** Even if you're planning to retire or cut back from full-time work, don't forget job possibilities with your current employer. GE's information unit in Rockville, Maryland, offers a Golden Opportunity program that lets retirees work up to 1,000 hours a year, and many firms in Southern California use retirees to help with special engineering projects.

*—Tim Smart*

work arrangements are the most common. Overall, older employees are rated highly for loyalty and dedication, commitment to doing quality work, reliability in a crisis, solid work performance, and experience. This has given rise to a new phenomenon, in which downsized older workers are coming back to the workplace as consultants, temps. or contingent workers hired to work on specific projects.

Many who possess skills that are high in demand, like computer experts or financial advisers are finding fresh opportunities: Brokerage firms, for example, have discovered that their clients enjoy having investment counselors whose life experience is written on their faces.

Other countries are grappling with this issue as well. The Danish government, for example now offers salaried one-year training programs to unemployed workers over age 50. The German government has made it more costly for companies to downsize. And the French government is experimenting with ways to reduce the hours people spend on the job, to spread the work around. For Americans, however, the likely solution will depend on the ability of older workers to take control of their careers as never before, to think of themselves as independent contractors—units of one, so to speak—and, to do whatever they can to enhance their value. At a time when work has become, all-encompassing for many of us, it remains an eminently desirable endeavor. And although much is uncertain about the future, one thing is clear: Work will be part of it.

*Mark Hunter is the author of five books, including* The Passions of Men: Work and Love in the Age of Stress *(Putnam, 1988). He lives in Paris.*

# Schools That Develop Children

## BY JAMES P. COMER

American schools are said to be failing. Like nineteenth-century medicine men, everybody is promoting everything, whether there is any evidence that it works or not. Over here we have vouchers, charters, privatization, longer school days, summer school, and merit pay. Over there we have the frequent testing of students, the testing of teachers, smaller class size, report cards on schools, and high-stakes accountability. And over here, a very special offer: student uniforms, flag-raising ceremonies every morning, the posting of the Ten Commandments on schoolhouse walls, and sophisticated diagnostic instruments to identify children at risk for acting violently—when many administrators and teachers can't even identify children who need glasses.

Most of these "cures"—traditional and reform—can't work or, at best, will have limited effectiveness. They all are based on flawed models. We will be able to create a successful system of education nationwide only when we base everything we do on what is known about how children and youths develop and learn. And this knowledge must be applied throughout the enterprise of education—in child rearing before school age, in schools and school districts, in schools of education, in state education departments, in legislatures, and everywhere else that personnel preparation takes place and school policy is made.

Given the purpose of education—to prepare students to become successful workers, family members, and citizens in a democratic society—even many "good" traditional schools, as measured by high test scores, are not doing their job adequately. But test scores alone are too narrow a measure. A good education should help students to solve problems encountered at work and in personal relationships, to take on the responsibility of caring for themselves and their families, to get along well in a variety of life settings, and to be motivated, contributing members of a democratic society. Such learning requires conditions that promote positive child-and-youth development.

Children begin to develop and learn through their first interactions with their consistent caretakers. And the eventual learning of basic academic skills—reading, writing,

mathematics—and development are inextricably linked. Indeed, learning is an aspect of development and simultaneously facilitates it. Basic academic skills grow out of the fertile soil of overall development; they provide the platform for higher-order learning.

Through the early interactions, a bond is established that enables the child to imitate, identify with, and internalize the attitudes, values, and ways of their caretakers, and then those of other people around them. These people become important because they mediate (help make sense of and manage) a child's experiences and protect the child and help him or her to grow along the important developmental pathways—physical, social-interactive, psycho-emotional, ethical, linguistic, intellectual-cognitive, and eventually academic. The more mature thus help the less mature to channel potentially harmful aggressive energy into the energy of constructive learning, work, and play. But good early development is not a kind of inoculation that will protect a child for life. Future good development builds on the past and is mediated continuously by more mature people, step by step.

Understanding this process is no longer a matter of conjecture or the whining of "fuzzy-headed" social scientists or, as in my case, psychiatrists. Hard science—brain research—has confirmed the nature and critical importance of this interactive process. Without it children can lose the "sense"—the intelligence potential—they were born with. Children who have had positive developmental experiences before starting school acquire a set of beliefs, attitudes, and values—as well as social, verbal, and problem-solving skills, connections, and power—that they can use to succeed in school. They are the ones best able to elicit a positive response from people at school and to bond with them.

People at school can then influence children's development in ways similar to competent parents. To be successful, schools must create the conditions that make good development and learning possible: positive and powerful social and academic interactions between students and staff. When this happens, students gain social and academic competence, confidence, and comfort. Also, when parents and their social networks value school success and school experiences are positive and powerful, students are likely to acquire an internal desire to be successful in school and in life, and to gain and express the skills and behavior necessary to do so.

---

## Vouchers do not address the challenge of child development. They simply change mechanisms of infrastructure, curriculum, and service delivery.

---

In order to realize the full potential of schools and students, we must create—and adequately support—a wide and deep pool of teachers and administrators who, in addition to having thorough knowledge of their disciplines, know how children develop generally and academically and how to support that development. They must be able to engage the families of students and the institutions and people in communities in a way that benefits student growth in school and society.

Vouchers and similar reforms currently being touted do not address these standards. They are simply changes in infrastructure, curriculum, and service delivery. They do not offer the potential for a nationwide transformation that a developmental focus does. And vouchers can reduce funds needed to improve the schools that must educate the majority of American children.

### THE CHALLENGE OF CHANGE

The function of promoting good child-and-youth development and achievement was once served in our society through families and their social networks and through community life in small towns and rural areas. If students did not do well in school, they could leave, earn a living, still take care of themselves and their families, and become positive, contributing members of their communities. Despite massive and rapid scientific, technological, and social change, children have the same needs they always did: They must be protected and their development must be guided and supported by the people around them. They cannot rear themselves.

High mobility and modern communication created by technological change have undermined supports for child-and-youth development. Children experience many stimulating models of potentially troublesome behaviors—often in the absence of emotionally meaningful, influential adults. As a result, too many young people receive too little help in learning to manage feelings and act appropriately on the increased and more stimulating information they re-

ceive. This makes adequate social, psychological, and ethical development difficult.

Meanwhile, the new economy has made a high level of development and education a necessity for 90 percent of the population instead of the 20 percent we got by with half a century ago. Yet the rise of technology has led to an overvaluation of measured intelligence rather than an appreciation of overall development and the kind of intellectual growth that promotes strong problem-solving capacities.

Many successful people are inclined to attribute their situations to their own ability and effort—making them, in their minds, more deserving than less successful people. They ignore the support they received from families, networks of friends and kin, schools, and powerful others. They see no need for improved support of youth development. These misperceptions influence many education policies and practices.

Adequate support for development must be restored. And school is the first place this can happen. It is the common pathway for all children—the only place where a significant number of adults are working with young people in a way that enables them to call on family and community resources to support growth systematically and continually. And school is one of the few places where students, staff, and community can create environments in which to help young people achieve the necessary levels of maturity.

In the early 1980s, James Coleman, the late and respected University of Chicago sociologist, called what children gain from their parents and their networks "social capital." I do not like this term in discussing humans, but it is much used. Many poor children grow up in primary social networks that are marginal to mainstream institutions and transmit social capital that is different from that needed for school success. School requires mainstream social capital. In a January 2000 *New York Times Magazine* article, James Traub said that "Coleman consistently pointed out that we now expect the school to provide all the child's human and social capital—an impossibility."

I agree that the school can't do it alone. But schools can do much more than what they now do. Most students, even those from very difficult social conditions, enter school with the potential needed to gain mainstream social capital. But traditional schools—and most reforms—fail such students.

Not long ago I asked approximately 300 experienced teachers and administrators from across the country if they'd taken a child development course; about half had. But when I asked how many had taken a school-based, supervised course in applied child development, only seven hands remained up. This lack of training is why many educators can't discuss the underlying factors involved in a playground fight or how to create social and academic experiences that motivate learning by tapping into the developmental needs and information level of today's students.

Even fewer could construct environments conducive to overcoming racial, ethnic, income, and gender barriers.

But schools can succeed if they are prepared to embrace poor or marginalized families and to provide their children with conditions that promote mainstream skills. And when these conditions are continued throughout the school years, children from low-income backgrounds can do well in school; they will have better life chances. I was first convinced that this was the case for very personal reasons.

My mother was born into the family of a sharecropper in rural Mississippi in 1904. Her father was a good man, but he was killed by lightning when she was six years old. There were no family assistance programs, and a cruel, abusive stepfather came into their lives. He would not allow the children to go to school, and they lived under conditions of extreme poverty. At about eight years of age, as a barefoot child in the cotton fields, my mother realized that education was the way to a better life. When she was 16, she ran away to live with a sister in East Chicago, Indiana, with the hope of getting an education. But that was not possible.

When she had to leave school, my mother declared that if she ever had children, she would make certain they all got a good education. And then she set out—very, very, very carefully—to find my father, a person of like mind and purpose. Her caution paid off. My father, with six or seven years of education, worked as a steel mill laborer; and my mother, with no education, worked as a domestic. The two of them eventually sent the five of us to college, where we earned a total of 13 degrees.

Our family was enmeshed in an African-American church culture that provided the necessary social, ethical, and emotional context. My parents took us to everything educational they could afford; they talked and interacted with us in a way that encouraged learning and promoted overall development. Working for and respected by some of the most powerful people in our community, my mother observed and acquired mainstream success skills and made useful social contacts. Most of the summer jobs that helped us pay our way through college came from those contacts. And I enjoyed caviar brought home after parties before my working-class friends knew that it existed. Indeed, many European, black, and brown immigrants "made it" through similar experiences.

My three best friends were as intelligent as anybody in our family and in the predominantly white working- and middle-class school we attended. On the playground and the street corner, they could think as fast and as well as students who were more successful in school. But all three went on a downhill course: one died early from alcoholism, one spent time in jail, and one was in and out of mental institutions until he died recently. My parents had the same kind of jobs as their parents did, and we all attended the same school. Why the difference? It was the more useful developmental experience we were provided.

This notion was confirmed a few years ago when I visited my mother in the hospital. My spry, 80-plus-year-old first-grade teacher, Ms. Walsh, was a hospital volunteer.

When she saw me, she threw her arms around me and said, "Oh, my little James." I was 55 years old going on six. She stepped back and said, "We just loved the Comer children. You came to school with those bright, eager eyes, and you got along so well with the other children, and you all were so smart," and more. She was describing the outcome of a home and community experience that provided adequate development and school readiness—social capital, if I must use the term.

I acknowledge that my parents, perhaps even my community and school, were not and are not typical. And again, the community conditions that supported family functioning, child rearing, and development to a much greater degree in the past are weaker today. The positive connections that the poor previously had with the more privileged in American society have decreased.

A few scattered programs make good education and life opportunities possible for poor and working-class children. Prep for Prep lays the groundwork for students to attend elite private schools; A Better Chance places students in good suburban schools; the Summer Study Skills Program prepares students for challenging academic courses. These "pull-out" programs provide the social capital, knowledge, and skills needed for mainstream participation. But they do not serve that large body of able young people, like my childhood friends, who are lost in elementary schools. Prepared and supported differently, such children could succeed.

## MODELS OF DEVELOPMENT

The Yale Child Study Center's School Development Program has been working with schools for the past 32 years. The outcomes suggest that by basing what we do in schools (and in the education enterprise beyond schools) on what we know about how children develop and learn, we can provide most children with what they need to succeed in school and in life.

I recently visited the Samuel Gompers Elementary School in one of the poorest neighborhoods in Detroit, a school with 97 percent student poverty. The Yale program has been used in this school for the past six years. The neighborhood was a disaster; the school was a pearl. The students were lively, spontaneous, and engaged in their work at appropriate times, yet quiet and attentive when they were supposed to be. They got along well with one another and were eager to demonstrate their skills to their parents and teachers. Eighty percent of the students passed the 1999 fourth-grade Michigan Educational Assessment Program (MEAP) test in reading and science, and 100 percent passed in mathematics. In 2000 they achieved the highest MEAP test scores among elementary schools in their size category in the state. Why here? It is not a mystery.

The Gompers School's success is related as much to the conditions that promote development and learning as it is to curriculum and instruction. How did it create these conditions and achieve good academic outcomes? The Yale program provided the conceptual and operational framework, child development–centered training for staff and parents, and very limited field support. The Skillman Foundation in Detroit, the Detroit Public Schools, Eastern Michigan University College of Education staff members, and parents (key members of the education enterprise) all came together to help the Gompers School and others provide the social capital the students need. The philosophy of the principal, Marilee Bylsma, is an important underpinning: "The school should be a safe haven for children, someplace that inspires learning." The staff, parents, and students did the work.

Committees, operations, and guidelines help schools create a culture of mutual respect and collaboration as well as social and academic programs that enable them to support students' development and learning. The transformation is gradual but frequent in schools that work to form good adult relationships. Good student relationships can follow.

At Gompers there is a 15-minute assembly every morning in which the students say the Pledge of Allegiance and make a school pledge. They sing a patriotic song and the school song. The custodian recognizes the "birthday boys and girls." (Message: It's everybody's school; we all play important roles.) The class with the best previous-day behavior gets "Gator points." Other recognitions take place. During the announcements, the students often discuss what's going on in their lives—the unexpected death of a teacher, problems in the neighborhood, and so on—and the adults help them learn to manage related feelings.

## In traditional high schools, teachers are often much more anchored in subject matter than in student development.

When the school basketball team lost a tournament they had expected to win, the principal gave much thought to how to help the players manage their disappointment and grow from the experience. The next morning, she talked about how important it is to try to be number one in all you do. But the team members should celebrate their effort, she explained—they came in third in a large field—and look forward to the next opportunity. The students can tell you that they participate in extracurricular activities to create a good community, a condition that they value.

Activities and interactions like those at Gompers can't be carried out very long, if at all, in a school where the staff members don't like, trust, or respect one another or the parents. And you can't just mandate these conditions. Child

development–oriented structures and processes must operate in a way that brings about these conditions.

Initially, the Yale program's work was just in elementary schools, but it is now being carried out in many middle schools and high schools. Admittedly, middle school is difficult, and high school is even more so. That's when teens are "placing" themselves in the world and establishing their identity. Young people who place themselves and their futures in family and social networks that are dysfunctional are likely to perform in school in ways that lead to similar poor or marginal outcomes for themselves. Additionally, they are physically able to engage in adult behaviors. Only a half-century ago, many teens were married, working, and raising families; but in these more complex times, they often lack the experiences and resultant judgment, personal control, discipline, and problem solving skills needed to manage adult living.

In traditional high schools, teachers are often much more anchored in subject matter than in student development. Peer groups provide belonging and therefore become very powerful. They are sometimes positive, but too often are troublesome—it's the inexperienced and immature leading the inexperienced and immature. Aside from athletic coaches and teachers in the arts and other special areas, too few mature adults can interact with students in sustained and meaningful ways. These are powder keg conditions. And in communities where there are too few constructive supports for good development both inside and outside school, bad things happen—among staff, students, and parents.

In all schools—but particularly in low-income and nonmainstream communities—it is important for the staff to expose students to mainstream work as well as civic activities so that the connection between learning and later expectations is clear. School should help young people to learn what is needed for life success. Social and academic skills, attitudes, management of feelings, and other attributes needed to participate successfully in the mainstream can then be developed.

West Mecklenberg High School in Charlotte, North Carolina, received an additional 222 students in 1992 from a competing high school; its enrollment went from 1,144 to 1,366, precipitating a crisis. The school was almost evenly divided between whites and African Americans. Most of the students were children of blue-collar workers. Fourteen guns and many knives were confiscated during the first year, and parents, teachers, and students were concerned about their safety. Dennis Williams was assigned to the school as principal; Haywood Homsley, then the guidance counselor and coach, became the Yale-program facilitator. Williams and Homsley began to focus on reducing intergroup tensions and creating a climate that enabled staff members to consider and respond to the developmental needs of the students.

The transformation was dramatic. On April 28, 1995, *The Leader*, Charlotte's major newspaper, highlighted the gains seen at West Mecklenberg since the Yale program was introduced: Scholastic Assessment Test (SAT) scores rose by an average of 16 points; the number of students who made the honor roll jumped 75 percent; the number of students enrolled in advanced courses increased 25 percent; and the average daily attendance rate for the year went from 89 percent to almost 94 percent. The process of change at West Mecklenberg was essentially the same as in elementary schools like Gompers except that the students themselves were more involved in the thinking and planning of the programs.

In the 1994–1995 academic year, West Mecklenberg was designated a "school of excellence" by the state of North Carolina for the high level at which it reached its benchmark goals, and it was the only high school of 11 in its district to attain this status. Despite the fact that there have been three principals since 1992, the school has held the "excellence" rating for three of the past five years.

## SUSTAINING GAINS

Are the academic gains large enough? Can they be sustained? What about the schools that do not improve? And what about middle- and upper-income young people, who face a more complex world? Even with developmentally based programs and other reform models, it's true that academic gains in schools serving students who are most in need do not quickly and routinely match those of more privileged students. Sometimes they can't be sustained; and sometimes there is no improvement at all. But when the process is well implemented, large gains have been achieved and sustained.

---

**Frequent changes in administrators or teachers can undo in several months or less a school culture that took years to create.**

---

For example, the Norman Weir K-8 school in Paterson, New Jersey, went from 34th to first in academic achievement among eighth-graders in 1995. They equaled or surpassed suburban schools for four consecutive years. A school in Virginia went from 24th to first but fell apart the next year because the principal and several key senior staff members were removed or left and were replaced by untrained staff. Weir escaped the same fate because a group of staff members went to the superintendent and asked for

and were assigned a good principal whose educational philosophy was grounded in child development.

Before a school can experience large, widespread, sustained achievement-test gains and adequately prepare students for adult life, it must be able to promote student development and manage its way to success, as Gompers, West Mecklenberg, and others have done. For this to be possible, we must produce large numbers of adequately prepared and supported staff. The policies and practices of the major players in the education enterprise nationwide— schools of education, legislators at all levels, state and federal departments of education, school districts, businesses—must be coherent by virtue of being based in child-and-youth development.

There are many obstacles to significant school improvement. Five in particular are very troublesome yet more accessible than the seemingly intransigent issues of race, class, and financial equity. These five are the ones that prevent the education enterprise as a whole from empowering school staffs, as in the case of the Gompers School. If these were addressed all at once, the United States could begin to foster widespread, sustained, high-level school improvement—and perhaps, eventually, could even address the most resistant issues.

First, frequent changes in personnel—particularly in districts and schools faced with great challenges—is a major problem. Child development–based strategies require continuity, training, and support of school staff. Frequent changes in administrators or governance at the district or building level, or in teachers—without careful selection and training of new people—can undo in several months or less a school culture that took three to five years to create. Understanding student and organization needs, developing resources and staff, and building community support isn't possible in the two-year tenure of most school superintendents.

Second, education policy is often fragmented rather than prioritized. This is because it is made everywhere—legislatures, state departments, districts, unions, city councils, businesses, and more. Many policy makers have no expertise in child development, teaching, and learning. And when crafting policy, most do not talk to one another, to students, or to school staff. Rarely are these policies guided by what we know about child growth and development and its relationship to learning.

And legislators, businesspeople, state departments, and others are—like school administrators—under great pressure to "Do something!" Because they widely believe that test scores alone can measure school effectiveness, that is what they focus on most. And without well-considered, evidence-based, coherent education policies, equitable funding will be impossible. In one city, eight of the 10 schools listed as "failing" had made the greatest gains in the system over the previous two years. The listing was demoralizing and led to harmful staff turnover and achievement setbacks, but it was the only way to get funds to help those schools.

Third, most schools of education do not provide future teachers or administrators with adequate knowledge or skills to promote a culture supportive of overall student development. Most focus—and in the college classroom, particularly—on curriculum, instruction, assessment, administration, and, sometimes, use of technology.

Sound knowledge of academic disciplines is important but not sufficient. Many schools of education provide courses in abnormal child development but no study of normal development. And the preparation to teach reading is often limited. Yet a child who has difficulty learning to read—the academic task that serves as a foundation for all future learning—is likely to experience feelings that limit emotional, psychological, ethical, and social developmental growth, or that promote troublesome growth.

Fourth, schools of education are seldom involved with other departments of the university in mutually enriching ways. Meaningful interaction between colleges of education and other university departments would be beneficial also to the institutions and the communities around them.

And fifth, there is no vehicle in universities or among research-and-development groups that will enable working educators to update their skills regularly and learn best practices. Also, there is no existing way to address these five most troublesome obstacles simultaneously so that synergy results.

Agricultural extension provides a useful model for educators. The Smith-Lever Act of 1914 created the Agricultural Extension Service to transmit knowledge to a large number of farmers through federal, state, and county partnerships. Farm agents, in addition to changing farmer practice, changed policy makers' and the public's understanding of best practice, as well as the policies needed to promote it. Improved agriculture enriched the economy and made America the breadbasket of the world.

Education is to the information-age economy of today what agriculture was to the economy at the turn of the twentieth century. Schools of education could create centers designed to overcome major obstacles in the education enterprise. Such centers would provide education agents. Schools of education will need to incorporate and institutionalize child development knowledge and expertise. But once this is done, education scholars and agents will be well positioned to share with and learn from colleagues at universities, to help future and current teachers and administrators become more effective practitioners, and to help policy makers and the public better understand and support good schooling.

Few schools of education or university programs are presently prepared to work in this way. We should not rush into such programs without sound pilot and infrastructure work. But knowledge, organization, and support can be acquired. The states—who are legally responsible for educating America's children—should support such efforts. Most, largely through their departments of education, have been involved in standard-setting as well as in regulatory and oversight activities. They are involved in takeovers of failing districts. Yet they have little experience in—and no mechanisms for—correcting the complex problems involved in school improvement.

The decisions we make in the next few years will involve significant amounts of money and will lock us into helpful or harmful directions. A miracle quick fix is not possible. But if we today begin to mount programs that connect to practice and to policy what we know about how children develop and learn, we could soon be well on our way to having better-functioning systems of education in five years and good ones in a decade. If we continue to be guided by tradition, ideology, and power, however, we will reach a point of no return—one where too many young people are undereducated, acting out, and gradually undermining our economy and our democracy.

JAMES P. COMER, M.D., is the Maurice Falk Professor of Child Psychiatry at the Yale University Child Study Center. He founded the Center's School Development Program in 1968.

# The future of humanity

"How beauteous mankind is!" said Miranda in *The Tempest*.
But can natural evolution or our own genetic engineering
improve on the present model?

## By **Colin Tudge**

Are we it? Have we already seen the best of humanity? Was Plato or Shakespeare or Einstein or Buddha or Lao Tzu or the prophet Mohammed as clever as any human being is ever likely to be? Modern athletes with their minutely cultured hearts and limbs don't run the 100 metres significantly faster than Jesse Owens did in 1936. So is this as fast as people can ever be? In short: has our evolution stopped: and if so, why, and if not, what lies in store? Or might genetic engineering allow us to breed our own superspecies, if not in God's image, at least according to the demands of market forces?

To begin at the beginning. Darwin's great contribution in *The Origin of Species* was to propose not simply evolution, but a plausible mechanism: it happens, he said, "by means of natural selection". The individuals best able to cope at any one time are those most likely to survive and leave offspring. So as the generations pass, each lineage of creatures becomes more and more closely adapted ("fitted") to its particualr surroundings. Natural selection requires an appropriate mechanism of inheritance—one that ensures "like begets like" (that cats have kittens, and horses give birth to foals), but also provides variation, so that not all kittens and foals are identical. Darwin's near contemporary, Gregor Mendel, working in what was then Moravia and is now the Czech Republic, provided just what was needed: he showed that inheritance works by transmitting units of information, now known as genes. Genes encapsulate the characters

of the parents, but they are recombined in the offspring through the machinations of sex and and are also prone to random change, of the kind known as mutation. So they provide all the variation that is required.

Darwin did not know of Mendel's work (he had Mendel's account on his desk, but failed to cut the pages), but 20th-century biologists put the two together and, by the 1940s, generated "neo-Darwinism". Creatures that reproduce through sex continually swap and recombine their genes, so all the genes in all the individuals in a sexually breeding population form one great "gene pool". Natural selection operates on the pool as a whole (these neo-Darwinists said). It knocks out individuals who contain less helpful genes, but favours those whose genes are especially advantageous. Thus the "bad" genes tend to be lost as time goes by, while the ones that promote survival and reproduction spread through the pool. Over time, the composition of the gene pool changes and so the creatures change as well. The neo-Darwinian model has been modified somewhat, but that general picture obtains.

There is no destiny in evolution, Darwinian or neo-Darwinian. Natural selection is opportunist and answers to the here and now; it has no mind for the distant future. The fossils tell us that our ancestors grew taller over the past five million years, from about a metre to nearly two, while our brains have puffed up from an apish 400ml or so to 1,400ml—easily the biggest in proportion to body weight of any animal. Perhaps this has made us more like God. But there is nothing in natural selection to suggest that our ancestors did more than adapt to whatever their surroundings threw at them, or to imply that we will grow more godlike as the future unfolds.

Neither will we go the way of *The Eagle's* Mekon, arch-enemy of Dan Dare: a green homunculus with a head as big as a dustbin and legs like cribbage pegs. Before Darwin, the Frenchman Jean-Baptiste Lamarck proposed a different mechanism of evolution, through "inheritance of acquired characteristics". He observed rightly enough that bodies adapt to whatever is demanded of them, so that blacksmiths, say, acquire bigger muscles. But he was wrong to propose that a blacksmith passes on his hard-earned biceps to his children. If the children want to be tough, they have to do their own smithying. By the same token, thinking won't make our brains grow bigger, in any heritable way, and physical indolence will not shrink our descendants' legs. So our evolution is not shaped by destiny, nor by our own endeavours, nor by our self-indulgence. Neo-Darwinian mutation and selection (plus large slices of chance) are all there is.

## The same techniques that made wheat from wild grasses could transform humanity, too

But in us, the neo-Darwinian mechanism seems logjammed. Some genetic variants are being lost, as small tribal groups continue to die out; and others are constantly gained by mutations, some of which persist. There are fluctuations: genes that confer resistance to Aids are gaining ground in Africa, for instance, while Kenyans are currently breeding faster than Italians, so any genetic variants that are peculiar to either group must be increasing or falling. But the permanent losses of genes through extinction of minorities are small compared to the whole pool, and while the particular genes of Kenyans may wax in one century, they may wane in another. Most importantly, there is no consistent pressure to push our gene pool in any particular direction. Nobel prize-winners and professional basketball players are lauded, but do not typically leave more offspring than the ordinary Joe. Infant mortality is still high in some societies but, in genetic terms, it strikes randomly because the poor are not genetically distinct.

Genetic logjams certainly happen, as is clear from the fossils. Some lineages of clams remained virtually unchanged for tens or even hundreds of millions of years. Today's leopards and impala are more agile and brainy than their ancestors of 50 million years ago, but they have not changed much in the past three million years. People anatomically undistinguishable from us were living in Africa at least 100,000 years ago.

Yet the deadlock could be broken. Through global war or some other ecological disaster, human beings could again become isolated into island groups, and natural selection could then go to work on each of them separately to produce a range of neo-humans, each adapted to its own island. We should not assume that any of the islands would especially favour brains, which require a great deal of nourishment. Agile climbers of fruit trees might fare best, and so we might again become more simian.

Or human beings might take their own genetic future in hand—which, in principle, has long been within our gift. The same techniques that made wheat from wild grasses and Aberdeen Angus from aurochs could transform humanity, too, in any direction we might care to prescribe—albeit over longer periods, given that we have such an extended generation interval, and many of the characters we might be most interested in undoubtedly have a complex genetic basis. Eugenics, the deliberate transformation of the human gene pool, was popular 100 years ago through most of Europe, and *de rigueur* in the US. Only the Catholics spoke out consistently against it, and the socialists H G Wells, George Bernard Shaw and Sidney and Beatrice Webb were among its most incongruous advocates. Up-to-date Edwardian matrons spoke approvingly of "eugenic" marriages.

The eugenicists were interested not so much in breeding super-people as in preventing the "decline" of the species through the perceived reproductive prodigality of the "feeble minded" (who were taken to include a great many foreigners and a large section of the working class). Hitler revealed the political perils, however, as he wiped out the people who did not meet his own particular criteria and matched blonds with blondes like prize porkers. So eugenics has gone out of fashion and now is virtually taboo. But in various ways, the new biotechnologies seem to open new possibilities and have concentrated minds afresh: cloning, genomics, genetic engineering.

Genetic engineering is the biggie: the transfer of particular stretches of DNA from one individual to another. The first phase of the Human Genome Project was completed last year, and it is already beginning to show which pieces of DNA correspond to which particular genes and which, therefore, are worth transferring. Cloning *qua* cloning is not directly pertinent, but it does provide techniques that will generally be necessary if genetic engineering is ever to progress beyond its simplest stages. Genetic engineering is already commonplace in bacteria, increasingly in food crops (GMOs), and in laboratory mice. It has at least been essayed in farm livestock and, in principle, is certainly applicable to humans. So where might it lead?

Most simply, doctors already try to repair the affected tissues in people with particular diseases: for example, to correct the damaged genes in the lungs of patients with cystic fibrosis (CF). Genetic changes made to the lungs (if and when this becomes possible) would not be reflected in the eggs and sperm, and so would not be passed on to future generations. Some argue that genetically transformed lung cells could escape, to be breathed in by the rest of us. But apart from this hypothetical hazard, no third parties are involved. The ethical problems therefore seem minimal.

More radical would be to repair the CF gene in a very young embryo, so that the whole person who subsequently develops would be genetically changed. His or her sperms or eggs would develop from cells that were already transformed, so the genetic alteration would be passed down the generations. Biologically and ethically, this is far more heavy-duty than *ad hoc* tissue repair.

Whether CF cells are repaired *ad hoc*, or in a young embryo and so passed on, such procedures are clearly in the realms of therapy. CF is a disease that causes suffering: to correct the gene is to attempt a cure. Western medicine is rooted in the belief that therapy, to correct unmistakable illness, is good.

But some already speak not simply of repairing what is obviously damaged, but of improving (according to their own or their clients' judgement) on what already works well enough. By analogy with traditional medicine, this would move us from physic to tonic—a distinction clearly spelled out by controllers of sports, who allow insulin to correct diabetes (some of the greatest athletes have had diabetes) but forbid steroids to pump up muscles that are already perfectly functional. At the end of the line lies the "designer baby", built to a specification in the way that Ferrari builds motor cars. In *Remaking Eden*, Professor Lee Silver of Princeton University in effect advocates such a course, proposing that "GenRich" (genetically enhanced) individuals, primed to gain honours at Princeton and/or to outreach Michael Jordan at the basketball hoop, will be tomorrow's elite. There are plenty of people with cash to spare for such indulgences, says Silver, and plenty of molecular biologists anxious to oblige; and, he says, where the market presses, reality should and indeed must follow.

Yet for all the hype and hand-wringing, the evolutionary impact of these new technologies will surely be virtually zero. The genetic repair of damaged embryos would affect the future, at least in a few families, but it is very difficult to see why anybody should ever want to do such a thing. A person may carry the CF gene (say) yet half of his or her sperm or eggs will be free of it. Even if a carrier marries another carrier, one in four of their embryos will be totally free of the damaged gene. It would be far easier in principle to induce superovulation, fertilise the eggs in vitro to produce a batch of embryos (as is already standard practice for IVF births), and then select the ones that do not contain the mutant gene at all. Only these healthy embryos would then be implanted into the mother. Techniques of the kind that have been developed largely in the context of genetic engineering are employed for diagnosis, but no actual genetic transformation takes place.

Critics, though, have perceived indirect evolutionary consequences if we contrive to rescue babies with damaged genes who would otherwise have died. Those damaged genes, they argue, would once have been purged from the human lineage, but now they survive, and surely this will weaken the pool as a whole. This argument is similar to that of the old eugenicists

who feared the genes of the "feeble minded", and is at least equally misguided.

Most of the genes that cause "single-gene disorders", including CF, have no adverse effects unless they are inherited from both parents. The unfortunate individuals with a double dose are called "homozygotes". The "heterozygotes"—those who inherit the "bad" gene from only one parent—carry that gene and may pass it on to their offspring, but they are not diseased themselves.

Most "bad" genes are rare, but a few are common. The genes that cause sickle-cell anemia occur frequently in people of African descent, while an astonishing one in 20 Caucasians carries the CF mutant. But assuming random mating (as biologists say), each CF carrier has only a one-in-20 chance of mating with another CF carrier; so only one in 400 Caucasian marriages will bring two carriers together. Only one in four of their offspring will inherit the bad gene from both parents, and so be homozygous for CF; so only one in 1,600 children in a Caucasian population will actually manifest the disease. It would be possible to sterilise those children (as if they did not have problems enough already) or to let them die, as they would do if neglected. But it makes no genetic sense to eliminate one in 1,600 children while leaving the carriers, who are so much more common, intact. Indeed, before modern medicine came along, nature had been assiduously eliminating the unfortunate homozygotes for many thousands of years (ever since the CF mutation first occurred) and yet it is still with us.

## To eliminate all "bad" genes, we would need to wipe out the entire human species

Some eugenic zealots could track down all the carriers, and eliminate them: although, if such zealots were Caucasian, they might well find that they themselves were carriers. It's easy to see intuitively, too, that the rarer the gene—and most are far rarer than CF—the more dramatically the heterozygous carriers outnumber the homozygous sufferers. Besides, at least 5,000 different syndromes have been described that are caused by mutations in single genes, and there must in reality be many more, because all our genes are prone to mutation. Thus it is estimated that every one of us is liable to carry an average of five damaged genes that would cause disease if we had children by some similar carrier. To eliminate all "bad genes", we would need to wipe out the entire human species. In short, genetic zealotry is born of nonsense. Humane, sensible medicine implies no genetic risk for our species as a whole.

The designer baby, however, the child conceived like a custom car, is metaphorical pornography that, we may note in passing, is perpetrated not by the much-maligned "press", but by the scientists themselves, many of whom have their eyes on megabucks and argue the market mantra that what people are prepared to pay for is by definition good. Fortunately, it is also ludicrous. This listing of genes through the Human Genome Project does not "open the book of life" as some idle geneticists (not the Cambridge scientists who actually did the work) have claimed.

If we think of genes as words, then what we have is an incomplete lexicon. An individual's apportionment of genes—the genome—should be construed as an arcane work of literature with its own syntax, puns, allusions, redundancies, colloquialisms and overall "meaning" of which we have almost no inkling, and may never understand exhaustively. On present knowledge, or even with what we are likely to know in the next two centuries, it would be as presumptuous to try to improve on the genes of a healthy human baby as it would be to edit sacred verse in medieval Chinese if all we had to go on was a bad dictionary.

So all in all, human beings seem likely to remain as they are, genetically speaking, barring some ecological disaster; and there doesn't seem to be much that meddling human beings can do about it. This, surely, is a mercy. We may have been shaped blindly by evolution. We may have been guided on our way by God. Whichever it was, or both, the job has been done a million times better than we are ever likely to do. Natural selection is far more subtle than human invention. "What a piece of work is a man!" said Hamlet. "How beauteous mankind is!" said Miranda. Both of them were absolutely right.

From *New Statesman*, April 8, 2002, pp. 25-27. © 2002 by New Statesman Ltd. Reprinted by permission.

# Seeking Abortion's Middle Ground

## *Why My Pro-Life Allies Should Revise Their Self-Defeating Rhetoric*

**Frederica Mathewes-Green**

*The following article is adapted from a talk the author gave May 31, [1996], in Madison, Wis., at the first national conference of the Common Ground Network for Life and Choice, an organization of antiabortion activists and abortion-rights supporters who are seeking new ways to discuss their differences.*

I WAS pro-choice at one point in my life, but I came over to a pro-life position years ago. I've been there ever since. Perhaps because of my background, I think there's a logic to the pro-choice position that deserves respect, even as we engage it critically. It is possible to disagree with somebody without calling them baby-killers, without believing that they are monsters or fiends. It is possible to disagree in an agreeable way.

The abortion argument is essentially an argument among women. It's been a bitter and ugly debate, and I find that embarrassing. For me, that gives a special urgency to this conference.

To reach agreement in any kind of conflict, you need to be able to back up and see far enough into the distance to locate a point you can actually agree on. What the two sides have in common is this: Each of us would like to see a world where women no longer want abortions.

I don't believe that even among the most fervent pro-choice people there is anybody who rejoices over abortion. I think we both wish that there were better solutions that could make abortion unnecessary, or prevent pregnancies in the first place. We'd like to see the demand for the procedure reduced, by resolving women's problems and alleviating the pressure for abortion. We can go along this road together as far as we can, and there will come a time when pro-choicers are satisfied, and pro-lifers want to keep going, but that doesn't mean we can't go together for now.

A few years ago, quite by accident, I discovered an important piece of common ground. Something I wrote in a conservative think-tank journal was picked up and quoted widely. I had written: "There is a tremendous sadness and loneliness in the cry 'A woman's right to choose.' No one wants an abortion as she wants an ice-cream cone or a Porsche. She wants an abortion as an animal, caught in a trap, wants to gnaw off its own leg."

What surprised me was where it appeared: I started getting clips in the mail from friends, showing the quote featured in pro-choice publications. I realized I had stumbled across one of those points of agreement: We all know that no one leaves the abortion clinic skipping. This made me think that there was common ground, that instead of marching against each other, maybe we could envision a world without abortion, a world we could reach by marching together.

The problem thus far, and I believe the pro-life movement has been especially complicit in this, is that we have focused only on abortion, and not on women's needs. We in the pro-life movement have perpetuated a dichotomy where it's the baby against the woman, and we're on the baby's side. You can look over 25 years of pro-life rhetoric and basically boil it down to three words: "It's a baby." We have our little-feet lapel pins, our "Abortion stops a beating heart" bumper stickers, and we've pounded on that message.

In the process we have contributed to what I think is a false concept—an unnatural and even bizarre concept—that women and their unborn children are mortal enemies. We have contributed to the idea that they've got to duke it out, it's going to be a fight to the finish. Either the woman is going to lose control of her life, or the child is going to lose its life.

It occurred to me that there's something wrong with this picture. When we presume this degree of conflict between women and their own children, we're locating the conflict in the wrong place. Women and their own children are not

In news coverage of the abortion controversy, The Washington Post has adopted the terms "anti-abortion" and "abortion rights" as more neutral descriptions of the opposing points of view. Frederica Mathewes-Green's article, however, is drawn from her talk at the network's recent conference and therefore is similar to a quotation; it would change the meaning and context of her remarks to use Post style, so the terms "pro-life" and "pro-choice" appear throughout.
—The Editors

naturally mortal enemies, and the problem is not located inside women's bodies, it's within society. Social expectations make unwanted pregnancy more likely to occur and harder for women to bear. Unwed mothers are supposed to have abortions, to save the rest of us from all the costs of bringing an "unwanted" child into the world.

There are three drawbacks to emphasizing "It's a baby" as the sole message. One is that it contributes to the present deadlock in this debate. We say "It's a baby," and our friends on the pro-choice side say, "No, it's her right," and the arguments don't even engage each other. It's an endless, interminable argument that can go on for another 25 years if we don't find a way to break through.

Second, the "It's a baby" message alienates the woman distressed by a difficult pregnancy. There's a pro-life message that I sometimes hear which makes me cringe: "Women only want abortions for convenience. They do this for frivolous reasons. She wants to fit into her prom dress. She wants to go on a cruise." But this alienates the very person to whom we need to show compassion. If we're going to begin finding ways to live without abortion, we need to understand her problems better.

Of course, there has been a wing of the pro-life movement that has been addressing itself to pregnant women's needs for a long time, and that is the crisis pregnancy center movement. Centers like these have been giving women maternity clothes, shelter, medical care, job training and other help for 30 years. But you wouldn't know that from the things the movement says. I once saw a breakdown of the money and time spent on various sorts of pro-life activities, and over half the movement's energy was go-

ing into direct aid to pregnant women. Yet you don't hear this in the rhetoric.

The third problem with this rhetoric is that it enables the people in the great mushy middle, the ones who are neither strongly pro-life or strongly pro-choice, to go on a shrugging off the problem. While both sides know that women don't actually want abortions in any positive sense, the middle is convinced they do. And that's because both sides are telling it they do. Pro-lifers say, "She wants an abortion because she's selfish"; pro-choicers say, "She wants an abortion because it will set her free." No wonder the middle believes us; it's one of the few things we appear to agree on.

But both sides know that abortion is usually a very unhappy choice. If women are lining up by the thousands every day to do something they do not want to do, it's not liberation we've won. But our rhetoric in the pro-life movement, our insistence that "It's a baby and she's just selfish," keeps the middle thinking that abortion really is what women want, so there's no need for change and nothing to fix. I want to recognize my side's complicity in contributing to this deadlock and confusion.

I can understand why my pro-life allies put the emphasis on "It's a baby." It's a powerful and essential message. Visualizing the violence against the unborn was the conversion point for me and many others. But it cannot be the sole message. Polls on American attitudes toward abortion show that between 70 and 80 percent already agree that it's a baby—especially since the advent of sonograms. So when we say, "It's a baby," we're answering a question nobody's asking any more. I believe there is a question they are asking about abortion, and the question is, "How could we live without abortion?"

The abortion rate in this country is about a million and a half a year, a rate that has held fairly stable for about 15 years. Divide that figure by 365 and that equals about 4,100 abortions every day.

Now imagine for a moment that in the middle of the country there is a big abortion store, and outside it 4,100 women got in a long line, one behind the other—and that's just today. It's a sobering image. And the short-sighted pro-life response has been, "Put a padlock on the abortion

store." But that's not going to solve the problem. You cannot reduce the demand by shutting off the supply. If 4,100 women were lining up every day to get breast implants, we'd be saying, "What's causing this demand? What's going on here?"

How can we solve the problems that contribute to the demand for abortion? If this were easy, we would have done it by now. It's not easy. There are two obvious components: preventing the unwanted pregnancy in the first place, and assisting women who slip through the cracks and become pregnant anyway.

The obvious tool for pregnancy prevention is contraception, but the pro-life movement has been very reluctant to support the contraceptive option. I come from a religious tradition that permits some forms of contraception, so it's not been a theological problem for me. So when I started considering this, I thought, "This is great! I'll get a helicopter, fill it with condoms, get a snow shovel, and just fly over the country tossing 'em out. We'll close all of the abortion clinics tomorrow!"

But then I began to analyze it a little deeper. While I believe the pro-life movement needs to make a strong stand in favor of preventing these unplanned pregnancies, I became skeptical of the contraceptive solution. For example, there's the recent study showing about two-thirds of births to teenage moms in California involved a dad who was an adult, and another one that found teen mothers had been forced into sex at a young age and that the men who molested them had an average age of 27. Closer to home, a friend of mine was brought to an abortion clinic by her older brother, who molested her when she was 12; they gave her a bag of condoms and told her to be more careful. You're not going to solve problems like these by tossing a handful of condoms at [them].

But leaving aside the question of sexual abuse, I think we need to look hard at the consequences of the sexual revolution that began in the 1960s. When I entered college in the early 1970s, the revolution was in full bloom. It seemed at the time a pretty care-free enterprise. Condoms, pills and diaphrams were readily available and abortion had just been legalized by the Supreme Court. But I gradually began to think that it was a con game being played on women. We were "expected to behave according to men's notions of sexuality," to use author Adrienne Rich's phrase. Instead of gaining respect and security in our bodies, we were expected to be more physically available, more vulnerable than before, with little offered in return.

What women found out is that we have hearts in here along with all our other physical equipment, and you can't put a condom on your heart. So in answering the question, "How do we live without abortion?," I'd say we need to look at restoring respect and righting the balance of power in male-female sexual relationships.

What can we do to help women who get pregnant and would rather not be? For a book I was writing, I went around the country talking to women who have had an abortion and to women who provide care for pregnant women. I had presumed that most abortions are prompted by problems that are financial or practical in nature.

But to my surprise, I found something very different. What I heard most frequently in my interviews was that the reason for the abortion was not financial or practical. The core reason I heard was, "I had the abortion because someone I love told me to." It was either the father of the child, or else her own mother, who was pressuring the woman to have the abortion.

Again and again, I learned that women had abortions because they felt abandoned, they felt isolated and afraid. As one woman said, "I felt like everyone would support me if I had the abortion, but if I had the baby I'd be alone." When I asked, "Is there anything anyone could have done? What would you have needed in order to have had that child?" I heard the same answer over and over: "I needed a friend. I felt so alone. I felt like I didn't have a choice. If only one person had stood by me, even a stranger, I would have had that baby."

We also must stop thinking about abortion in terms of pregnancy. We harp on pregnancy and forget all about what comes next. Getting through the pregnancy isn't nearly the dilemma that raising a child for 18 years is. In most families, marriage lightens the load, but for some people that isn't the best solution. A neglected option is adoption, which can free the woman to resume her life, while giving the child a loving home.

The numbers on this, however, are shocking. Only 2 percent of unwed pregnant women choose to place their babies for adoptions. Among clients at crisis pregnancy centers, it's 1 to 2 percent. Adoption is a difficult sell to make for a number of complex reasons, but the bottom line is that 80 to 90 percent of the clients who go through pregnancy care centers and have their babies end by setting up single-parent homes. This is very serious. Pregnancy care centers know this, but aren't sure what to do about it. I've been strongly encouraging that there be more emphasis on presenting adoption to clients, and equipping center volunteers so they feel comfortable with the topic and enabled to dis-cuss it. Adoption is not a one-size-fits-all solution, but it's got to fit more than 1 or 2 percent. More women should try it on for size.

**L**et me finish with these thoughts. I want to encourage us to view the pregnant woman and child as a naturally-linked pair that we strive to keep together and support. Nature puts the mother and the child together, it doesn't make them enemies, it doesn't set one against the other in a battle to the death. If our rhetoric is tearing them apart, we're the ones who are out of step. The pro-life movement should be answering the question "How can we live without abortion?" by keeping mother and child together, looking into pregnant women's needs and examining how to meet them, and encouraging responsible sexual behavior that will prevent those pregnancies in the first place.

*Frederica Mathewes-Green is a columnist for Religion News Service and does commentary on National Public Radio. She is the author of "Real Choices," a book on alternatives to abortion (Questar, 1994). She lives in Baltimore with her husband and three teenaged children.*

# THE FUTURE OF RELIGION IN AMERICA

*Andrew M. Greeley*

In this year marking the start of a new millennium, there will be many efforts to peer into the fog of the future and predict what will happen in various areas of American life. The purpose of this article will be to attempt to see in the fog what will happen to religion in the United States.

Let me begin by proposing a number of unexceptionable assertions about contemporary religion in this country as we begin the 21st century, assertions which will provide a frame for my remarks. The data I will cite in this presentation are taken from the National Opinion Research Center's General Social Survey (GSS), an annual, more recently biennial, survey of a probability sample of Americans, funded in part by the National Science Foundation. The GSS began in 1972 and has used full probability samples since 1975. Block quotas were used from 1972 to 1974.

## Propositions

1) Belief in a supernatural reality will slowly erode as educational levels rise and the impact of scientific thinking expands. Belief in life after death, for example, can be expected to continue to erode.

2) As the possibility of combining rationality and religion declines, the fundamentalist denominations will continue their steady growth in recruits from the mainline denominations.

3) Hence America's religious "exceptionalism" will diminish as American religious belief and practice converges with that of Europe.

4) The destabilization of the Catholic Church launched by the Second Vatican Council will continue to produce substantial losses for the Catholic Church. While dissent in American Catholicism may not lead to an open break with the Vatican, Catholics will increasingly display little difference from American Protestants.

5) Moreover, denominational differences among mainline Protestants will continue to diminish, so that the non-fundamentalist segment of American religion will be increasingly homogenized, save perhaps for those Catholics who might choose to make alliances with the fundamentalists. Religious boundaries are eroding and men and women—a generation of seekers as one author calls them, now make their own religion out of the primal plasma created by the implosion of denominationalism.

6) The political power of the evangelical right will continue to grow in American politics which will mean pressure on abortion rights and gay and lesbian rights.

7) Immigration from Asia will substantially increase the proportions of Americans who belong to religious denominations which are not part of the Jewish and Christian traditions. Hence, as the *New York Times* has reported, serious study of religion in America must consider these "new religions" because they have changed the map of American religion.

8) Like the fundamentalists, the "New Age" religious movements, unique to our time, will continue to grow as more people opt for non-rational religion in a climate of post-modernity.

9) Religion's impact on life in America will continue to decline as the influences of the churches on their membership will become less important.

Now these propositions may seem to be so obvious that to repeat them is trite, not to say trivial. They sum up the not always expressed assumptions of both the academy (including especially many religion and theology departments) and the higher media. How can anyone challenge at least the general picture they present? Are not these the trends we all know about? The only trouble is that none of the nine propositions are true.

1) Belief in life after death has *increased* over the years of the General Social Survey by some five percentage points. When that increase is spread out over age cohorts from the beginning of the century, there has been a twenty percentage point increase in belief in life after death among American Catholics

and a doubling (to over fifty percent) for American Jews. This totally unexpected increase is not the result of increase in fundamentalism or the rise of the "New Age" religion or changes in any of the other "usual suspects" of demographic variables.

As Michael Hout and I have demonstrated in an article in the *American Sociological Review*, the increase for Catholics is a function of generation in America, as the eastern and southern European immigrant groups of the third and fourth generation "catch up" with the Irish orthodoxy. It would appear that this "catching up" is the result of the fierce resistance of the Catholic Church to (as it saw it) attempts at conversion of Catholic immigrants to the host culture. Those who "caught up" were either members of Catholic organizations (which proliferated in the immigrant parishes) or had attended Catholic schools. Despite the mythology, the religion of the immigrants is less orthodox than that of the third and fourth generation. We found that the increase in belief in the life after death (which is taught in the Mishna by the way) among Jews is harder to explain because even in a sample of almost forty thousand respondents there are not all that many Jews. However, the increase seems to occur especially among those who attend services more often, describe themselves as strongly Jewish, and are either Orthodox or conservatives. These findings are obviously counterintuitive. Belief is supposed to go down. In fact belief in this particular (central) item of faith has increased.

2) The increase in fundamentalists which virtually every author has attributed to dissatisfaction with the modernist tendencies of liberal and mainline Protestant denominations is in fact the result of higher levels of fertility among the fundamentalists. Fertility accounts for approximately 75% of the increase in the mainline proportion of American Protestants. There is very little change across denominational lines between the mainline and the fundamentalists. Mainline religious change is mostly either to no religion or to Catholicism. The net flow from mainline to fundamentalism is +4%, to Catholics +6%, and to no religion +10%. We conclude from these findings that one should not indulge in sweeping generalizations about cultural change until one has taken into account demographic factors.

3) Sweeping generalizations about religion in Europe (particularly from scholars who are in the United Kingdom or The Netherlands) do not stand up to the test of data from other countries. Thus, since the fall of socialism in Eastern Europe there has been a significant increase in religious faith in Hungary, Slovenia, East Germany, and the Soviet Union, particularly in matters of religious faith like belief in God, life after death, heaven, hell, and religious miracles. The argument here is not that there are never any changes in religion. Quite the contrary there are constant changes. However, they are not unidirectionally downward. "What about The Netherlands?", one is asked. "What about Russia?", I respond. In some countries religion seems to decrease and in others to increase. Why that is so is a fascinating question but it cannot be answered in a perspective which insists that all religious change is in the direction of decline.

4) Reports of the death of Catholicism in the United States are premature. Catholics continue to be a quarter of the American population. Moreover since the second birth cohort (the 1910s) approximately 2/3 of every cohort of those raised Catholic choose spouses who were also raised Catholic. The Catholic religious imagination, emphasizing the graciousness of God with its components of community, sacramentality, and hierarchy is still strikingly different from that of Protestants (as I have argued in my book, *Religion as Poetry*) and in the years since the council, the difference has significantly *increased*. Catholics, apparently because of this religious imagination, also have sex more often than do other Americans, even as reported by their spouses who are not Catholic. Indeed, their sex is on the average more playful. For Catholics church attendance and fine arts participation is positive, for Protestants it's negative. I do not contend that Catholics have not changed in the last three decades, but only that they are still Catholic and show no signs of not being Catholic.

Indeed, we who are their leaders, despite our best efforts, have not been able to drive them out. Moreover, while the Vatican Council II may be an easy target to blame for the turbulence in Catholicism (and the 1968 birth control encyclical perhaps a more appropriate target), one must ask whether the educational change in the Catholic population might also account for the freedom many Catholics feel to dissent from some of the Church's sexual teaching. In fact education does, but not respondent's education, spouse's education, or father's education. Mother's education, however, accounts for at least a third of the changes on measures of sexual attitudes across the twenty five years of the General Social Survey. Finally there are more Catholic churches in this country than there were in 1968.

5) Denominational affiliation continues to be important in distinguishing among American Protestants. Only eight of the 40,000 respondents cannot give an answer to Will Herberg's famous question of what their religion is (Protestant, Catholic, Jew, other, or none). While over 20% of GSS respondents were raised in mixed marriages, less than 1% cannot give an answer to the question, "In what denomination were you raised?" 70% of Americans continue to belong to the denomination in which they were raised. Denominational affiliation is an important correlate of political, religious, and cultural attitudes and behaviors not only among the broad divisions reaching from fundamentalism to liberalism, but even among the "moderate" denominations.

In particular, statistically significant differences exist among the two large denominational families, Lutherans and Methodists. The latter for example are more likely than the former to support national policies which would spend more money on education, drugs, and African Americans, to believe that you can expect people to be fair, trustworthy and helpful, and to think the lot of the working man is not declining and it is safe to bring children into the world. Lutherans go to church more often, Methodists are more likely to support school prayer and bible reading. Lutherans are more likely to have been confirmed, Methodists are more likely to say that their church attendance lapsed at one time. Lutherans are more afraid of science breaking down morality, Methodists are more likely to be born again and to like Gospel music. Lutherans are more likely to appreciate oldies Rock, to have visited an art museum, to have attended a classic concert or opera, and to have seen a movie during the past year. Methodists are more likely to think that only a few people can judge art. In questions of national policy, then, Methodists are more likely to tilt to the left in comparison with the Lutherans, and in religious and cultural matters more likely to tilt in a fundamentalist direction. Further analysis will be required to sort out these differences in detail. Yet it certainly seems to be true that differences persist among the five major Protestant denominational families—Baptist, Methodist, Lutheran, Presbyterian, and Episcopalian.

One is tempted to say after writing the previous paragraph that we knew about these differences all along—or at least we did if we associated much with Lutherans and Methodists. But the assumption of contemporary social science (and higher media) that Protestants can be divided between fundamentalist and all others misses much of the fine grained but important differences among denominations. Equally important is the strength of denominationalism.

Some writers (Robert Wuthnow, Clark Roof, and Christian Smith) are busily promoting a post-denominational analysis. The observations in the preceding paragraph contradict them. Churches organize religion, and people seem to like them. They need them for ritual devotions, but they are far from indifferent among the choices available. They cling surprisingly strongly to the denominations of their youth. They bring their children to the church they were raised in. Even after moving to a new city or state, when they are most likely to "shop around' they "choose" the denomination they're familiar with.

6) Although the fundamentalist (or evangelical) denominations have increased, Protestants who believe in the literal interpretation of scripture have declined six percentage points since the question was first asked in 1984. Only 57% of the Southern Baptists (who have been unfairly treated by the elite media which persist in identifying statements of the annual Southern Baptist Convention with the actual beliefs of Southern Baptists) believe in the literal interpretation of the bible, as do only 40% of Southern Baptists under 40 who attend church every week. The Evangelical component of American religion has always been substantial, around 20% of the population. Just as Catholics are different from the rest of us, so the evangelicals are different from the rest of us (and the Catholics and the evangelicals are different from one another). However, most evangelicals are not members of the hard line religious right.

Thus if one combines belief in the literal interpretation of the bible, opposition to abortion, belief that premarital sex is always wrong, and belief that abortion is always wrong, one finds that only about 5% of the American people share the agenda of the religious right (even as that is generously defined), as do only 13% of the Southern Baptists. Moreover the religious right is not even the majority or a large minority of committed Republicans, though somehow they have managed to create the illusion that they are. Most of them are hard core Republicans who would vote for a conservative Republican regardless of their religious convictions. Playing the evangelical card is not a wise strategy for the GOP, though it is one that, Irish Catholic Democrat from Chicago that I am, I hope it follows.

7) The impact of Asian migration on American religion has been greatly exaggerated. While Asian American religion is a fascinating subject for study as Asians adjust to American cul-

ture, it does not follow that the map of American religion has changed as greatly as the *New York Times* (with its usual search for the best of the received wisdom on the subject of religion) contends. In the 1998 General Social Survey only 1.1% of Americans report that they are Hindu, Moslem, Buddhist, or "other Eastern."

8) It is hard to know exactly what "New Age" stands for. However, it is very difficult to find traces of membership in the General Social Survey. The proportion of Americans who say that their religion is "other" has hovered around 3% and that includes, for example, Mormons and Eastern Orthodox. Anyone who knows the history of religion in this country, realizes that in addition to various "Great Awakenings," America is always in a state of religious revival and that many interesting movements begin in our "mess" of religious pluralism. Some survive and grow—the Unitarians, the Disciples, the Mormons, the Adventists, and the Christian Scientists for example—most do not. These "new" religions are fascinating subjects for research, but they do not represent a phenomenon on the American religious scene which is radically new.

9) The last assertion—the decline of the influence of religion on American life—is the last refuge of those who think that religion is not as important as it used to be—a classic expression of the so-called "Golden Age" fallacy. Has not the ability of the churches to control sexual behavior almost vanished? Perhaps it has. However, as ought to be patent, religion still strongly influences the civil rights movement, the pro-life movement, the environmental movement, and the volunteer movement. Indeed church membership and church attendance explain completely the higher rates of volunteerism in the United States in comparison with those of European countries.

## Reflections

There surely have been changes in American religion in the last thirty years, and there may even be some trends (belief in the literal interpretation of the bible has gone down, for example, but only among Catholics). However none of the phenomena which the received wisdom knows to be true are in fact true. To paraphrase an Irish member of parliament, "The right honorable conventional wisdom has said much that is true and much that is new. Alas, that which is true is not new and that which is new is not true."

Unless and until American social scientists (and their elite media acolytes) are ready to abandon their conviction that there is an overarching religious trend and that it is downward, we will know very little in a systematic way about the religious phenomena in this country or anywhere else. It will be hard for social scientists to abandon this often vague and deep-seated assumption because there is rarely an occasion to question it—and when someone dares to question it, they are dismissed as unworthy of attention. Moreover there still exists in our profession the belief that there are "social laws" which can account for social change—or at least for religious change. William Sewell, Jr. argues convincingly that the search for such laws is illusory:

Sociology's epic quest for social laws is illusory, whether the search is for timeless truths about all societies, ineluctable trends of more limited historical epochs, or inductively derived laws of certain classes of social phenomena. Social processes are inherently contingent, discontinuous, and open-ended. Big and ponderous social processes are never entirely immune from being transformed by small alterations in volatile and local social processes. "Structures" are constructed by human action, and "societies" or "social formations or social systems" are continually shaped and reshaped by the creativity and stubbornness of their human creators.

I believe that such words as modernization, secularization, globalization, etc., etc., (to say nothing of "post-modernity") are labels under which we subsume a wide variety of contrasting and contrary phenomena which are ill served by being lumped together. They may be useful hooks for undergraduate instruction and dinner party conversation, but when they become reified so that they are taken as dynamisms which actually exist in the outside world they are an excuse for thought, indeed a substitute for thought. One who uses such words as if they were realities with an existence of their own may sound profound but actually reveals himself to be shallow and superficial, someone who, for the sake of a convenient labels, loses all sense of the complex realities of social life.

Sewell argues for "well-honed stories," which are perhaps not all that different from Robert K. Merton's "theories of the middle range." You can't tell a well honed story about religion if you believe that the only story to tell is one of decline—particularly of groups you don't happen to like, such as Catholics. All the findings I have reported above are stories told in response to the current conventional wisdom, whether well-honed is not for me to say. At any rate the story of the increase in belief in life after death described above owes nothing to the overarching theory of religious decline. It owes quite a bit to the perspective of a competitive market place in religion, though that theory hardly predicted the finding. If we were not sufficiently immunized to the social law of the decline of religion, I doubt that we would have even noticed the surprising increase in belief in life after death in this country. After considerable struggle we managed to persuade the editor of the *American Sociological Review* that it was sufficiently well-honed to be published.

Why the social law? The answer is easy, religion is not supposed to survive in an age of science and reason. Voltaire said it. Durkheim said it. Most social scientists today, especially those at the elite institutions of higher learning, say it. Therefore, how can it be wrong? It can, patently, be wrong if the data rarely verify it.

The explanation, I think, is fairly easy. The law is more a norm than a law: Religion should be in decline. Those who say it is not are violating the norm. I recall my astonishment when I presented in seminars the findings from ISSP study of religion in Russia which indicated that one of the great religious revivals in history was going on there. Colleagues with indecent haste leaped to their feet to explain why it wouldn't last, even

couldn't last—without any data to support their speculations. One young woman from Harvard explained it as a desire by young Russians to have their weddings in church, as though that accounted for everything without having to ask why such weddings were still important after three-quarters of a century of socialist rule. These young Russians, incidentally, also state their firm intention to raise their children in religion).

The social law of the decline of religion is both a dogma and a norm. It is an iron curtain that one can rarely tear open with a well-honed story which either refutes the law or cheerfully ignores it. We will not have good social science study of religion in this country until the anti-religious norms and biases are abandoned. I don't expect that will happen for a long time. I've often wondered why no one thought of studying the thousand Southern Baptists in the GSS to see how the two top executives in our land could both be devout Southern Baptists and still hold the political and social positions to which they are committed. The answer is that the denomination (ten percent of the American people) is pluralistic like every other large religious group) and that the local clergy and members take their orders from the Convention the way Catholic lower clergy and laity take their orders from the Vatican. If pressed Messrs. Clinton and Gore would finesse the question of the literal, word for word interpretation of the bible, in a way similar to the way that Senators Kennedy and Moynihan would finesse questions about how they can be Catholic and not oppose abortion legislation. However, the false myth about Southern Baptists is part of the larger law of the decline of religion. Hence there is no need to question it.

Why has religion survived when everyone knew that it wouldn't? I believe the answer might go something like this. Men and women still want something in which to believe and to which to belong. They aspire to faith and community. Humans are caught between the two possibilities. Perhaps Macbeth was right when he said that life is a tale told by an idiot full of sound and fury and signifying nothing. Or perhaps Pere Teilhard was right when he said that something is afoot in the universe, something that looks like gestation and birth. Uncertain which to believe, they incline to the more hopeful bet proposed by Blaise Pascal and bet on purpose rather than absurdity because in such a bet there seems nothing to lose. They walk on air, in Seamus Heaney's words, against their better judgment.

So they tend, as they always have, to believe with their fingers crossed. For some this is an agonizing decision, to be renewed perhaps every day. Or others it is a minor matter. For most it is something important but not always all-important. There are those who cannot believe and those who believe more or less, and finally, the God haunted who believe fiercely and are haunted by fierce doubts. As Edward Shils once remarked, as long as humans worry seriously about the meaning of life, there will always be some who choose a religious option. One may dismiss religion as wish fulfillment. It may well be that, though it does not follow that because we wish something to be true (e.g., that our beloved really loves us) it is thereby false. Nonetheless, even if we think religion is nothing more than wish fulfillment, we are not thereby excused from objective social science study of religion.

Such an approach is, I would submit, a more useful model than the patient assumption that if one waits long enough religion will disappear—arguably also a form of wish fulfillment. Finally I will repeat a few predictions for the next thirty years that I have made elsewhere.

1. Religion will not lose its adherents.
2. Nor is religion likely to lose its influence on non-religious dimensions of human life.
3. Religious institutions will no more wither away than did the Marxist state.
4. There will be considerably more sympathetic understanding of the wisdom of other religious traditions and of those who profess such traditions.
5. There will be a further understanding both in theory and in practice of the responsibility of the individual as the ultimate religious and ethical agent in the context of the circumstances in which he finds himself and of his personal relationships with those around him.
6. Denominations will not cease to be characteristic of the Western religious scene.
7. The local congregations will not perish.

Not very exciting predictions, are they? Am I not saying that American religion thirty years from now will be pretty much what it's like today? That's indeed what I'm saying and thus arguing for the well-honed story approach to the study of American religion rather then the "mega-trend" approach.

I should add one note. Those predictions were not made this year. Rather they appeared in a book I called *Religion in the Year 2000* and wrote in 1968, around the time it was announced (*Time* magazine Easter Issue 1968) to one and all that God was dead. It turned out that God was not dead but alive and well and living in Moscow! As the French would say, *plus ça change, plus c'est la même chose!* I don't expect to be around, however, to check on the accuracy of these predictions! Nonetheless, I will be watching from somewhere and laughing.

---

*Andrew Greeley is a Catholic priest and best-selling novelist. He is professor of social science at the University of Chicago and a member of its National Opinion Research Center. Greeley is also a visiting professor at the University of Arizona. Among his books are* Faithful Attraction, The Denominational Society, Unsecular Man, Death and Beyond, *and* The Church and the Suburbs.

From *Society,* March/April 2001, pp. 32-37. © 2001 by Transaction Publishers. Reprinted by permission.

# UNIT 6
# Social Change and the Future

## Unit Selections

## Key Points to Consider

- What are the advantages of slowing world population growth? How can it be done?

- What dangers does humankind's overexploitation of the environment create?

- What are some of the major problems that technology is creating?

- How bright is America's future? What are the main threats to it? What are some of its main challenges?

- Would you say that both democracy and capitalism are triumphant today? Explain your answer. What kind of problems can democracy and capitalism cause?

 **Links: www.dushkin.com/online/**
These sites are annotated in the World Wide Web pages.

**Communications for a Sustainable Future**
  *http://csf.colorado.edu*
**Gil Gordon Associates**
  *http://www.gilgordon.com*
**Human Rights and Humanitarian Assistance**
  *http://www.etown.edu/vl/humrts.html*
**The Hunger Project**
  *http://www.thp.org*
**National Immigrant Forum**
  *http://www.immigrationforum.org/index.htm*
**Terrorism Research Center**
  *http://www.terrorism.com/index.shtml*
**United Nations Environment Program (UNEP)**
  *http://www.unep.ch*
**William Davidson Institute**
  *http://www.wdi.bus.umich.edu*

Fascination with the future is an enduring theme in literature, art, poetry, and religion. Human beings are anxious to know if tomorrow will be different from today and in what ways it might differ. Coping with change has become a top priority in the lives of many. One result of change is stress. When the future is uncertain and the individual appears to have little control over what happens, stress can be a serious problem. On the other hand, stress can have positive effects on people's lives if they can perceive changes as challenges and opportunities.

Any discussion of the future must begin with a look at the interface of population and the environment. Some scholars are very concerned about population's impact on the environment and others are confident that technological developments will solve most of the problems. Since the debate is about the future, neither view can be "proved." Nevertheless, it is important to understand the seriousness of the problem. In the first unit article, Lester Brown, Gary Gardner, and Brian Halweil discuss 16 impacts of population growth. The way societies are providing for the present 6 billion people is badly damaging Earth's ecosystems and crowding or overshooting environmental limits. Many changes are needed in the next few decades to achieve sustainability, including stabilizing world population.

The next article discusses current scientific thinking about global warming. The environment is in trouble in many ways from overplowing, overgrazing, overfishing, overtimbering, and species loss to resource depletion, toxic wastes, and water shortages, but the focal issue today is global warming. The predictions are scary. The low estimates of warmer world temperatures would cause considerable trouble, but the high estimates "could be disastrous." Michael Lemonick reviews many of the possible impacts and urges that the world take steps now to substantially reduce greenhouse gasses to prevent these impacts.

The next subsection in unit 6 addresses the linkage between technological change and society. Both articles in this section raise concerns about the possible negative effects of supposedly beneficial technologies. The first article, by Eduardo Goncalves, evaluates another sophisticated technology—nuclear power. It can win wars and supply useful electrical energy, but it may have already killed 175 million people. Furthermore, the way scientists and governments have acted regarding nuclear energy shows that they cannot always be trusted to pursue the public good in their decisions regarding new technologies. One big technology story concerns genetic engineering, and one of its important areas of application is agriculture. The crucial question is whether it produces great agricultural advances or ecological nightmares. J. Madeleine Nash tells teh story of the noble efforts to engineer beta-carotine into rice to make children in developing countries more resistant to diseases. Many lives would be saved or improved, but the haunting question is whether this new technology will have harmful unintended consequences.

The next section focuses on the new crisis of terrorism. It begins with an article by L. Paul Bremer, which discusses how terrorism has changed from limited violence as a tactic in political struggles to indiscriminate mass killings to inflict maximum harm on a hated people. Now certain extremist groups are willing to murder millions of people. Bremer points out that the new terror-

ism requires a new strategy for countering it. We must end state support for terrorism, delegitimize terrorism, and build an international consensus against it. It is necessary that fellow members of ethnic and religious groups to which the terrorists belong must frequently and strongly condemn terrorism. The next article explores the motives behind terrorist acts against the United States. Stanley Hoffmann explores the question "Why Don't They Like Us?" Hatreds between groups are based on biased and selective perceptions of events and this typical pattern is true for the current hatred toward the United States by many peoples of the world. Hoffmann concludes that "Perhaps the principal criticism is of the contrast between our ideology of universal liberalism and policies that have all too often consisted of supporting and sometimes installing singularly authoritarian and repressive regimes." Also, antiglobalism so often becomes anti-Americanism.

The final subsection looks at the future in terms of some of the most important trends and how to create a good future out of them. William Van Dusen Wishard, president of a firm that does research on trends, has authored the first of these articles. Armed with many interesting statistics on trends he argues that the world is undergoing a great transition that is based on globalization, rapid technological development, and "a long-term spiritual and psychological reorientation that's increasingly generating uncertainty and instability." As a result, "the soul of America—indeed, of the world—is in a giant search for some deeper and greater expression of life." Next, Amitai Etzioni describes the trends toward greater inequality and diversity in the United States and asks whether these trends threaten the integration of American society. Since the 1960s, identity politics have succeeded in reducing past injustices but also "have divided the nation along group lines." Then he draws on sociological theory to propose ways to build community by reducing inequalities, increasing bonds, and generating stronger value commitments.

# 16 Impacts of Population Growth

Ongoing global population growth may be THE most critical issue of today.
Here are 16 ways it affects human prospects.

By Lester R. Brown, Gary Gardner, and Brian Halweil

The world's population has doubled during the last half century, climbing from 2.5 billion in 1950 to 5.9 billion in 1998. This unprecedented surge in population, combined with rising individual consumption, is pushing our claims on the planet beyond its natural limits.

The United Nations projects that human population in 2050 will range between 7.7 billion and 11.2 billion people. We use the United Nation's middle-level projection of 9.4 billion (from *World Population Prospects: The 1996 Revision*) to give an idea of the strain this "most likely" outcome would place on ecosystems and governments in the future and of the urgent need to break from the business-as-usual scenario.

Our study looks at 16 dimensions or effects of population growth in order to gain a better perspective on how future population trends are likely to affect human prospects:

## Impacts on Food and Agriculture

### 1. Grain Production

From 1950 to 1984, growth in the world grain harvest easily exceeded that of population. But since then, the growth in the grain harvest has fallen behind that of population, so per-person output has dropped by 7% (0.5% a year), according to the U.S. Department of Agriculture.

The slower growth in the world grain harvest since 1984 is due to the lack of new land and to slower growth in irrigation and fertilizer use because of the diminishing returns of these inputs.

Now that the frontiers of agricultural settlement have disappeared, future growth in grain production must come almost entirely from raising land productivity. Unfortu-nately, this is becoming more difficult. The challenge for the world's farmers is to reverse this decline at a time when cropland area per person is shrinking, the amount of irrigation water per person is dropping, and the crop yield response to additional fertilizer use is falling.

### 2. Cropland

Since mid-century, grain area—which serves as a proxy for cropland in general—has increased by some 19%, but global population has grown by 132%. Population growth can degrade farmland, reducing its productivity or even eliminating it from production. As grain area per person falls, more and more nations risk losing the capacity to feed themselves.

The trend is illustrated starkly in the world's four fastest-growing

U.S. AID

**Shanty town life in Bangladesh.** Countries that fail to reduce population growth will endure the breakdown of their economic and social systems, according to the authors.

large countries. Having already seen per capita grain area shrink by 40%–50% between 1960 and 1998, Pakistan, Nigeria, Ethiopia, and Iran can expect a further 60%–70% loss by 2050—a conservative projection that assumes no further losses of agricultural land. The result will be four countries with a combined population of more than 1 billion whose grain area per person will be only 300–600 square meters—less than a quarter of the area in 1950.

### 3. Fresh Water

Spreading water scarcity may be the most underrated resource issue in the world today. Wherever population is growing, the supply of fresh water per person is declining.

Evidence of water stress can be seen as rivers are drained dry and water tables fall. Rivers such as the Nile, the Yellow, and the Colorado have little water left when they reach the sea. Water tables are now falling on every continent, including in major food-producing regions. Aquifers are being depleted in the U.S. southern Great Plains, the North China Plain, and most of India.

The International Water Management Institute projects that a billion people will be living in countries facing absolute water scarcity by 2025. These countries will have to reduce water use in agriculture in order to satisfy residential and industrial water needs. In both China and India, the two countries that together dominate world irrigated agriculture, substantial cutbacks in irrigation water supplies lie ahead.

### 4. Oceanic Fish Catch

A fivefold growth in the human appetite for seafood since 1950 has pushed the catch of most oceanic fisheries to their sustainable limits or beyond. Marine biologists believe that the oceans cannot sustain an annual catch of much more than 93 million tons, the current take.

As we near the end of the twentieth century, overfishing has become the rule, not the exception. Of the 15 major oceanic fisheries, 11 are in decline. The catch of Atlantic cod—long a dietary mainstay for western Europeans—has fallen by 70% since peaking in 1968. Since 1970, bluefin tuna stocks in the West Atlantic have dropped by 80%.

With the oceans now pushed to their limits, future growth in the demand for seafood can be satisfied only by fish farming. But as the world turns to aquaculture to satisfy its needs, fish begin to compete with livestock and poultry for feedstuffs such as grain, soybean meal, and fish meal.

The next half century is likely to be marked by the disappearance of some species from markets, a decline in the quality of seafood caught, higher prices, and more conflicts among countries over access to fisheries. Each year, the future oceanic catch per person will decline by roughly the amount of population growth, dropping to 9.9 kilograms (22 pounds) per person in 2050, compared with the 1988 peak of 17.2 kilograms (37.8 pounds).

### 5. Meat Production

When incomes begin to rise in traditional low-income societies, one of the first things people do is diversify their diets, consuming more livestock products.

World meat production since 1950 has increased almost twice as fast as population. Growth in meat

ANNUAL EDITIONS

©PHOTODISC, INC.

**The demand for energy will grow faster than population** and create even more pollution as developing countries try to become as affluent as industrialized nations.

production was originally concentrated in western industrial countries and Japan, but over the last two decades it has increased rapidly in East Asia, the Middle East, and Latin America. Beef, pork, and poultry account for the bulk of world consumption.

Of the world grain harvest of 1.87 billion tons in 1998, an estimated 37% will be used to feed livestock and poultry, producing milk and eggs as well as meat, according to the U.S. Department of Agriculture. Grain fed to livestock and poultry is now the principal food reserve in the event of a world food emergency.

Total meat consumption will rise from 211 million tons in 1997 to 513 million tons in 2050, increasing pressures on the supply of grain.

## Environment and Resources

### 6. Natural Recreation Areas

From Buenos Aires to Bangkok, dramatic population growth in the world's major cities—and the sprawl and pollution they bring—threaten natural recreation areas that lie beyond city limits. On every continent, human encroachment has reduced both the size and the quality of natural recreation areas.

In nations where rapid population growth has outstripped the carrying capacity of local resources, protected areas become especially vulnerable. Although in industrial nations these areas are synonymous with camping, hiking, and picnics in the country, in Asia, Africa, and Latin America most national parks, forests, and preserves are inhabited or used for natural resources by local populations.

Migration-driven population growth also endangers natural recreation areas in many industrial nations. Everglades National Park, for example, faces collapse as millions of newcomers move into southern Florida.

Longer waiting lists and higher user fees for fewer secluded spots are likely to be the tip of the iceberg, as population growth threatens to eliminate the diversity of habitats and cultures in addition to the peace and quiet that protected areas currently offer.

### 7. Forests

Global losses of forest area have marched in step with population growth for much of human history, but an estimated 75% of the loss in global forests has occurred in the twentieth century.

In Latin America, ranching is the single largest cause of deforestation. In addition, overgrazing and overcollection of firewood—which are often a function of growing population—are degrading 14% of the world's remaining large areas of virgin forest.

Deforestation created by the demand for forest products tracks closely with rising per capita consumption in recent decades. Global use of paper and paperboard per person has doubled (or nearly tripled) since 1961.

The loss of forest areas leads to a decline of forest services. These include habitat for wildlife; carbon storage, which is a key to regulating climate; and erosion control, provision of water across rainy and dry seasons, and regulation of rainfall.

### 8. Biodiversity

We live amid the greatest extinction of plant and animal life since the dinosaurs disappeared 65 million years ago, at the end of the Cretaceous period, with species losses at 100 to 1,000 times the natural rate. The principal cause of species extinction is habitat loss, which tends to accelerate with an increase in a country's population density.

A particularly productive but vulnerable habitat is found in coastal areas, home to 60% of the world's population. Coastal wetlands nurture two-thirds of all commercially caught fish, for example. And coral reefs have the second-highest concentration of biodiversity in the world, after tropical rain forests. But human encroachment and pollution are degrading these areas: Roughly half of the world's salt marshes and mangrove swamps have been eliminated or radically altered, and two-thirds of the world's coral reefs have been degraded, 10% of them "beyond recognition." As coastal migration continues—coastal dwellers could account for 75% of world population within 30 years—the pressures on these productive habitats will likely increase.

### 9. Climate Change

Over the last half century, carbon emissions from fossil-fuel burning expanded at nearly twice the rate of population, boosting atmospheric concentrations of carbon dioxide, the principal greenhouse gas, by 30% over preindustrial levels.

## The 20 Largest Countries Ranked According to Population Size (in millions)

| 1998 Rank | Country | Population | 2050 Country | Population |
|---|---|---|---|---|
| 1 | China | 1,255 | India | 1,533 |
| 2 | India | 976 | China | 1,517 |
| 3 | United States | 274 | Pakistan | 357 |
| 4 | Indonesia | 207 | United States | 348 |
| 5 | Brazil | 165 | Nigeria | 339 |
| 6 | Pakistan | 148 | Indonesia | 318 |
| 7 | Russia | 147 | Brazil | 243 |
| 8 | Japan | 126 | Bangladesh | 218 |
| 9 | Bangladesh | 124 | Ethiopia | 213 |
| 10 | Nigeria | 122 | Iran | 170 |
| 11 | Mexico | 96 | The Congo | 165 |
| 12 | Germany | 82 | Mexico | 154 |
| 13 | Vietnam | 78 | Philippines | 131 |
| 14 | Iran | 73 | Vietnam | 130 |
| 15 | Philippines | 72 | Egypt | 115 |
| 16 | Egypt | 66 | Russia | 114 |
| 17 | Turkey | 64 | Japan | 110 |
| 18 | Ethiopia | 62 | Turkey | 98 |
| 19 | Thailand | 60 | South Africa | 91 |
| 20 | France | 59 | Tanzania | 89 |

*SOURCE: UNITED NATIONS, WORLD POPULATION PROSPECTS: THE 1996 REVISION.*

Fossil-fuel use accounts for roughly three-quarters of world carbon emissions. As a result, regional growth in carbon emissions tend to occur where economic activity and related energy use is projected to grow most rapidly. Emissions in China are projected to grow over three times faster than population in the next 50 years due to a booming economy that is heavily reliant on coal and other carbon-rich energy sources.

Emissions from developing countries will nearly quadruple over the next half century, while those from industrial nations will increase by 30%, according to the Intergovernmental Panel on Climate Change and the U.S. Department of Energy. Although annual emissions from industrial countries are currently twice as high as from developing ones, the latter are on target to eclipse the industrial world by 2020.

## 10. Energy

The global demand for energy grew twice as fast as population over the last 50 years. By 2050, developing countries will be consuming much more energy as their populations increase and become more affluent.

When per capita energy consumption is high, even a low rate of population growth can have significant effects on total energy demand. In the United States, for example, the 75 million people projected to be added to the population by 2050 will boost energy demand to roughly the present energy consumption of Africa and Latin America.

World oil production per person reached a high in 1979 and has since declined by 23%. Estimates of when global oil production will peak range from 2011 to 2025, signaling future price shocks as long as oil remains the world's dominant fuel.

In the next 50 years, the greatest growth in energy demands will come where economic activity is projected to be highest: in Asia, where consumption is expected to

## Demographic Fatigue

To assess the likelihood that the U.N. population projections will actually occur, it is useful to bear in mind the concept of the demographic transition, formulated by Princeton demographer Frank Notestein in 1945. Its three stages help to explain widely disparate population-growth rates.

The first stage describes pre-industrial societies: Birthrates and death rates are both high, offsetting each other and leading to little or no population growth. In stage two, countries reach an unsustainable state as they begin to modernize: Death rates fall to low levels while birthrates remain high. In the third state, modernization continues: Birth and death rates are again in balance, but at lower levels, and populations are essentially stable. All countries today are in either stage two or stage three.

One key question now facing the world is whether the 150 or so countries that are still in stage two, with continuing population growth, can make it into stage three by quickly reducing births. Governments of countries that have been in stage two for several decades are typically worn down and drained of financial resources by the consequences of rapid population growth, in effect suffering from "demographic fatigue." Such countries are losing the struggle to educate their children, create jobs, and cope with environmental problems such as erosion, deforestation, and aquifer depletion.

Demographic fatigue is perhaps most evident in the inability of many governments to combat the resurgence of traditional diseases, such as malaria or tuberculosis, and new diseases, such as AIDS. If these threats are not dealt with, they can force countries back into stage one. For several African countries with high HIV infection levels, this is no longer a hypothetical prospect. Although most industrialized nations have held infection levels under 1%, governments overwhelmed by population pressures have not.

Zimbabwe, for example, has a 26% adult HIV infection rate and cannot pay for the costly drugs needed to treat the disease. Zimbabwe is expected to reach population stability in 2002 as death rates from the HIV/AIDS epidemic climb to offset birthrates, essentially falling back into stage one. Other African countries that are likely to follow include Botswana, Namibia, Zambia, and Swaziland.

*—Lester R. Brown, Gary Gardner, and Brian Halweil*

grow 361%, though population will grow by just 50%. Energy consumption is also expected to increase in Latin America (by 340%) and Africa (by 326%). In all three regions, local pressures on energy sources, ranging from forests to fossil fuel reserves to waterways, will be significant.

### 11. Waste

Local and global environmental effects of waste disposal will likely worsen as 3.4 billion people are added to the world's population over the next half century. Prospects for providing access to sanitation are dismal in the near to medium term.

A growing population increases society's disposal headaches—the garbage, sewage, and industrial waste that must be gotten rid of. Even where population is largely stable—the case in many industrialized countries—the flow of waste products into landfills and waterways generally continues to increase. Where high rates of economic and population growth coincide in coming decades, as they will in many developing countries, mountains of waste will likely pose difficult disposal challenges for municipal and national authorities.

## Economic Impacts and Quality of Life

### 12. Jobs

Since 1950, the world's labor force has more than doubled—from 1.2 billion people to 2.7 billion—outstripping the growth in job creation. Over the next half century, the world will need to create more than 1.9 billion jobs in the developing world just to maintain current levels of employment.

While population growth may boost labor demand (through economic activity and demand for goods), it will most definitely boost labor supply. As the balance between the demand and supply of labor is tipped by population growth, wages tend to decrease. And in a situation of labor surplus, the quality of jobs may not improve as fast, for workers will settle for longer hours, fewer benefits, and less control over work activities.

As the children of today represent the workers of tomorrow, the interaction between population growth and jobs is most acute in nations with young populations. Nations with more than half their population below the age of 25 (e.g., Peru, Mexico, Indonesia, and Zambia) will feel the burden of this labor flood. Employment is the key to obtaining food, housing, health services, and education, in addition to providing self-respect and self-fulfillment.

### 13. Income

Incomes have risen most rapidly in developing countries where population has slowed the most, including South Korea, Taiwan, China, Indonesia, and Malaysia. African countries, largely ignoring family planning, have been overwhelmed by the sheer numbers of young people who need to be educated and employed.

**Small families are the key to stabilizing population.** Convincing couples everywhere to restrict their childbearing to replacement-level fertility is important enough to warrant a worldwide campaign, according to the authors.

If the world cannot simultaneously convert the economy to one that is environmentally sustainable and move to a lower population trajectory, economic decline will be hard to avoid.

### 14. Housing

The ultimate manifestation of population growth outstripping the supply of housing is homelessness. The United Nations estimates that at least 100 million of the world's people—roughly equal to the population of Mexico—have no home; the number tops 1 billion if squatters and others with insecure or temporary accommodations are included.

Unless population growth can be checked worldwide, the ranks of the homeless are likely to swell dramatically.

### 15. Education

In nations that have increasing child-age populations, the base pressures on the educational system will be severe. In the world's 10 fastest-growing countries, most of which

are in Africa and the Middle East, the child-age population will increase an average of 93% over the next 50 years. Africa as a whole will see its school-age population grow by 75% through 2040.

If national education systems begin to stress lifelong learning for a rapidly changing world of the twenty-first century, then extensive provision for adult education will be necessary, affecting even those countries with shrinking child-age populations.

Such a development means that countries which started population-stabilization programs earliest will be in the best position to educate their entire citizenry.

### 16. Urbanization

Today's cities are growing faster: It took London 130 years to get from 1 million to 8 million inhabitants; Mexico City made this jump in just 30 years. The world's urban population as a whole is growing by just over 1 million people each week. This urban growth is fed by the natural increase of urban populations, by net migration from the country-

side, and by villages or towns expanding to the point where they become cities or they are absorbed by the spread of existing cities.

If recent trends continue, 6.5 billion people will live in cities by 2050, more than the world's total population today.

## Actions for Slowing Growth

As we look to the future, the challenge for world leaders is to help countries maximize the prospects for achieving sustainability by keeping both birth and death rates low. In a world where both grain output and fish catch per person are falling, a strong case can be made on humanitarian grounds to stabilize world population.

What is needed is an all-out effort to lower fertility, particularly in the high-fertility countries, while there is still time. We see four key steps in doing this:

**Assess carrying capacity.** Every national government needs a carefully articulated and adequately supported population policy, one that takes into account the country's carrying capacity at whatever consumption level citizens decide on.

Without long-term estimates of available cropland, water for irrigation, and likely yields, governments are simply flying blind into the future, allowing their nations to drift into a world in which population growth and environmental degradation can lead to social disintegration.

**Fill the family-planning gap**. This is a high-payoff area. In a world where population pressures are mounting, the inability of 120 million of the world's women to get family-planning services is inexcusable. A stumbling block: At the International Conference on Population and Development in Cairo in 1994, the industrialized countries agreed to pay one-third of the costs for reproductive-health services in developing countries. So far they have failed to do so.

**Educate young women**. Educating girls is a key to accelerating the shift to smaller families. In every society for which data are available, the more education women have, the fewer children they have. Closely related to the need for education of young females is the need to provide equal opportunities for women in all phases of national life.

**Have just two children.** If we are facing a population emergency, it should be treated as such. It may be time for a campaign to convince couples everywhere to restrict their childbearing to replacement-level fertility.

**About the Authors**

Lester R. Brown is founder, president, and a senior researcher at the Worldwatch Institute, 1776 Massachusetts Avenue, N.W., Washington, D.C. 20036. Telephone 1-202-452-1999; Web site www.worldwatch.org.

Gary Gardner is a senior Worldwatch researcher and has written on agriculture, waste, and materials issues for *State of the World* and *World Watch* magazine.

Brian Halweil is a Worldwatch staff researcher and writes on issues related to food and agriculture, HIV/AIDS, cigarettes, and biotechnology.

This article is drawn from their report *Beyond Malthus: Sixteen Dimensions of the Population Problem*. Worldwatch Institute. 1998. 98 pages. Paperback. $5.

Originally published in the February 1999 issue of *The Futurist*, pp. 36-41. © 1999, World Future Society, 7910 Woodmont Ave, Bethesda, MD 20814, 301-656-8274. Used with permission.

SPECIAL REPORT • GLOBAL WARMING

# FEELING THE HEAT
# LIFE IN THE GREENHOUSE

Except for nuclear war or a collision with an asteroid, no force has more potential to damage our planet's web of life than global warming. It's a "serious" issue, the White House admits, but nonetheless George W. Bush has decided to abandon the 1997 Kyoto treaty to combat climate change—an agreement the U.S. signed but the new President believes is fatally flawed. His dismissal last week of almost nine years of international negotiations sparked protests around the world and a face-to-face disagreement with German Chancellor Gerhard Schröder. Our special report examines the signs of global warming that are already apparent, the possible consequences for our future, what we can do about the threat and why we have failed to take action so far.

By MICHAEL D. LEMONICK

There is no such thing as normal weather. The average daytime high temperature for New York City this week should be 57°F, but on any given day the mercury will almost certainly fall short of that mark or overshoot it, perhaps by a lot. Manhattan thermometers can reach 65° in January every so often and plunge to 50° in July. And seasons are rarely normal. Winter snowfall and summer heat waves beat the average some years and fail to reach it in others. It's tough to pick out overall changes in climate in the face of these natural fluctuations. An unusually warm year, for example, or even three in a row don't necessarily signal a general trend.

Yet the earth's climate does change. Ice ages have frosted the planet for tens of thousands of years at a stretch, and periods of warmth have pushed the tropics well into what is now the temperate zone. But given the normal year-to-year variations, the only reliable signal that such changes may be in the works is a long-term shift in worldwide temperature.

And that is precisely what's happening. A decade ago, the idea that the planet was warming up as a result of human activity was largely theoretical. We knew that since the Industrial Revolution began in the 18th century, factories and power plants and automobiles and farms have been loading the atmosphere with heat-trapping gases, including carbon dioxide and methane. But evidence that the climate was actually getting hotter was still murky.

Not anymore. As an authoritative report issued a few weeks ago by the United Nations-sponsored Intergovernmental Panel on Climate Change makes plain, the trend toward a warmer world has unquestionably begun. Worldwide temperatures have climbed more than 1°F over the past

# MAKING THE CASE THAT OUR CLIMATE IS CHANGING

From melting glaciers to rising oceans, the signs are everywhere. Global warming can't be blamed for any particular heat wave, drought or deluge, but scientists say a hotter world will make such extreme weather more frequent—and deadly.

## EXHIBIT A

### Thinning Ice

ANTARCTICA, home to these Adélie penguins, is heating up. The annual melt season has increased up to three weeks in 20 years.

MOUNT KILIMANJARO has lost 75% of its ice cap since 1912. The ice on Africa's tallest peak could vanish entirely within 15 years.

LAKE BAIKAL in eastern Siberia now feezes for the winter 1.1 days later than it did a century ago.

VENEZUELAN mountaintops had six glaciers in 1972. Today only two remain.

## EXHIBIT B

### Hotter Times

TEMPERATURES SIZZLED from Kansas to New England last May.

CROPS WITHERED and Dallas temperatures topped 100°F for 29 days-sstraight in a Texas hot spell that struck during the summer of 1998.

INDIA'S WORST heat shock in 50 years killed more than 2,500 people in May 1998.

CHERRY BLOSSOMS in Washington bloom seven days earlier in the spring than they did in 1970.

## EXHIBIT C

### Wild Weather

HEAVY RAINS in England and Wales made last fall Britain's wettest three-month period on record.

FIRES due to dry conditions and record-breaking heat consumed 20% of Samos Island, Greece, last July.

FLOODS along the Ohio River in March 1997 caused 30 deaths and at least $500 million in property damage.

HURRICAN FLOYD brought flooding rains and 130-m.p.h. winds through the Atlantic seabord in September1999, killing 77 people and leaving thousands homeless.

## EXHIBIT D

### Nature's Pain

PACIFIC SALMON populations fell sharply in 1997 and 1998, when local ocean temperatures rose 6°F.

POLAR BEARS in Hudson Bay are having fewer cubs, possibly as a result of earlier spring ice breakup.CORAL REEFS suffer from the loss of algae that color and nourish them. The process, called bleaching, is caused by warmer oceans.DISEASES like dengue fever are expanding their reach northward in the U.S.

BUTTERFLIES are relocating to higher latitudes. The Edith's Checkerspot butterfly of western North America has moved almost 60 miles north in 100 years.

## EXHIBIT E

### Rising Sea Levels

CAPE HATTERAS Lighthouse was 1,500 ft. from the North Carolina shoreline when it was built in 1870. By the late 1980s teh ocean had crept to within 160 ft., and the lighthouse had to be moved to avoid collapse.

JAPANESE FORTIFICATIONS were built on Kosrae Island in the southwest Pacific Ocean during World War II to guard against U.S. Marines' invading the beach. Today the fortifications are awash at high tide.

FLORIDA FARMLAND up to 1,000 ft. inland from Biscayne Bay is being infiltrated by salt water, rendering the land too toxic for crops. Salt water is also nibbling at the edges of farms on Maryland's Eastern Shore.

BRAZILIAN SHORELINE in the region of Recife receded more than 6 ft. a year from 1915 to 1950 and more than 8 ft. a year from 1985 to 1995.

century, and the 1990s were the hottest decade on record. After analyzing data going back at least two decades on everything from air and ocean temperatures to the spread and retreat of wildlife, the IPCC asserts that this slow but steady warming has had an impact on no fewer than 420 physical processes and animal and plant species on all continents.

Glaciers, including the legendary snows of Kilimanjaro, are disappearing from mountaintops around the globe. Coral reefs are dying off as the seas get too warm for comfort. Drought is the norm in parts of Asia and Africa. El Niño events, which trigger devastating weather in the eastern Pacific, are more frequent. The Arctic permafrost is starting to melt. Lakes and rivers in colder climates are freezing later and thawing earlier each year. Plants and animals are shifting their ranges poleward and to higher altitudes, and migration patterns for animals as diverse as polar bears, butterflies and beluga whales are being disrupted.

Faced with these hard facts, scientists no longer doubt that global warming is happening, and almost nobody questions the fact that humans are at least partly responsible. Nor are the changes over. Already, humans have increased the concentration of carbon dioxide, the most abundant heat-trapping gas in the atmosphere, to 30% above pre-industrial levels—and each year the

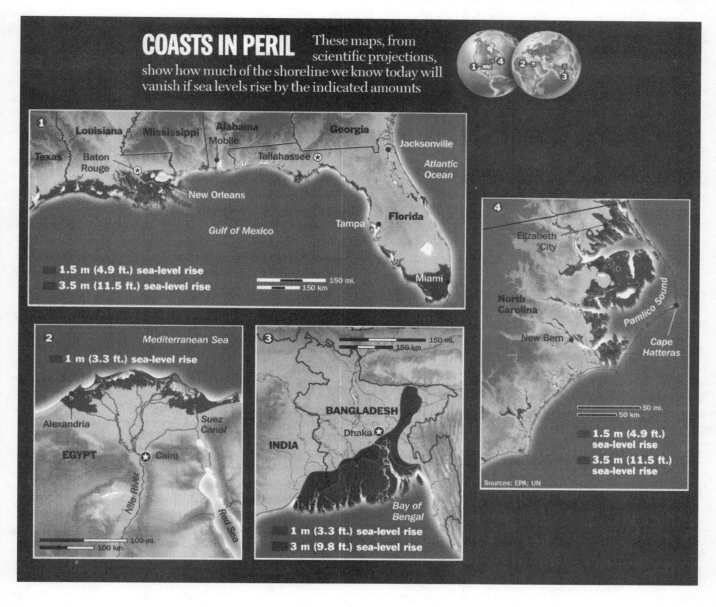

**COASTS IN PERIL** These maps, from scientific projections, show how much of the shoreline we know today will vanish if sea levels rise by the indicated amounts

1
Louisiana    Mississippi    Alabama    Georgia
Mobile
Texas    Baton Rouge    Tallahassee    Jacksonville
Atlantic Ocean
New Orleans
Gulf of Mexico    Tampa    Florida
Miami
1.5 m (4.9 ft.) sea-level rise
3.5 m (11.5 ft.) sea-level rise
150 mi.
150 km

2
Mediterranean Sea
1 m (3.3 ft.) sea-level rise
Alexandria    Suez Canal
EGYPT    Cairo
Nile River    Red Sea
100 mi.
100 km

3
150 mi.
150 km
BANGLADESH
INDIA    Dhaka
Bay of Bengal
1 m (3.3 ft.) sea-level rise
3 m (9.8 ft.) sea-level rise

4
Elizabeth City
North Carolina    Pamlico Sound
New Bern    Cape Hatteras
50 mi.
50 km
1.5 m (4.9 ft.) sea-level rise
3.5 m (11.5 ft.) sea-level rise
Sources: EPA; UN

rate of increase gets faster. The obvious conclusion: temperatures will keep going up.

Unfortunately, they may be rising faster and heading higher than anyone expected. By 2100, says the IPCC, average temperatures will increase between 2.5°F and 10.4°F—more than 50% higher than predictions of just a half-decade ago. That may not seem like much, but consider that it took only a 9°F shift to end the last ice age. Even at the low end, the changes could be problematic enough, with storms getting more frequent and intense, droughts more pronounced,

coastal areas ever more severely eroded by rising seas, rainfall scarcer on agricultural land and ecosystems thrown out of balance.

But if the rise is significantly larger, the result could be disastrous. With seas rising as much as 3 ft., enormous areas of densely populated land—coastal Florida, much of Louisiana, the Nile Delta, the Maldives, Bangladesh—would become uninhabitable. Entire climatic zones might shift dramatically, making central Canada look more like central Illinois, Georgia more like Guatemala. Agriculture would be

thrown into turmoil. Hundreds of millions of people would have to migrate out of unlivable regions.

Public health could suffer. Rising seas would contaminate water supplies with salt. Higher levels of urban ozone, the result of stronger sunlight and warmer temperatures, could worsen respiratory illnesses. More frequent hot spells could lead to a rise in heat-related deaths. Warmer temperatures could widen the range of disease-carrying rodents and bugs, such as mosquitoes and ticks, increasing the incidence of dengue fever, malaria, encephalitis,

Lyme disease and other afflictions. Worst of all, this increase in temperatures is happening at a pace that outstrips anything the earth has seen in the past 100 million years. Humans will have a hard enough time adjusting, especially in poorer countries, but for wildlife, the changes could be devastating.

Like any other area of science, the case for human-induced global warming has uncertainties—and like many pro-business lobbyists, President Bush has proclaimed those uncertainties a reason to study the problem further rather than act. But while the evidence is circumstantial, it is powerful, thanks to the IPCC's painstaking research. The U.N.-sponsored group was organized in the late 1980s. Its mission: to sift through climate-related studies from a dozen different fields and integrate them into a coherent picture. "It isn't just the work of a few green people," says Sir John Houghton, one of the early leaders who at the time ran the British Meteorological Office. "The IPCC scientists come from a wide range of backgrounds and countries."

Measuring the warming that has already taken place is relatively simple; the trick is unraveling the causes and projecting what will happen over the next century. To do that, IPCC scientists fed a wide range of scenarios involving varying estimates of population and economic growth, changes in technology and other factors into computers. That process gave them about 35 estimates, ranging from 6 billion to 35 billion tons, of how much excess carbon dioxide will enter the atmosphere.

Then they loaded those estimates into the even larger, more powerful computer programs that attempt to model the planet's climate. Because no one climate model is considered definitive, they used seven different versions, which yielded 235 independent predictions of global temperature increase. That's where the range of 2.5°F to 10.4°F (1.4°C to 5.8°C) comes from.

The computer models were criticized in the past largely because the climate is so complex that the limited hardware and software of even a half-decade ago couldn't do an adequate simulation. Today's climate models, however, are able to take into account the heat-trapping effects not just of $CO_2$ but also of other greenhouse gases, including methane. They can also factor in natural variations in the sun's energy and the effect of substances like dust from volcanic eruptions and particulate matter spewed from smokestacks.

That is one reason the latest IPCC predictions for temperature increase are higher than they were five years ago. Back in the mid-1990s, climate models didn't include the effects of the El Chichon and Mount Pinatubo volcanic eruptions, which threw enough dust into the air to block out some sunlight and slow down the rate of warming. That effect has dissipated, and the heating should start to accelerate. Moreover, the IPCC noted, many countries have begun to reduce their emissions of sulfur dioxide in order to fight acid rain. But sulfur dioxide particles, too, reflect sunlight; without this shield, temperatures should go up even faster.

The models still aren't perfect. One major flaw, agree critics and champions alike, is that they don't adequately account for clouds. In a warmer world, more water will evaporate from the oceans and presumably form more clouds. If they are billowy cumulus clouds, they will tend to shade the planet and slow down warming; if they are high, feathery cirrus clouds, they will trap even more heat.

Research by M.I.T. atmospheric scientist Richard Lindzen suggests that warming will tend to make cirrus clouds go away. Another critic, John Christy of the University of Alabama in Huntsville, says that while the models reproduce the current climate in a general way, they fail to get right the amount of warming at different levels in the atmosphere. Neither Lindzen nor Christy (both IPCC authors) doubts, however, that humans are influencing the climate. But they question how much—and how high temperatures will go. Both scientists are distressed that only the most extreme scenarios, based on huge population growth and the maximum use of dirty fuels like coal, have made headlines.

It won't take the greatest extremes of warming to make life uncomfortable for large numbers of people. Even slightly higher temperatures in regions that are already drought- or flood-prone would exacerbate those conditions. In temperate zones, warmth and increased $CO_2$ would make some crops flourish—at first. But beyond 3° of warming, says Bill Easterling, a professor of geography and agronomy at Penn State and a lead author of the IPCC report, "there would be a dramatic turning point. U.S. crop yields would start to decline rapidly." In the tropics, where crops are already at the limit of their temperature range, the decrease would start right away.

Even if temperatures rise only moderately, some scientists fear, the climate would reach a "tipping point"—a point at which even a tiny additional increase would throw the system into violent change. If peat bogs and Arctic permafrost warm enough to start releasing the methane stored within them, for example, that potent greenhouse gas would suddenly accelerate the heat-trapping process.

By contrast, if melting ice caps dilute the salt content of the sea, major ocean currents like the Gulf Stream could slow or even stop, and so would their warming effects on northern regions. More snowfall reflecting more sunlight back into space could actually cause a net cooling. Global warming could, paradoxically, throw the planet into another ice age.

Even if such a tipping point doesn't materialize, the more drastic effects of global warming might be only postponed rather than avoided. The IPCC's calculations end with the year 2100, but the warming won't.

World Bank chief scientist, Robert Watson, currently serving as IPCC chair, points out that the $CO_2$ entering the atmosphere today will be there for a century. Says Watson: "If we stabilize ($CO_2$ emissions) now, the concentration will continue to go up for hundreds of years. Temperatures will rise over that time."

That could be truly catastrophic. The ongoing disruption of ecosystems and weather patterns would be bad enough. But if temperatures reach the IPCC's worst-case levels and stay there for as long as 1,000 years, says Michael Oppenheimer, chief scientist at Environmental De-

fense, vast ice sheets in Greenland and Antarctica could melt, raising sea level more than 30 ft. Florida would be history, and every city on the U.S. Eastern seaboard would be inundated.

In the short run, there's not much chance of halting global warming, not even if every nation in the world ratifies the Kyoto Protocol tomorrow. The treaty doesn't require reductions in carbon dioxide emissions until 2008. By that time, a great deal of damage will already have been done. But we can slow things down. If action today can keep the climate from eventually reaching an unsta-

ble tipping point or can finally begin to reverse the warming trend a century from now, the effort would hardly be futile. Humanity embarked unknowingly on the dangerous experiment of tinkering with the climate of our planet. Now that we know what we're doing, it would be utterly foolish to continue.

*Reported by David Bjerklie,*
*Robert H. Boyle and*
*Andrea Dorfman/New York and*
*Dick Thompson/Washington*

# The secret nuclear war

The equivalent of a nuclear war has already happened. Over the last half-century, millions have died as a result of accidents, experiments, lies and cover-ups by the nuclear industry. **Eduardo Goncalves** pulls together a number of examples, and counts the fearful total cost.

Hugo Paulino was proud to be a fusilier. He was even prouder to be serving as a UN peacekeeper in Kosovo. It was his chance to help the innocent casualties of war. His parents did not expect him to become one.

Hugo, says his father Luis, died of leukaemia caused by radiation from depleted uranium (DU) shells fired by NATO during the Kosovo war. He was one of hundreds of Portuguese peacekeepers sent to Klina, an area heavily bombed with these munitions. Their patrol detail included the local lorry park, bombed because it had served as a Serb tank reserve, and the Valujak mines, which sheltered Serbian troops.

In their time off, the soldiers bathed in the river and gratefully supplemented their tasteless rations with local fruit and cheeses given to them by thankful nuns from the convent they guarded. Out of curiosity, they would climb inside the destroyed Serbian tanks littering the area.

Hugo arrived back in Portugal from his tour of duty on 12 February 2000, complaining of headaches, nausea and 'flu-like symptoms'. Ten days later, on 22 February, he suffered a major seizure. He was rushed to Lisbon's military hospital, where his condition rapidly deteriorated. On 9 March, he died. He was 21.

The military autopsy, which was kept secret for 10 months, claimed his death was due to septicaemia and 'herpes of the brain'. Not so, says Luis Paulino. 'When he was undergoing tests, a doctor called me over and said he thought it could be from radiation.'

It was only then that Luis learnt about the uranium shells—something his son had never been warned about or given protective clothing against. He contacted doctors and relatives of Belgian and Italian soldiers suspected of having succumbed to radiation poisoning.

'The similarities were extraordinary', he said. 'My son had died from leukaemia. That is why the military classified the autopsy report and wanted me to sign over all rights to its release.'

Today, Kosovo is littered with destroyed tanks, and pieces of radioactive shrapnel. NATO forces fired 31,000 depleted uranium shells during the Kosovo campaign, and 10,800 into neighbouring Bosnia. The people NATO set out to protect—and the soldiers it sent out to protect them—are now dying. According to Bosnia's health minister, Boza Ljubic, cancer deaths among civilians have risen to 230 cases per 100,000 last year, up from 152 in 1999. Leukaemia cases, he added, had doubled.

Scientists predict that the use of DU in Serbia will lead to more than 10,000 deaths from cancer among local residents, aid workers, and peacekeepers. Belated confessions that plutonium was also used may prompt these estimates to be revised. But while NATO struggles to stave off accusations of a cover-up, the Balkans are merely the newest battlefield in a silent world war that has claimed millions of lives. Most of its victims have died not in war-zones, but in ordinary communities scattered across the globe.

## The hidden deaths of Newbury

Far away from the war-torn Balkans is Newbury, a prosperous white-collar industrial town in London's commuter belt. On its outskirts is Greenham Common, the former US Air Force station that was one of America's most important strategic bases during the Cold War. The base was closed down after the signing of the INF (Intermediate Nuclear Forces) Treaty by Ronald Reagan and Mikhail Gorbachev. The nuclear threat was over. Or so people thought.

In August 1993, Ann Capewell—who lived just one mile away from the base's former runway—died of acute myeloid leukaemia. She was 16 when she passed away, just 40 days after diagnosis. As they were coming to terms with their sudden loss, her parents—Richard and Elizabeth—were surprised to find a number of other cases of leukaemia in their locality.

The more they looked, the more cases they found. 'Many were just a stone's throw from our front door,' says Richard, 'mainly cases of myeloid leukaemia in young people.' What none of them knew was that they were the victims of a nuclear accident at Greenham Common that had been carefully covered up by successive British and American administrations.

## 'It is believed that the estimated 1,900 nuclear tests conducted during the Cold War released fallout equivalent to 40,000 Hiroshimas in every corner of the globe.'

On February 28 1958, a laden B-47 nuclear bomber was awaiting clearance for take-off when it was suddenly engulfed in a huge fireball. Another bomber flying overhead had dropped a full fuel tank just 65 feet away. The plane exploded and burnt uncontrollably for days. As did its deadly payload.

A secret study by scientists at Britain's nearby nuclear bomb laboratory at Aldermaston documented the fallout, but the findings were never disclosed. The report showed how radioactive particles had been 'glued' to the runway surface by fire-fighters attempting to extinguish the blazing bomber—and that these were now being slowly blown into Newbury and over other local communities by aircraft jet blast.

'Virtually all the cases of leukaemias and lymphomas are in a band stretching from Greenham Common into south Newbury,' says Elizabeth. However, the British government continues to deny the cluster's existence, whilst the Americans still insist there was no accident.

Yet this was just one of countless disasters, experiments and officially-sanctioned activities which the nuclear powers have kept a closely-guarded secret. Between them, they have caused a global human death toll which is utterly unprecedented and profoundly shocking.

## Broken Arrows

In 1981, the Pentagon publicly released a list of 32 'Broken Arrows—official military terminology for an accident involving a nuclear weapon. The report gave few details and did not divulge the location of some accidents. It was prepared in response to mounting media pressure about possible accident cover-ups.

But another US government document, this time secret, indicates that the official report may be seriously misleading. It states that 'a total of 1,250 nuclear weapons have been involved in accidents during handling, storage and transportation', a number of which 'resulted in, or had high potential for, plutonium dispersal.'[1]

Washington has never acknowledged the human consequences of even those few accidents it admits to, such as the Thule disaster in Greenland in 1968. When a B-52 bomber crashed at this secret nuclear base, all four bombs detonated, and a cloud of plutonium rose 800 metres in the air, blowing deadly radioactive particles hundreds of miles. The authorities downplayed the possibility of any health risks. But today, many local Eskimos, and their huskies, suffer from cancer, and over 300 people involved in the clean-up operation alone have since died of cancer and mysterious illnesses.

We may never know the true toll from all the bomb accidents, as the nuclear powers classify these disasters not as matters of public interest but of 'national security' instead. Indeed, it is only now that details are beginning to emerge of some accidents at bomb factories and nuclear plants that took place several decades ago.

## Soviet sins

In 1991, Polish film-maker Slawomir Grunberg was invited to a little-known town in Russia's Ural mountains that was once part of a top-secret Soviet nuclear bomb-making complex. What he found was a tragedy of extraordinary dimensions, largely unknown to the outside world, and ignored by post-Cold War leaders.

His film—*Chelyabinsk: The Most Contaminated Spot on the Planet*—tells the story of the disasters at the Soviet Union's first plutonium factory, and the poisoning of hundreds of thousands of people. For years, the complex dumped its nuclear waste—totalling 76 million cubic metres—into the Techa River, the sole water source for scores of local communities that line its banks. According to a local doctor, people received an average radiation dose 57 times higher than that of Chernobyl's inhabitants.

In 1957, there was an explosion at a waste storage facility that blew 2 million curies of radiation into the atmosphere. The kilometre-high cloud drifted over three

## The cancer epidemic

Scientists at St Andrew's University recently found that cells exposed to a dose of just two alpha particles of radiation produced as many cancers as much higher doses of radiation. They concluded that a single alpha particle of radiation could be carcinogenic.

Herman Muller, who has received a Nobel Prize for his work, has shown how the human race's continuous exposure to so-called 'low-level' radiation is causing a gradual reduction in its ability to survive, as successive generations are genetically damaged. The spreading and accumulation of even tiny genetic mutations pass through family lines, provoking allergies, asthma, juvenile diabetes, hypertension, arthritis, high blood cholesterol conditions, and muscular and bone defects.

Dr Chris Busby, who has extensively researched the low-level radiation threat, has made a link between everyday radiation exposure and a range of modern ailments: 'There have been tremendous increases in diseases resulting from the breakdown of the immune system in the last 20 years: diabetes, asthma, AIDS and others which may have an immune-system link, such as MS and ME. A whole spectrum of neurological conditions of unknown origin has developed'.[10]

Around the world, a pattern is emerging. For the first time in modern history, mortality rates among adults between the ages of 15 and 54 are actually increasing, and have been since 1982. In July 1983, the US Center for Birth Defects in Atlanta, Georgia, reported that physical and mental disabilities in the under-17s had doubled—despite a reduction in diseases such as polio, and improved vaccines and medical care.

Defects in new-born babies doubled between the 1950s and 1980s, as did long-term debilitating diseases. The US Environmental Protection Agency adds that 23 per cent of US males were sterile in 1980, compared to 0.5 per cent in 1938.

Above all, cancer is now an epidemic. In 1900, cancer accounted for only 4 per cent of deaths in the US. Now it is the second leading cause of premature mortality. Worldwide, the World Health Organisation (WHO) estimates the number of cancers will double in most countries over the next 25 years.

Within a few years, the chances of getting cancer in Britain will be as high as 40 per cent—virtually the toss of a coin.

---

Soviet provinces, contaminating over 250,000 people living in 217 towns and villages. Only a handful of local inhabitants were ever evacuated.

10 years later, Lake Karachay, also used as a waste dump, began to dry up. The sediment around its shores blew 5 million curies of radioactive dust over 25,000 square kilometres, irradiating 500,000 people. Even today, the lake is so 'hot' that standing on its shore will kill a person within one hour.

Grunberg's film tells of the terrible toll of these disasters on local families, such as that of Idris Sunrasin, whose grandmother, parents and three siblings have died of cancer. Leukaemia cases increased by 41 per cent after the plant began operations, and the average life span for women in 1993 was 47, compared to 72 nationally. For men it was just 45.

### The secret nuclear war

Russia's nuclear industry is commonly regarded as cavalier in regard to health and safety. But the fact is that the nuclear military-industrial complex everywhere has been quite willing to deliberately endanger and sacrifice the lives of innocent civilians to further its ambitions.

The US government, for example, recently admitted its nuclear scientists carried out over 4,000 experiments on live humans between 1944 and 1974. They included feeding radioactive food to disabled children, irradiating prisoners' testicles, and trials on new-born babies and pregnant mothers. Scientists involved with the Manhat-

tan Project injected people with plutonium without telling them. An autopsy of one of the victims reportedly showed that his bones 'looked like Swiss cheese'. At the University of Cincinnati, 88 mainly low-income, black women were subjected to huge doses of radiation in an experiment funded by the military. They suffered acute radiation sickness. Nineteen of them died.

## 'Scientists predict that millions will die in centuries to come from nuclear tests that happened in the 1950s and 1960s.'

Details of many experiments still remain shrouded in secrecy, whilst little is known of the more shocking ones to come to light—such as one when a man was injected with what a report described as 'about a lethal dose' of strontium-89.[2]

In Britain too, scientists have experimented with plutonium on new-born babies, ethnic minorities and the disabled. When American colleagues reviewed a British proposal for a joint experiment, they concluded: 'What is the worst thing that can happen to a human being as a result of being a subject? Death.'[3]

They also conducted experiments similar to America's 'Green Run' programme, in which 'dirty' radiation was released over populated areas in the western states of Washington and Oregon contaminating farmland, crops and water. The 'scrubber' filters in Hanford's nuclear stacks were deliberately switched off first. Scientists, posing as agriculture department officials, found radiation contamination levels on farms hundreds of times above 'safety' levels.

But America's farmers and consumers were not told this, and the British public has never been officially told about experiments on its own soil.

## Forty thousand Hiroshimas

It is believed that the estimated 1,900 nuclear tests conducted during the Cold War released fallout equivalent to 40,000 Hiroshimas in every corner of the globe. Fission products from the Nevada Test site can be detected in the ecosystems of countries as far apart as South Africa, Brazil, and Malaysia. Here, too, ordinary people were guinea pigs in a global nuclear experiment. The public health hazards were known right from the beginning, but concealed from the public. A 1957 US government study predicted that recent American tests had produced an extra 2,000 'genetically defective' babies in the US each year, and up to 35,000 every year around the globe. They continued regardless.

Ernest Sternglass's research shows how, in 1964, between 10,000 and 15,000 children were lost by miscarriage and stillbirth in New York state alone—and that there were some 10 to 15 times this number of foetal deaths across America.[4]

## 'Over the years, the Harwell, Aldermaston and Amersham plants have pumped millions of gallons of liquid contaminated with radioactive waste into the River Thames.'

Those who lived closest to the test sites have seen their families decimated. Such as the 100,000 people who were directly downwind of Nevada's fallout. They included the Mormon community of St George in Utah, 100 miles away from 'Ground Zero'—the spot where the bombs were detonated. Cancer used to be virtually unheard of among its population. Mormons do not smoke or drink alcohol or coffee, and live largely off their own homegrown produce.

Mormons are also highly patriotic. They believe government to be 'God-given', and do not protest. The military could afford to wait until the wind was blowing from the test site towards St George before detonating a device. After all, President Eisenhower had said: 'We can afford to sacrifice a few thousand people out there in defence of national security.'[5]

When the leukaemia cases suddenly appeared, doctors—unused to the disease—literally had no idea what it was. A nine-year-old boy, misdiagnosed with diabetes,

died after a single shot of insulin. Women who complained of radiation sickness symptoms were told they had 'housewife syndrome'. Many gave birth to terribly deformed babies that became known as 'the sacrifice babies'. Elmer Pickett, the local mortician, had to learn new embalming techniques for the small bodies of wasted children killed by leukaemia. He himself was to lose no fewer than 16 members of his immediate family to cancer.

By the mid-1950s, just a few years after the tests began, St George had a leukaemia rate 2.5 times the national average, whereas before it was virtually non-existent. The total number of radiation deaths are said to have totalled 1,600—in a town with a population of just 5,000.

The military simply lied about the radiation doses people were getting. Former army medic Van Brandon later revealed how his unit kept two sets of radiation readings for test fallout in the area. 'One set was to show that no one received an [elevated] exposure' whilst 'the other set of books showed the actual reading. That set was brought in a locked briefcase every morning.'[6]

## Continuous fallout

The world's population is still being subjected to the continuous fallout of the 170 megatons of long-lived nuclear fission products blasted into the atmosphere and returned daily to earth by wind and rain—slowly poisoning our bodies via the air we breathe, the food we eat, and the water we drink. Scientists predict that millions will die in centuries to come from tests that happened in the 1950s and 1960s.

But whilst atmospheric testing is now banned, over 400 nuclear bomb factories and power plants around the world make 'routine discharges' of nuclear waste into the environment. Thousands of nuclear waste dumping grounds, many of them leaking, are contaminating soil and water every day. The production of America's nuclear weapons arsenal alone has produced 100 million cubic metres of long-lived radioactive waste.

The notorious Hanford plutonium factory—which produced the fissile materials for the Trinity test and Nagasaki bomb—has discharged over 440 billion gallons of contaminated liquid into the surrounding area, contaminating 200 square miles of groundwater, but concealed the dangers from the public. Officials knew as early as the late 1940s that the nearby Columbia River was becoming seriously contaminated and a hazard to local fishermen. They chose to keep information about discharges secret and not to issue warnings.

In Britain, there are 7,000 sites licensed to use nuclear materials, 1,000 of which are allowed to discharge wastes. Three of them, closely involved in Britain's nuclear bomb programme, are located near the River Thames. Over the years, the Harwell, Aldermaston and Amersham plants have pumped millions of gallons of liquid contaminated with radioactive waste into the river.

They did so in the face of opposition from government ministers and officials who said 'the 6 million inhabitants of London derive their drinking water from this source. Any increase in [radio-]activity of the water supply would increase the genetic load on this comparatively large group.'[7] One government minister even wrote of his fears that the dumping 'would produce between 10 and 300 severely abnormal individuals per generation'.

Public relations officers at Harwell themselves added: 'the potential sufferers are 8 million in number, including both Houses of Parliament, Fleet Street and Whitehall'. These discharges continue to this day.

Study after study has uncovered 'clusters' of cancers and high rates of other unusual illnesses near nuclear plants, including deformities and Down Syndrome. Exposure to radiation among Sellafield's workers, in northwest England, has been linked to a greater risk of fathering a stillborn child and leukaemia among off-spring. Reports also suggest a higher risk of babies developing spina bifida in the womb.

Although the plant denies any link, even official MAFF studies have shown high levels of contamination in locally-grown fruit and vegetables, as well as wild animals. The pollution from Sellafield alone is such that it has coated the shores of the whole of Britain—from Wales to Scotland, and even Hartlepool in north-eastern England. A nationwide study organised by Harwell found that Sellafield 'is a source of plutonium contamination in the wider population of the British Isles'.[8]

> **'Study after study has uncovered 'clusters' of cancers and high rates of other illnesses near nuclear plants, including deformities and Down Syndrome. Exposure to radiation among Sellafield's workers, in NW England, has been linked to a greater risk of fathering a stillborn child and leukaemia among off-spring.'**

Those who live nearest the plant face the greatest threat. A study of autopsy tissue by the National Radiological Protection Board (NRPB) found high plutonium levels in the lungs of local Cumbrians—350 per cent higher than people in other parts of the country. 'Cancer clusters' have been found around nuclear plants across the globe—from France to Taiwan, Germany to Canada. A joint White House/US Department of Energy investigation recently found a high incidence of 22 different kinds of cancer at 14 different US nuclear weapons facilities around the country.

Meanwhile, a Greenpeace USA study of the toxicity of the Mississippi river showed that from 1968-83 there were 66,000 radiation deaths in the counties lining its banks—more than the number of Americans who died during the Vietnam war.

## Don't blame us

Despite the growing catalogue of tragedy, the nuclear establishment has consistently tried to deny responsibility. It claims that only high doses of radiation—such as those experienced by the victims of the Hiroshima and Nagasaki bombs—are dangerous, though even here they have misrepresented the data. They say that the everyday doses from nuclear plant discharges, bomb factories and transportation of radioactive materials are 'insignificant', and that accidents are virtually impossible.

The truth, however, is that the real number and seriousness of accidents has never been disclosed, and that the damage from fallout has been covered up. The nuclear establishment now grudgingly (and belatedly) accepts that there is no such thing as a safe dose of radiation, however 'low', yet the poisonous discharges continue. When those within the nuclear establishment try to speak out, they are harassed, intimidated—and even threatened.

John Gofman, former head of Lawrence Livermore's biomedical unit, who helped produce the world's first plutonium for the bomb, was for years at the heart of the nuclear complex. He recalls painfully the time he was called to give evidence before a Congressional inquiry set up to defuse mounting concern over radiation's dangers.

'Chet Holifield and Craig Hosmer of the Joint Committee (on Atomic Energy) came in and turned to me and said: "Just what the hell do you think you two are doing, getting all those little old ladies in tennis shoes up in arms about our atomic energy program? There are people like you who have tried to hurt the Atomic Energy Commission program before. We got them, and we'll get you."'[9]

Gofman was eventually forced out of his job. But the facts of his research—and that of many other scientists—speak for themselves.

## The final reckoning

But could radiation really be to blame for these deaths? Are the health costs really that great? The latest research suggests they are.

It is only very recently that clues have surfaced as to the massive destructive power of radiation in terms of human health. The accident at Chernobyl will kill an estimated half a million people worldwide from cancer, and perhaps more. 90 per cent of children in the neighbouring former Soviet republic of Belarus are contaminated for life—the poisoning of an entire country's gene pool.

Ernest Sternglass calculates that, at the height of nuclear testing, there were as many as 3 million foetal deaths, spontaneous abortions and stillbirths in the US alone. In addition, 375,000 babies died in their first year of life from radiation-linked diseases.[11]

## The final reckoning

How many deaths is the nuclear industry responsible for? The following calculations of numbers of cancers caused by radiation are the latest and most accurate:[*]

from nuclear bomb production and testing:     385 million

from bomb and plant accidents:     9.7 million

from the 'routine discharges' of nuclear power plants
(5 million of them among populations living nearby):     6.6 million

likely number of total cancer fatalities worldwide:     175 million

[Added to this number are 235 million genetically damaged and diseased people, and 588 million children born with diseases such as brain damage, mental disabilities, spina bifida, genital deformities, and childhood cancers.]

[*]*Calculated by Rosalie Bertell, using the official 'radiation risk' estimates published in 1991 by the International Commission on Radiological Protection (ICRP), and the total radiation exposure data to the global population calculated by the UN Scientific Committee on the Effects of Atomic Radiation (UNSCEAR) in 1993.*

Rosalie Bertell, author of the classic book *No Immediate Danger*, now revised and re-released, has attempted to piece together a global casualty list from the nuclear establishment's own data. The figures she has come up with are chilling—but entirely plausible.

Using the official 'radiation risk' estimates published in 1991 by the International Commission on Radiological Protection (ICRP), and the total radiation exposure data to the global population calculated by the UN Scientific Committee on the Effects of Atomic Radiation (UNSCEAR) in 1993, she has come up with a terrifying tally:

- 358 million cancers from nuclear bomb production and testing
- 9.7 million cancers from bomb and plant accidents
- 6.6 million cancers from the 'routine discharges' of nuclear power plants (5 million of them among populations living nearby).
- As many as 175 million of these cancers could be fatal.

Added to this number are no fewer than 235 million genetically damaged and diseased people, and a staggering 588 million children born with what are called 'teratogenic effects'—diseases such as brain damage, mental disabilities, spina bifida, genital deformities, and childhood cancers.

Furthermore, says Bertell, we should include the problem of nonfatal cancers and of other damage which is debilitating but not counted for insurance and liability purposes'[12]—such as the 500 million babies lost as stillbirths because they were exposed to radiation whilst still in the womb, but are not counted as 'official' radiation victims.

It is what the nuclear holocaust peace campaigners always warned of if war between the old superpowers broke out, yet it has already happened and with barely a shot being fired. Its toll is greater than that of all the wars in history put together, yet no-one is counted as among the war dead.

## 'It is the nuclear holocaust that peace campaigners always warned of if war between the old superpowers broke out, yet it has already happened and with barely a shot being fired.'

Its virtually infinite killing and maiming power leads Rosalie Bertell to demand that we learn a new language to express a terrifying possibility: 'The concept of species annihilation means a relatively swift, deliberately induced end to history, culture, science, biological reproduction and memory. It is the ultimate human rejection of the gift of life, an act which requires a new word to describe it: omnicide'.[13]

*Eduardo Goncalves is a freelance journalist and environmental researcher. He is author of tile reports **Broken Arrow—Greenham Common's Secret Nuclear Accident** and **Nuclear Guinea Pigs—British Human Radiation Experiments**, published by CND (UK), and was researcher to the film **The Dragon that Slew St George**. He is currently writing a book about the hidden history of the nuclear age.*

## Notes

1. 'Report of the safety criteria for plutonium-bearing weapons—summary', US Department of Energy, February 14, 1973, document RS5640/1035.

2. Strontium metabolism meeting, Atomic Energy Division–Division of Biology and Medicine, January 17,1954.

3. memorandum to Bart Gledhill, chairman, Human Subjects Committee. LLNL, from Larry Anderson, LLNL, February 21,1989.

4. see 'Secret Fallout, Low-Level Radiation from Hiroshima to Three-Mile Island'. Ernest Sternglass, McGraw-Hill, New York, 1981.

5. see 'American Ground Zero; The Secret Nuclear War', Carole Gallagher, MIT Press. Boston, 1993.

6. Washington Post, February 24, 1994.

7. see PRO files AB 6/1379 and AB 6/2453 and 3584.

8. 'Variations in the concentration of plutonium, strontium-90 and total alpha-emitters in human teeth', RG. O'Donnell et al, Sd. Tot. Env, 201 (1997) 235–243.

9. interview with Gofman, DOE/OHRE Oral History Project, December 1994, pp 49-50 of official transcripts.

10. 'Wings of Death—nuclear pollution and human health', Dr. Chris Busby, Green Audit, Wales, 1995

11. see 'Secret Fallout, Low-Level Radiation from Hiroshima to Three-Mile Island', Ernest Sternglass, McGraw-Hill, New York, 1981.

12. from 'No Immediate Danger— Prognosis for a Radioactive Earth', Dr Rosalie Bertell. Women's Press. London 1985 (revised 2001)

13. pers. Comm. 4 February 2001

## Further reading:

'No Immediate Danger—Prognosis for a Radioactive Earth', Dr Rosalie Bertell, Women's Press, London (revised 2001)

'Deadly Deceit—low-level radiation, high-level cover-up', Dr. Jay Gould and Benjamin A. Goldman, Four Walls Eight Windows, New York, 1991

'Wings of Death—nuclear pollution and human health', Dr. Chris Busby, Green Audit, Wales, 1995

'American Ground Zero: The Secret Nuclear War', Carole Gallagher, MIT Press, Boston, 1993

'Radioactive Heaven and Earth—the health effects of nuclear weapons testing in, on, and above the earth', a report of the IPPNW International Commission, Zed Books, 1991 'Secret Fallout. Low-Level Radiation from Hiroshima to Three-Mile Island', Ernest Sternglass, McGraw-Hill, New York, 1981

'Clouds of Deceit—the deadly legacy of Britain's bomb tests', Joan Smith, Faber and Faber, London, 1985

'Nuclear Wastelands', Arjun Makhijani et al (eds), MIT Press, Boston, 1995 'Radiation and Human Health', Dr. John W. Gofman, Sierra Book Club, San Francisco, 1981

'The Greenpeace Book of the Nuclear Age—The Hidden History, the Human Cost', John May, Victor Gollancz, 1989

'The Unsinkable Aircraft Carrier—American military power in Britain', Duncan Campbell, Michael Joseph, London 1984

# GRAINS OF
# HOPE

**GENETICALLY ENGINEERED CROPS could revolutionize farming.
Protesters fear they could also destroy the ecosystem. You decide**

**By J. MADELEINE NASH**

ZURICH

AT FIRST, THE GRAINS OF RICE that Ingo Potrykus sifted through his fingers did not seem at all special, but that was because they were still encased in their dark, crinkly husks. Once those drab coverings were stripped away and the interiors polished to a glossy sheen, Potrykus and his colleagues would behold the seeds' golden secret. At their core, these grains were not pearly white, as ordinary rice is, but a very pale yellow—courtesy of beta-carotene, the nutrient that serves as a building block for vitamin A.

Potrykus was elated. For more than a decade he had dreamed of creating such a rice: a golden rice that would improve the lives of millions of the poorest people in the world. He'd visualized peasant farmers wading into paddies to set out the tender seedlings and winnowing the grain at harvest time in handwoven baskets. He'd pictured small children consuming the golden gruel their

mothers would make, knowing that it would sharpen their eyesight and strengthen their resistance to infectious diseases.

And he saw his rice as the first modest start of a new green revolution, in which ancient food crops would acquire all manner of useful properties: bananas that wouldn't rot on the way to market; corn that could supply its own fertilizer; wheat that could thrive in drought-ridden soil.

But imagining a golden rice, Potrykus soon found, was one thing and bringing one into existence quite another. Year after year, he and his colleagues ran into one unexpected obstacle after another, beginning with the finicky growing habits of the rice they transplanted to a greenhouse near the foothills of the Swiss Alps. When success finally came, in the spring of 1999, Potrykus was 65 and about to retire as a full professor at the Swiss Federal Institute of Technology in Zurich. At that point, he tackled an even more formidable challenge.

Having created golden rice, Potrykus wanted to make sure it reached those for whom it was intended: malnourished children of the developing world. And that, he knew, was not likely to be easy. Why? Because in addition to a full complement of genes from Oryza sativa—the Latin name for the most commonly consumed species of rice—the golden grains also contained snippets of DNA borrowed from bacteria and daffodils. It was what some would call Frankenfood, a product of genetic engineering. As such, it was entangled in a web of hopes and fears and political baggage, not to mention a fistful of ironclad patents.

For about a year now—ever since Potrykus and his chief collaborator, Peter Beyer of the University of Freiburg in Germany, announced their achievement—their golden grain has illuminated an increasingly polarized public debate. At issue is the question of what genetically engineered crops represent. Are they, as their proponents argue, a technological leap forward that will bestow in-

# HOW TO MAKE GOLDEN RICE
A four-step process to feed the poor

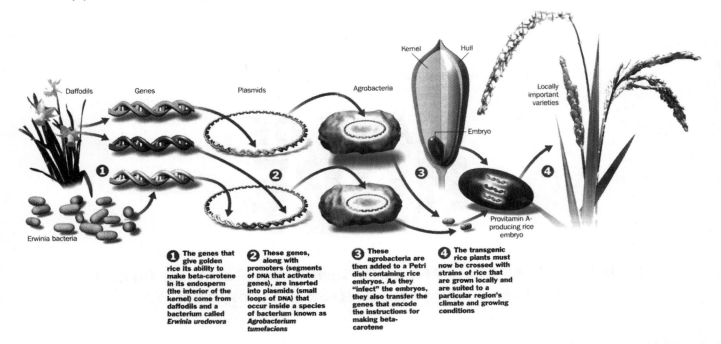

**1** The genes that give golden rice its ability to make beta-carotene in its endosperm (the interior of the kernel) come from daffodils and a bacterium called *Erwinia uredovora*

**2** These genes, along with promoters (segments of DNA that activate genes), are inserted into plasmids (small loops of DNA) that occur inside a species of bacterium known as *Agrobacterium tumefaciens*

**3** These agrobacteria are then added to a Petri dish containing rice embryos. As they "infect" the embryos, they also transfer the genes that encode the instructions for making beta-carotene

**4** The transgenic rice plants must now be crossed with strains of rice that are grown locally and are suited to a particular region's climate and growing conditions

SOURCE: DR. PETER BEYER, CENTER FOR APPLIED BIOSCIENCES, UNIVERSITY OF FREIBURG

calculable benefits on the world and its people? Or do they represent a perilous step down a slippery slope that will lead to ecological and agricultural ruin? Is genetic engineering just a more efficient way to do the business of conventional crossbreeding? Or does the ability to mix the genes of any species—even plants and animals—give man more power than he should have?

The debate erupted the moment genetically engineered crops made their commercial debut in the mid-1990s, and it has escalated ever since. First to launch major protests against biotechnology were European environmentalists and consumer-advocacy groups. They were soon followed by their U.S. counterparts, who made a big splash at last fall's World Trade Organization meeting in Seattle and last week launched an offensive designed to target one company after another (see accompanying story). Over the coming months, charges that transgenic crops pose grave dangers will be raised in petitions, editorials, mass mailings and protest marches. As a result, golden rice, de-spite its humanitarian intent, will probably be subjected to the same kind of hostile scrutiny that has already led to curbs on the commercialization of these crops in Britain, Germany, Switzerland and Brazil.

The hostility is understandable. Most of the genetically engineered crops introduced so far represent minor variations on the same two themes: resistance to insect pests and to herbicides used to control the growth of weeds. And they are often marketed by large, multinational corporations that produce and sell the very agricultural chemicals farmers are spraying on their fields. So while many farmers have embraced such crops as Monsanto's Roundup Ready soybeans, with their genetically engineered resistance to Monsanto's Roundup-brand herbicide, that let them spray weed killer without harming crops, consumers have come to regard such things with mounting suspicion. Why resort to a strange new technology that might harm the biosphere, they ask, when the benefits of doing so seem small?

## FROM THE TRANSGENIC GARDEN

**COTTON**
**BEAUTIFUL BOLL**: This plant has been given a bacterial gene to help it fight off worms that infest cotton crops

**CORN**
**HEALTHY KERNEL**: These corn seeds are protected by the same bacterial gene, one that ecologists fear could harm butterflies

**PAPAYA**
**VIRAL RESISTANCE**: Fruit carrying a gene from the ringspot virus are better able to withstand ringspot outbreaks

**CANOLA**
**PROBLEM POLLEN**: When transgenic seeds contaminated a non-transgenic shipment from Canada, European farmers cried foul

**SOYBEANS**
**ROUNDUP READY**: Will crops designed to take frequent spraying with Monsanto's top weed killer lead to Roundup-resistant weeds?

# Taking It to Main Street

**By MARGOT ROOSEVELT** SAN FRANCISCO

It WAS THE SORT OF KITSCHY STREET THEATER YOU EXPECT IN A city like San Francisco. A gaggle of protesters in front of a grocery store, some dressed as monarch butterflies, others as Frankenstein's monster. Signs reading HELL NO, WE WON'T GROW IT! People in white biohazard jumpsuits pitching Campbell's soup and Kellogg's cornflakes into a mock toxic-waste bin. The crowd shouting, "Hey, hey, ho, ho—GMO has got to go!" And, at the podium, Jesse Cool, a popular restaurant owner, wondering what would happen if she served a tomato spliced with an oyster gene and a customer got sick. "I could get sued," she says.

But just as the California activists were revving up last week, similar rants and chants were reverberating in such unlikely places as Grand Forks, N.D., Augusta, Maine, and Miami—19 U.S. cities in all. This was no frolicking radical fringe but the carefully coordinated start of a nationwide campaign to force the premarket safety testing and labeling of those GMOs, or genetically modified organisms. Seven organizations— including such media-savvy veterans as the Sierra Club, Friends of the Earth and the Public Interest Research Groups— were launching the Genetically Engineered Food Alert, a million-dollar, multiyear organizing effort to pressure Congress, the Food and Drug Administration and individual companies, one at a time, starting with Campbell's soup.

The offensive represents the seeds of what could grow into a serious problem for U.S. agribusiness, which had been betting that science-friendly American consumers would remain immune to any "Frankenfood" backlash cross-pollinating from Europe or Japan. After all, this is (mostly) U.S. technology, and it has spread so quickly and so quietly that the proportion of U.S. farmland planted in genetically altered corn now stands at nearly 25%. Some 70% of processed food in American supermarkets, from soup to sandwich meat, contains ingredients derived from transgenic corn, soybeans and other plants. Yet all of a sudden, activists are "yelling fire in a movie theater," says Dan Eramian, spokesman for the Biotechnology Industry Organization (BIO).

How widespread is this protest movement? And how deep are its roots? We may soon find out, for it's emergence is a study in the warp-speed politics of the age of the Internet. This is a time when a Web designer named Craig Winters can start an organization called the Campaign to Label Genetically Engineered Food with a staff of one (himself), mount a website and sell 160,000 "Take Action Packets" in nine weeks. Want to know what the Chileans are doing about transgenic grain shipments? How South Korean labeling laws work? Just subscribe to one of the four biotech e-mail lists of the Institute for Agriculture and Trade Policy, based in Minneapolis, Minn.

Even so-called ecoterrorists who have uprooted scores of university test plots across the country in the past year use the Net to organize their lawbreaking protests. In an Internet posting from Santa Cruz last week, Earth First! beckons, "You're all invited to sunny California for a weekend of workshops, training and fun! We also have plenty of [genetically engineered] crops waiting for your night time gardening efforts." Says Carl Pope, the Sierra Club's executive director: "I've never seen an issue go so quickly."

It started about two years ago, when the buzz from European anti-biotech protest groups began to ricochet throughout the Net, reaching the community groups that were springing up across the U.S. Many were galvanized by proposed FDA regulations that would have allowed food certified as "organic" to contain genetically modified ingredients—an effort shouted down by angry consumers. Meanwhile, Greenpeace began to target U.S. companies such as Gerber, which quickly renounced the use of transgenic ingredients, and Kellogg's, which has yet to do so. With so-called Frankenfoods making headlines, several other companies cut back on biotech: McDonald's forswore genetically engineered potatoes, and Frito-Lay decreed it would buy no more genetically modified corn.

But the issue that is now on the front burner dates back to 1992, when the FDA decided that biotech ingredients did not materially alter food and therefore did not require labeling. Nor, the agency declared, was premarket safety testing required, because biotech additives were presumed to be benign. Last March the Center for Food Safety and 53 other groups, including the Union of Concerned Scientists, filed a petition to force the FDA to change its policy.

Meanwhile, the biotech issue is gathering steam in Congress, where safety and labeling bills have been introduced by Democratic Representative Dennis Kucinich of Ohio and 55 co-sponsors in the House, and by Daniel Patrick Moynihan and Barbara Boxer in the Senate. Similar statewide bills are pending in Maine, Colorado and Oregon. Shareholder resolutions demanding safety testing and labeling have targeted a score of companies from life-science giants to supermarket chains.

Surveys indicate that between two-thirds and three-quarters of Americans want biotech food to be labeled. Then why not do it? Because companies fear such disclosure could spell disaster. "Our data show that 60% of consumers would consider a mandatory biotech label as a warning that it is unsafe," says Gene Grabowski, spokesman for the Grocery Manufacturers of America. "It is easier," BIO's Eramian points out, "to scare people about biotechnology than to educate them."

The labeling threat finally spurred a hitherto complacent industry into action. Last April, Monsanto, Novartis and five other biotech companies rolled out a $50 million television advertising campaign, with soft-focus fields and smiling children, pitching "solutions that could improve our world tomorrow."

But by then the opposition was morphing from inchoate splinter groups into something that looks like a mainstream coalition. In July 1999, some 40 environmentalists, consumer advocates and organic-food activists met in Bolinas, Calif., to map a national campaign. Rather than endorse a total ban on genetically modified foods that Greenpeace was pushing, says Wendy Wendlandt, political director of the state Public Interest Research Groups, "it was more practical to call for a moratorium until the stuff is safety tested and labeled, and companies are held responsible for any harmful effects."

In May the FDA announced that in the fall it would propose new rules for genetically engineered crops and products. Instead of safety testing, it would require only that companies publicly disclose their new biotech crops before they are planted. Labeling would be voluntary.

The critics' response came last week: a campaign to muster public opposition to the FDA's new rules and to target individual companies and their previous trademarks. The mock advertisements for "Campbull's Experimental Vegetable Soup," with the advisory, "Warning: This Product Is Untested," is only the first salvo. Some 18 other brand-name U.S. companies are on a tentative hit list, including General Mills, Coca-Cola and Kraft.

Will the companies succumb to the pressure, as they have in Europe? As of last week, Campbell claimed to be unfazed, with few customers registering concern, despite the spotlight. Even at the San Francisco rally, there was some ambivalence. "I may not eat Campbell's soup as much," offered Shanae Walls, 19, a student at Contra Costa College who was there with her Environmental Science and Thought class. But as the protesters tossed products from Pepperidge Farm—a Campbell subsidiary—into the toxic-waste bin, she had second thoughts. "I love those cookies," she said wistfully. "That might take some time."

# THE GLOBAL FOOD FIGHT

**① BRUSSELS, 1998**
France, Italy, Greece, Denmark and Luxembourg team up to block introduction of all new GM products in the European Union— including those approved by E.U. scientific advisory committees and even a few developed in these five countries. Several E.U. countries have also banned the importation and use of 18 GM crops and foods approved before the blockade went into effect. New safety rules could eventually break this logjam.

**② SEATTLE, NOVEMBER 1999**
Taking to the streets to protest the spread of "Frankenfoods," among other issues, demonstrators trying to disrupt the World Trade Organization summit are tear-gassed and beaten by police.

**③ MIDWESTERN U.S., 1999**
A coalition of agricultural groups calls for a freeze on government approval of new GM seeds in light of dwindling markets in anti-GM European countries. Planting of GM corn drops from 25 million acres (10 million hectares) in 1999 to 19.9 million acres (8 million hectares) in 2000.

**④ MONTREAL, JANUARY 2000**
130 nations, including Mexico, Australia and Japan, sign the Cartagena Protocol on Biosafety, which requires an exporting country to obtain permission from an importing country before shipping GM seeds and organisms and to label such shipments with warnings that they "may contain" GM products.

## Key
▶ Strongly in favor of GM foods
▶ Somewhat in favor of GM foods
▶ Opposed to GM foods

### Canada
**POPULATION** 31,147,000
**ATTITUDE** Generally pro, though consumers are wary
*Grains make up 24.8% of diet*
**REASON** Second biggest producer of GM products, after the U.S., and a major food exporter.

–By Michael D. Lemonick. With reporting by Yudhijit Bhattacharjee and Max Rust/New York, with other bureaus

### U.S.
**POPULATION** 278,357,000
**ATTITUDE** Cautiously pro
**REASON** As a major food exporter and home to giant agribiotech businesses, led by Monsanto, the country stands to reap huge profits from GM foods.
*Grains make up 23.6% of diet*

### Argentina
**POPULATION** 37,031,000
**ATTITUDE** Pro
**REASON** Third largest producer of biotech crops in the world, after the U.S. and Canada.
*Grains make up 29.5% of diet*

### Brazil
**POPULATION** 170,116,000
**ATTITUDE** Very cautiously pro
**REASON** The country is eager to participate in the potentially profitable biotech revolution but is worried about alienating anti-GM customers in Europe.
*Grains make up 30.9% of diet*

### Britain
**POPULATION** 58,830,000
**ATTITUDE** Strongly anti
**REASON** "Mad cow" disease in beef and a report that GM potatoes caused immune-system damage in rats have alarmed most Brits. Markets ban GM foods, and experiments are tightly controlled.
*Grains make up 22.8% of diet*

### France
**POPULATION** 59,079,000
**ATTITUDE** Strongly anti
**REASON** Like Britain, France has been stung by incidents with tainted food. Its attitude is also colored by hostility to U.S. imports and a desire to protect French farmers.
*Grains make up 24.3% of diet*

(CONTINUED)

190

(CONTINUED)

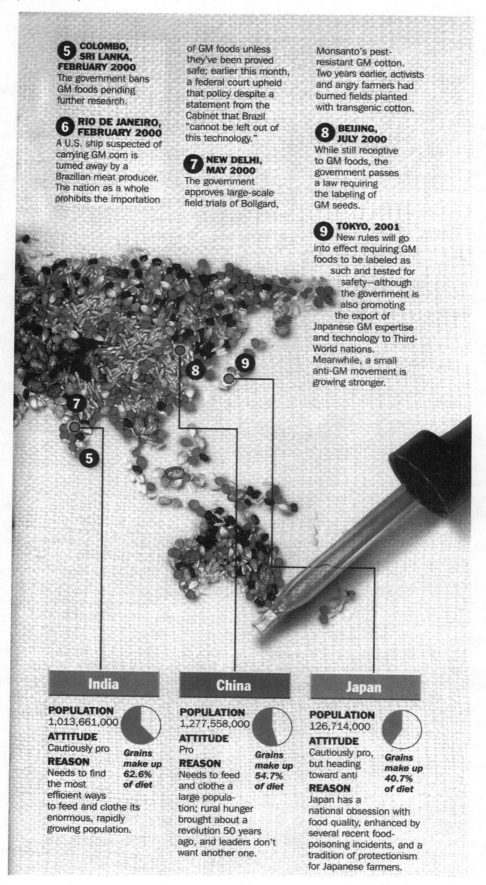

**5** COLOMBO, SRI LANKA, FEBRUARY 2000
The government bans GM foods pending further research.

**6** RIO DE JANEIRO, FEBRUARY 2000
A U.S. ship suspected of carrying GM corn is turned away by a Brazilian meat producer. The nation as a whole prohibits the importation of GM foods unless they've been proved safe; earlier this month, a federal court upheld that policy despite a statement from the Cabinet that Brazil "cannot be left out of this technology."

**7** NEW DELHI, MAY 2000
The government approves large-scale field trials of Bollgard, Monsanto's pest-resistant GM cotton. Two years earlier, activists and angry farmers had burned fields planted with transgenic cotton.

**8** BEIJING, JULY 2000
While still receptive to GM foods, the government passes a law requiring the labeling of GM seeds.

**9** TOKYO, 2001
New rules will go into effect requiring GM foods to be labeled as such and tested for safety—although the government is also promoting the export of Japanese GM expertise and technology to Third-World nations. Meanwhile, a small anti-GM movement is growing stronger.

### India

**POPULATION**
1,013,661,000

**ATTITUDE**
Cautiously pro

**REASON**
Needs to find the most efficient ways to feed and clothe its enormous, rapidly growing population.

*Grains make up 62.6% of diet*

### China

**POPULATION**
1,277,558,000

**ATTITUDE**
Pro

**REASON**
Needs to feed and clothe a large population; rural hunger brought about a revolution 50 years ago, and leaders don't want another one.

*Grains make up 54.7% of diet*

### Japan

**POPULATION**
126,714,000

**ATTITUDE**
Cautiously pro, but heading toward anti

**REASON**
Japan has a national obsession with food quality, enhanced by several recent food-poisoning incidents, and a tradition of protectionism for Japanese farmers.

*Grains make up 40.7% of diet*

Indeed, the benefits have seemed small—until golden rice came along to suggest otherwise. Golden rice is clearly not the moral equivalent of Roundup Ready beans. Quite the contrary, it is an example—the first compelling example—of a genetically engineered crop that may benefit not just the farmers who grow it but also the consumers who eat it. In this case, the consumers include at least a million children who die every year because they are weakened by vitamin-A deficiency and an additional 350,000 who go blind.

No wonder the biotech industry sees golden rice as a powerful ally in its struggle to win public acceptance. No wonder its critics see it as a cynical ploy. And no wonder so many of those concerned about the twin evils of poverty and hunger look at golden rice and see reflected in it their own passionate conviction that genetically engineered crops can be made to serve the greater public good—that in fact such crops have a critical role to play in feeding a world that is about to add to its present population of 6 billion. As former President Jimmy Carter put it, "Responsible biotechnology is not the enemy; starvation is."

Indeed, by the year 2020, the demand for grain, both for human consumption and for animal feed, is projected to go up by nearly half, while the amount of arable land available to satisfy that demand will not only grow much more slowly but also, in some areas, will probably dwindle. Add to that the need to conserve overstressed water resources and reduce the use of polluting chemicals, and the enormity of the challenge becomes apparent. In order to meet it, believes Gordon Conway, the agricultural ecologist who heads the Rockefeller Foundation, 21st century farmers will have to draw on every arrow in their agricultural quiver, including genetic engineering. And contrary to public perception, he says, those who have the least to lose and the most to gain are not well-fed Americans and Europeans but the hollow-bellied citizens of the developing world.

## GOING FOR THE GOLD

IT WAS IN THE LATE 1980s, AFTER HE became a full professor of plant science at the Swiss Federal Institute of Technology, that Ingo Potrykus started to think about using genetic engineering to improve the nutritional qualities of rice. He knew that of some 3 billion people who depend on rice as their major staple, around 10% risk some degree of vitamin-A deficiency and the health problems that result. The reason, some alleged, was an overreliance on rice ushered in by the green revolution. Whatever its cause, the result was distressing: these people were so poor that they ate a few bowls of rice a day and almost nothing more.

The problem interested Potrykus for a number of reasons. For starters, he was attracted by the scientific challenge of transferring not just a single gene, as many had already done, but a group of genes that represented a key part of a biochemical pathway. He was also motivated by complex emotions, among them empathy. Potrykus knew more than most what it meant not to have enough to eat. As a child growing up in war-ravaged Germany, he and his brothers were often so desperately hungry that they ate what they could steal.

Around 1990, Potrykus hooked up with Gary Toenniessen, director of food security for the Rockefeller Foundation. Toenniessen had identified the lack of beta-carotene in polished rice grains as an appropriate target for gene scientists like Potrykus to tackle because it lay beyond the ability of traditional plant breeding to address. For while rice, like other green plants, contains light-trapping beta-carotene in its external tissues, no plant in the entire *Oryza* genus—as far as anyone knew—produced beta-carotene in its endosperm (the starchy interior part of the rice grain that is all most people eat).

It was at a Rockefeller-sponsored meeting that Potrykus met the University of Freiburg's Peter Beyer, an expert on the beta-carotene pathway in daffodils. By combining their expertise, the two scientists figured, they might be able to remedy this unfortunate oversight in nature. So in 1993, with some $100,000 in seed money from the Rockefeller Foundation, Potrykus and Beyer launched what turned into a seven-year, $2.6 million project, backed also by the Swiss government and the European Union. "I was in a privileged situation," reflects Potrykus, "because I was able to operate without industrial support. Only in that situation can you think of giving away your work free."

That indeed is what Potrykus announced he and Beyer planned to do. The two scientists soon discovered, however, that giving away golden rice was not going to be as easy as they thought. The genes they transferred and the bacteria they used to transfer those genes were all encumbered by patents and proprietary rights. Three months ago, the two scientists struck a deal with AstraZeneca, which is based in London and holds an exclusive license to one of the genes Potrykus and Beyer used to create golden rice. In exchange for commercial marketing rights in the U.S. and other affluent markets, AstraZeneca agreed to lend its financial muscle and legal expertise to the cause of putting the seeds into the hands of poor farmers at no charge.

No sooner had the deal been made than the critics of agricultural biotechnology erupted. "A rip-off of the public trust," grumbled the Rural Advancement Foundation International, an advocacy group based in Winnipeg, Canada. "Asian farmers get (unproved) genetically modified rice, and AstraZeneca gets the 'gold.'" Potrykus was dismayed by such negative reaction. "It would be irresponsible," he exclaimed, "not to say immoral, not to use biotechnology to try to solve this problem!" But such expressions of good intentions would not be enough to allay his opponents' fears.

## WEIGHING THE PERILS

BENEATH THE HYPERBOLIC TALK OF Frankenfoods and Superweeds, even proponents of agricultural biotechnology agree, lie a number of real concerns. To begin with, all foods, including the transgenic foods created through genetic engineering, are potential sources of allergens. That's because the transferred genes contain instructions for making proteins, and not all proteins are equal. Some—those in peanuts, for example—are well known for causing allergic reactions. To many, the possibility that golden rice might cause such a problem seems farfetched, but it nonetheless needs to be considered.

Then there is the problem of "genetic pollution," as opponents of biotechnology term it. Pollen grains from such wind-pollinated plants as corn and canola, for instance, are carried far and wide. To farmers, this mainly poses a nuisance. Transgenic canola grown in one field, for example, can very easily pollinate nontransgenic plants grown in the next. Indeed this is the reason behind the furor that recently erupted in Europe when it was discovered that canola seeds from Canada—unwittingly planted by farmers in England, France, Germany and Sweden—contained transgenic contaminants.

The continuing flap over Bt corn and cotton—now grown not only in the U.S. but also in Argentina and China—has provided more fodder for debate. Bt stands for a common soil bacteria, *Bacillus thuringiensis*, different strains of which produce toxins that target specific insects. By transferring to corn and cotton the bacterial gene responsible for making this toxin, Monsanto and other companies have produced crops that are resistant to the European corn borer and the cotton bollworm. An immediate concern, raised by a number of ecologists, is whether or not widespread planting of these crops

will spur the development of resistance to Bt among crop pests. That would be unfortunate, they point out, because Bt is a safe and effective natural insecticide that is popular with organic farmers.

## SQUEEZE ME: Scientists turned off the gene that makes tomatoes soft and squishy

Even more worrisome are ecological concerns. In 1999 Cornell University entomologist John Losey performed a provocative, "seat-of-the-pants" laboratory experiment. He dusted Bt corn pollen on plants populated by monarch-butterfly caterpillars. Many of the caterpillars died. Could what happened in Losey's laboratory happen in cornfields across the Midwest? Were these lovely butterflies, already under pressure owing to human encroachment on their Mexican wintering grounds, about to face a new threat from high-tech farmers in the north?

The upshot: despite studies pro and con—and countless save-the-monarch protests acted out by children dressed in butterfly costumes—a conclusive answer to this question has yet to come. Losey himself is not yet convinced that Bt corn poses a grave danger to North America's monarch-butterfly population, but he does think the issue deserves attention. And others agree. "I'm not anti biotechnology per se," says biologist Rebecca Goldberg, a senior scientist with the Environmental Defense Fund, "but I would like to have a tougher regulatory regime. These crops should be subject to more careful screening before they are released."

Are there more potential pitfalls? There are. Among other things, there is the possibility that as transgenes in pollen drift, they will fertilize wild plants, and weeds will emerge that

are hardier and even more difficult to control. No one knows how common the exchange of genes between domestic plants and their wild relatives really is, but Margaret Mellon, director of the Union of Concerned Scientists' agriculture and biotechnology program, is certainly not alone in thinking that it's high time we find out. Says she: "People should be responding to these concerns with experiments, not assurances."

And that is beginning to happen, although—contrary to expectations—the reports coming in are not necessarily that scary. For three years now, University of Arizona entomologist Bruce Tabashnik has been monitoring fields of Bt cotton that farmers have planted in his state. And in this instance at least, he says, "the environmental risks seem minimal, and the benefits seem great." First of all, cotton is self-pollinated rather than wind-pollinated, so that the spread of the Bt gene is of less concern. And because the Bt gene is so effective, he notes, Arizona farmers have reduced their use of chemical insecticides 75%. So far, the pink bollworm population has not rebounded, indicating that the feared resistance to Bt has not yet developed.

## ASSESSING THE PROMISE

ARE THE CRITICS OF AGRICULtural biotechnology right? Is biotech's promise nothing more than overblown corporate hype? The papaya growers in Hawaii's Puna district clamor to disagree. In 1992 a wildfire epidemic of papaya ringspot virus threatened to destroy the state's papaya industry; by 1994, nearly half the state's papaya acreage had been infected, their owners forced to seek outside employment. But then help arrived, in the form of a virus-resistant transgenic papaya developed by Cornell University plant pathologist Dennis Gonsalves. In 1995 a team of scientists set up a field trial of two transgenic lines—UH SunUP and UH Rainbow—and by 1996, the verdict had been rendered. As everyone could see, the nontransgenic plants in the field trial were a stunted mess, and the transgenic plants were healthy. In 1998, after negotiations with four patent holders, the papaya growers switched en masse to the transgenic seeds and reclaimed their orchards. "Consumer acceptance has been great," reports Rusty Perry, who runs a papaya farm near Puna. "We've found that customers are more concerned with how the fruits look and taste than with whether they are transgenic or not."

Viral diseases, along with insect infestations, are a major cause of crop loss in Africa, observes Kenyan plant scientist Florence Wambugu. African sweet-potato fields, for example, yield only 2.4 tons per acre, vs. more than double that in the rest of the world. Soon Wambugu hopes to start raising those yields by introducing a transgenic sweet potato that is resistant to the feathery mottle virus. There really is no other option, explains Wambugu, who currently directs the International Service for the Acquisition of Agri-biotech Applications in Nairobi. "You can't control the virus in the field, and you can't breed in resistance through conventional means."

To Wambugu, the flap in the U.S. and Europe over genetically engineered crops seems almost ludicrous. In Africa, she notes, nearly half the fruit and vegetable harvest is lost because it rots on the way to market. "If we had a transgenic banana that ripened more slowly," she says, "we could have 40% more bananas than now." Wambugu also dreams of getting access to herbicide-resistant crops. Says she: "We could liberate so many people if our crops were resistant to herbicides that we could then spray on the surrounding weeds. Weeding enslaves Africans; it keeps children from school."

In Wambugu's view, there are more benefits to be derived from agricultural biotechnology in Africa than practically anywhere else on the planet—and this may be so. Among the genetic-engineering projects funded by the Rockefeller Foundation is one aimed at controlling striga, a weed that parasitizes the roots of African corn plants. At present there is little farmers can do about striga infestation, so tightly intertwined are the weed's roots with the roots of the corn plants it targets. But scientists have come to understand the source of the problem: corn roots exude chemicals that attract striga. So it may prove possible to identify the genes that are responsible and turn them off.

The widespread perception that agricultural biotechnology is intrinsically inimical to the environment perplexes the Rockefeller Foundation's Conway, who views genetic engineering as an important tool for achieving what he has termed a "doubly green revolution." If the technology can marshal a plant's natural defenses against weeds and viruses, if it can induce crops to flourish with minimal application of chemical fertilizers, if it can make dryland agriculture more productive without straining local water supplies, then what's wrong with it?

Of course, these particular breakthroughs have not happened yet. But as the genomes of major crops are ever more finely mapped, and as the tools for transferring genes become ever more precise, the possibility for tinkering with complex biochemical pathways can be expected to expand rapidly. As Potrykus sees it, there is no question that agricultural biotechnology can be harnessed for the good of humankind. The only question is whether there is the collective will to do so. And the answer may well emerge as the people of the world weigh the future of golden rice.

*—With reporting by Simon Robinson/Nairobi*

# A New Strategy for the New Face of Terrorism

L. Paul Bremer, III

"THE THIRD World War was begun on Tuesday, September 11, on the East Coast of the United States"—so began the French magazine *L'Express* two days later. Whether these words turn out to be prediction or exaggeration will depend on how the world now reacts to the new face of terrorism represented by the vicious attacks of that day.

The September 11 atrocities made for the most dramatic day in American history, dwarfing even the events at Pearl Harbor sixty years ago. Three times as many Americans died in New York and Washington as died at Pearl Harbor. And this time innocent civilians, not military men, were the intended targets. But this was not just an attack on America. Citizens of at least eighty countries died in the collapsed World Trade towers. We are all, in a direct way, victims of the new terrorism.

## The Changing Nature of Terrorism

WHILE THE attacks were shocking for their audacity and effectiveness, they should have surprised no serious student of terrorism. A large-scale attack on American soil has been widely predicted by experts. For years they have drawn attention to a disturbing paradox: while the number of international terrorist incidents has been declining over the past decade, the number of casualties has risen. This trend reflects the changing motives of terrorists.

During the 1970s and 1980s, most terrorist groups had limited political motives. For them, terrorism was a tactic mainly to draw attention to their "cause." These groups reasoned that many people would sympathize with that cause if only they were made aware of it. Designing their tactics to support this objective, these "old-style" terrorists rarely engaged in indiscriminate mass killing. They rightly concluded such attacks would disgust the very audiences they were trying to convert to their cause. So most terrorist groups designed their attacks to kill enough people to draw in the press but not so many as to repel the public. Often they used terror to force negotia-

tions on some issue, such as the release of jailed comrades. As one terrorism expert put it, these groups were seeking a place at the negotiating table.

Eventually, most terrorist groups in Europe overplayed their hands and the publics turned against them. But anti-terrorism policies helped win the day. With vigorous American leadership, European countries and the United States developed a counter-terrorist strategy to deal with this threat. At the heart of that strategy were three principles: make no concessions to terrorists; treat terrorists as criminals to be brought to justice; and punish states that support terrorism. On balance, this strategy worked.

Over the past decade, however, it has become clear that many terrorist groups are motivated less by narrow political goals and more by ideological, apocalyptic or religious fanaticism. Sometimes their goal is simply hatred or revenge, and tactics have changed to reflect these motives. Rather than avoiding large-scale casualties, these terrorists seek to kill as many people as possible. They are unconstrained by the respect for human life that undergirds all the world's great religions. including Islam.

Beginning with the downing of Pan Am Flight 103 in December 1988, through the first World Trade Center bombing in 1993, to the chemical attacks in the Tokyo subways in 1995 and the attacks on two U.S. embassies in East Africa in 1998, terrorist actions have resulted in increasing numbers of casualties. The September 11 attacks killed more than 5,000 people, making it the single worst terrorist attack in world history.

Things could get even worse. During the 1990s, concerns arose that terrorists might use chemical, biological, radiological or nuclear agents. In the 1980s, terrorist groups could have developed such weapons, but they did not do so, apparently calculating that their use would make public support for their causes less likely. But far from steering away from such agents, the new terrorists might find these weapons attractive precisely because they can kill tens of thousands. This was the goal, fortunately unrealized, of Aum Shinrikyo's chemical attack on the Tokyo subway. Indeed, there is evidence that some new terrorist groups, including bin Laden's Al-Qaeda, have tried to acquire nuclear, biological and chemical agents. It is known that the terrorist states of North Korea, Iraq, Iran, Libya and Syria all have tried to develop nuclear, chemical and biological weapons. Moreover, in the 1990s, information about chemical and biological agents became widely available on the Internet. The recent anthrax attacks may foreshadow a major escalation to bioterrorism by Islamist and perhaps other terrorists.

The changed motives of these "new-style" terrorists mean that at least two-thirds of the West's old strategy is out-moded. One pillar of that strategy, not making concessions to terrorists, remains valid. But it may be irrelevant when faced with groups like Al-Qaeda. Such groups are not trying to start negotiations. They make no negotiable "demands" that the West can comply with to forestall further attacks. These men do not seek a seat at the table; they want to overturn the table and kill everybody at it.

It is an honorable reflection of the basic friendliness of the American people that most of us find it difficult to believe that anybody hates Americans. Many find it especially confusing that men who lived among us, sometimes for years, attending our schools and shopping in our malls, should hate the very society whose freedoms they enjoyed. That they somehow must not understand us is the first reaction of many.

But this reaction reflects a misunderstanding about the new terrorists. They hate America precisely because they *do* understand our society; they hate its freedoms, its commitment to equal rights and universal suffrage, its material successes and its appeal to so many non-Americans. Thus, the question of whether or not to make concessions in the face of such hatred is simply irrelevant. Nothing America can say or do, short of ceasing to exist, will satisfy these terrorists.

Our long-standing objective of "bringing terrorists to justice", the second pillar of U.S. strategy, is also irrelevant to the new fight. During the past decade, an increasing percentage of terrorist attacks, especially those conducted by Middle Eastern groups, have involved suicides. This underscores the perpetrators' extraordinary commitment to terror, but it also shows the futility of relying on the concept of using criminal justice to punish them. Men who are prepared to die in an airplane crash are not going to be deterred by the threat of being locked in a prison cell. We need to revise our thinking; now our goal should be, as President Bush has suggested, "bringing justice to the terrorists."

*Terrorism—The New Face of War*

IN THE BROADER sense, the September 11 attacks preview the kind of security threat America will face in the 21st century. Terrorism allows the weak to attack the

strong. It is relatively inexpensive to conduct, and devilishly difficult to counter.

Relative to all the other powers in the world, America is stronger than any country has ever been in history. The Gulf War showed that even a lavishly equipped conventional force (at the time, Iraq possessed the world's fifth largest army) was no match for America. The lesson for would-be tyrants and terrorists was clear: America could only be attacked by unconventional means, and terrorism is a fundamental tactic of asymmetrical warfare.

Terrorists take advantage of two important asymmetries. First, in the fight against terrorism, defenders have to protect all their points of vulnerability around the world; the terrorist has only to attack the weakest point. This lesson was brought home to the U.S. government when Al-Qaeda attacked the American embassies in Nairobi and Dar es-Salaam in August 1998, two embassies thought to be in little danger and thus ill-protected.

Secondly, the costs of launching a terrorist attack are a fraction of the costs required to defend against it. To shoot up an airport, a terrorist needs only an AK-47 assault rifle; defending that same airport costs millions of dollars. The September 11 attacks probably cost less than $2 million and caused over $100 billion in damage and business interruption. Thus, the new terrorism reverses the conventional wisdom that, in military operations, the offense must be three times as strong as the defense.

How, then, are we to fight this new and increasingly dangerous threat?

The proper objective of a counter-terrorist policy is to prevent attacks before they happen. So, more than in any other field of foreign and national security affairs, success in the fight against terrorism depends on having good intelligence. But there is no more difficult or dangerous kind of intelligence to collect. The surest way to know about an attack ahead of time is to have somebody tell you the plans. That means having a spy in the terrorist group itself.

Inserting an agent inside a terrorist group is among any intelligence agency's most difficult task. These groups are by nature clandestine and suspicious, even paranoid. Membership is often based on ethnic, tribal, clan or family ties, so Western intelligence agencies can rarely use their own nationals to infiltrate such groups.

There are two other possibilities for getting this valuable "human intelligence." Our agencies can, and do, work with friendly intelligence agencies in the Middle East. Often those organizations can use their own nationals to infiltrate terrorist cells. And if we handle such a relationship properly, our government can get useful and timely information about terrorist plans that enables us to disrupt them before they can be carried out. Such a relationship helped foil Al-Qaeda's planned millennium celebration attacks.

The second path is for the CIA itself to recruit a member of the group. This is exceptionally dangerous since the penalty, if caught spying, is certain death. We have also made the task more difficult for ourselves. Over the past 25 years, the United States has seriously undermined its capability to acquire "human intelligence." In the mid-1970s, politicized attacks by Congress damaged CIA operations and morale. In the late 1970s, a large number of the Agency's best officers specializing in collecting human intelligence were fired. These trends were exacerbated when, in 1995, the Clinton Administration imposed rigid and bureaucratic procedures governing the Agency's recruitment of spies who themselves have been involved with terrorist organizations. These new guidelines had the effect of making such recruitments even more difficult than they already were.

The bipartisan National Commission on Terrorism, which I chaired, carefully investigated the effect of these 1995 "guidelines." During our work in 2000, we heard testimony from serving CIA officers, at home and abroad, from first-tour case officers to station chiefs. Their testimony was unambiguous, unanimous and conclusive: the "guidelines" were an obstacle to the recruitment of effective spies in the struggle against terrorism. We strongly recommended their immediate cancellation.

The CIA's response to this recommendation was curious. Its leaders stated that they had never turned down a proposal *presented to them* to recruit a terrorist spy. But this entirely misses the point. By the time a proposed recruitment makes it to the CIA's leadership, it has already passed through a welter of rules, regulations, procedures, committees and lawyers that essentially guarantees that only the least suspect person will be suggested (assuming that after this tortuous and time-consuming process the terrorist is still around to recruit).

As the Bremer Commission noted, the major problem with the "guidelines" is the effect they have in the field. Officer after officer confirmed to our commissioners that the prospect of having to navigate Washington's bureaucratic jungle-gym was a clear disincentive even to begin the process of such recruitments. Many officers told us that they simply decided to go after easier targets. The "guidelines" have become an effective, though undesirable, bureaucratic prophylactic against risk-taking. They must be changed.

## A New Strategy for Countering Terrorism

THE ELEMENTS of a new strategy to deal with the new threat are at hand. We need only the will to implement that strategy.

Our strategic objective must be to deny terrorist groups safe havens from which they can operate and garner various kinds of support from governments. As President Bush stated in his September 20 address, America intends to punish not just the terrorists but any group or state that has in any way supported them.

We must apply this strategy ruthlessly and creatively. Our tactics should range across the entire spectrum of activity from diplomacy, political pressure and economic measures, to military, psychological and covert operations. As the President has emphasized, this will be a long campaign demanding patience and cunning. The battle will be less like an American football game, with its fixed "battle lines" and clearly defined moves (as in the Gulf War), and more like European football: open, fluid and improvisational.

American actions must move beyond the episodic and limp-wristed attacks of the past decade, actions that seemed designed to "signal" our seriousness to the terrorists without inflicting any real damage on them. Naturally, their feebleness demonstrated the opposite. This time the terrorists and their supporters must be eliminated.

Our strategy should operate in three concentric circles. In the first and innermost circle, we must deal decisively with those most immediately responsible for the September attack. This means destroying all the terrorist camps, personnel and infrastructure in Afghanistan and getting rid of the Taliban regime. We must avoid thinking that the fight is only about bin Laden. It is one of the habitual failings of U.S. policy to over-emphasize one individual terrorist and ignore the broader dangers. In the late 1970s, Libya's Muammar Qaddafi was America's enemy number one. In the mid-1980's, Abu Nidal took his place. Ten years later, it was, and remains today, bin Laden.

There are two dangers with this approach. First, it tends to build up the terrorist leader, in his own eyes and in the eyes of his supporters. The concentration on one individual may thus paradoxically make it easier for him to find new recruits. Secondly, over-emphasis on one man may mislead the public into thinking that if only the "bad guy" could be eliminated, the terrorist problem would go away. It's just not so. Even if bin Laden were to die today, our problems would not end, for Afghanistan has become a cesspool of terrorism, much as Lebanon was in the 1980s. At least a half dozen other terrorist groups have training camps and facilities in the country, all welcomed by the Taliban. That is why our initial actions must go beyond destroying the terrorist camps. As long as the Taliban rule in Afghanistan, the terrorists' infrastructure can be quickly reconstituted.

It would be preferable if the Afghan people, who have suffered greatly under the harsh rule of the Taliban, could throw that regime out themselves. Certainly, the West should encourage this by supporting the exiled king, Mohammed Zahir, in his call for an uprising. Still popular among the Afghan people, the king is a Pashtun and thus has a crucial role to play in the establishment of a credible alternative government (though we must respect his need to avoid being seen as an American puppet).

This political strategy must be wedded to a three-pronged military plan. Our military forces and those of our allies must first degrade the Taliban's military capabilities. This will bring about a new balance of forces on the ground. Then we must encourage the creation and arming of an effective Pashtun military force, using as its core those Taliban commanders who have already defected. Finally, we and our allies should support the Northern Alliance, which still controls 10 to 15 percent of the country and which has support among the Tajik, Uzbek and Hazara communities.

The harsh reality is that any campaign that does not result in a change of regime in Kabul will be a failure. This is the *sine qua non* of our entire strategy. We therefore cannot exclude the possibility that it may be necessary to introduce ground troops into this hostile topography.

America's seriousness of purpose in the new war on terrorism will be demonstrated by U.S. and allied actions in this first phase. If we are weak, hesitant or ineffective, we will pay a heavy price later.

## Ending State Support for Terrorism

THE SECOND objective of our strategy must be to deny terrorists operating bases. This means rooting out terrorist camps, bases and cells wherever they are, including the United States. It is likely that some of the Al-Qaeda terrorists will escape us in Afghanistan. They will try to relocate elsewhere, perhaps seeking out friendly governments or weak states in the Middle East, Central Asia or in Africa. We must pursue them and destroy them, with or without the help of the relevant governments.

The President made clear in his address to the American people on September 20 that any state that harbors or supports terrorist groups will be henceforth considered "a hostile regime." This statement has important implications beyond the obvious countries of Iran and Iraq. Syria, with which our European allies and we have regular diplomatic relations, still hosts over a dozen terrorist groups. So do Sudan and Lebanon.

Yet for too long American policy has contented itself with merely identifying states that support terrorism without forcing any serious consequences upon them in turn. Our European allies have been even less forceful, seeming to ignore state involvement in terrorism, often in the hopes of winning commercial advantage. For example, the European Union's long running "constructive dialogue" with Iran may have won European firms handsome contracts to develop Iranian energy resources, but it has not in any respect altered Iran's continued and open support for Middle East terrorist groups. Iran remains the world's leading state sponsor of terrorism. Groups such as Hamas, the Palestinian Islamic Jihad and Hizballah, which regularly target innocent civilians, all depend on Iranian support. In fact, as the State Department has pointed out, Iranian involvement in terror has actually increased since the election of Mohammad Khatemi as president four years ago.

Some commentators argue that the new terrorism is caused by discontent with America's role in supporting Israel. The implication is that if America would just weaken that support, the terrorism would end. This argument is wrong on two counts. First, bin Laden has made clear in his own words, for years, that he attacks America because he hates who we are, not because of whom we support. Secondly, dealing effectively with radical Islam is the prerequisite to moving toward a broader regional peace, not the other way around. It was America's decisive (though incomplete) victory over Iraq in 1991 that was the necessary precondition for the Oslo peace process. Now as then, countries in the Middle East and Europe will pay attention to American ideas for regional security when we have shown that we are prepared to act decisively against threats to that security.

## A War on Islam?

PRESIDENT BUSH and all his senior advisors have been clear: We do not consider the American response to the September 11 attacks to be a war against Islam. He is right. Bin Laden and his allies in the Taliban are a fringe minority far removed from the teachings of mainstream Islam. But there is a real danger now that "moderate" Muslims are allowing these radicals to hijack Islam, and thus to define Islam as an enemy of the West. Until now, we have heard too few voices of restraint from the Islamic world. Quite the contrary. For example, through their controlled media, the Palestinians and even some "moderate" Arab governments have spewed out anti-American hatred with impunity for years. On the very day of the suicide attacks, the newspaper of the Palestinian Authority, *al-Hayat al-Jadida,* praised suicide bombers as "noble… the salt of the earth, the engines of history…. They are the most honorable among us." Inflammatory articles like this have contributed to an environment that made possible the appalling spectacle of schoolchildren in Gaza and Ramallah cheering the news of the American tragedies.

Europeans, who provide the bulk of money to the Palestinians, should make clear that until such inflammatory rhetoric stops, there will be no more euros for Yasir Arafat. Nor should American taxpayers be expected to send another penny to the Palestinian Authority until Arafat roots out, expels or imprisons the Hamas, Hizballah and Islamic Jihad terrorists who oeprate from his territory.

In Pakistan, Islamic *madrassas* regularly indoctrinate young boys to hate America. At one school, after the September 11 attack, eight year-old boys vied with one another to be the one who would grow up to bring down the Sears Tower in Chicago. Here in America, some Islamic leaders have said that the September 11 attacks violate the Quran. But several have then made the astonishing statement that, this being the case, Israelis or Americans themselves must have conducted the attacks.

Moderate Islam is on the front line now. Its leaders have a solemn responsibility to make clear, in public, that the purposeful slaughter of innocent civilians is anathema to Islamic beliefs and that those who commit such acts are apostates who will go to hell, not to heaven. Unless they speak out now, there is a real risk that Islam will be defined by the radicals at war with the West. And then this *will* become a war with Islam, delcared *by* Islam.

## Delegitimizing Terror

FINALLY, American strategy must have as a broader objective rebuilding the international consensus against terrorism that flourished briefly during the 1980s, but then fell into neglect. If done effectively, this can delegitimize terror.

There are many areas where better cooperation will prove useful. Intelligence cooperation is the most urgent need. Clearly, no matter how good its intelligence organization, no one nation alone can hope to gather enough specific information on a worldwide terrorist network. In the wake of the September 11 attacks, it has become clear that America's intelligence failure was mirrored in many other countries: none seemed to be taking seriously enough the clear declarations of war by bin Laden, and none was sufficiently attentive to the activities of suspicious people. Sharing intelligence with friendly countries is an essential step in developing a common strategy. As noted, during the 1980s America and its European partners found ways to deepen cooperation in this vital area. This effort must now be accelerated and broadened to include cooperation with friendly Muslim states.

There must also be more vigorous and persistent efforts to track terrorist funds. Too often, terrorist groups have been able to use front organizations, nongovernmental organizations and willing dupes to raise and distribute money. Out of ignorance, laziness or cowardice, most governments have looked the other way. The recent U.S. decision to seize terrorist assets is a good first step. So is the UN Security Council resolution calling on all states to take robust action against terrorist finances.

To maintain broad support for the struggle against terrorism, the United States will have to accept that the problem goes beyond those terrorist groups with a "global reach." While such groups are the proper objective of our initial strategy, we will have to show that we share the concerns of our allies who are subjected to Irish and Basque terrorism, for example, if we are to get continuing support from Britain and Spain in the fight.

As to legal matters, no doubt there will be proposals for new international conventions and treaties concerning terrorism and state support for it. Each of these should be examined on its merits and pursued where useful. But we should not let the search for an illusive international legal consensus stop us from vigorous action against known terrorist groups or states.

WE HAVE seen the face of the new threat to our security in the 21st century. Under Article 51 of the United Nations Charter, the United States is fully justified in taking any and all means of self-defense against that threat. The United States has made clear that it welcomes the assistance of any country in anti-terrorist military operations, and so far the American government has done a masterful job of assembling broad support for the initial phase of the campaign in Afghanistan. The challenge will be to sustain that support as the battle wears on, and especially when the campaign enters the second phase, after we have dealt with Afghanistan.

We must destroy the terrorists before they destroy us. They hate us and are so dangerous that they must be stopped before they can take the battle to a still higher plane of lethality. We must disrupt, dismantle or destroy terrorist groups wherever they are and deny them safe havens. Americans should therefore be under no illusions about the campaign we have embarked upon. There will be war with more than one country. As in all wars, there will be civilian casualties. America will win some battles but lose others. More Americans will die. But neither our allies nor our enemies should be in any doubt: We shall prevail.

---

### "The Martyr"

There is sobbing of the strong,
And a pall upon the land;
But the People in their weeping
Bare the iron hand:
Beware the People weeping
When they bare the iron hand.

—Herman Melville

---

Ambassador L. Paul Bremer, III is chairman and chief executive officer of Marsh Crisis Consulting. He served as chairman of the National Commission on Terrorism.

Reprinted with permission of *The National Interest*, No. 65-s (Thanksgiving 2001), pp. 23-30. © 2001 by The National Interest, Washington, DC.

# Why Don't They Like Us?

How America Has Become the Object of Much of the Planet's Genuine Grievances—and Displaced Discontents

BY STANLEY HOFFMANN

It wasn't its innocence that the United States lost on September 11, 2001. It was its naïveté. Americans have tended to believe that in the eyes of others the United States has lived up to the boastful clichés propagated during the Cold War (especially under Ronald Reagan) and during the Clinton administration. We were seen, we thought, as the champions of freedom against fascism and communism, as the advocates of decolonization, economic development, and social progress, as the technical innovators whose mastery of technology, science, and advanced education was going to unify the world.

Some officials and academics explained that U.S. hegemony was the best thing for a troubled world and unlike past hegemonies would last—not only because there were no challengers strong enough to steal the crown but, above all, because we were benign rulers who threatened no one.

But we have avoided looking at the hegemon's clay feet, at what might neutralize our vaunted soft power and undermine our hard power. Like swarming insects exposed when a fallen tree is lifted, millions who dislike or distrust the hegemon have suddenly appeared after September 11, much to our horror and disbelief. America became a great power after World War II, when we faced a rival that seemed to stand for everything we had been fighting against—tyranny, terror, brainwashing—and we thought that our international reputation would benefit from our standing for liberty and stability (as it still does in much of Eastern Europe). We were not sufficiently marinated in history to know that, through the ages, nobody—or almost nobody—has ever loved a hegemon.

Past hegemons, from Rome to Great Britain, tended to be quite realistic about this. They wanted to be obeyed or, as in the case of France, admired. They rarely wanted to be loved. But as a combination of high-noon sheriff and proselytizing missionary, the United States expects gratitude and affection. It was bound to be disappointed; gratitude is not an emotion that one associates with the behavior of states.

## THE NEW WORLD DISORDER

This is an old story. Two sets of factors make the current twist a new one. First, the so-called Westphalian world has collapsed. The world of sovereign states, the universe of Hans Morgenthau's and Henry Kissinger's Realism, is no longer. The unpopularity of the hegemonic power has been heightened to incandescence by two aspects of this collapse. One is the irruption of the public, the masses, in international affairs. Foreign policy is no longer, as Raymond Aron had written in *Peace and War*, the closed domain of the soldier and the diplomat. Domestic publics—along with their interest groups, religious organizations, and ideological chapels—either dictate or constrain the imperatives and preferences that the governments fight for. This puts the hegemon in a difficult position: It often must work with governments that represent but a small percentage of a country's people—but if it fishes for public support abroad, it risks alienating leaders whose cooperation it needs. The United States paid heavily for not having had enough contacts with the opposition to the shah of Iran in the 1970s. It discovers today that there is an abyss in Pakistan, Saudi Arabia, Egypt, and Indonesia between our official allies and the populace in these countries. Diplomacy in a world where the masses, so to speak, stayed indoors, was a much easier game.

The collapse of the barrier between domestic and foreign affairs in the state system is now accompanied by a disease that attacks the state system itself. Many of the "states" that are members of the United Nations are pseudo-states with shaky or shabby institutions, no basic consensus on values or on procedures among their heterogeneous components, and no sense of national identity. Thus the hegemon—in addition to suffering the hostility of the government in certain countries (like Cuba, Iraq, and North Korea) and of the public in others (like, in varying degrees, Pakistan, Egypt, and even France)—can now easily become both the target of factions fighting one another in disintegrating countries and the pawn in their quarrels (which range over such increasingly borderless issues as drug trafficking, arms trading, money laundering, and other criminal enterprises). In addition, today's hegemon suffers from the volatility and turbulence of a global system in which ethnic, religious, and ideological sympathies have become transnational and in which groups and individuals uncontrolled by states can act on their own. The world of the nineteenth century, when hegemons could impose their order, their institutions, has been supplanted by the world of the twenty-first century: Where once there was order, there is now often a vacuum.

What makes the American Empire especially vulnerable is its historically unique combination of assets and liabilities. One has to go back to the Roman Empire to find a comparable set of resources. Britain, France, and Spain had to operate in multipolar systems; the United States is the only superpower.

But if America's means are vast, the limits of its power are also considerable. The United States, unlike Rome, cannot simply impose its will by force or through satellite states. Small "rogue" states can defy the hegemon (remember Vietnam?). And chaos can easily result from the large new role of nonstate actors. Meanwhile, the reluctance of Americans to take on the Herculean tasks of policing, "nation building," democratizing autocracies, and providing environmental protection and economic growth for billions of human beings stokes both resentment and hostility, especially among those who discover that one can count on American presence and leadership only when America's material interests are gravely threatened. (It is not surprising that the "defense of the national interest" approach of Realism was developed for a multipolar world. In an empire, as well as in a bipolar system, almost anything can be described as a vital interest, since even peripheral disorder can unravel the superpower's eminence.) Moreover, the complexities of America's process for making foreign-policy decisions can produce disappointments abroad when policies that the international community counted on—such as the Kyoto Protocol and the International Criminal Court—are thwarted. Also, the fickleness of U.S. foreign-policy making in arenas like the Balkans has convinced many American enemies that this country is basically incapable of pursuing long-term policies consistently.

NONE OF THIS MEANS, OF COURSE, THAT THE UNITED STATES has no friends in the world. Europeans have not forgotten the liberating role played by Americans in the war against Hitler and in the Cold War. Israel remembers how President Harry Truman sided with the founders of the Zionist state; nor has it forgotten all the help the United States has given it since then. The democratizations of postwar Germany and Japan were huge successes. The Marshall Plan and the Point Four Program were revolutionary initiatives. The decisions to resist aggression in Korea and in Kuwait demonstrated a commendable farsightedness.

But Americans have a tendency to overlook the dark sides of their course (except on the protesting left, which is thus constantly accused of being un-American), perhaps because they perceive international affairs in terms of crusades between good and evil, endeavors that entail formidable pressures for unanimity. It is not surprising that the decade following the Gulf

War was marked both by nostalgia for the clear days of the Cold War and by a lot of floundering and hesitating in a world without an overwhelming foe.

## STRAINS OF ANTI-AMERICANISM

The main criticisms of American behavior have mostly been around for a long time. When we look at anti-Americanism today, we must first distinguish between those who attack the United States for what it does, or fails to do, and those who attack it for what it is. (Some, like the Islamic fundamentalists and terrorists, attack it for both reasons.) Perhaps the principal criticism is of the contrast between our ideology of universal liberalism and policies that have all too often consisted of supporting and sometimes installing singularly authoritarian and repressive regimes. (One reason why these policies often elicited more reproaches than Soviet control over satellites was that, as time went by, Stalinism became more and more cynical and thus the gap between words and deeds became far less wide than in the United States. One no longer expected much from Moscow.) The list of places where America failed at times to live up to its proclaimed ideals is long: Guatemala, Panama, El Salvador, Chile, Santo Domingo in 1965, the Greece of the colonels, Pakistan, the Philippines of Ferdinand Marcos, Indonesia after 1965, the shah's Iran, Saudi Arabia, Zaire, and, of course, South Vietnam. Enemies of these regimes were shocked by U.S. support for them—and even those whom we supported were disappointed, or worse, when America's cost-benefit analysis changed and we dropped our erstwhile allies. This Machiavellian scheming behind a Wilsonian facade has alienated many clients, as well as potential friends, and bred strains of anti-Americanism around the world.

A second grievance concerns America's frequent unilateralism and the difficult relationship between the United States and the United Nations. For many countries, the United Nations is, for all its flaws, the essential agency of cooperation and the protector of its members' sovereignty. The way U.S. diplomacy has "insulted" the UN system—sometimes by ignoring it and sometimes by rudely imposing its views and policies on it—has been costly in terms of foreign support.

Third, the United States' sorry record in international development has recently become a source of dissatisfaction abroad. Not only have America's financial contributions for narrowing the gap between the rich and the poor declined since the end of the Cold War, but American-dominated institutions such as the International Monetary Fund and the World Bank have often dictated financial policies that turned out to be disastrous for developing countries—most notably, before and during the Asian economic crisis of the mid-1990s.

Finally, there is the issue of American support of Israel. Much of the world—and not only the Arab world—considers America's Israel policy to be biased. Despite occasional American attempts at evenhandedness, the world sees that the Palestinians remain under occupation, Israeli settlements continue to expand, and individual acts of Arab terrorism—acts that Yasir Arafat can't completely control—are condemned more harshly than the killings of Palestinians by the Israeli army or by Israeli-sanctioned assassination squads. It is interesting to note that Israel, the smaller and dependent power, has been more successful in circumscribing the United States' freedom to maneuver diplomatically in the region than the United States has been at getting Israel to enforce the UN resolutions adopted after the 1967 war (which called for the withdrawal of Israeli forces from then-occupied territories, solving the refugee crisis, and establishing inviolate territorial zones for all states in the region). Many in the Arab world, and some outside, use this state of affairs to stoke paranoia of the "Jewish lobby" in the United States.

## ANTIGLOBALISM AND ANTI-AMERICANISM

Those who attack specific American policies are often more ambivalent than hostile. They often envy the qualities and institutions that have helped the United States grow rich, powerful, and influential.

The real United States haters are those whose anti-Americanism is provoked by dislike of America's values, institutions, and society—and their enormous impact abroad. Many who despise America see us as representing the vanguard of globalization—even as they themselves use globalization to promote their hatred. The Islamic fundamentalists of al-Qaeda—like Iran's Ayatollah Khomeini 20 years ago—make excellent use of the communication technologies that are so essential to the spread of global trade and economic influence.

We must be careful here, for there are distinctions among the antiglobalist strains that fuel anti-Americanism. To some of our detractors, the most eloquent spokesman is bin Laden, for whom America and the globalization it promotes relentlessly through free trade and institutions under its control represent evil. To them, American-fueled globalism symbolizes the domination of the Christian-Jewish infidels or the triumph of pure secularism: They look at the United States and see a society of materialism, moral laxity, corruption in all its forms, fierce selfishness, and so on. (The charges are familiar to us because we know them as an exacerbated form of right-wing anti-Americanism in nineteenth- and twentieth-century Europe.) But there are also those who, while accepting the inevitability of globalization and seem eager to benefit from it, are incensed by the contrast between America's promises and the realities of American life. Looking at the United States and the countries we support, they see insufficient social protection, vast pockets of poverty amidst plenty, racial discrimination, the large role of money in politics, the domination of the elites—and they call us hypocrites. (And these charges, too, are familiar, because they are an exacerbated version of the left-wing anti-Americanism still powerful in Western Europe.)

On the one hand, those who see themselves as underdogs of the world condemn the United States for being an evil force because its dynamism makes it naturally and endlessly imperialistic—a behemoth that imposes its culture (often seen as debased), its democracy (often seen as flawed), and its conception of individual human rights (often seen as a threat to more communitarian and more socially concerned approaches) on other societies. The United States is perceived as a bully ready to use all means, including overwhelming force, against those who resist it: Hence, Hiroshima, the horrors of Vietnam, the rage against Iraq, the war on Afghanistan.

On the other hand, the underdogs draw hope from their conviction that the giant has a heel like Achilles'. They view America as a society that cannot tolerate high casualties and prolonged sacrifices and discomforts, one whose impatience with protracted and undecisive conflicts should encourage its victims to be patient and relentless in their challenges and assaults. They look at American foreign policy as one that is often incapable of overcoming obstacles and of sticking to a course that is fraught with high risks—as with the conflict with Iraq's Saddam Hussein at the end of the Gulf War; as in the flight from Lebanon after the terrorist attacks of 1982; as in Somalia in 1993; as in the attempts to strike back at bin Laden in the Clinton years.

Thus America stands condemned not because our enemies necessarily hate our freedoms but because they resent what they fear are our Darwinian aspects, and often because they deplore what they see as the softness at our core. Those who, on our side, note and celebrate America's power of attraction, its openness to immigrants and refugees, the uniqueness of a society based on common principles rather than on ethnicity or on an old culture, are not wrong. But many of the foreign students, for instance, who fall in love with the gifts of American education return home, where the attraction often fades. Those who stay sometimes feel that the price they have to pay in order to assimilate and be accepted is too high.

## WHAT BRED BIN LADEN

This long catalog of grievances obviously needs to be picked apart. The complaints vary in intensity; different cultures, countries, and parties emphasize different flaws, and the criticism is often wildly excessive and unfair. But we are not dealing here with purely rational arguments; we are dealing with emotional responses to the omnipresence of a hegemon, to the sense that many people outside this country have that the United States dominates their lives.

Complaints are often contradictory: Consider "America has neglected us, or dropped us" versus "America's attentions corrupt our culture." The result can be a gestalt of resentment that strikes Americans as absurd: We are damned, for instance, both for failing to intervene to protect Muslims in the Balkans and for using force to do so.

But the extraordinary array of roles that America plays in the world—along with its boastful attitude and, especially recently, its cavalier unilateralism—ensures that many wrongs caused by local regimes and societies will be blamed on the United States. We even end up being seen as responsible not only for anything bad that our "protectorates" do—it is no coincidence that many of the September 11 terrorists came from America's protégés, Saudi Arabia and Egypt—but for what our allies do, as when Arabs incensed by racism and joblessness in France take up bin Laden's cause, or when Muslims talk about American violence against the Palestinians. Bin Laden's extraordinary appeal and prestige in the Muslim world do not mean that his apocalyptic nihilism (to use Michael Ignatieff's term) is fully endorsed by all those who chant his name. Yet to many, he plays the role of a bloody Robin Hood, inflicting pain and humiliation on the superpower that they believe torments them.

Bin Laden fills the need for people who, rightly or not, feel collectively humiliated and individually in despair to attach themselves to a savior. They may in fact avert their eyes from the most unsavory of his deeds. This need on the part of the poor and dispossessed to connect their own feeble lot to a charismatic and single-minded leader was at the core of fascism and of communism. After the failure of pan-Arabism, the fiasco of nationalism, the dashed hopes of democratization, and the fall of Soviet communism, many young people in the Muslim world who might have once turned to these visions for succor turned instead to Islamic fundamentalism and terrorism.

One almost always finds the same psychological dynamics at work in such behavior: the search for simple explanations—and what is simpler and more inflammatory than the machinations of the Jews and the evils of America—and a highly selective approach to history. Islamic fundamentalists remember the promises made by the British to the Arabs in World War I and the imposition of British and French imperialism after 1918 rather than the support the United States gave to anticolonialists in French North Africa in the late 1940s and in the 1950s. They remember British opposition to and American reluctance toward intervention in Bosnia before Srebrenica, but they forget about NATO's actions to save Bosnian Muslims in 1995, to help Albanians in Kosovo in 1999, and to preserve and improve Albanians' rights in Macedonia in 2001. Such distortions are manufactured and maintained by the controlled media and schools of totalitarian regimes, and through the religious schools, conspiracy mills, and propaganda of fundamentalism.

## WHAT CAN BE DONE?

Americans can do very little about the most extreme and violent forms of anti-American hatred—but they can try to limit its spread by addressing grievances that are justified. There are a number of ways to do this:

- First—and most difficult—drastically reorient U.S. policy in the Palestinian-Israeli conflict.
- Second, replace the ideologically market-based trickle-down economics that permeate American-led development institutions today with a kind of social safety net. (Even *New York*

*Times* columnist Thomas Friedman, that ur-celebrator of the global market, believes that such a safety net is indispensable.)

- Third, prod our allies and protégés to democratize their regimes, and stop condoning violations of essential rights (an approach that can only, in the long run, breed more terrorists and anti-Americans).
- Fourth, return to internationalist policies, pay greater attention to the representatives of the developing world, and make fairness prevail over arrogance.
- Finally, focus more sharply on the needs and frustrations of the people suffering in undemocratic societies than on the authoritarian regimes that govern them.

America's self-image today is derived more from what Reinhold Niebuhr would have called pride than from reality, and this exacerbates the clash between how we see ourselves and foreign perceptions and misperceptions of the United States. If we want to affect those external perceptions (and that will be very difficult to do in extreme cases), we need to readjust our self-image. This means reinvigorating our curiosity about the outside world, even though our media have tended to downgrade foreign coverage since the Cold War. And it means listening carefully to views that we may find outrageous, both for the kernel of truth that may be present in them and for the stark realities (of fear, poverty, hunger, and social hopelessness) that may account for the excesses of these views.

Terrorism aimed at the innocent is, of course, intolerable. Safety precautions and the difficult task of eradicating the threat are not enough. If we want to limit terrorism's appeal, we must keep our eyes and ears open to conditions abroad, revise our perceptions of ourselves, and alter our world image through our actions. There is nothing un-American about this. We should not meet the Manichaeanism of our foes with a Manichaeanism of self-righteousness. Indeed, self-examination and self-criticism have been the not-so-secret weapons of America's historical success. Those who demand that we close ranks not only against murderers but also against shocking opinions and emotions, against dissenters at home and critics abroad, do a disservice to America.

STANLEY HOFFMANN *is the Paul and Catherine Buttenwieser University Professor at Harvard University.*

Reprinted with permission from *The American Prospect,* November 19, 2001, Vol. 12, No. 20, pp. 18-21. © 2001 by The American Prospect, 5 Broad Street, Boston, MA 02109. All rights reserved.

# Between Two Ages

## GET USED TO IT

Address by WILLIAM VAN DUSEN WISHARD, *President, World Trends Research*
*Delivered to the Coudert Institute, Palm Beach, Florida, December 1, 2001*

Your topic of study "Living in an age of transition" couldn't be more appropriate to what we have been, are, and will continue to be living through probably for the rest of our lives.

In 2000, I published a new book, Between Two Ages. On the front cover appears this sentence: "The next three decades may be the most decisive 30 year period in the history of mankind." Then there's another sentence describing how the book examines that suggestion.

Nothing so dramatizes living between two ages as does the image of the fireball engulfing the World Trade Center, an image burned into the world's psyche September 11th. I'm not going to dwell on that event, except to say this. The image of the imploding World Trade Center must be seen as part of a panorama of images for its full significance to best be understood. The image, for instance, of death camps and crematoriums in Central Europe. The image of a mushroom cloud rising over the Pacific. Of Neil Armstrong stepping onto the Moon. Of Louise Brown, the first human to be conceived outside of the human body. Of a man standing near the summit of Mt. Everest talking on his cell phone to his wife in Australia. Of the first human embryo to be cloned. Of a computer performing billions of calculations in a second, calculations that could not have been performed by all the mathematicians who ever lived, even in their combined lifetimes. These are some of the images, representing both human greatness and depravity, that mark the end of one age and the approach of a new time in human experience.

It was in 1957 that Peter Drucker, who, more than any other person, defined management as a discipline, wrote: "No one born after the turn of the 20th century has ever known anything but a world uprooting its foundations, overturning its values and toppling its idols." So today I'm going to pursue Drucker's thought and suggest why I believe we're living at probably the most critical turning point of human history.

Between two ages. How are we to visualize the difference between those two ages? I offer some contrasts. From the dom-inance of print communication, to the emergence of electronic communication. From American immigration coming primarily from Europe, to immigration coming mainly from Asia and Latin America. From a time of relatively slow change, to change at an exponential rate. From economic development as a national endeavor, to economic development as part of a global system. From ultimate destructive power being confined to the state, to such power available to the individual. We could continue, but I think you see what I mean. We're in what the ancient Greeks called Kairos—the "right moment" for a fundamental change in principles and symbols.

Exactly what kind of era is opening up is far from clear. The only obvious fact is that it's going to be global, whatever else it is.

In the next few minutes I want to comment on three trends that are part of this shift between two ages. Let me start by stating my bias: I am bullish on the future. We've got unprecedented challenges ahead, clearly the most difficult humanity has ever faced. But I believe in the capacity of the human spirit to surmount any challenge if given the vision, the will and the leadership.

With this in mind, let's look at some trends that are moving us from one age to the next.

First trend: For the first time in human history, the world is forging an awareness of our existence as a single entity. Nations are incorporating the planetary dimensions of life into the fabric of our economics, politics, culture and international relations. The shorthand for this is "globalization."

We all have some idea of what globalization means. In my view, globalization represents the world's best chance to enrich the lives of the greatest number of people. The specter of terrorism, however, raises the question as to globalization's future. Will the 1990's "go-go" version be one of the casualties of terrorism? Yes and no. The economic pace of globalization may slow down, and certainly reaction to America's "soft power"— what other nations see as the "Americanization" of world culture—will continue to grow. But other aspects may actually accelerate. For example, we're already seeing the increased globalization of intelligence, security and humanitarian concerns.

Aside from that, globalization is far more than just economics and politics: more than non-western nations adopting free markets and democratic political systems. At its core, globalization means that western ideas are gradually seeping into the social and political fabric of the world. And even deeper, globalization is about culture, tradition and historic relationships; it's about existing institutions and why and how they evolved. In short, globalization goes to the very psychological foundations of a people.

Look at what's happening. Nations are adopting such ideas as the sanctity of the individual, due process of law, universal education, the equality of women, human rights, private property, legal safeguards governing business and finance, science as the engine of social growth, concepts of civil society, and perhaps most importantly, the ability of people to take charge of their destiny and not simply accept the hand dealt them in life. For millions of people these concepts are new modes of thought, which open undreamt of possibilities.

Is this good? From our perspective it is. But what do other nations feel as America's idea of creative destruction and entrepreneurship press deeper into the social fabric of countries such as China and India; as American cultural products uproot historic traditions?

In the Middle East, American culture as exemplified by a TV program such as Baywatch generates a unique resentment. Such a program presents Islamic civilization with a different nuance of feminine beauty and the dignity of women. Baywatch, and American culture in general, lure Muslims into an awkward position. On the one hand, their basic human appetites respond at a primal level. So it becomes part of them. Yet on another level, they fear the invasion of this new culture is undermining something sacred and irreplaceable in their very social fabric. Yes, it's their own fault; they don't have to import such entertainment. Yet it all seems to be part of so-called "modernization."

All of which illustrates how hard it is for us Americans to appreciate the underlying differences between western ideas and the foundations of other nations. Take some of the basic contrasts between Asia and the west. The west prizes individuality, while the east emphasizes relationships and community. The west sees humans dominating nature, while the east sees humans as part of nature. In the west there is a division between mind and heart, while in the east mind and heart are unified.

I mention this to illustrate the deep psychological trauma nations are experiencing as they confront the effects of globalization. We Americans, raised on the instinct of change, say, "Great. Let tradition go. Embrace the new." But much of the world says, "Wait a minute. Traditions are our connection to the past; they're part of our psychic roots. If we jettison them, we'll endanger our social coherence and stability."

Remember, it took centuries for our political, social and economic concepts to evolve in the West. They are the product of a unique western psychology and experience. Thus we cannot expect non-western nations to graft alien social attitudes onto an indigenous societal structure overnight.

Part of the upheaval created by globalization is the largest migration the world has ever seen, which is now under way. In China alone, 100 million people are on the move from the countryside to the city. In Europe, the OECD tells us that no country is reproducing its population; that the EU will need 180 million immigrants in the next three decades simply to keep its population at 1995 levels, as well as to keep the current ratio of retirees to workers.

As European population growth declines, and as immigration increases, the historic legends that are the basis of national identities tend to wane. As one British historian put it, "A white majority that invented the national mythologies underpinning modern European culture lives in an almost perpetual state of fear that it and its way of life are about to disappear." You realize what he means when you hear that the Church of England expects England to have more practicing Muslims than practicing Anglicans by next year. In Italy, the Archbishop of Bologna recently warned Italy is in danger of "losing its identity" due to the immigration from North Africa and Central Europe. This fear is the subtext for everything else we see happening in Europe today.

The question of identity is at the core of the world problem as globalization accelerates. It came sharply into focus in the 1960's when, for the first time in human history, we saw Earth from space, from the moon. An idea that had only existed in the minds of poets and philosophers suddenly became geopolitical reality—the human family is a single entity. We began to see national, cultural and ethnic distinctions for what they are—projections in our minds. We lost the clarity of identity—Herder's "collective soul"—that had given birth and meaning to nations and civilizations for centuries.

In my view, it's this continuing loss of identity—or the threat of it—that helps fuel terrorism. Granted, there's an individual psychotic aspect to any terrorist. But the context in which they live is a loss of a personal sense of identity, as well as a subsequent psychological identification with the God-image.

One aspect of globalization we sometimes find irritating is America's global role and the resulting world perception of America. This perception is shaped by many factors, some of which we control, many of which we don't. For example, nations have historically felt a natural antipathy toward the world's strongest empire, whoever it happened to be at the time. And make no mistake, we are perceived, at a minimum, as an empire of influence. That said, in my view no great nation has used its power as generously and with as little intention of territorial gain as has America. Nonetheless, if we don't understand what other nations feel about America, globalization will not succeed, and neither will the war on terrorism.

Consider a comment by the Norwegian newspaper, Aftenposten: "in Norway, Nepal, and New Zealand, all of us live in a world that is increasingly shaped by the United States." Now let's play with that thought for a moment and consider a hypothetical situation.

Imagine how we would feel if the world were increasingly shaped by, say, China. Suppose China had produced the information technology that is the engine of globalization, technology that we had to buy and incorporate into our social structure. Picture Chinese currency as the medium of world trade. Further envision Chinese as the international language of commerce. What if Chinese films and TV programs were flooding global entertainment markets, undermining bedrock American beliefs and values. Suppose China were the dominant military and economic world power. Imagine the Chinese having troops stationed for security and peacekeeping in over thirty countries around the world. What if the IMF and World Bank were primarily influenced by Chinese power and pressure. Suppose China had developed the economic and management theories that we had to adopt in order to compete in the global marketplace.

If this were the case, how would Americans feel? I'm not suggesting there's anything inherently wrong with U.S. world influence, I'm trying to illustrate the all pervasiveness of America's reach in the world in order to suggest why even our allies manifest uneasy concerns about America. Understanding this, and adjusting where warranted, is essential to the success of globalization, to say nothing of the future of America.

Consider another example. Think what it looks like to the rest of the world when we judge other nations on the basis of human rights and democracy, while at the same time systematically feeding our children a cultural diet considered by all religions and civilizations throughout history to be destructive of personal character and social cohesion. Two of America's foremost diplomats have commented on this anomaly. Zbigniew Brzezinski, former National Security Advisor to the president, writes, "I don't think Western secularism in its present shape is the best standard for human rights." He mentions consumption, self-gratification and hedonism as three characteristics of America's definition of the "good life," and then says, "The defense of the political individual doesn't mean a whole lot in such a spiritual and moral vacuum."

George F. Kennan, one of the giant U.S. diplomatic figures of the past half century, says simply, "This whole tendency to see ourselves as the center of political enlightenment and as teachers to a great part of the rest of the world strikes me as unthought-through, vainglorious and undesirable." I might add these comments were made before September 11th.

Such comments perhaps seem almost unpatriotic. But America's ability to provide world leadership may depend on whether we have the capacity to consider such reactions, and see what truth there may be in them. It's what the Scottish poet Robert Burns wrote: "Oh would some power the gift to give us, to see ourselves as others see us!"

I emphasize these points because if we're going to build a global age, it's got to be built on more than free markets and the Internet. Even more, it's got to be built on some view of life far broader than "my nation," "my race" or "my religion" is the greatest. Such views gave dynamism and meaning to the empires of the past. But the task now is to bring into being a global consciousness. It must have as its foundation some shared psychological and, ultimately, spiritual experience and expression. At the end of the day, globalization must have a legitimacy that validates itself in terms of a true democratic and moral order.

The second trend moving us between two ages is a new stage of technology development. This new phase is without precedent in the history of science and technology.

At least since Francis Bacon in the 1600's we have viewed the purpose of science and technology as being to improve the human condition. As Bacon put it, the "true and lawful end of the sciences is that human life be enriched by new discoveries and powers."

And indeed it has. Take America. During the last century, the real GDP, in constant dollars, increased by $48 trillion, much of this wealth built on the marvels of technology.

But along with technological wonders, uncertainties arise. Let me interject here that in 1997 I had a quadruple heart bypass operation using the most sophisticated medical technology in the world. So I'm a believer. Nonetheless, the question today is whether we're creating certain technologies not to improve the human condition, but for purposes that seem to be to replace human meaning and significance altogether.

The experts tell us is that by the year 2035, artificial robotic intelligence will surpass human intelligence. (Let's leave aside for a moment the question of what constitutes "intelligence.") And a decade after that, we shall have a robot with all the emotional and spiritual sensitivities of a human being.

Not long after that, computers—will go at such a speed that the totality of human existence will change so dramatically that it's beyond our capability to envision what life will be like. But never fear, we're told. The eventual marriage of human and machine will mean that humans will continue as a species, albeit not in a form we would recognize today.

Thus arrives what some would-be scientific intellectuals call the "Post-human Age." I emphasize, this is not science fiction. It is the projection of some of our foremost scientists.

Let's move from the general to the specific. Consider a remark by the co-founder of MIT's artificial intelligence lab and one of the world's leading authorities on artificial intelligence: "Suppose that the robot had all of the virtues of people and was smarter and understood things better. Then why would we want to prefer those grubby, old people? I don't see anything wrong with human life being devalued if we have something better." Now just absorb that thought for a moment. One of the world's leading scientists ready to "devalue human life" if we can create something he thinks is better. Setting aside the question of who decides what "better" is, to me, devaluing human life is a form of self-destruction.

The editor of Wired magazine says we're in the process of the "wiring of human and artificial minds into one planetary soul." Thus, he believes, we,ll be the first species "to create our own successors." He sees artificial intelligence "creating its own civilization."

These are not "mad scientists." They're America's best and brightest, and they believe they're ushering in the next stage of evolution.

In sum, we're creating technology that forces us to ask what are humans for once we've created super intelligent robots that can do anything humans can do, only do it a thousand times faster? Why do we need robots with emotional and spiritual capability, and what does that have to do with the seventy percent of humanity that simply seeks the basic necessities of life? What will it mean to be able to change the genetic structure not just of an individual child, but also of all future generations? Do we really want to be able to make genetic changes so subtle that it may be generations before we know what we've done to ourselves?

What we're talking about is a potential alteration of the human being at the level of the soul. This is a work proceeding absent any political debate, certainly without the assent of elected leaders. Yet it will change the definition of what it means to be a human being. It's the silent loss of freedom masquerading as technological progress.

Many other questions come to mind, but two in particular. Will it happen, and what is driving this self-destructive technological imperative?

On the first question—will it happen—my guess is probably not. In my judgment, there is a major issue the technological visionaries disregard. That is the question of how much manipulation and accelerated change the human being can take before he/she disintegrates psychologically and physiologically.

What we're experiencing is not simply the acceleration of the pace of change, but the acceleration of acceleration itself. In other words, change growing at an exponential rate. The experts tell us that the rate of change doubles every decade; that at today's rate of change, we'll experience 100 calendar years of change in the next twenty-five years; and that due to the nature of exponential growth, the 21st century as a whole will experience almost one thousand times greater technological change than did the 20th century.

I hasten to add that these are not my projections. They are the views of some of America's most accomplished and respected experts in computer science and artificial intelligence.

Onrushing change is already producing mounting dysfunction. The suicide rate among women has increased 200% in the past two decades. Thirty years ago, major corporations didn't have to think much about mental health programs for employees. Now, mental health is the fastest growing component of corporate health insurance programs. Think of the corporations that now provide special rooms for relaxation, naps, music or prayer and meditation. The issue now for corporations is not so much how to deal with stress; it's how to maintain the psychological integrity of the individual employee.

Other indicators of dysfunction tell us that teen suicide jumped 300% between 1960-90. Books are now written for eight and nine year old children advising them how to recognize the symptoms of stress, and to deal with it in their own lives. Anti-depressants and other character-controlling drugs are taken like aspirin. Rage has assumed a culture-like place in the national fabric, whether rage on the road, in stores, in schools and even in a popular video game called "Primal Rage," and, most tragically, in families.

Now, project forward the predicted increased speed of computers and the resulting ratcheting up of the pace of life over the next decades, and you end up asking, "How much more of this can the human metabolism take?" It's not the case that sooner or later something will give way. The multiplying social pathol-

ogies indicate that individual and collective psychological integrity is already giving way.

The second question is, what's driving this self-destructive activity? Certainly we as consumers are a major part of it. We're addicted to the latest electronic gizmo; whether it's the ubiquitous cell phone to keep us in touch with everyone everywhere, or one of those Sharper Image CD players you hang on the shower head so you can listen to Beethoven while taking a shower.

But let me offer three views that suggest a deeper story. Consider the comment of a former Carnegie-Mellon University computer scientist hired by Microsoft as a researcher. In an interview with the Washington Post, the good professor said, "This corporation is my power tool. It is the tool I wield to allow my ideas to shape the world."

My power tool. What clearer expression of ego-inflation could there be?

A second comment comes from the editor of Wired magazine, who famously wrote, "We are as gods, and we might as well be good at it." The Greeks had a word for identifying ourselves with the gods—hubris, pride reaching beyond proper human limits.

Perspective on all this comes from within the scientific community itself.

Freeman Dyson is one of the world's preeminent theoretical physicists. He talks about the "technical arrogance" that overcomes people "when they see what they can do with their minds."

My power tool; we are as gods; technical arrogance. The Greeks had another word that was even stronger than hubris. Pleonexia. An overweening resolve to reach beyond the limits, an insatiable greed for the unattainable. It is what one writer terms the "Masculine Sublime," which he describes as the "gendered characteristics out of which the myths of science are molded-myths of masculine power, control, rationality, objectivity."

From the earliest times, everything in human myth and religion warns us about overreaching. From the myths of Prometheus in ancient Greece, to the Hebrew story of Adam and Eve; from the Faust legend to Milton's Paradise Lost; from Mary Shelly's Frankenstein to Stevenson's Dr. Jekyll and Mr. Hyde; from Emily Dickinson to Robert Oppenheimer's lament that "in some sort of crude sense, the physicists have known sin"; through all these stories and experiences that come from the deepest level of the human soul, there has been a warning that limits exist on both human knowledge and endeavor; that to go beyond those limits is self-destructive.

No one knows exactly where such limits might be. But if they don't include the effort to create some technical/ human life form supposedly superior to human beings, if they don't include the capacity to genetically reconfigure human nature, if they don't include the attempt to introduce a "post-human" civilization, then it's hard to imagine where such limits would be drawn.

Keep in mind that myths are more than fanciful stories left over from the childhood of man. They emanate from the unconscious level of the psyche; that level which connects us to whatever transpersonal wisdom may exist. It's a level at which, as quantum physics suggests, there may exist some relationship between the human psyche and external matter. There may be some fundamental pattern of life common to both that is operating outside the understanding of contemporary science. In other words, we may be fooling around with phenomena that are, in fact, beyond human awareness; possibly even beyond the ability of humans to grasp. For at the heart of life is a great mystery which does not yield to rational interpretation. This eternal mystery induces a sense of wonder out of which all that humanity has of religion, art and science is born. The mystery is the giver of these gifts, and we only lose the gifts when we grasp at the mystery itself. In my view, Nature will not permit arrogant man to defy that mystery, that transcendent wisdom. In the end, Nature's going to win out.

Some people are already searching for the wisest way to approach such potential challenges as the new technologies present. Bill Joy, co-founder and former chief scientist of Sun Microsystems, suggests we've reached the point where we must "limit development of technologies that are too dangerous, by limiting our pursuit of certain kinds of knowledge." His concerns are based on the unknown potential of genetics, nanotechnology and robotics, driven by computers capable of infinite speeds, and the possible uncontrollable self-replication of these technologies this might pose. Joy acknowledges the pursuit of knowledge as one of the primary human goals since earliest times. But, he says, "If open access to, and unlimited development of, knowledge henceforth puts us all in clear danger of extinction, then common sense demands that we re-examine even these basic, long-held beliefs."

The third trend moving us between two ages is a longterm spiritual and psychological reorientation that's increasingly generating uncertainty and instability. This affects all of us, for we're all part of America's collective psychology, whether we realize it or not.

The best measure of America's psychological and spiritual life is not public opinion polls telling us what percentage of the population believes in God. Rather, it's the content and quality of our culture. For culture is to a nation what dreams are to an individual—an indication of what's going on in the inner life.

In my judgment, what's really going on is that the world is experiencing a long-term spiritual and psychological reorientation similar to what happened when the Greco-Roman era gave way to the start of the Feudal Age. That was a time of great disorientation and searching. The cry "Great Pan is dead," was heard throughout the ancient world as the traditional gods lost their hold on the collective psyche. The Greco-Roman world became awash in countless new religions and sects vying for supremacy.

Not too different from our times, beginning with Nietzsche's cry, "God is dead." When we look at what's happening today we see 1500 religions in America, including such anomalies as "Catholic-Buddhists." Beyond that, we see a smorgasbord of spiritual/psychological fare as seen in the popularity of books such as The Celestine Prophecy or the Chicken Soup series, in the rise of worldwide fundamentalism, in numerous cults such as "Heaven's Gate," in the New Age phenomenon, in interest in Nostradamus, in crop circles, in the supposed "Bible Code," in conspiracy theories, in fascination with the "other" as seen in movies such as "Planet of the Apes" or "Tomb Raiders," in the search for some extraterrestrial intelligence to save us from ourselves, and last but certainly not least, in terrorism, which, at its core, is a demonic hatred expressed in spiritual terms.

What happened in the Rome—early Feudal Age shift was played out over centuries. What's happening today has, yes, been evolving over the past few centuries. We see it first manifested in the emergence of the Faust legend; then in the Enlightenment's enthronement of the Goddess of Reason in Notre Dame and the ensuing acceptance of rationalism as life's highest authority; and in our own time in the ethos of "meaninglessness" that has virtually defined 20th century Western culture. But what's happening today—due to the 20th century electronic information technologies—is probably unfolding at a more rapid pace than the shift in the fourth-fifth-sixth centuries. For information technologies transmit not only information, but psychological dynamics as well.

While there are millions of devout Christians and Jews in America and Europe, the Judeo-Christian impulse is no longer the formative dynamic of Western culture, especially among the so-called "creative minority." Even so calm a journal as the Economist opines, "The West is secular." One need only look at the changing relationship between the roles of the priest and the psychologist to see what has been happening. Earlier in the 20th century, if someone had personal problems, he or she went to the priest for advice. Gradually that changed, and people started going to their psychologist. Recently, the leader of the Roman Catholic Church in England and Wales said that as a background for people's lives, Christianity "has almost been vanquished." His language mirrored a statement by the Archbishop of Canterbury who declared Britain to be a country where "tacit atheism prevails." Newsweek recently described Europe as a "post-Christian civilization." Throughout the continent, Newsweek reported, "churches stand empty."

Part of the psychological reorientation taking place is the breakup of our collective inner images of wholeness. For example, we used to talk about "heaven," which denoted the transcendent realm, eternity, the dwelling place of the gods. Now we just speak of "space," which has no spiritual connotation. We used to talk of "mother earth," which had a vital emotional association. From time immemorial, nature was filled with spirit. Now we just speak of "matter," a lifeless nature bereft of gods.

Thus transcendent meaning—which is the source of psychological wholeness is diminished. The function of symbolic language-words like "heaven" and "mother earth"— is to link our consciousness to the roots of our being, to link our consciousness to its base in the unconscious. When that link is devalued or discarded, there is little to sustain the inner life of the individual. So, few people are inwardly fed by any primal source of wholeness. In effect, our symbolic life and language have been displaced by a vocabulary of technology, a vocabulary that's increasingly devoid of transcendent meaning. The effect is a weakening of the structures that organize and, regulate our life-religion, self-government, education, culture and the family.

As a result, the soul of America—indeed, of the world—is in a giant search for some deeper and greater expression of life. Despite the benefits of modernization, technological society offers no underlying meaning to life. Thus the search taking place is both healthy and normal—given the seminal shift to an entirely new epoch that is occurring as we speak.

What we're discussing is at the core of the crisis of meaning that afflicts not only America and Europe, but Asia as well. For example, the Washington Post reports from Beijing, "Across China people are struggling to redefine notions of success and failure, right and wrong. The quest for something to believe in is one of the unifying characteristics of China today." A report from the East/West Center in Hawaii notes the decline in family and authority in Asia, and concludes by saying, "Eastern religion no longer is the binding force in Asian society." So it's a global crisis of meaning we're talking about.

Let me briefly summarize what we've been discussing. (1) Globalization possibly the most ambitious collective human experiment in history; (2) a new stage of technology the objective of which is to supplant human meaning and significance; and (3) a long-term psychological and spiritual reorientation. These are only three of the basic changes determining the future. And it's because of the magnitude and significance of such trends that I suggest the next three decades may be the most decisive thirty-year period in human history.

How do we respond to such a situation? We're already responding in the most sweeping redefinition of life America has ever known. We're redefining and restructuring all our institutions. Corporations are redefining their mission, structure and modus operandi. In education, we're trying countless new experiments, from vouchers to charter schools to home schooling. Alternative dispute resolution is helping lift the burden off the back of our legal system. Civic and charitable organizations are assuming functions formerly undertaken by local governments. More people are involved in efforts to help the elderly and those in poverty. In fact, it's estimated that well over fifty percent of all adult Americans donate a portion of their time to non-profit social efforts. Most importantly, there are countless efforts underway to redress the severe environmental imbalance we've created.

Against the background of the three trends I mentioned, perhaps this is a modest start, but at least it's a start. Clearly, there's another level of effort to move to, As Bill Joy suggests, such efforts must include a decision whether or not to continue research and development of technologies that could, in Joy's words, "bring the world to the edge of extinction." Obviously, such an examination must be done in a global context if it's to be valid.

But another question is, how are you and I to live in a world that's changing faster than individuals and institutions can assimilate? How do we maintain anchorage and balance when we're in between two ages?

I believe the starting place is understanding; simply to understand the fundamental changes taking place. That takes time and work.

As the most basic change taking place is in us as individuals, we must understand ourselves at a wholly new level. For the individual is the carrier of civilization. In the West, we tend to think in abstract categories of generality, such as civilizations, nations, historic trends, economic imperatives, social theories and philosophical concepts. These, we say, are the factors that make history. In my view, they're not. People make history, and all our concepts, theories and imperatives are projections of one kind or another that emanate from deep within the human psyche. It's what we are as individuals that shapes the future. So the issue boils down to how well do we know ourselves, both as individuals and as a nation?

We all know Socrates advice, "Know thyself." And most of us, if we pay any attention to that suggestion, think of knowing ourselves as knowing our conscious self. We think in terms of ego-consciousness. We think in terms of our persona, the mask we present to the world. The persona, however, is not the true, individual "me." The persona is usually a social identity—being a teacher, lawyer, banker or businessperson. As such, the persona derives from the collective psyche, not from any individual uniqueness.

But who we really are does not derive from our social role, from the work we do or our position on the social scale. Most of what we truly are resides in the unconscious, in the shadow side of our lives. My persona is who I like to think I am. My shadow is who I really am. My persona is the conscious "me." The shadow is the unconscious me. So getting to know the shadow is a prerequisite to knowing ourselves and who we truly are.

By and large, the shadow is a collection of repressed desires and "uncivilized" impulses. It's that part of our character we're not especially proud of and we'd rather not admit to. The British psychiatrist Anthony Stevens suggests that if you want to know what your shadow looks like, just write down a description of the sort of person you simply cannot stand. That description is your shadow. Everyone has a shadow. The problem is we easily see the other person's shadow, but not our own.

So what do we do with our shadow? Because we don't want to confront it, we usually project it on to others. We see our own devils in other people. This projection has been going on for millennia. It caused Christ to say, "And why do you see the mote that is in your brother's eye, but fail to see the beam that is in your own eye?" It's a form of denial, and there can be national denial as well as individual denial.

This failure to see our shadow is responsible for any amount of acrimony in relationships in a family, between friends or in an organization. On a collective level, it gives rise to political polarization, racial tension and international conflict. Hitler's projected shadow was a prime cause of the Holocaust. Every international conflict is, to some extent, a shadow projection. One reason we fail to resolve such international crises is because we don't recognize the critical dimension that is at the center of every crisis—the human psyche and its archetypal shadow. So how can you and I deal with our shadow, something that is unconscious?

The best way I've discovered is to study my reactions to other people. Reactions have two parts: First, an objective assessment of another person's character or actions; and second, the emotional intensity with which I react. No matter how accurate my assessment may be, that emotional intensity represents my shadow. So the instructive question to ask is not, "Why did the other person do what he or she did?" It's "Why am I reacting the way I am? What can my reaction tell me about my shadow?"

Let me make it personal. I have constant reactions to my wife. We've been married forty-four years, and I love her dearly. But that doesn't alter the fact that we react to each other. It's human nature. So when I react to her, no matter what the issue, I've learned to ask myself, "Where's the emotional steam coming from? Why am I reacting so strongly?" And I usually get an answer. And more often than not, the answer has to do with my loss of control of some particular situation. Something has happened that has taken away my control of my plan.

There's another feature of our shadow: the shadow includes aspects of ourselves that contain our unlived life-talents and abilities that, for various reasons, have been buried or never been made conscious. So the more we understand our shadow, the more likely these positive attributes are to develop.

As we confront our shadow, over time our negative qualities can be integrated with our positive qualities to make us more complete personalities. Becoming complete personalities is the whole object of life. That's what healing is all about; it's what growth is all about. It's a process of making conscious what has been unconscious. It's what one author wrote: "The full and joyful acceptance of the worst in oneself may be the only way of transforming it."

My task as a human being is to discover who I really am, and that means getting behind the persona and confronting the shadow. We can live on our persona only so long before life becomes stale and inauthentic, at which point we turn to trivia for distraction and entertainment. The same is true for nations. And while we Americans see our persona, the rest of the world sees our shadow. Indeed, Hollywood has made our shadow America's primary cultural export to the world.

Between two ages. There's a new epoch of human meaning struggling to take shape. Through the chaos and the killing, through the heartache and inner emptiness, the birth of a height-ened consciousness is fighting its way out of the womb into the light.

The womb that nurtures this New Time is nothing less than the human unconscious, especially the deepest strata that is common to all humankind, the collective unconscious. The key to unlocking this deeper realm is to know ourselves in a new and deeper way; to become aware of life's opposites—the persona and the shadow, the good and evil, the loves and hatreds — that dwell within each of us, all of which constitute the totality of who we really are. The task is to strengthen the dialogue between consciousness and the limitless creative powers of the collective unconscious, wherein resides life's highest meaning.

A new time in history requires a fresh affirmation of the meaning and coherence of the human journey. That will not come from a speechwriter's pen or Madison Avenue. It must be born in the depths of the psyche of each one of us as we individually seek our own deeper meaning and relevance at a time of opportunity and danger unequaled in history. As we do this, we affirm that the sacred continuity of life continues. But it does not continue in a way we think of as normal. A new epoch will not emerge from conventional attitudes and habits. Living between two ages requires us to redefine what constitutes normalcy. A new normalcy can only come if we face our shadow so it can—over time—be integrated into a greater wholeness of personality. That's the price that must be paid in order that a new spiritual dispensation, a fresh expression of life's highest meaning, can come into being, and can shape the era that is to be.

Some eternal, infinite power is at work in each of us, as well as in the universe. This power is the source of renewal of all man's most vital and creative energies. With all our problems and possibilities, the future depends on how we—each in his or her own unique way-tap into that eternal renewing dynamic that dwells in the deepest reaches of the human soul.

In my view, this is some of what it means to live in an age of transition. Thank you.

From *Vital Speeches of the Day*, January 15, 2002, pp. 203-211. © 2002 by City News Publishing Company, Inc.

# COMMUNITY BUILDING
## STEPS TOWARD A GOOD SOCIETY

*AMITAI ETZIONI*

**W**ell-formed national societies are not composed of millions of individuals but are constituted as communities of communities. These societies provide a framework within which diverse social groups as well as various subcultures find shared bonds and values. When this framework falls apart, we find communities at each other's throats or even in vicious civil war, as we sadly see in many parts of the world. (Arthur Schlesinger Jr. provides an alarming picture of such a future for our society in his book, *The Disuniting of America*.)

Our community of communities is particularly threatened in two ways that ought to command more of our attention in the next years. First, our society has been growing more diverse by leaps and bounds over recent decades, as immigration has increased and Americans have become more aware of their social and cultural differences. Many on the left celebrate diversity because they see it as ending white European hegemony in our society. Many on the right call for "bleaching out" ethnic differences to ensure a united, homogenous America.

A second challenge to the community of communities emanates from the fact that economic and social inequality has long been rising. Some see a whole new divide caused by the new digital technologies, although others believe that the Internet will bridge these differences. It is time to ask how much inequality the community of communities can tolerate while still flourishing. If we are exceeding these limits, what centrist corrections are available to us?

## DIVERSITY WITHIN UNITY

As a multiethnic society, America has long debated the merit of unity versus pluralism, of national identity versus identity politics, of assimilation of immigrants into mainstream culture versus maintaining their national heritages. All of these choices are incompatible with a centrist, communitarian approach to a good society. Assimilation is unnecessarily homogenizing, forcing people to give up important parts of their selves; unbounded ra-

cial, ethnic, and cultural diversity is too conflict-prone for a society in which all are fully respected. The concept of a community of communities provides a third model.

The community of communities builds on the observation that loyalty to one's group, to its particular culture and heritage, is compatible with sustaining national unity as long as the society is perceived not as an arena of conflict but as a society that has some community-like features. (Some refer to a community of communities as an imagined community.) Members of such a society maintain layered loyalties. "Lower" commitments are to one's immediate community, often an ethnic group; "higher" ones are to the community of communities, to the nation as a whole. These include a commitment to a democratic way of life, to a constitution and more generally to a government by law, and above all to treating others—not merely the members of one's group—as ends in themselves and not merely as instruments. Approached this way, one realizes that up to a point, *diversity can avoid being the opposite of unity and can exist within it.*

Moreover, sustaining a particular community of communities does not contradict the gradual development of still more encompassing communities, such as the European Union, a North American community including Canada and Mexico, or, one day, a world community.

During the last decades of the 20th century, the U.S. was racked by identity politics that, in part, have served to partially correct past injustices committed against women and minorities, but have also divided the nation along group lines. Other sharp divisions have appeared between the religious right and much of the rest of the country. One of the merits of the centrist, communitarian approach has been that it has combined efforts to expand the common ground and to cool intergroup rhetoric. Thus communitarians helped call off the "war" between the genders, as Betty Friedan—who was one of the original endorsers of the Communitarian Platform—did in 1997.

New flexibility in involving faith-based groups in the provision of welfare, health care, and other social services, and even allowing some forms of religious activities in public schools, has defused some of the tension between the religious right and the rest of society. The national guidelines on religious expression in public schools, first released by the U.S. Department of Education on the directive of President Clinton in August of 1995, worked to this end. For example, in July of 1996, these guidelines spurred the St. Louis School Board to implement a clearly defined, districtwide policy on school prayer. This policy helped allay the confusion—and litigation—that had previously plagued the role of religion in this school district.

The tendency of blacks and whites not to dialogue openly about racial issues, highlighted by Andrew Hacker, has to some degree been overcome. The main, albeit far from successful, effort in this direction has been made by President Clinton's Advisory Board on Race. And for the first time in U.S. history, a Jew was nominated by a major political party for the post of vice president.

In the next years, intensified efforts are called for to balance the legitimate concerns and needs of various communities that constitute the American society on one hand, and the need to shore up our society as a community of communities on the other. Prayers truly initiated by students might be allowed in public schools as long as sufficient arrangements are made for students who do not wish to participate to spend time in other organized activities. There are no compelling reasons to oppose "after hours" religious clubs establishing themselves in the midst of numerous secular programs. Renewed efforts for honest dialogues among the races are particularly difficult and needed. None of these steps will cause the differences among various communities—many of which serve to enrich our culture and social life—to disappear. But they may go a long way toward reinforcing the framework that keeps American society together while it is being recast.

## UNIFYING INEQUALITY

Society cannot long sustain its status as a community of communities if general increases in well-being, even including those that trickle down to the poorest segments of the society, keep increasing the economic distance between the elites and the common people. Fortunately, it seems that at least by some measures, economic inequality has not increased in the United States between 1996 and 2000. And by several measures, the federal income tax has grown surprisingly progressive. (The opposite must be said about rising payroll taxes.) About a third of those who filed income tax returns in 2000 paid no taxes or even got a net refund from the Internal Revenue Service (IRS). However, the level of inequality in income at the end of the 20th century was substantially higher than it was in earlier periods. Between 1977 and 1999, the after-tax income of the top 1 percent of the U.S. population increased by 115 percent, whereas the after-tax income of the U.S. population's lowest fifth decreased by 9 per-

cent. There is little reason to expect that this trend will not continue.

### SOCIAL JUSTICE

We may debate what social justice calls for; however, there is little doubt about what community requires. If some members of a community are increasingly distanced from the standard of living of most other members, they will lose contact with the rest of the community. The more those in charge of private and public institutions lead lives of hyper-affluence—replete with gated communities and estates, chauffeured limousines, servants and personal trainers—the less in touch they are with other community members. Such isolation not only frays social bonds and insulates privileged people from the moral cultures of the community, but it also blinds them to the realities of the lives of their fellow citizens. This, in turn, tends to cause them to favor unrealistic policies ("let them eat cake") that backfire and undermine the trust of the members of the society in those who lead and in the institutions they head.

The argument has been made that for the state to provide equality of outcomes undermines the motivation to achieve and to work, stymies creativity and excellence, and is unfair to those who do apply themselves. It is also said that equality of outcomes would raise labor costs so high that a society would be rendered uncompetitive in the new age of global competition. Equality of opportunity has been extolled as a substitute. However, to ensure equality of opportunity, some equality of outcome must be provided. As has often been pointed out, for all to have similar opportunities, they must have similar starting points. These can be reached only if all are accorded certain basics. Special education efforts such as Head Start, created to bring children from disadvantaged backgrounds up to par, and training for workers released from obsolescent industries are examples of programs that provide some equality of results to make equality of opportunity possible.

Additional policies to further curb inequality can be made to work at both ends of the scale. Policies that ensure a rich basic minimum serve this goal by lifting those at the lower levels of the economic pyramid. Reference is often made to education and training programs that focus on those most in need of catching up. However, these work very slowly. Therefore, in the short run more effects will be achieved by raising the Earned Income Tax Credit and the minimum wage, and by implementing new intercommunity sharing initiatives.

The poor will remain poor no matter how much they work as long as they own no assets. This is especially damaging because people who own assets, especially a place of residence (even if only an apartment), are most likely to "buy" into a society—to feel and be part of a community. By numerous measures, homeowners are more involved in the life of their communities, and their children are less likely to drop out of school. Roughly one-third of Americans do not own their residence; 73 percent of whites do, compared to 47 percent of African Americans and Hispanics.

## MORTGAGES

Various provisions allowing those with limited resources to get mortgages through federally chartered corporations like Fannie Mae, which helps finance mortgages for many lower-income people, have been helpful in increasing ownership. More needs to be done on this front, especially for those of little means. This might be achieved by following the same model used in the Earned Income Tax Credit in the U.S. and the Working Families Tax Credit in the United Kingdom: providing people who earn below a defined income level with "earned interest on mortgages," effectively granting them two dollars for every dollar set aside to provide seed money for a mortgage. And sweat equity might be used as the future owner's contribution—for instance, if they work on their own housing site. (Those who benefit from the houses that Habitat for Humanity builds are required to either make some kind of a financial contribution themselves or help in the construction of their homes.) Far from implausible, various ideas along these lines were offered by both George W. Bush and Al Gore during the 2000 election campaign, as well as by various policy researchers.

Reducing hard core unemployment by trying to bring jobs to poor neighborhoods (through "enterprise zones") or by training the long-unemployed in entrepreneurial skills is often expensive and slow, and is frequently unsuccessful. The opposite approach, moving people from poor areas to places where jobs are, often encounters objections by the neighborhoods into which they are moved, as well as by those poor who feel more comfortable living in their home communities. A third approach should be tried much more extensively: providing ready transportation to and from places of employment.

Measures to cap the higher levels of wealth include progressive income taxes, some forms of inheritance tax, closing numerous loopholes in the tax codes, and ensuring that tax on capital is paid as it is on labor. Given that several of these inequality curbing measures cannot be adopted on a significant scale if they seriously endanger the competitive state of a country, steps to introduce many of them should be undertaken jointly with other Organization for Economic Cooperation and Development (OECD) countries, or better yet, among all the nations that are our major competitors and trade partners.

One need not be a liberal—one can be a solid communitarian—and still be quite dismayed to learn that the IRS audits the poor (defined as income below $25,000) more than the rich (defined as income above $100,000). In 1999, the IRS audited 1.36 percent of poor taxpayers, compared to 1.15 percent of rich taxpayers. In 1988, the percentage for the rich was 11.4. In one decade, there was thus a decline of about 90 percent in auditing the rich. This oc-

curred because Congress did not authorize the necessary funds, despite the General Accounting Office's finding that the rich are more likely to evade taxes than are the poor. This change in audit patterns also reflects the concern of Republican members of Congress that the poor will abuse the Earned Income Tax Credit that the Clinton administration has introduced. It should not take a decade to correct this imbalance.

Ultimately, this matter and many others will not be properly attended to until there is a basic change in the moral culture of the society and in the purposes that animate it. Without such a change, a major reallocation of wealth can be achieved only by force, which is incompatible with a democratic society and will cause a wealth flight and other damage to the economy. In contrast, history from early Christianity to Fabian socialism teaches us that people who share progressive values will be inclined to share their wealth voluntarily. A good society seeks to promote such values through a grand dialogue rather than by dictates.

## THE NEW GRAND DIALOGUE

The great success of the economy in the 1990s made Americans pay more attention to the fact that there are numerous moral and social questions of concern to the good society that capitalism has never aspired to answer and that the state should not promote. These include moral questions such as what we owe our children, our parents, our friends, and our neighbors, as well as people from other communities, including those in far away places. Most important, we must address this question: What is the ultimate purpose our personal and collective endeavors? Is ever greater material affluence our ultimate goal and the source of meaning? When is enough—enough? What are we considering the good life? *Can a good society be built on ever increasing levels of affluence? Or should we strive to center it around other values, those of mutuality and spirituality?*

The journey to the good society can benefit greatly from the observation, supported by a great deal of social science data, that ever increasing levels of material goods are not a reliable source of human well-being or contentment—let alone the basis for a morally sound society. To cite but a few studies of a large body of findings: Frank M. Andrews and Stephen B. Withey found that the level of one's socioeconomic status had meager effects on one's "sense of well-being" and no significant effect on "satisfaction with life-as-a-whole." Jonathan L. Freedman discovered that levels of reported happiness did not vary greatly among the members of different economic classes, with the exception of the very poor, who tended to be less happy than others. David G. Myers reported that although per capita disposable (after-tax) income in inflation-adjusted dollars almost exactly doubled between 1960 and 1990, 32 percent of Americans reported that they were "very happy" in 1993, almost the same proportion as did in 1957 (35 percent). Although economic growth slowed after the mid-1970s, Americans' reported happiness was remarkably stable (nearly always between 30 and 35 percent) across both high-growth and low-growth periods.

## HAPPINESS

These and other such data help us realize that the pursuit of well-being through ever higher levels of consumption is Sisyphean. When it comes to material goods, enough is never enough. This is not an argument in favor of a life of sackcloth and ashes, of poverty and self-denial. The argument is that once basic material needs (what Abraham Maslow called "creature comforts") are well sated and securely provided for, additional income does not add to happiness. On the contrary, hard evidence—not some hippie, touchy-feely, LSD-induced hallucination—shows that profound contentment is found in nourishing ends-based relationships, in bonding with others, in community building and public service, and in cultural and spiritual pursuits. Capitalism, the engine of affluence, has never aspired to address the whole person; typically it treats the person as *Homo economicus.* And of course, statist socialism subjugated rather than inspired. It is left to the evolving values and cultures of centrist societies to fill the void.

Nobel laureate Robert Fogel showed that periods of great affluence are regularly followed by what he calls Great Awakenings, and that we are due for one in the near future. Although it is quite evident that there is a growing thirst for a purpose deeper than conspicuous consumption, we may not have the ability to predict which specific form this yearning for spiritual fulfillment will take.

There are some who hold firmly that the form must be a religious one because no other speaks to the most profound matters that trouble the human soul, nor do others provide sound moral guidance. These believers find good support in numerous indicators that there was a considerable measure of religious revival in practically all forms of American religion over the last decades of the 20th century. The revival is said to be evident not merely in the number of people who participate in religious activities and the frequency of their participation in these activities, but also in the stronger, more involving, and stricter kinds of commitments many are making to religion. (Margaret Talbot has argued effectively that conservative Christians, especially fundamentalists, constitute the true counterculture of our age; they know and live a life rich in fulfillment, not centered around consumer goods.) Others see the spiritual revival as taking more secular forms, ranging from New Age cults to a growing interest in applied ethics.

## PRIORITIES

Aside from making people more profoundly and truly content individuals, a major and broadly based upward shift on the Maslovian scale is a prerequisite for being able to better address some of the most tantalizing problems plaguing modern societies, whatever form such a shift may take. That is what is required before we can come into harmony with our environment, because these higher priorities put much less demand on scarce resources than do lower ones. And such a new set of priorities may well be the only conditions under which those who are well endowed would be willing to support serious reallocation of wealth and power, as their personal fortunes would no longer be based on amassing ever larger amounts of consumer goods. In addition, transitioning to a knowledge-based economy would free millions of people (one hopes all of them, gradually) to relate to each other mainly as members of families and communities, thus laying the social foundations for a society in which ends-based relationships dominate while instrumental ones are well contained.

The upward shift in priorities, a return to a sort of moderate counterculture, a turn toward voluntary simplicity—these require a grand dialogue about our personal and shared goals. (A return to a counterculture is not a recommendation for more abuse of controlled substances, promiscuity, and self-indulgence—which is about the last thing America needs—but the realization that one can find profound contentment in reflection, friendship, love, sunsets, and walks on the beach rather than in the pursuit of ever more control over ever more goods.) Intellectuals and the media can help launch such a dialogue and model the new forms of behavior. Public leaders can nurse the recognition of these values by moderating consumption at public events and ceremonies, and by celebrating those whose achievements are compatible with a good society rather than with a merely affluent one.

But ultimately, such a shift lies in changes in our hearts and minds, in our values and conduct—what Robert Bellah called the "habits of the heart." We shall not travel far toward a good society unless such a dialogue is soon launched and advanced to a good, spiritually uplifting conclusion.

*Mr. Etzioni is editor of* The Responsive Community. *From "Next: Three Steps Towards A Good Society," by Amitai Etzioni,* The Responsive Community, *Winter 2000–01, pages 49–58.*

Reprinted from *Current*, January 2001, pp. 29–33. Originally printed in *The Responsive Community*, Vol. II, No. 1, Winter 2000/01, pp. 49–58 which was adapted from the author's book *Next: The Road to the Good Society* (New York: Basic Books, 2001).

# Index

# Index

# Test Your Knowledge Form

We encourage you to photocopy and use this page as a tool to assess how the articles in *Annual Editions* expand on the information in your textbook. By reflecting on the articles you will gain enhanced text information. You can also access this useful form on a product's book support Web site at *http://www.dushkin.com/online/*.

NAME:                                            DATE:

_____

TITLE AND NUMBER OF ARTICLE:

_____

BRIEFLY STATE THE MAIN IDEA OF THIS ARTICLE:

_____

LIST THREE IMPORTANT FACTS THAT THE AUTHOR USES TO SUPPORT THE MAIN IDEA:



_____

WHAT INFORMATION OR IDEAS DISCUSSED IN THIS ARTICLE ARE ALSO DISCUSSED IN YOUR TEXTBOOK OR OTHER READINGS THAT YOU HAVE DONE? LIST THE TEXTBOOK CHAPTERS AND PAGE NUMBERS:



_____

LIST ANY EXAMPLES OF BIAS OR FAULTY REASONING THAT YOU FOUND IN THE ARTICLE:



_____

LIST ANY NEW TERMS/CONCEPTS THAT WERE DISCUSSED IN THE ARTICLE, AND WRITE A SHORT DEFINITION:

# We Want Your Advice

ANNUAL EDITIONS revisions depend on two major opinion sources: one is our Advisory Board, listed in the front of this volume, which works with us in scanning the thousands of articles published in the public press each year; the other is you—the person actually using the book. Please help us and the users of the next edition by completing the prepaid article rating form on this page and returning it to us. Thank you for your help!

**ANNUAL EDITIONS:** Sociology 03/04

## ARTICLE RATING FORM

Here is an opportunity for you to have direct input into the next revision of this volume.
We would like you to rate each of the articles listed below, using the following scale:

1. **Excellent: should definitely be retained**
2. **Above average: should probably be retained**
3. **Below average: should probably be deleted**
4. **Poor: should definitely be deleted**

Your ratings will play a vital part in the next revision.
Please mail this prepaid form to us as soon as possible.
Thanks for your help!

| RATING | ARTICLE |
|---|---|
| | 1. Modernization's Challenge to Traditional Values: Who's Afraid of Ronald McDonald? |
| | 2. The Mountain People |
| | 3. More Moral |
| | 4. American Culture Goes Global, or Does It? |
| | 5. What's So Great About America? |
| | 6. Boys Will Be Boys |
| | 7. Born to Be Good? |
| | 8. Preventing Crime: The Promising Road Ahead |
| | 9. Pedophilia |
| | 10. The American Family |
| | 11. Divorce and Cohabitation: Why We Don't Marry |
| | 12. Should You Stay Together for the Kids? |
| | 13. Now for the Truth About Americans and Sex |
| | 14. Shades of Gay |
| | 15. When Careers Collide |
| | 16. Where Everyone's a Minority |
| | 17. Still the Land of Opportunity? |
| | 18. The Great CEO Pay Heist |
| | 19. Corporate Welfare |
| | 20. From Welfare to Work |
| | 21. Racism Isn't What It Used to Be |
| | 22. Why We Hate |
| | 23. The Melting Pot, Part I: Are We There Yet? |
| | 24. The Past and Prologue |
| | 25. Violence Against Women |
| | 26. Who Rules America? |
| | 27. Where the Public Good Prevailed |
| | 28. In Corporate America, It's Cleanup Time |
| | 29. Work, Work, Work, Work! |
| | 30. Schools That Develop Children |
| | 31. The Future of Humanity |
| | 32. Seeking Abortion's Middle Ground |
| | 33. The Future of Religion in America |
| | 34. Sixteen Impacts of Population Growth |
| | 35. Feeling the Heat: Life in the Greenhouse |
| | 36. The Secret Nuclear War |
| | 37. Grains of Hope |
| | 38. A New Strategy for the New Face of Terrorism |

| RATING | ARTICLE |
|---|---|
| | 39. Why Don't They Like Us? |
| | 40. Between Two Ages |
| | 41. Community Building: Steps Toward a Good Society |

*(Continued on next page)*

ANNUAL EDITIONS: SOCIOLOGY 03/04

## BUSINESS REPLY MAIL
FIRST-CLASS MAIL  PERMIT NO. 84  GUILFORD CT

POSTAGE WILL BE PAID BY ADDRESSEE

**McGraw-Hill/Dushkin**
**530 Old Whitfield Street**
**Guilford, Ct 06437-9989**

NO POSTAGE
NECESSARY
IF MAILED
IN THE
UNITED STATES

# ABOUT YOU

Name

Date

Are you a teacher? ☐  A student? ☐
Your school's name

Department

Address          City          State     Zip

School telephone #

# YOUR COMMENTS ARE IMPORTANT TO US!

Please fill in the following information:
For which course did you use this book?

Did you use a text with this ANNUAL EDITION? ☐ yes ☐ no
What was the title of the text?

What are your general reactions to the *Annual Editions* concept?

Have you read any pertinent articles recently that you think should be included in the next edition? Explain.

Are there any articles that you feel should be replaced in the next edition? Why?

Are there any World Wide Web sites that you feel should be included in the next edition? Please annotate.

May we contact you for editorial input? ☐ yes ☐ no
May we quote your comments? ☐ yes ☐ no